AMERICAN POLITICAL IDEALS AND REALITIES

AMERICAN POLITICAL IDEALS AND REALITIES

Peter Woll
Brandeis University

Stephen J. Rockwell
Brookings Institution

 LONGMAN

An imprint of Addison Wesley Longman, Inc.

New York • Reading, Massachusetts • Menlo Park, California • Harlow, England
Don Mills, Ontario • Sydney • Mexico City • Madrid • Amsterdam

Editor in Chief: Priscilla McGechon
Acquisitions Editor: Eric Stano
Marketing Manager: Megan Galvin-Falc
Supplements Editor: Mark Toews
Design Manager: Rubina Yeh
Project Manager: Ellen MacElree
Cover Design: Kay Petronio
Text Design: David Munger and Dianne Hall, The Davidson Group
Electronic Page Makeup: Dianne Hall, The Davidson Group
Electronic Project Management: David Munger, The Davidson Group
Senior Print Buyer: Hugh Crawford
Printer and Binder: The Maple-Vail Book Manufacturing Group
Cover Printer: Coral Graphic Services, Inc.

Library of Congress Cataloging-in-Publication Data

American political ideals and realities / [edited by] Peter Woll, Stephen J. Rockwell.
    p. cm.
   ISBN 0-321-02946-1
   1. United States—Politics and government. I. Woll, Peter, 1933- II. Rockwell,
Stephen J., 1966-

JK21 .A4614 1999
320.473 21—dc21

                                  99-044973

Please visit our Website at http://www.awlonline.com

ISBN: 0-321-02946-1

12345678910—MA—02010099

For Wesley Peter Nugent,
at the Threshold of Ideals and
Realities

and

For Jean Glaab,
my Grandmother,
who will always be "Nanny"

CONTENTS

Chapter 2

POLITICS AND PUBLIC DEBATE: WHY DON'T THE MEDIA JUST REPORT THE FACTS?   31

Chapter 3
BUREAUCRACY AND ADMINISTRATION: WHY IS RUNNING A GOVERNMENT TOUGHER THAN RUNNING A BUSINESS? 63

Chapter 4
THE SEPARATION OF POWERS: HOW INDEPENDENT IS THE JUDICIARY?   97

Supreme Court opinions will be implemented. In the judiciary, as elsewhere, the implementation process can shape policy in a way that diverges from the Supreme Court's original intent.

Chapter 5
THE SEPARATION OF CHURCH AND STATE: MUST PUBLIC DUTY REPLACE PRIVATE BELIEF?   137

beliefs are fundamental in American society. Our political ideals protect freedom of expression, including religious expression, but our politics pushes religion aside.

Chapter 6

CAMPAIGN FINANCE:
WHY IS A FREE COUNTRY SO EXPENSIVE?   173

Chapter 7
FOREIGN POLICY: WHAT'S THE "RIGHT"
THING TO DO, AND HOW DO WE DO IT?   217

Chapter 9
PLURALISM, DIVERSITY, AND IMMIGRATION: HOW DO WE ALL GET ALONG?   293

The contrasting forces of assimilation and ethnic pluralism have at different times affected American Indians for good and ill. The civil rights movement of the 1960s eventually led to the passage of legislation that sought to protect the rights of Indians as individuals. Unique tribal rights continue to complicate Indian affairs, and upholding Indian civil and tribal rights continues to challenge government.

Competition and even conflict are stages in the process by which diverse groups learn to get along with one another. A commitment to diversity requires us to tolerate contention in American society.

PREFACE

Overview

American Political Ideals and Realities is a collection of essays by scholars and government leaders aimed at bridging the gap between theoretical understandings of the American system, on the one hand, and the realities of governing, on the other. This new collection of essays and scholarly works demonstrates the dilemmas, difficulties, and consequences of political decision making.

The readings focus on traditional topics of introductory political science courses, while challenging students to see how aspects of the American system complicate the design and implementation of policies. *Ideals and Realities* is a suitable basic text for introductory courses, and it can also be used to supplement established texts or to provide a foundation for class discussion and paper assignments. The readings are organized to encourage debate and discussion, and to lead students to compare ideas within and across different chapters.

Ideals and Realities moves beyond traditional American government readers by highlighting the relationship of the nation's democratic ideals to the dynamics of its political institutions. Anthologies on government too often focus on academic perspectives that assume we can easily achieve the lofty ideals embodied in the Constitution and in the Declaration of Independence; other anthologies tackling specific issues too often propose policy options that ignore the difficulties of decision making in a fragmented and decentralized system. Issue-based anthologies often present two "sides" of an issue, creating artificial dichotomies and overlooking the compromise necessary for effective governing. *Ideals and Realities* focuses on those compromises, and on the problems faced by leaders trying to design and implement policies that will satisfy American ideals and work in reality.

The Readings

Each chapter in *Ideals and Realities* addresses a particular aspect of American governance from a unique perspective. Selections by top scholars outline complexities and constraints facing government action, in a framework designed to answer the kinds of basic questions that college students ask about American government. The cornerstones of each chapter are selections written by public officials that tie real-world experience to the topics discussed by the scholars. This bridging of the gap between academic debate and realistic decisionmaking sets *Ideals and Realities* apart, giving students insight into both the world of academic debate and the world of public service.

Chapter One, "Conflict and Governance: Does Politics Have To Be So Political?," serves as an introduction. This chapter outlines the fundamentally conflicted nature of American ideals, and examines how those ideals are constrained by the necessities of real-world governance. The chapter begins with James Madison's classic analysis of factions and the extended republic from *Federalist 10*. *Federalist 51* follows, in which Madison turns to the premises and operations of the separation of powers and the checks and balances system. This is followed by a selection from Samuel Huntington's *American Politics: The Promise of Disharmony*, in which Huntington discusses the American creed and the ways in which political ideals and values intersect actual governing institutions. The next reading, from Elliott Richardson's memoir, *Reflections of a Radical Moderate*, looks at power in Washington from the inside. Richardson's thoughtful essay offers a compellingly sympathetic view of public officials, one which serves as a corrective to negative stereotypes of government and its employees. David Stockman's classic account of his years as Director of the Office of Management and Budget under President Reagan follows. Stockman relates how his ideals about governance and decision making succumbed to the real politics and needs of the American system, and how he learned to accept that system with all its flaws. Finally, the chapter concludes with Theda Skocpol's recent analysis of the failure of health care reform in President Clinton's first term. A plan ultimately based on the universal right to health care, Skocpol argues, fell victim to the dynamics of a fragmented system characterized by a wide variety of interest groups and individuals.

Chapter Two, "Politics and Public Debate: Why Don't the Media Just Report the Facts?," examines the ideal of objective reporting and the reality of the media's intimate relationship with politics. Scholar Timothy Cook opens the chapter with a discussion of the media as a political institution tied to the activities and operations of government. An excerpt from Walter Lippmann's classic work, *Public Opinion*, follows, explaining the nature and limits of the concepts of "news" and "truth." The third selection is from James Fallows' recent book, *Breaking the News*, in which Fallows examines the public journalism movement and the role of media personnel in influencing the character and direction of the news they report. Finally, veteran reporter David Broder concludes the chapter with a discussion of the competing loyalties journalists face when they become deeply involved with the activities of public officials.

Chapter Three, "Bureaucracy and Administration: Why Is Running a Government Tougher than Running a Business?," highlights the competing demands placed on public agencies. These selections examine the most overlooked aspect of American politics and outline the realities of implementing policy in the American system. Peter Woll's essay places the bureaucracy in its constitutional context, underscoring the important point that the Constitution creates a balanced, deliberative government, not a pure democracy. James Q. Wilson follows this selection with an excerpt from his instant classic, *Bureaucracy: What Government Agencies Do and Why They Do It*. Wilson outlines the conflicting demands faced by government agencies, highlighting the ways in which administering public policy differs from implementing initiatives in the private sector. Next, Michael D. Reagan looks at how regulation is a political process, and why ideals like "merit" and "public interest" cannot form a realistic foundation for actual policy. Martin A. Levin follows with a speculative essay, "The Day After an AIDS Vaccine is Discovered: Management Matters." In this clever and honest piece, Levin demonstrates how even the best and most supported public policy initiatives still face myriad difficulties and obstacles in the real world of administration. The chapter concludes with an entry from President Clinton's chief advisor on AIDS policy, Sandra Thurman. Thurman reinforces Levin's case, noting that formulating and implementing AIDS policy has become more difficult, not easier, with the passage of time.

Chapter Four, "The Separation of Powers: How Independent Is the Judiciary?," illustrates the limits on our ideal of an "independent" judiciary. Robert McCloskey opens the chapter, in a selection from his classic book on the Supreme Court. McCloskey notes that the Court must constantly navigate between conflicting ideals, especially the competing demands of a higher justice, on the one hand, and popular sovereignty, on the other. Robert Katzmann then advances the analysis of the external demands made on the Court by focusing on the involvement of Congress in the Court's operations. Lawrence Baum discusses the numerous factors that play a role in implementing Court decisions, explaining why Court rulings are far from the end of any issue: the implementation process is crucial in shaping the impacts of Court rulings. Finally, former Chief Justice Earl Warren, in a selection from his memoirs, acknowledges the extent to which political factors helped mold the Court's activity when it considered and issued the landmark *Brown v. Board of Education* decisions. Like Baum, Warren notes the important role played by other factors after the Court has issued its rulings. The Courts are hardly "independent" in our system of shared powers, and implementing decisions relies on much more than the simple issuance of a ruling.

Chapter Five, "The Separation of Church and State: Must Public Duty Replace Private Belief?," examines a perennially thorny issue. Our idealized "wall of separation" between church and state does not accurately reflect reality. Mario Cuomo's landmark 1984 speech on abortion indicates the seriousness with which our public officials strive to reconcile their beliefs and their duties. This is followed by a selection from Ronald Thiemann, former Dean of the Harvard Divinity School, in which he argues that religious expression has much to bring to discussions of public issues. The next selection is excerpted from Stephen L. Carter's instant classic, *The Culture of Disbelief*, in which he argues that the marginalization of belief from public discourse presents serious threats to our nation. The chapter concludes with a piece by Laurence Tribe, arguing that the courts have a legitimate role to play in deciding critical debates like that surrounding abortion. Tribe's piece demonstrates that the debate of abstract ideals can only take us so far; sooner or later, official engines of government have an obligation to become involved.

In Chapter Six, five top writers engage the question, "Campaign Finance: Why Is a Free Country So Expensive?" Our ideals often tell us that money is a corrupting influence on politics, and they suggest that if we could control the flow of money we might regain certain positive aspects of campaigning and governing: a role for the small independent voter, for example. The reality is more complex, however, and Greg Kubiak's opening piece illustrates the world of practical politics and how it diverges from the constitutional ideal. Brooks Jackson then illustrates how the influence of money can push debate of issues aside, as candidates seek new sources of funds. Following these pieces is a very interesting analysis by Bradley Smith, in which he examines the extent to which common assumptions about campaign financing are really true. The final two selections, one by veteran campaigner Ed Rollins and one by former United States Senator Bill Bradley, offer inside views of how money really affects campaigning and politics.

Chapter Seven, "Foreign Policy: What's the 'Right' Thing to Do, and How Do We Do It?," addresses the true complexity of formulating and implementing foreign policy. Henry Kissinger opens the chapter with an examination of how our nation's conflicting foreign policy ideals complicate our conduct abroad. David Gergen outlines the numerous forces that influence foreign policy and make the formulation of a grand, coherent foreign policy extremely difficult. Edward Luttwak then takes this idea a step further. Noting that observers frequently criticize U.S. policy toward China as ambiguous and often arbitrary, Luttwak argues that an incoherent foreign policy can make very good sense. Finally, the chapter concludes with an excerpt from Richard C. Holbrooke's memoirs of his service in the Bosnia conflict, in which he notes that the assumption that human rights interests and national security interests conflict can be a false one: in Bosnia, he writes, these interests overlapped.

Chapter Eight, "Civil Society and Community: Who Are We and What Do We Want from Each Other?," addresses a recurring theme in American politics: the relationship of the individual to the greater society. Alexis de Tocqueville opens the chapter with a classic analysis of how self-interest in America has impacted the course of public affairs. Tocqueville suggests that the idealized formulation of "individual vs. society" is overstated. William J. Bennett argues, in the following selection, that serious consideration of issues of right and wrong and of personal character are crucial to our functioning as a community. The next piece, by Seymour Martin Lipset, observes neatly that many of the ideals we hold as Americans contribute to some of our worst social problems. The final two selections, one by Benjamin R. Barber and one by Lawrence K. Grossman, look at the ways in which technology and the Internet may affect our republic. Both argue that these impacts are not as simple or as predictable as we often imagine, and that the ideal of a true electronic democracy in our future warrants careful consideration.

Chapter Nine, "Pluralism, Diversity, and Immigration: How Do We All Get Along?," looks at the nature of group conflict in America. John Higham's opening selection points out that the usual terms of debate—pluralism and assimilation—are often oversimplified and misunderstood. Stephan Thernstrom and Abigail Thernstrom then discuss racial gerrymandering in political districts, arguing that the results of such actions are also often misunderstood. The very practice of race-based districting, they write, poses serious risks to our ability to get along as a diverse society. In the next selection, Peter Schuck argues that the immigration question is never as clear-cut as we sometimes think: the nation is ambivalent about immigration. Schuck notes that, historically, we are neither as open to immigration as we'd like to believe nor as xenophobic as we sometimes fear. Nathan Glazer follows with a discussion of how recent changes have helped reshape the immigration debate. W. Richard West, Jr. and Kevin Gover then examine an often overlooked piece of the race puzzle in America: American Indians. Adding another twist to the nation's efforts to realize its ideals in a diverse society, West and Gover write that while many groups' claims of rights and privileges, and their charges of discrimination, flow from racial or ethnic status, the claims of American Indians also involve the unique political status of Indian communities. The book's final selection is a brief, provocative essay in which Peter Skerry argues that group conflict is a necessary part of the American reality.

Acknowledgments

We are grateful for the insights and the support of Sidney Milkis, Shep Melnick, Peter Skerry, and Stephanie Greco Larson, who have offered invaluable suggestions over the years that have contributed greatly to this collection of writings. We would also like to thank our dedicated and professional assistant, Trudy Crosby, who handled the multiple tasks required in preparation of the manuscript; and Eric J. Broxmeyer, who transcribed the radio interview for Chapter 15. In addition, we would like to thank those reviewers who provided invaluable feedback in the development of this book in various styles: Richard Adinaro of Seton Hall University; Sean Anderson of Idaho State University; Anthony Champagne of University of Texas–Dallas; Gloria Cohen-Dion of Bloomsburg University; Martin Gruberg of University of Wisconsin–Oshkosh; John Haskell of Drake University; Willoughby Jarell of Kennesaco State University; Coleman H. McGinnis of Tennessee State University; Jacqueline Vaughn-Switzer of Southern Oregon State College; and John West of Seattle Pacific University.

Steve Rockwell also wishes to acknowledge a number of people who have helped this book along in thousands of unseen ways: First and foremost, my deepest respect and gratitude go to my parents, Patricia and Ronald Rockwell, who have encouraged me and supported me for many more years, I'm sure, than they ever expected. My thanks also to Joseph Glaab, my grandfather, who contributed more, probably, than he ever realized. I offer my sincere appreciation to my brothers, David and Kenny, who offer new perspectives on the world every day and without whom this book would never have been finished. Finally, I have been blessed with friends and families whose contributions to this book underlie every page: Patricia and John Schmitt and their wonderful family; Matt Rorke; Zoe and Sam Gedal; Hank Lutton; Fred Dews; Paula Kelly; Jon Shields; Nicole and Steve Pierce; Cheryl and Tal Ninyo and their family; Glen Weiss and Ann Ginsberg; Lonnie Meiner; and Karen and Jordan Breslow and their family. Special appreciation is due to Peter Skerry and Martha Bayles for their invaluable input and encouragement; and to Peter Woll, who gave me this job and who continues to provide a model of dedication, enjoyment, and true professionalism.

Chapter 1

Conflict and Governance

Does Politics Have To Be So Political?

To the framers of the Constitution the ideal form of government was one that would be balanced, deliberative, and nonpartisan. The constitutional framers supported the Lockean social contract under which government could exist only with the consent of the people. Consent of the people, however, did not mean majority rule. Majorities as well as minorities pursue selfish interests that undermine a government by consent of all the people.

James Madison's argument against factions in *Federalist 10* has persisted in American political thought and practice. Liberty of political expression guarantees factions and protects them against intrusive government regulation. Madison points out in the following selection that the causes of faction cannot be removed in a free society, but a large representative republic can filter and control the effects of faction.

At the age of 36, James Madison represented Virginia at the Constitutional Convention of 1787 in Philadelphia. He was instrumental in persuading his fellow delegates to establish a strong national government. Although the delegates voted to keep their proceedings secret, Madison fortunately kept extensive notes of their deliberations which became the only record of the historic and unique Convention debates. After the Convention he joined New York delegate Alexander Hamilton in 1788 to write *The Federalist*, first published as a series of newspaper articles in New York, to explain the Constitution and persuade New York to ratify it. As a member of the first Congress in 1791, Madison led Congress in drafting the Bill of Rights. President Thomas Jefferson appointed him to be Secretary of State in 1801.

At the end of his administration Jefferson anointed Madison to be his successor. In 1809 the electoral college chose Madison as President, and re-elected him in 1813. The

War of 1812 was the major event of Madison's administration. On the domestic front he created the first national bank, which the Supreme Court upheld in the historic case of *McCulloch v. Maryland* (1819).

The following selection is the most famous of the *Federalist* papers. The major points Madison makes are:

1. "Factions," whether large or small, represent special interests in opposition to the rights of citizens and the aggregate interest of the community.
2. Factions can be controlled either by removing their causes or by controlling their effects.
3. Liberty inevitably breeds factions as people join groups to advance their self-interest. The unequal distribution of wealth is the principal cause of faction.
4. Liberty is a natural right; therefore to curtail liberty in order to control faction makes that remedy for factions worse than the disease. Since the causes of faction cannot be removed, the Constitution should control their effects.
5. A large republic is the best means to control the effects of faction. Such a republic, by incorporating a large number of states, and establishing a representative government, both disperses and filters factions. In a large representative republic a single faction may temporarily be able to seize control of a state, but will be unable to spread its influence throughout the nation.

1

James Madison

FEDERALIST 10

Among the numerous advantages promised by a well constructed Union, none deserves to be more accurately developed than its tendency to break and control the violence of faction. The friend of popular governments never finds himself so much alarmed for their character and fate as when he contemplates their propensity to this dangerous vice. He will not fail, therefore, to set a due value on any plan which, without violating the principles to which he is attached, provides a proper cure for it. The instability, injustice, and confusion, introduced into the public councils, have, in truth been the mortal diseases under which popular governments have everywhere perished; as they continue to be the favorite and fruitful topics from which the adversaries to liberty derive their most specious declamations. The valuable improvements made by the American constitutions on the popular models, both ancient and modern, cannot certainly be too much admired; but it would be an unwarrantable partiality, to contend that they have as effectually obviated the danger on this side, as was wished and expected. Complaints are everywhere heard from our most considerate and virtuous citizens, equally the friends of public and private faith, and of public and personal liberty, that our governments are too unstable; that the public good is disregarded in the conflicts of rival parties; and that measures are too often decided, not according to the rules of justice, and the rights of the minor party, but by the superior force of an interested and overbearing majority. However anxiously we may wish that these complaints had no foundation, the evidence of known facts will not permit us to deny that they are in some degree true. It will be found, indeed, on a candid review of our situation, that some of the distresses under which we labor, have been erroneously charged on the operation of our governments; but it will be found, at the same time, that other causes will not alone account for many of our heaviest misfortunes; and, particularly, for the prevailing and increasing distrust of public engagements, and alarm for private rights, which are echoed from one end of the continent to the other. These must be chiefly, if not wholly, effects of the unsteadiness and injustice, with which a factious spirit has tainted our public administrations.

By a faction, I understand a number of citizens, whether amounting to a majority or minority of the whole, who are united and actuated by some common impulse of passion, or of interest, adverse to the rights of other citizens, or to the permanent and aggregate interest of the community.

There are two methods of curing the mischiefs of faction: the one, by removing its causes; the other, by controlling its effects.

There are again two methods of removing the causes of faction: the one, by destroying the liberty which is essential to its existence; the other, by giving to every citizen the same opinions, the same passions, and the same interests.

It could never be more truly said, than of the first remedy, that it was worse than the disease. Liberty is to faction what air is to fire, an ailment, without which it instantly expires. But it could not be a less folly to abolish liberty, which is essential to political life because it nourishes faction, than it would be to wish the annihilation of air, which is essential to animal life, because it imparts to fire its destructive agency.

The second expedient is as impracticable, as the first would be unwise. As long as the reason of man continues fallible, and he is at liberty to exercise it, different opinions will be formed. As long as the connection subsists between his reason and his self-love, his opinions and his passions will have a reciprocal influence on each other; and the former will be objects to which the latter will attach themselves. The diversity in the faculties of men, from which the rights of property originate, is not less an insuperable obstacle to a uniformity of interests. The protection of those faculties is the first object of government. From the protection of different and unequal faculties of acquiring property, the possession of different degrees and kinds of property immediately results; and from the influence of these on the sentiments and views of the respective proprietors, ensues a division of the society into different interests and parties.

The latent causes of faction are thus sown in the nature of man; and we see them everywhere brought into different degrees of activity, according to the different circumstances of civil society. A zeal for different opinions concerning religion, concerning government, and many other points, as well of speculation as of practice; an attachment to different leaders, ambitiously contending for preeminence and power; or to persons of other descriptions, whose fortunes have been interesting to the human passions, have, in turn, divided mankind into parties, inflamed them with mutual animosity, and rendered them much more disposed to vex and oppress each other, than to cooperate for their common good. So strong is this propensity of mankind, to fall into mutual animosities, that where no substantial occasion presents itself, the most frivolous and fanciful distinctions have been sufficient to kindle their unfriendly passions, and excite their most violent conflicts. But the most common and durable source of factions has been the various and unequal distribution of property. Those who hold, and those who are without property, have ever formed distinct interests in society. Those who are creditors, and those who are debtors, fall under a like discrimination. A landed interest, a manufacturing interest, a mercantile interest, a moneyed interest, with many lesser interests, grow up of necessity in civilized nations, and divide them into different classes, actuated by different sentiments and views. The regulation of these various and interfering interests forms the principal task of modern legislation, and involves the spirit of party and faction in the necessary and ordinary operations of government.

No man is allowed to be a judge in his own cause; because his interest will certainly bias his judgment, and, not improbably, corrupt his integrity. With equal, nay, with greater reason, a body of men are unfit to be both judges and parties at the same time; yet what are many of the most important acts of legislation, but so many judicial determinations, not indeed concerning the rights of single persons, but concerning the rights of large bodies of citizens? And what are the different classes of legislators, but advocates and parties to the cause which they determine? Is a law proposed concerning private debts? It is a question to which the creditors are parties on one side, and the debtors on the other. Justice ought to hold the balance between them. Yet the parties are, and must be, themselves the judges; and the most numerous party, or, in other words, the most powerful faction, must be expected to prevail. Shall domestic manufactures be encouraged, and in what degree, by restrictions on foreign manufactures are questions which would be differently decided by the landed and the manufacturing classes; and probably by neither with a sole regard to justice and the public good. . . .

It is vain to say, that enlightened statesmen will be able to adjust these clashing interests, and render them all subservient to the public good. Enlightened statesmen will not always be at the helm; nor, in many cases, can such an adjustment be made at all, without taking into view indirect and remote considerations, which will rarely prevail over the immediate interest which one party may find in disregarding the rights of another, or the good of the whole.

The inference to which we are brought is, that the *causes* of faction cannot be removed; and that relief is only to be sought in the means of controlling its *effects*.

If a faction consists of less than a majority, relief is supplied by the republican principle, which enables the majority to defeat its sinister views, by regular vote. It may clog the administration, it may convulse the society; but it will be unable to execute and mask its violence under the forms of the constitution. When a majority is included in a faction, the form of popular government, on the other hand, enables it to sacrifice to its ruling passion or interest, both the public good and the rights of other citizens. To secure the public good, and private rights, against the danger of such a faction, and at the same time to preserve the spirit and the form of popular government, is then the great object to which our inquiries are directed. Let me add, that it is the great desideratum, by which alone this form of government can be rescued from the opprobrium under which it has so long labored, and be recommended to the esteem and adoption of mankind.

By what means is this object attainable? Evidently by one of two only. Either the existence of the same passion or interest in a majority, at the same time must be prevented; or the majority, having such coexistent passion or interest, must be rendered, by their number and local situation, unable to concert and carry into effect schemes of oppression. If the impulse and the opportunity be suffered to coincide, we well know, that neither moral nor religious motives can be relied on as an adequate control. They are not found to be such on the injustice and violence of individuals, and lose their efficacy in proportion to the number combined together; that is, in proportion as their efficacy becomes needful.

From this view of the subject, it may be concluded, that a pure democracy, by which I mean a society consisting of a small number of citizens, who assemble and administer the government in person, can admit of no cure from the mischiefs of faction. A common passion or interest will, in almost every case, be felt by a majority of the whole; a communication and concert results from the form of government itself; and there is nothing to check the inducements to sacrifice the weaker party, or an obnoxious individual. Hence it is, that such democracies have ever been spectacles of turbulence and contention; have ever been found incompatible with personal security, or the rights of property; and have, in general, been as short in their lives, as they have been violent in their deaths. Theoretic politicians, who have patronized this species of government, have erroneously supposed that by reducing mankind to a perfect equality in their political rights, they would, at the same time, be perfectly equalized and assimilated in their possessions, their opinions, and their passions.

A republic, by which I mean a government in which the scheme of representation takes place, opens a different prospect, and promises the cure for which we are seeking. Let us examine the points in which it varies from pure democracy, and we shall comprehend both the nature of the cure and the efficacy which it must derive from the union.

The two great points of difference, between a democracy and a republic, are, first, the delegation of the government, in the latter, to a small number of citizens elected by the rest; secondly, the greater number of citizens, and greater sphere of country, over which the latter may be extended.

The effect of the first difference is on the one hand, to refine and enlarge the public views, by passing them through the medium of a chosen body of citizens, whose wisdom may best discern the true interest in their country, and whose patriotism and love of justice will be least likely to sacrifice it to temporary or partial considerations. Under such a regulation, it may well happen, that the public voice, pronounced by the representatives of the people, will be more consonant to the public good, than if pronounced by the people themselves, convened for the purpose. On the other hand, the effect may be inverted. Men of factious tempers, of local prejudices, or of sinister designs, may by intrigue, by corruption, or by other means, first obtain the suffrages, and then betray the interest of the people. The question resulting is, whether small or extensive republics are most favorable to the election of proper guardians of the public weal; and it is clearly decided in favor of the latter by two obvious considerations.

In the first place, it is to be remarked, that however small the republic may be, the representatives must be raised to a certain number, in order to guard against the cabals of a few; and that however large it may be, they must be limited to a certain number, in order to guard against the confusion of a multitude. Hence, the number of representatives in the two cases not being in proportion to that of the constituents, and being proportionally greatest in the small republic, it follows that if the proportion of fit characters be not less in the large than in the small republic, the former will present a greater option, and consequently a greater probability of a fit choice.

In the next place, as each representative will be chosen by a greater number of citizens in the large than in the small republic, it will be more difficult for unworthy candidates to practice with success the vicious arts, by which elections are too often carried; and the suffrages of the people being more free, will be more likely to center in men who possess the most attractive merit, and the most diffusive and established characters. . . .

The other point of difference is, the greater number of citizens, and extent of territory, which may be brought within the compass of republican, than of democratic government; and it is this circumstance principally which renders factious combinations less to be dreaded in the former, than in the latter. The smaller the society, the fewer probably will be the distinct parties and interests composing it; the fewer the distinct parties and interests, the more frequently will a majority be found of the same party; and the smaller the number of individuals composing a majority, and the smaller the compass within which they are placed, the more easily they will concert and execute their plans of oppression. Extend the sphere, and you take in a greater variety of parties and interests; you make it less probable that a majority of the whole will have a common motive to invade the rights of other citizens; or if such a common motive exists, it will be more difficult for all who feel it to discover their own strength, and to act in unison with each other. . . .

Hence, it clearly appears, that the same advantage, which a republic has over a democracy, in controlling the effects of faction, is enjoyed by a large over a small republic—is enjoyed by the union over the states composing it. Does this advantage consist in the substitution of representatives, whose enlightened views and virtuous sentiments render them superior to local prejudices, and to schemes of injustice? It will not be denied, that the representation of the union will be most likely to possess these requisite endowments. Does it consist in the greater security afforded by a greater variety of parties, against the event of any one party being able to outnumber and oppress the rest? In an equal degree does the increased variety of parties, comprised within the union, increase this security? Does it, in fine, consist in the greater obstacles opposed to the concert and accomplishment of the secret wishes of an unjust and interested majority? Here, again, the extent of the union gives it the most palpable advantage.

The influence of factious leaders may kindle a flame within their particular states, but will be unable to spread a general conflagration through the other states; a religious sect may degenerate into a political faction in a part of the confederacy; but the variety of sects dispersed over the entire face of it, must secure the national councils against any danger from the source; a rage for paper money, for an abolition of debts, for an equal division of property, or for any other improper or wicked project, will be less apt to pervade the whole body of the union, than a particular member of it; in the same proportion as such a malady is more likely to taint a particular county or district, than an entire state.

In the extent and proper structure of the union, therefore, we behold a republican remedy for the diseases most incident to republican government. And according to the degree of pleasure and pride we feel in being republicans, ought to be our zeal in cherishing the spirit, and supporting the character of Federalists.

In the previous selection, Madison argues for a large republic to curtail the evil effects of faction. Madison's and the framers' basic premise was that concentrated power, especially in the hands of a majority, would threaten individual liberties and undermine the national interest. A large republic would help to disperse political power and prevent unbridled majority rule.

The framers also created the separation of powers and a system of checks and balances to assure balanced and deliberative government. Madison wrote in *Federalist 47*, citing Montesquieu, "The accumulation of all powers, legislative, executive, and judiciary, in the same hands, whether of one, a few, or many, and whether hereditary, self-appointed, or elective, may justly be pronounced the very definition of tyranny." Madison pointed out that the separation of powers "did not mean that [the three branches of government] ought to have no partial agency in, or no control over, the acts of each other. Montesquieu's meaning . . . can amount to no more than this, that where the *whole* power of one department is exercised by the same hands which possess the *whole* power of another department, the fundamental principles of a free constitution are subverted."

Madison describes how the checks and balances system operates in the following selection from *The Federalist*. The components of Madison's argument are:

1. Since the accumulation of all power in the same hands is the definition of tyranny, liberty requires a separation of powers among the branches of government.
2. Checks and balances are essential to the separation of powers. Each branch of the government must have the constitutional means and incentives to resist encroachments by coordinate branches.
3. While a dependence on the people is the primary control on government, auxiliary precautions against governmental despotism must be put into place.
4. The legislative power predominates in government, facilitating the possibility of legislative encroachments upon executive power. A bicameral legislature inhibits unilateral legislative action and helps to equalize legislative and executive power in the system of checks and balances.

2

James Madison

FEDERALIST 51

★★★

To what expedient then shall we finally resort, for maintaining in practice the necessary partition of power among the several departments, as laid down in the constitution? The only answer that can be given is, that as all these exterior provisions are found to be inadequate, the defect must be supplied, by so contriving the interior structure of the government, as that its several constituent parts may, by their mutual relations, be the means of keeping each other in their proper places. . . .

In order to lay a due foundation for that separate and distinct exercise of the different powers of government, which, to a certain extent, is admitted on all hands to be essential to the preservation of liberty, it is evident that each department should have a will of its own; and consequently should be so constituted, that the members of each should have as little agency as possible in the appointment of the members of the others. . . .

It is equally evident, that the members of each department should be as little dependent as possible on those of the others, for the emoluments annexed to their offices. Were the executive magistrate, or the judges, not independent of the legislature in this particular, their independence in every other, would be merely nominal.

But the great security against a gradual concentration of the several powers in the same department, consists in giving to those who administer each department, the necessary constitutional means, and personal motives, to resist encroachments of the others. The provision for defense must in this, as in all other cases, be made commensurate to the danger of attack. Ambition must be made to counteract ambition. The interest of the man must be connected with the constitutional rights of the place. It may be a reflection on human nature, that such devices should be necessary to control the abuses of government. But what is government itself, but the greatest of all reflections on human nature? If men were angels, no government would be necessary. If angels were to govern men, neither external nor internal controls on government would be necessary. In framing a government, which is to be administered by men over men, the great difficulty lies in this: you must first enable the government to control the governed; and in the next place, oblige it to control itself. A dependence on the people is, no doubt, the primary control on the government; but experience has taught mankind the necessity of auxiliary precautions.

This policy of supplying by opposite and rival interests, the defect of better motives, might be traced through the whole system of human affairs, private as well as public. We see it particularly displayed in all the subordinate distributions of power; where the constant aim is, to divide and arrange the several offices in such a manner, as that each may be a check on the other; that the private interest of every individual, may be a sentinel over the public rights. These inventions of prudence cannot be less requisite to the distribution of the supreme powers of the state.

But it is not possible to give each department an equal power of self-defense. In republican government, the legislative authority necessarily predominates. The remedy for this inconvenience is, to divide the legislature into different branches; and to render them by different modes of election, and different principles of action, as little connected with each other, as the nature of their common functions, and their common dependence on the society will admit. It may even be necessary to guard against dangerous encroachments, by still further precautions. As the weight of the legislative authority requires that it should be thus divided, the weakness of the executive may require, on the other hand, that it should be fortified. An absolute negative on the legislature, appears, at first view, to be the natural defense with which the executive magistrate should be armed. But perhaps it would be neither altogether safe, nor alone sufficient. On ordinary occasions, it might not be exerted with the requisite firmness; and on extraordinary occasions, it might be perfidiously abused. May not this defect of an absolute negative be supplied by some qualified connection between this weaker department, and the weaker branch of the stronger department, by which the latter may be led to support the constitutional rights of the former without being too much detached from the rights of its own department?

The following selection analyzes the values that form the core of what the author calls "the American Creed." Individual liberty and equality are important components of the creed, giving it an anti-government cast. We will see later in this chapter that President Reagan both in rhetoric and action drew upon the deeply-rooted values of individualism and liberty to attack big government.

The political ideals that Americans share often conflict with political practices and public policies. Political rhetoric and reality diverge, as do political ideals and many of the traditional theories that explain American politics.

Samuel P. Huntington is a political scientist who has had a long and distinguished career. The major points he makes in the following reading are:

1. The gap between political ideals and realities in American politics is greater than in any other country.
2. The American Creed reflects a broad consensus that is essentially anti-authoritarian and anti-government. Individualism is the central value of the Creed.
3. Traditional explanations of American politics overlook the importance of the American Creed in shaping political values and actions. The class-conflict, consensus, and pluralist models explain American politics differently. None of these models can explain "the passion, upheaval, or moral intensity that at times envelopes the American political scene."

3

Samuel P. Huntington

THE DISHARMONIC POLITY

★★★

[The] gap between political ideal and political reality is a continuing central phenomenon of American politics in a way that is not true of any other major state. The importance of the gap stems from three distinctive characteristics of American political ideals. First is the *scope* of the agreement on these ideals. In contrast to most European societies, a broad consensus exists and has existed in the United States on basic political values and beliefs. These values and beliefs, which constitute what is often referred to as "the American Creed," have historically served as a distinctive source of American national identity. Second is the *substance* of those ideals. In contrast to the values of most other societies, the values of this creed are liberal, individualistic, democratic, egalitarian, and hence basically antigovernment and antiauthority in character. Whereas other ideologies legitimate established authority and institutions, the American Creed serves to delegitimate any hierarchical, coercive, authoritarian structures, including American ones. Third is the changing *intensity* with which Americans believe in these basic ideals, an intensity that varies from time to time and from group to group. Historically, American society seems to evolve through periods of creedal passion and of creedal passivity. . . .

THE ONE, THE TWO, AND THE MANY:
STRUCTURAL PARADIGMS OF AMERICAN POLITICS

This central characteristic of American politics has received little notice in the traditional theories or paradigms of American politics. Over the years, the prevailing images of American politics have been shaped by three such paradigms.

What is often referred to as the "Progressive" theory emphasizes the continuing conflict between the few who are rich and the many who are poor. It is, indeed, better referred to as the "class-conflict" theory of American politics, since it has been espoused by many others in addition to early-twentieth-century Progressive historians. Federalist thinkers such as John Adams assumed that "there is no special providence for Americans, and their nature is the same with that of others." Consequently, they also assumed that the social divisions that existed elsewhere would be reproduced in America. "The people, in all nations," Adams said, "are naturally divided into two sorts, the gentlemen and the simplemen . . . The great and perpetual distinction in civilized societies has been between the rich, who are few, and the poor, who are many." In similar terms, Alexander Hamilton agreed that "all communities divide themselves into the few and the many." In postulating this image, Hamilton's sympathies were with the rich, while Adams was deeply and equally suspicious of both rich and poor. At the end of the nineteenth century the Progressive historians attacked Federalist politics and identified themselves with the poor, while retaining the Federalist picture of American society. . . .

The consensus theory of American politics posits an image of American politics that is, in many respects, the polar opposite of the Federalist-Progressive approach. According to this theory, the key to understanding American history is not the conflict between two classes but rather the overwhelming predominance of the middle class. For a variety of reasons—the absence of feudalism, the abundance of free land, the shortage of labor, the resulting opportunities for vertical and horizontal mobility, the early introduction of universal manhood suffrage, and the prevalence of a "Lockean" ethos of liberty, equality, individualism—class consciousness and class conflict never developed in the United States as it did in Europe. Instead there was the "pleasing uniformity" that had struck Crèvecoeur and the social and political equality that had so impressed Tocqueville. As a result, class-based ideologies never developed in American politics as they did in European politics. A consensus on middle-class values prevailed, and the conflicts that have existed in American politics have been over relatively narrow issues of economics and personality within the framework of the all-pervading basic consensus. . . .

A third theory, the pluralist paradigm, holds that the central feature of American politics is the competition among interest groups. The process version of this approach sees politics as a struggle among large numbers of relatively small interest groups. The organization version emphasizes the dominant role of a small number of large, well-organized groups in shaping public policy. Proponents of the process theory tend to be favorably disposed toward that process, seeing a rough approximation of the public interest emerge out of open, competitive struggle in the political free market, where it can be assumed that constitutional and governmental structures do not significantly discriminate among groups in terms of their access to the political process. Proponents of the organization version, on the other hand, usually emphasize the extent to which the established groups control the political process and make meaningless many of the pretensions of the democratic system premised on individual equality. At the extreme, this version of the pluralist approach can have many resemblances to the class-conflict theory.

The pluralist paradigm received its classic statement by James Madison in *The Federalist* (particularly Number 10). It was reformulated by Arthur F. Bentley in the early twentieth century, and it reemerged as the dominant interpretation of American politics among political scientists after World War II. It is, in some measure, quite compatible with the consensus paradigm, since the conflicts among interest groups over particular issues can be conceived of as occurring within the framework of a broad agreement on basic political values. In fact, one paradigm almost implies the existence of the other: they differ in that one stresses the basic agreement and the other the specific issues that are fought over within the context of this agreement.

Each of these three theories has its strengths and its weaknesses, The class-conflict theory points accurately to the existence in America of significant inequalities in wealth and income. It argues inaccurately, however, that these differences have been a principal continuing basis for political cleavage in American society. While American politics has at times been polarized, it has seldom, if ever (the New Deal was the most notable exception), been polarized between rich and poor. More generally, in attempting to sandwich American political struggle into a simple, dualistic framework, the class-conflict theory does scant justice to the complexity and variability of the struggle. For many of the class-conflict theorists, class conflict more accurately describes what they think American politics should be like rather than what it actually has been like over the course of centuries. The consensus theory, on the other hand, rightly acknowledges the absence of European class-based ideologies and the widespread agreement in the United States on liberal, democratic, individualistic, Lockean political values. Particularly in [Louis Hartz's] formulation, however, it also tended to suggest that the existence of an ideological consensus meant the absence of any form of significant social conflict. In fact, the United States has had more sociopolitical conflict and violence than many European countries. "Americans," as Hofstadter neatly put it, "do not *need* ideological conflict to shed blood on a large scale." Why this should be the case is ignored by consensus theory. Finally, the pluralist paradigm—in both its process and organizational versions—clearly describes the way in which American politics functions a good part of the time. It does not, however, anymore than the consensus theory, provide for or explain the passion, upheaval, or moral intensity that at times envelops the American political scene. . . .

IDEALS VERSUS INSTITUTIONS

. . . When foreigners ask, "What is American politics all about?" it cannot be explained to them simply in terms of a . . . struggle of faction and group, or a Marxist-like confrontation of classes, or a complacent consensus. It is, in some measure, all of these things, but it is also much more. To see American politics purely as a reflection of social structure is to miss the teleological—as distinguished from the mechanistic—dimension of that politics. The ways in which individuals, groups, and classes act in politics are decisively shaped not only by their own perceptions of their immediate interests but also by the ideological climate and the common political values and purposes that they all recognize as legitimate. The United States has lacked European-style ideological conflict, yet its politics has been infused with more moral passion than those of any European country. "America," Santayana once observed, "is all one prairie, swept by a universal tornado." The consensus theory posits the uniformity of the prairie but not the fury of the tornado that the prairie's very flatness engenders. In the United States, ideological consensus is the source of political conflict, polarization occurs over moral issues rather than economic ones, and the politics of interest groups is supplemented and at times supplanted by the politics of moralistic reform. America has been spared class conflicts in order to have moral convulsions. It is precisely the central role of moral passion that distinguishes American politics from the politics of most other societies, and it is this characteristic that is most difficult for foreigners to understand.

The importance of political ideas and values in shaping the course of American development has not always been neglected in historical writing, and in part for this reason it tended to become discredited. The progressive realization of American ideals was a familiar theme among nineteenth-century "Patriotic" historians. "The unifying principle" of history for George Bancroft, as Hofstadter points out, "was progress ordained and planned by God—the advance of liberty, justice, and humanity, all of which were peculiarly exemplified in American history, where providential guidance had brought together a singularly fit people and fit institutions . . . American history could be seen as a kind of consummation of all history." The same theme, viewed considerably more ambivalently, was also present in Tocqueville. Common to both was the concept of American history as a gradual but steady unfolding and realization of the ideals of liberty, equality, and democracy.

This interpretation accurately highlighted the extent to which the pursuit of these ideals was central to the American political experience. What it did not highlight, however, was the extent to which the failure to realize those ideals was equally central to that experience. The image of the triumphant realization of the American promise or ideal was an exercise in patriotic unreality at best and hypocrisy at worst. The history of American politics is the repetition of new beginnings and flawed outcomes, promise and disillusion, reform and reaction. American history is the history of the efforts of groups to promote their interests by realizing American ideals. What is important, however, is not that they succeed but that they fail, not that the dream is realized but that it is not and never can be realized completely or satisfactorily. In the American context there will always be those who say that the institutional glass is half-empty and who will spill much passion attempting to fill it to the brim from the spring of idealism. But in the nature of things, particularly in America, it can never be much more than half-full. . . .

Social, economic, and political inequalities may well be more limited and political liberties more extensive in the United States than they are in most other societies. Yet the commitment to equality and liberty and the opposition to hierarchy and authority are so widespread and deep that the incongruity between the normative and existential orders is far greater in the United States than elsewhere. Traditional India was clearly more unequal than modern America, but modern America is clearly more disharmonic than traditional India. The extent to which a society or a political system is harmonic or disharmonic depends as much upon the values of its people as upon the structure of its institutions. Any society, moreover, necessarily involves a certain irreducible minimum of inequality and hierarchy. The variations in attitudes toward inequality, hierarchy, and authority among the peoples of different societies are likely to be at least as great as the variations in actual inequality, hierarchy, and authority among those societies, particularly in the modern world. With its unique consensus on and commitment to liberal, democratic, and egalitarian political values, the United States is the modern disharmonic polity par excellence.

... Critics say that America is a lie because its reality falls so far short of its ideals. They are wrong. America is not a lie; it is a disappointment. But it can be a disappointment only because it is also a hope.

The framers of the Constitution agreed with Lord Acton's maxim that "power corrupts, and absolute power corrupts absolutely." The Madisonian system of separation of powers and checks and balances was in part based upon a skeptical view of *unchecked* political power. Madison and the framers saw the proper and deliberate exercise of political power as essential to the preservation of a union. The eighteenth-century model of government based upon checks and balances and separation of powers was not negative as it is often portrayed, but a positive and essential way to channel political power in the national interest.

The Madisonian ideal seems to have worked, according to the author of the following selection, who over his long career engaged in Washington politics at the highest levels. "The truth about power in Washington," he writes, "is that no individual has much.... The dispersal of power has from the outset been a source of vitality and resilience." The Madisonian model lives.

Elliot Richardson had a distinguished political career in Massachusetts and in Washington. In Massachusetts he became Lieutenant Governor in 1965, and served as Attorney General from 1967–1969. He served as President Richard M. Nixon's Secretary of Health, Education, and Welfare from 1970–1973, then briefly as Secretary of Defense. In 1973 he became Nixon's Attorney General, but after Nixon fired special Watergate prosecutor Archibald Cox, Richardson resigned in protest. He returned to Washington as President Jimmy Carter's Secretary of Commerce in 1976–1977. He is the only person in history to have served in four different Cabinet posts.

Richardson makes the following arguments:

1. A widely held belief is that to get to the top in Washington one must pursue power ruthlessly.
2. The media fortifies the popular belief that only power is the name of the Washington game because they focus almost exclusively on the dramatic side of the power game to capture public attention.
3. The reality is that Machiavelli would be confused by Washington politics. He would find a world more of cocker spaniels then pit bulls. Washington players seek power to achieve worthy ends, not for its own sake.
4. Fragmented power is a Washington reality. No single individual, not even the President, has a monopoly on power. The constitutional separation of powers and the system of checks and balances works. The constitutional and political dispersion of power encourages the compromises that are necessary to support a viable democratic system.

4

Elliot Richardson

Power in Washington

★ ★ ★

Do you believe that the pursuit of power is the national capital's favorite form of exercise? That wielding power is Washington's most gratifying occupation? That skill in its manipulation is the key to effectiveness? That to get to the top of the Washington heap you have to have a streak of ruthlessness, even meanness?

If your answers are affirmative, you share a set of widely held beliefs. That they happen to be wrong should not embarrass you. It's quite understandable, in fact, that you and so many others should think this way. Events that are "newsworthy," which is to say exciting or dramatic, are more likely to seize your attention than those that are merely important. Power, in any case, has an exciting aura (while still new to Washington Henry Kissinger called it "the great aphrodisiac"). There is drama in its capture, manipulation, curtailment, or loss. These are things we all read about in the morning paper and watch on the evening news. No matter how conscientious, we could not possibly give proportionate attention to the remainder—89 percent perhaps—of what the Washington complex is actually chewing away on day by day.

History has scarcely more time than journalism for the ordinary and undramatic. Just as good news is no news, uneventful times have no history. And while Washington's history has not been uneventful, its hardest-fought struggles have been over purposes and policies rather than power. By comparison with that of other great capitals, Washington's past has been tame. Every national election has been held on the appointed day. Every transfer of power from one administration to the next has proceeded without incident. No American politician has ever gone to the chopping block, forfeited his estates, or been sent into exile. There has never been even a hint of a conspiracy to take over the White House and oust the president. And only one president has been forced to resign.

Machiavelli would be confused by Washington. He would find it hard to believe that it is in reality a city of cocker spaniels more eager to be loved, petted, and admired than to wield power. He would wonder where the pit bulls are. And while Machiavelli might see encouraging signs that the nation's capital is on its way toward becoming a place in which he might eventually feel at home, he would encounter little immediate use for his skills. The reason for his disappointment, of course, would be that our system has throughout its history been strikingly successful in cutting down to size those who seek personal aggrandizement. It has also done very well in harnessing political power to the security and welfare of the American people.

But past success is small solace for future failure, and the system is indeed coming under increasing strain. It is important, therefore, for us to try to understand how and why it has worked so well up to now. This essay records the outcome of my own efforts to reach such understanding. What I have to report will, I hope, help us stay the course.

One clue to the system's success that struck me early on is a clue like that of the dog that *didn't* bark in the Sherlock Holmes story: it is the scarcity in Washington of individuals who are recognizably driven by the pursuit of power for its own sake. Your typical cynic will, of course, reject this observation, but that need not trouble us; cynics are not distinguished for their realism. Journalists and fiction writers (the difference between the two is not always clear) would also have us believe that Washington is full of power-hungry monomaniacs, but they have, after all, a certain interest in encouraging this belief.

In the real Washington, even the most ambitious people I know would insist that they seek power only for the sake of worthy ends. It goes without saying that they want to win as well as to achieve recognition, enjoy respect, and make a comfortable living. They realize, however, that being perceived as too aggressive or too self-seeking could jeopardize these aims. Besides, in Washington as elsewhere, success seldom confers esteem unless it appears to have been won in accordance with the rules. Why otherwise would those who are known to have broken them on the way up later feel compelled to try to cultivate social acceptance?

The truth about power in Washington is that no individual has much. The system works, not in spite of that fact, but because of it. The dispersal of power has from the outset been a source of vitality and resilience. The system is constantly renewed, indeed, by the perennial necessity both to combine the efforts of people who share an objective they cannot accomplish on their own and to head off the opposition of people any of whom could block it on their own. You see these processes going on at every point around the circle linking voters with interest groups with the presidency with executive branch agencies with Congress with voters and so around the circle again.

Let's break into the circle at the presidency. The president is, of course, much more powerful than anybody else in the system. But what does he actually do with his time? Mostly, he tries to build support. When Theodore Roosevelt referred to the "bully pulpit," he was not exulting in the power of his office but making the point that the White House is a good platform from which to win converts and rally the faithful. The later Roosevelt's "fireside chats," JFK's press conferences, Clinton's town meetings, and every recent president's nationally televised speeches have all been means not simply of explaining presidential policies but of building broader support. This has to go on continually and on many levels: with the general public, interest groups, members of Congress, businessmen, religious leaders, educators, the medical profession, heads of other governments, and on and on and on.

The president has to have his own pollsters to tell him what the people want and how to get across to them what he thinks they should want. He has to have his own lobbyists to track developments on the Hill, sell his programs, and spot the senators and congressmen who need his personal massaging. The president has to answer critics, mollify interest groups, and cultivate the media. He has to be image-conscious twenty-four hours a day. His fellow citizens' dislike or distrust can reduce him to impotence.

The people who work for the president at high levels in executive branch departments and agencies have to operate in the same kind of way, although of course on a smaller and narrower scale. Making decisions and issuing orders won't cut it. For every important initiative it is essential to seek and win support. Indeed, this conspicuous difference between the day-to-day roles of government managers and corporate executives may explain why success in business is no guarantee of success in government.

From the president on down, people in the executive branch used to take what advantage they could of a limited supply of carrots and sticks. Both the sticks and the carrots were fashioned from the same material—government grants and contracts, presidential appointments, bills or appropriations of special interest to a constituency, pork-barrel projects, and the like. Where inducing congressional cooperation was concerned, the carrot held out support for some such interest; the stick warned of opposition to it. These carrot-and-stick combinations, however, are of limited utility. For one thing, there were often larger public interests at stake that inhibited their use. For another, there was at any one time only a limited number of interests unique to an individual senator or congressman that the executive branch could legitimately advance or impede. Moreover, any given carrot or stick could be used only once. The risk of making a permanent enemy also had to be weighed.

The executive branch's lobbying resources, in any case, had to be spread thinly over a very broad agenda. The White House had first claim on the valuable items. Those left over were useful only for secondary issues. Back in the days of President Eisenhower's second term, when I was responsible for the Department of Health, Education, and Welfare's legislative program, the goodies at my disposal were so insignificant that to mention them would have been more likely to derail my appeal on the merits than to win a congressman's support. That experience set a precedent for all my later contacts with Congress. . . .

Every new Congress reconfirms the saying "The president proposes and Congress disposes." The House's exclusive power to originate revenue bills, the Senate's tolerance of unlimited debate, and both bodies' delaying tactics can be maddening to a president who thinks he knows what he was elected to accomplish. Given these frustrations, it's easy to see why presidents have been so anxious to get the line-item veto and why the present Congress has not yet let them have even a watered-down version of it.

Despite all the time and money that other people give to winning their support, senators and congressmen have no time to enjoy the possession of power. Other than butlers and firemen, they're the only people I know of who are constantly being summoned by bells. An executive branch supplicant is surprised only the first time when a committee chairman suspends a meeting in his office to take a call from an important constituent. And no matter how often you've testified at committee hearings you don't get used to being stopped in midsentence so that members can answer a roll call.

But the surest way to lose one's awe of congressional power is to expose oneself to the apparatus that Congress has assembled to handle communications with constituents. The audio and video facilities, the computerized files, the mail-handling machinery, and the copying, faxing, and word-processing equipment—all these show whom Congress holds in awe.

Most House members have between four and ten staffers who do nothing but sort and answer mail and another three or four who do nothing but handle casework. Most members spend an average of fifteen to twenty hours a week meeting with constituents, taking them to lunch, or showing them around the Capitol. All members have local offices at which citizens can make their requests and voice their complaints, and most have regular office hours and town meetings back home on weekends. Even the unremitting necessity of raising money pays homage to people power. According to a *Congressional Quarterly* study of all reported expenditures in the 1992 House and Senate campaigns, the share that went into communicating with the electorate was 44 percent for House incumbents and 56 percent for House challengers, 53 percent for Senate incumbents and 62 percent for Senate challengers.

And what about the constituents themselves? Do they feel good about all the attention lavished on them by the suitors for their support? Not if you can believe the opinion surveys. The proportion of the adult public who think that people running the country don't really care what happens to them has risen steadily year by year for a long time. So too has the proportion who think that most people with power try to take advantage of people like themselves. This is a deeply disturbing development. It reflects a sense of inefficacy and helplessness which, though the product of factors quite different from those to which it is attributed, is meat for a demagogue like Ross Perot.

The designers of our constitutional system would be astonished and perhaps dismayed by the scale and complexity of the society to which their inventions are being applied. Showing them Washington would be like showing a Boeing 747 to the Wright brothers. But the framers would surely be gratified to learn that, thanks to their devices for limiting, dispersing, and checking the use of power, ours is the only major country in the world which, in the last two hundred years, has never been ruled by a dictator or an oligarchy.

At this point the cynic breaks in. Though almost always wrong, he can be astute. He observes that the dispersal of power, rather than supporting my view of its limited motivating force, proves nothing more than that the game engages a great many players. Knowing my weakness for constitutional history, he then throws in my face *The Federalist*, no. 51's famous dictum on the separation of powers: "The great security . . . consists in giving to those who administer each department, the necessary constitutional means, and personal motives, to resist encroachments of the others. . . . Ambition must be made to counteract ambition." Following up this thrust, the cynic then goes on to cite Madison's exposition in *The Federalist*, no. 10, of the manner in which groups and interests ("factions") are bound to struggle for advantage.

The cynic has a point. The framers, however, did not assume that self-interest alone would assure outcomes in the general interest of everyone. Self-government could not succeed unless, as Madison put it, there were "other qualities in human nature which justify a certain portion of esteem and confidence." "Republican government," Madison added, "presupposes the existence of these qualities in a higher degree than any other form." Were it otherwise, "the inference would be, that there is not sufficient virtue among men for self-government . . ." (*The Federalist*, no. 55). As to factions, "a multiplicity of interests" would tend to make "a coalition of a majority of the whole society" unlikely "on any other principles than those of justice and the general good" (*The Federalist*, no. 51).

If it were not for the common bonds of human decency, ours would be a far nastier society—and Washington, D.C., would be a far less tame capital—than they actually are. Not to acknowledge these facts would be palpably unrealistic. Indeed, it is just such a lack of touch with reality that discredits cynicism. My conception of our system, in any case, is not confined to the self-adjusting mechanisms of its constitutional machinery and the psychological insights that inspired its design. The dispersal of power has never been the only contributor to the prevention of its abuse. To account for the survival of our system of government in essentially unchanged form for more than two hundred years it is also necessary to grasp the indispensable role of certain uniquely American ways of looking at and approaching things. What I have in mind aren't traits or characteristics exactly, or values, though they're related to values. I call them "attitudes."

The first and most basic of these attitudes is the demand for accountability. The generation that shaped the constitutions of the first thirteen states and then gave birth to the Federal Constitution did in fact ordain and establish governments of a new kind: governments that derived their just—and limited—powers from the consent of the governed. "We the People" are the continually renewed body of citizens of the United States of America who hold accountable those of their fellow citizens who at any given time occupy elected or appointed public offices.

The second attitude is almost equally basic. An offshoot of the first, it is our insistence on openness and transparency in the conduct of governmental affairs.

The third attitude keeps us focused on what works and on what really matters. The result is a blend of idealism and practicality. This attitude explains why few Americans have been drawn into struggles between competing ideologies.

Partly contributing to and partly generated by the system shaped by the framers' genius, these three attitudes have throughout our history held government to the service of the American people. They made it adaptable to change, resilient in surmounting adversity, and resourceful in accommodating clashing interests. Little by little they transformed the system into a democracy. And, perhaps above all, more than "supplying the defect of better qualities," these attitudes called forth better qualities.

The attitudes I have identified were, I believe, the keys to the ability of our form of representative democracy to disperse and limit power while at the same time making possible the practical resolution of contentious issues. . . .

[O]ur constitutional system has again and again demonstrated its powers of self-correction and renewal. We, its masters, being both optimistic and otherwise occupied, are slow in reacting to a developing threat and even slower in coming to a consensus as to how to deal with it. Like a spring whose power to recoil increases with the pressure exerted against it, the distinctively American attitudes discussed in this essay can reassert themselves. But whether or not they do so must not be left to chance. . .

✯✯✯

The Reagan administration in the 1980s had a Grand Doctrine. We pointed out in our introduction to selection three in this chapter that many of the values comprising the American Creed surfaced in Reagan's Grand Doctrine. Individualism, self-reliance, and freedom supported Reagan's attack on big government.

Reagan's Grand Doctrine bolstered laissez-faire economics, which at the time was called supply-side economics. The plan was to cut government spending through the elimination of the New Deal and Great Society programs of the past, and market forces would take up the slack and produce a booming economy.

David A. Stockman had served Michigan's fourth district in Congress from 1977–1981. He strongly opposed the welfare state, which continued the tradition of the Republican representatives from the district. Stockman became Washington's Republican expert on the budget during the Carter years, which led Reagan to appoint him as his Budget Director in 1981. Stockman's ideal was supply-side economics, but he soon learned that political realities would intrude upon the Grand Doctrine's implementation.

In the following selection Stockman describes what he found out about Washington politics as he sought to implement the Grand Doctrine.

1. Comprehensive doctrines that reflect economic or political ideals, such as supply-side economics, have a logical and sometimes even simplistic appeal.
2. Practical politics always overwhelms ideological blueprints.
3. The practical politics of American democracy will always defeat an anti-welfare state theory that adversely impacts powerful economic and political interests.
4. Members of Congress pursue reelection, not grand theories. Economic theories must bend to political realities in the budgetary process.
5. The American political system has balanced capitalism and social democracy. Economic competition exists side by side with stability and social security.

5

David A. Stockman

THE TRIUMPH OF POLITICS

[T]he supply-side synthesis closed the final loop in my quest for the Grand Doctrine.

As an intellectual and moral matter, this comprehensive supply-side doctrine had a powerful appeal. It offered a rigorous standard of justice and fairness, and provided a recipe for economic growth and prosperity—the only viable way to truly eliminate poverty and social deprivation. But its elegant idealism was hostile to all the messy, expedient compromises of daily governance.

This was made dramatically evident when, toward the end of my second term, the Chrysler Corporation demanded that the federal government rescue it from its own mismanagement. The action was justified by an army of lobbyists who represented every imaginable local interest group and no discernible policy principle.

The notion that the federal government should, on demand, refinance inefficient, bankrupt private enterprises was so loathsome to me that I resolved not only to vote against it, but to take the lead in trying to stop it. So I took the floor of the House to speak out against this abomination that was about to pass. I preached to the politicians my most fevered anti-statist sermon. Both the fevers and the sermon were still with me when I moved into the White House a year later:

> We have to be pragmatic. Fix it up now and worry about the consequences later. Don't bother yourself with elegant theories about whether it's sound public policy.
> Don't trouble yourself with the economic effects of catapulting Chrysler from the back of the credit line to the front. Somebody else is going to be squeezed out of the credit market—small manufacturers, construction firms, auto dealers, farmers—with reduced production and employment elsewhere in the economy as a result.
> These latter firms and workers are not speculative. They are just politically invisible.
> No one on the globe with real money to invest is willing to come forward to Chrysler's rescue: not the banks, insurance companies, or the bond markets. . . . Unless Uncle Sam promises to underwrite the risk.
> Well, P.T. Barnum once said, "There's one born every day—you can count on it." Apparently the U.S. Congress is the only one left.

Despite its disdainful tone and righteous indignation, my speech was applauded even by some of those who had declared they would vote for the bailout (while holding their noses). For my opposition I was oxymoronically hailed by many as an "intelligent" politician.

Looking back on that, I am not at all sure I deserve the praise. I spoke of economic doctrine but did not manage to see a stark, dramatic truth. The Chrysler bailout passed by a margin of over one hundred votes because the impacted voters wanted it. And if the House of Representatives would go for the raw, unprincipled expediency of that measure, why should I have assumed, only a year later, that the institution, and the electorates it represented, would accept the kind of sweeping austere ideological blueprint the Reagan Revolution called for? I finally had my Grand Doctrine, but it completely overwhelmed my grasp of what the politics of American governance was all about. . . .

THE TRIUMPH OF POLITICS

"You ain't seen nothing yet." The White House made that its official campaign slogan for 1984. When it did, I knew that my own days were numbered, and that even the reluctant loyalty I had maintained during the long battle to reverse the President's tax policy was no longer defensible. Now I had to resort to out-and-out subversion—

scheming with the congressional leaders during the first half of 1985 to force a tax hike. But that failed too, leaving me with no choice but to resign in the knowledge that my original ideological excesses had given rise to a fiscal and political disorder that was probably beyond correction.

Politics had triumphed: first by blocking spending cuts and then by stopping revenue increases. There was nothing left to do but follow former Governor Hugh Carey's example and head out of town, whupped.

That the politics of American democracy made a shambles of my anti-welfare state theory I can now understand. Whatever its substantive merit, it rested on the illusion that the will of the people was at drastic variance with the actions of the politicians.

But the political history of the past five years mostly invalidates that proposition. We have had a tumultuous national referendum on everything in our half-trillion-dollar welfare state budget. By virtue of experiencing the battle day after day in the legislative and bureaucratic trenches, I am as qualified as anyone to discern the verdict. Lavish Social Security benefits, wasteful dairy subsidies, futile UDAG grants, and all the remainder of the federal subventions do not persist solely due to weak-kneed politicians or the nefarious graspings of special-interest groups.

Despite their often fuzzy rhetoric and twisted rationalizations, congressmen and senators ultimately deliver what their constituencies demand. The notion that Washington amounts to a puzzle palace on the Potomac, divorced from the genuine desires of the voters, thus constitutes more myth than truth. So does the related proposition eloquently expressed in the editorial pages of *The Wall Street Journal*. Somehow it manages to divine a great unwashed mass of the citizenry demanding the opposite of the spending agendas presented by the Claude Peppers, the homebuilders' lobby, and the other hired guns of K Street.

But those who suggest the existence of an anti-statist electorate are in fact demanding that national policy be harnessed to their own particular doctrine of the public good. The actual electorate, however, is not interested in this doctrine; when it is interested at all, it is interested in getting help from the government to compensate for a perceived disadvantage. Consequently, the spending politics of Washington do reflect the heterogeneous and parochial demands that arise from the diverse, activated fragments of the electorate scattered across the land. What you see done in the halls of the politicians may not be wise, but it is the only real and viable definition of what the electorate wants.

I cannot be so patient with the White House. By 1984 it had become a dreamland. It was holding the American economy hostage to a reckless, unstable fiscal policy based on the politics of high spending and the doctrine of low taxes. Yet rather than acknowledge that the resulting massive buildup of public debt would eventually generate serious economic troubles, the White House proclaimed a roaring economic success. It bragged that its policies had worked as never before when, in fact, they had produced fiscal excesses that had never before been imagined.

The brash phrasemakers of the White House had given George Orwell a new resonance—and right on schedule. In 1984 we were plainly drifting into unprecedented economic peril. But they had the audacity to proclaim a golden age of prosperity.

What economic success there was had almost nothing to do with our original supply-side doctrine. Instead, [Federal Reserve Board Chairman] Paul Volcker and the business cycle had brought inflation down and economic activity surging back. But there was nothing new, revolutionary, or sustainable about this favorable turn of events. The cycle of economic boom and bust had been going on for decades, and by election day its oscillations had reached the high end of the charts. That was all. . . .

. . . Ronald Reagan had been induced by his advisers and his own illusions to embrace one of the more irresponsible platforms of modern times. He had promised, as it were, to alter the laws of arithmetic. No program that had a name or line in the budget would be cut; no taxes would be raised. Yet the deficit was pronounced intolerable and it was pledged to be eliminated.

This was the essence of the unreality. The President and his retainers promised to eliminate the monster deficit with spending cuts when for all practical purposes they had already embraced or endorsed 95 percent of all the spending there was to cut.

The White House itself had surrendered to the political necessities of the welfare state early on. By 1985, only the White House speechwriters carried on a lonely war of words, hurling a stream of presidential rhetoric at a ghostly abstraction called Big Government.

The White House's claim to be serious about cutting the budget had, in fact, become an institutionalized fantasy. I had tried diplomatically and delicately to convey the facts that made this so, but the only response I got was a new whispering campaign led by Ed Meese: Stockman is too pessimistic; he's been on the Hill too long; he's one of *them!*

Maybe so. Ever since September 1981 I'd been reduced to making one-sided spending deals. The politicians mostly got what their constituents wanted, but here and there we trimmed the edges. But my relentless dealmaking inherently yielded savings that amounted to rounding errors in a trillion-dollar budget because it was based on bluff and searching out for obscure tidbits of spending that could be excised without arousing massive political resistance. Thus, for example, we did get the second-tier COLA in the railroad retirement program capped below the inflation rate. This reduced overall spending by 0.0001 percent!

But nothing meaningful could be done about federal spending because even the President no longer had a plausible program to do anything about it. The White House had thrown in the towel on all the big spending components that could make a difference on the deficit. And it had abandoned nearly every policy principle that could have been the basis for organizing a renewed anti-spending coalition.

The domestic budget is huge, but nearly 90 percent of it is accounted for by a handful of big programs: Social Security and other social insurance; Medicare; the safety net, veterans, agriculture and transportation.

By 1984, the White House had explicitly decided not to challenge these big components of the welfare state budget in any significant way. Jim Baker had been proven correct about the political consequences of attacking the basic entitlement and COLA of the 36 million citizens receiving Social Security and Medicare. So I had eventually been reduced to trying to get the Congress to modestly trim the Medicare entitlement. But in the election/budget year of 1984 even the President rejected proposals for increased patient cost sharing, and then went on to plant his feet in concrete against any cuts in Social Security at all.

These two programs accounted for half of the welfare state budget, yet by 1985 the only option we had left was to squeeze a few percent of their massive $270 billion cost from the doctors and hospitals that delivered the services the old folks were now guaranteed to receive. Right then and there the fiscal arithmetic of coping with a $200 billion deficit through spending cuts alone had become prohibitive.

The President had also inadvertently safeguarded the smaller civil service retirement system from cuts, too. The administration budget carried a proposal to cap civil service COLAs and penalize early retirement (before age sixty-two), but its legislative prospects depended crucially on applying the same concept to the even more generous military retirement program. Both proposals were put in the President's budget, but the Joint Chiefs of Staff soon complained loudly. The President then cancelled the military reforms, buttressing the $25 billion civil service retirement program as he did so.

Likewise, the $27 billion complex of veterans' programs was also given immunity in a curious way. The White House appointed a VA administrator, by the name of Harry Walters, who spent a large part of his time denouncing the President's budget director at American Legion conventions. Whatever tiny veterans' cuts I managed to stuff into the budget were made instantly non-operative by Mr. Walters's ability to claim with impunity that he spoke for the President. No one at the White House ever said he didn't.

After the first round of cuts in the $75 billion complex of welfare, food stamp, and safety net programs, the White House raised the white flag there, too. The President promised the governors not to tamper seriously with Medicaid—the largest program—and appointed a task force which recommended that we repeal some of the nutrition program reforms we had already made. While we continued to send up to the Hill small, technical proposals to nick a billion or two, the clear White House message was that the safety net was now inviolate.

That position reflected the overwhelming sentiment of the public, and in that sense was justifiable. But it also constituted another big block of evidence that the President's antispending rhetoric amounted to an illusion. . . .

As I prepared to make one last run at the deficit monster in late 1984, I soon found myself impaled upon an awful dilemma. Given the fiscal facts of life, I somehow believed that the White House would be prepared to wriggle out of its militant no-tax-increase campaign pledges. With everyone for the welfare state and no one against it, the only thing left to do was to pay for it. But I was mistaken once again. . . .

Some will be tempted to read into the failure of the Reagan Revolution more than is warranted. It represents the triumph of politics over a particular doctrine of economic governance and that is all. It does not mean American democracy is fatally flawed: special interest groups do wield great power, but their influence is deeply rooted in local popular support. Certainly, it does not mechanically guarantee the inevitability of permanent massive budget deficits or economic doom.

Its implications are deeply pessimistic only for the small and politically insignificant set of anti-statist conservatives who inhabit niches in the world of government, academia, business, and journalism. For us, there is no room for equivocation. The Reagan Revolution amounted to the clearest test of doctrine ever likely to occur in a heterogeneous democracy like our own. And the anti-statist position was utterly repudiated by the combined forces of the politicians—Republican and Democrat, those in the executive branch as well as the legislative.

This verdict has implications, however, which go well beyond the invalidation of anti-statist doctrine. The triumphant welfare state principle means that economic governance must consist of a fundamental trade-off between capitalist prosperity and social security. As a nation we have chosen to have less of the former in order to have more of the latter.

Social Security, trade protectionism, safety net programs, UDAG, and farm price supports all have one thing in common. They seek to bolster the lot of less productive industries, regions, and citizens by taxing the wealth and income of everyone else.

The case for all this redistributionism is lodged in the modern tradition of social democracy. In America we have seldom explicitly acknowledged this principle of governance, but it is in fact what we have. And to some degree it works. On the basis of private cash income alone, more than 55 million Americans would end up below the so-called poverty line. But after all the welfare state's cash and in-kind benefits are paid and taxes are collected, the number of the statistically poor drops by nearly two thirds. So although it is riddled with inefficiency and injustice, the American welfare state does fulfill at least some of its promises.

But it does so at the expense of a less dynamic and productive capitalism. The kind of high growth and constant economic change envisioned by the supply-side doctrine is not possible if government taxes away economic rewards, blocks capital and labor reallocations, and funds a high safety net.

Social democracy also encourages the electorate to fragment into narrow interest groups designed to thwart and override market outcomes. That these pressure groups prevail most of the time should not be surprising. The essential welfare state principle of modern American governance sanctions both their role and their claims.

Viewed in this light, our political system performs its intended function fairly well. Its search to balance and calibrate the requisites of capitalism with social democracy's quest for stability and security has produced a surprising result. By any comparative standard, American politicians have created a more favorable balance between the two than in any other advanced industrial democracy.

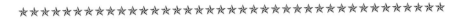

The preceding selection described how politics as usual defeated Reagan's Grand Doctrine. That Doctrine would have downsized government by reducing spending and government programs, and at the same time reducing taxes. The Grand Doctrine clashed with powerful political interests that benefited from government subsidies.

President Clinton also had a grand design. He dedicated his first term to the achievement of comprehensive health care, and put his wife Hillary Clinton in charge. Unlike Reagan's Grand Doctrine, Clinton's grand design was perceived by the American people to enlarge government, expand governmental regulations, and take away individual freedom to choose one's own doctor. Reagan's program conformed to the American Creed the first selection of this chapter describes. But Clinton's grand design clashed with American values of individualism and freedom that are anti-government. While politics as usual was probably the major reason for Clinton's defeat, the author of the following selection interestingly attributes Clinton's failure to the conflict between comprehensive health care and American ideals.

Theda Skocpol is a Professor of Government and Sociology at Harvard University. She is an expert on, among other things, health care reform, an area in which she has written extensively.

Skocpol's conclusions in the following selection on the failure of Clinton's health plan are:

1. Personality flaws and "stupid" decisions did not defeat Clinton's health plan.
2. Elite opinion opposed the democratic inclusiveness that Clinton's health plan incorporated.
3. The anti-government Reagan legacies helped to defeat Clinton's comprehensive health plan that would have raised taxes and expanded government regulation.

6

Theda Skocpol

BOOMERANG

★★★

A PIVOTAL EPISODE

On September 22, 1993, President Bill Clinton gave a stirring speech about "Health Security." As he stood before Congress and reached out via television to all the American people, Mr. Clinton was launching the most important initiative of his presidency. He called for legislators and citizens to work with him "to fix a health care system that is badly broken . . . giving every American health security—health care that's always there, health care that can never be taken away." "Despite the dedication of millions of talented health professionals," the President explained, health care "is too uncertain and too expensive. . . . Our health care system takes 35 percent more of our income than any other country, insures fewer people, requires more Americans to pay more and more for less and less, and gives them fewer choices. There is no excuse for that kind of system, and it's time to fix it."

Historic associations resonated as President Clinton spoke that September evening, particularly with the broad-based federal initiatives launched by another Democratic president, Franklin Delano Roosevelt, half a century earlier during the New Deal. The very title of Clinton's "Health Security" proposal harkened back to the Social Security Act of 1935. And the "Health Security card" that the president said every American would receive if his reforms were enacted was obviously meant to encourage a sense of safe and honorable entitlement such as Americans feel they have in Social Security. . . .

What Went Wrong?

Some have argued that there is little to investigate about the failure of the Clinton Health Security plan. Soon after George Mitchell, then the Democratic Majority Leader of the Senate, called it quits in the quest for any health legislation in September 1994, "obvious" explanations spewed forth to account for an attempted reform that backfired. Instant judgments came above all from Washington insiders and members of the "punditocracy" of media commentators and policy experts who appear daily on television and in the editorial and op-ed pages of newspapers and magazines. A year before, such commentators had been certain that President Clinton had irreversibly aroused a national commitment to some sort of universal health insurance. After the President's effort failed, the pundits became equally sure that his venture had never had any chance of popular acceptance or legislative enactment. We knew it all along, they said.

For many commentators, flaws in the personalities of key actors in the Clinton administration make sense of what happened. According to this story line, foolish and arrogant policy planners launched a liberal, government-takeover scheme that was doomed to fail. . . .

We should not, however, allow our attention to be directed away from the nation's major institutions—its government, mass media, political parties, and health care and economic enterprises. These were the arenas within which our leaders—not just those in the Clinton administration, but also corporate leaders, journalists, health care providers, and Democrats and Republicans in Congress and beyond—defined their goals and maneuvered in relation to each other. Within and at the intersections of these institutions, America's leaders failed to come up with reasonable ways to address pressing national concerns about the financing of health care for everyone.

As for explanations that highlight the personality flaws and supposed "awesome stupidity" of certain people in the Clinton administration, surely these miss the forest for a few trees. Various people in and around the Clinton administration did indeed take missteps. . . . But most of their errors were not stupid ones. Most of the mistakes made by the President and his allies need to be understood in terms of the difficult choices these people inexorably faced—given sensitive economic circumstances, artificially draconian federal budgetary constraints, and the flawed modalities of politics in the United States today. . . .

President Clinton and the Democrats struggled to extend health coverage to all Americans within a climate of elite opinion that is in principle unsympathetic to democratic inclusiveness. . . .

Despite the difficulties of advocating universal coverage in [this] climate of opinion, during 1992 and 1993 Bill Clinton came to believe that effective cost controls in health care financing were impossible without including all Americans. . . .

As a candidate and then as president, Bill Clinton searched assiduously for an approach to health care reform that would allow him to bridge the contradictions he had to face by achieving a new synthesis of previously opposed views. He looked for a middle way between Republicans and Democrats and between conservative and liberal factions in the Democratic Party and the Congress. He looked for a compromise between U.S. business and other private-sector elites who wanted to control rising health care costs, and average citizens who wanted secure coverage without personally having to pay much more for it. Perhaps most important, Mr. Clinton looked for a way to reform the financing of health care for everyone in the United States without increasing the size of the federal budget deficit or creating an open-ended new public "entitlement."

During 1993, many commentators, politicians, and members of the U.S. public thought that President Clinton was appropriately pointing the way toward feasible and moderate comprehensive health care reforms. So it does no good to pretend now, in retrospect, that all along the Clinton administration was off on an obviously unrealistic "liberal," "big government" tangent. . . .

Although I do not accept the notion that President Clinton or his health planners were "awesomely stupid" or excessively "liberal," we do need to probe into constraints and pitfalls that supporters of comprehensive health care reform did not adequately understand or cope with between 1992 and 1994. Things certainly went very wrong for the Clinton Health Security plan! It ended up furthering legislative and political outcomes that were exactly the opposite of what its promoters intended. Instead of cementing new intraparty coalitions and mobilizing renewed electoral support for the Democrats, the Clinton Health Security plan backfired on the Democrats. Instead of renewing and extending the federal government's capacity to ensure security for all Americans, the Clinton plan helped to trigger an extraordinary electoral and ideological backlash against federal social provision in general. . . .

. . . Bill Clinton's Health Security initiative was affected by Reagan's revenge. As a 1992 Democratic presidential contender, Governor Clinton had excellent reasons for promising comprehensive health care reform. His fellow citizens wanted it, and comprehensive reform was a way simultaneously to make Americans more secure and the national economy more efficient. Inclusive health reform also promised to overcome class and racial divisions within the Democratic Party; and its favorable results might well, over time, rekindle faith in government as an agent of the common good.

Still, even the original promises Clinton made about health care reform were influenced by antigovernment Reagan legacies. Clinton and his 1992 campaign advisors were obsessed with avoiding the word "taxes," so the candidate had to find a road to national health reform that appeared not to involve direct taxing and spending by government. Furthermore, after Clinton settled on managed competition within a budget as his "way through the middle," he refused openly to discuss the inevitable role of public rules of the game in his reform plan. So determined was Clinton to avoid the delegitimated subject of "government," that he and his advisors could barely acknowledge the governmental contents of their health care plan to themselves, let alone talk openly and convincingly about them to the American citizenry.

It wasn't just avoidance of "taxes" and "government" that mattered for Health Security, though. In a supreme irony, federal budgetary procedures put in place in the wake of the Reagan fiscal debacle pushed the Clinton administration toward including more rather than less governmental regulation in the full-fledged Health Security legislation. Reagan's revenge was a double bind, and it delivered a double whammy. In order to avoid a highly visible role for the federal government while still extending health coverage and dealing with the problem of the deficit, the Clinton planners substituted regulations for revenues, and governmental indirection for an out-front public presence in health care financing.

As we have learned, the Clinton Health Security proposal was no simple triumph of liberalism. Big cuts in two existing public health insurance programs, Medicaid and Medicare, were included in Health Security to help make the out-year budget projections look convincing. Still more telling, encompassing regional health alliances, contingent premium caps, and all sorts of charges to "recapture" private-sector health savings for the federal budget were included in the Health Security legislation largely in order to satisfy the deficit-neutrality rules of the Congressional Budget Office. CBO rules and other budget procedures had been devised as a response to the wild fiscal excesses of the Reagan era. Operating within these rules, and pursuing his own fiscal goals, President Clinton had to make a convincing case that health care reform would reduce the huge, looming national debts bequeathed to him (and all of us) from the 1980s.

A political boomerang resulted from President Clinton's efforts at governmental indirection and fiscal stringency. In large part because the Clinton administration's Health Security proposal was intricately designed as a series of interlocking regulations, right-wing government haters could argue that this set of reforms would hurt businesses, individuals, and health providers, interfering with their "liberties." Proclaimed threats of possibly rising taxes and governmental inefficiency could be spiced with pronouncements that big, intrusive government would destroy our freedom and the quality of the "best health care system in the world." Designed to get around and through the antigovernment and fiscal legacies of the Reagan era, the Clinton Health Security proposal—in its ultimate irony—gave new life to the outcries about "governmental tyranny" that Barry Goldwater had once presented so ineffectively. . . .

CHAPTER 2

***

POLITICS AND PUBLIC DEBATE

Why Don't the Media Just Report the Facts?

The media have become an important part of the governmental process itself, as the following selection reveals. The media are a fourth branch of the government, and reporters are important political actors. The media shape the flow of information among the branches of the government, and between government and the people. Effective communication between the President and the Congress is essential if anything is to be done. After public policies are passed, the media supplies information and analysis to the people to ease the way for effective implementation.

The media's importance also results from the way politicians use newsmaking to exercise political power. Reelection, power and influence within government, and the passage of legislation depend upon skillful management of the news.

The following selection analyzes the role of the media in politics, and concludes that journalistic demands diverge at many points from the need for a deliberative, informed, and effective democratic process.

Timothy E. Cook is a political scientist who has written extensively on the media. He argues in this reading:

1. The news media are a political institution that have become a fourth branch of the government.
2. Reporters have become important political actors.
3. Politicians achieve their goals through newsmaking, which enhances media power in the political process.
4. The media have always to a greater or lesser degree enhanced and enriched democratic participation through an informed electorate. Contemporary news organizations, however, are often more oriented to their audiences as consumers rather then as citizens. Media economic incentives do not match the needs of a democratic polity.

5. Politicians and the media strive to make news to achieve personal and institutional goals that have little to do with informing the electorate about important issues of public policy.

7

Timothy E. Cook

GOVERNING WITH THE NEWS

★★★

INTRODUCTION:
WHY DON'T WE CALL JOURNALISTS POLITICAL ACTORS?

To paraphrase Mark Twain's famous bon mot about the weather, all observers of American politics nowadays talk about the news media's power in government, but nobody does anything about it—or, at least, no one has yet figured out just how to make sense of that power. This is a bit of a puzzle, particularly given that, almost forty years ago, Douglass Cater wrote a slender volume entitled simply *The Fourth Branch of Government.* Here was his theme:

> The reporter is the recorder of government but he is also a participant. He operates in a system in which power is divided. He as much as anyone . . . helps to shape the course of government. He is the indispensable broker and middleman among the subgovernments of Washington. . . . He can illumine policy and notably assist in giving it sharpness and clarity; just as easily, he can prematurely expose policy and, as with an undeveloped film, cause its destruction. At his worst, operating with arbitrary and faulty standards, he can be an agent of disorder and confusion. At his best, he can exert a creative influence on Washington politics.

In the essay-writing tradition of another journalist-intellectual, Walter Lippmann, Cater pointed to the news media's power in the American political system. But his true insight was that he saw journalists as playing not only a political but a governmental role. He argued that a separation-of-powers system, where each institution controls significant resources, requires both communication between the branches and the imprimatur of public opinion if anything is to get done.

The news media, said Cater, provide a way to fulfill that task. Getting into the news provides a means to communicate quickly and directly across and within branches in a way otherwise denied to officials. Likewise, public opinion may be called upon to arbitrate between branches but is not readily available except through the surrogate of the news media. But because of the corporate sponsorship of their operations, the media are at least partially autonomous of the other three branches. With this independence, political actors in the three branches who wish to use the media's power for their own goals must accommodate themselves to the institutional needs of the news media—much as each branch must do when they wish to do the same with one of the other three established constitutional branches. The net effect, Cater warned, is that "government by publicity" may be an increasingly important focus for political actors in Washington who seek to accomplish policy goals, but that gain may be made at a high cost: further implicating journalistic standards of news into political standards of governance.

Cater did not set forth (and did not intend to set forth) a developed theoretical model; instead, his book is a series of discrete essays on a variety of topics related to the interaction of the press and government. Yet his idea deserves close attention as a spur to our attention and imagination. For one, Cater's notions presage, in the years before the dominance of television and before the rise of a media-savvy political class, our contemporary preoccupation with mass-mediated politics.

Most important, although we might quibble with the notion of a "fourth branch," Cater's sketch of the news media acting as an intermediary institution in Washington provides us with a new and productive way to make sense of the place of journalism in today's American political life. It is particularly beneficial, because for all the bounty of scholarship in political science, sociology, communication, and beyond on the news media and politics, no one has yet come up with an overarching model that would take all this enormously useful work and place it into a larger context that tells us something about the news media's political role. Instead, while there is controversy, confusion, and combat, scholars have tended to speak past each other. Some have proceeded from different definitions of "politics." Others have chosen case studies that cover only one part of the process of newsmaking or that deal with only certain kinds of news content and then extrapolate incorrectly to statements about the news media and politics.

In particular, our ability to make sense of the political power of the American news media has foundered on difficulties we have encountered in thinking productively of the news media as a "political institution." Many scholars have pointed to political and governmental roles for reporters and newspersons. But none has set forth . . . a clear model that sees the news media as a coherent intermediary institution without which the three branches established by the Constitution could not act and could not work. . . . [T]he news media are recognizable as a political institution because of their historical development, because of shared processes and predictable products across news organizations, and because of the way in which the work of newspersons is so intertwined with the work of official Washington that the news itself performs governmental tasks.

And not only is the news a "coproduction" of the news media and government, but policy today is likewise the result of collaboration and conflict among newspersons, officials, and other political actors, And none of this requires expanding the definition of "politics" past its customary definition in scholarship. Indeed . . . the American news media today are not merely part of politics; they are part of government.

. . . Explanation is one of my goals; evaluation is another. If indeed we can term the news media a "political institution," then we must begin to ask questions about their structure, function, and responsibilities much as political scientists have already done (exhaustively) for the other three branches. In particular, the ascent of the news media as an unelected intermediary institution raises problems of capacity and accountability.

Stated differently, I pose three questions. Does the growth of the media's influence in American politics empower an institution that is poorly equipped to assist in governance, given the prominence of journalistic rather than overtly political goals therein? Who elected reporters to represent them in government and politics, and can we think of the news media as politically accountable for the political choices and impacts they have? Does this then mean that perhaps it is time to start thinking about creating a new, more coherent policy regarding the news media to ensure that the news we receive gets us toward the politics and toward the democracy we want?

Now, readers may well protest: But surely, if this is such a good idea, why hasn't anyone thought of it before? Why didn't anyone take a cue from Cater in all the time since 1959? The answer is twofold. First, journalists work hard to discourage people from thinking of them as political actors. Indeed, they may be so successful at this attempt that they have convinced even themselves. Second, the study of political communication developed amidst a tradition emphasizing "media effects," and the disciplines most involved in the study of the politics of the news media have held back from implications of their work. In particular, while political scientists have been quite comfortable referring to the media's political contribution, they have been less willing to see the news media as an institution; conversely, while sociologists have had little problem referring to the news media as a social institution, they have not been as persuasive in outlining the news media's political role.

CONCLUSION:
THE FIRST AMENDMENT AND THE FOURTH BRANCH—
TOWARD REDESIGNING A NEWS MEDIA POLICY

[I have] investigated the possibility that the news media in the United States nowadays constitute a political institution in their own right. Drawing initial inspiration from Douglass Cater's 1959 book, *The Fourth Branch of Government*, I have argued that the news media are an intermediary institution in Washington, D.C., and a crucial one in a separation-of-powers system where action does not come easily. We have seen how the development of the current news media has always been closely fostered by practices and public policy, how the news media perform governmental tasks, how reporters themselves (like it or not) are political actors, and how government officials attempt to use the news as part of their daily jobs of governing. So the American news media do not only constitute a political institution; they are part of government.

To review the argument: the historical evidence . . . demonstrates that the development of the American news media was never free from politics. The history that is most often told concerns the demise of governmental control in the form of licensing, seditious libel, and censorship, and the decline of the individually sponsored partisan press. This story of the widening "progress" of freedom of the press must be joined by a less frequently recounted tale, whereby the news media have long been (and continue to be) subsidized by a variety of governmental policies and practices. The shapes, formats, and contents of the news, in other words, were never "free" from governmental intervention. On the contrary, a good case can be made that the news might not be possible if it weren't for what government does for and to the media.

To be sure, such governmental involvement is true of other institutions that would not readily be termed "political" by most observers (such as the corporation). . . . [T]he news media constitute a political institution, not merely in the sense that individual news outlets reinforce each other's coverage, not simply in the way that processes of newsmaking are similar from one organization to the next, but most centrally, in having been bequeathed a central role in a political and social process, that of communication. Yet the irony and the paradox of journalistic power is how it is hidden even (or especially) from its practitioners. By applying standards of objectivity, importance, and interest, and judging stories by how well they fit the "production values" of the news, journalists may believe they are contributing no political bias. The content suggests otherwise. And . . . the news media are political because the choices they end up making do not equally favor all political actors, processes, and messages. Far from holding up a mirror to external political actions, the news media are directly involved in instigating them.

The most impressive evidence, however, on the news media as a political institution comes not from what journalists and their organizations do, but instead from the increasing attention that political actors in other institutions give to newsmaking as a central part of their own job. Newsmaking is now a central way for governmental actors to accomplish political and policy goals. In that sense, the news media may well be an "unwitting adjunct" to power. And incumbents in every institution devote more time and energy to newsmaking than did their predecessors a few decades before. Making news, in other words, is not merely a way to get elected or reelected, to boost one's own ego or to be a show horse instead of a work horse; instead, it is a way to govern. The constitutional framework specified that when the executive, the legislature, or the judiciary acts, it needs the assistance, or at least the passive consent, of the other two for their decision to stand. Nowadays, the same may be said of the news media, which require aid and assistance from other political institutions to accomplish their task, but which in turn themselves participate directly in the Washington politics of "separated institutions sharing power. "

What is the Problem?

All this is not necessarily such a problem. The mere facts that the news media or that journalists embed bias in the news or that the news media exercise political power might disconcert some. So would the idea that the practice of American politics is increasingly centered on getting into the news. Yet these possibilities do not bother me in the abstract.

I do not share the apparent conviction on the part of journalists that they can approximate or even approach an objective, unfiltered account of what is going on in the world. Instead, my view of social science—let alone a more intuitive enterprise such as journalism—would lead me to indicate that our ability to understand social and political processes hinge on making arguments and marshaling evidence behind those arguments, and that lone facts cannot be judged in the absence of the framework of understanding that generated them. Individual journalists' biases and omissions seem less of a concern than the very real possibility that journalism, as a collective enterprise across individuals and indeed across organizations, implicitly contains an entire series of assumptions about how the world works, and how the world should work, that bring with it a limited set of political interpretations. This homogeneity across news outlets and repetition over time makes for the political force of the news. As the assumptions and routines produce predictable news over time and homogenized news across news outlets, their worth is reinforced. The tools of journalism are rarely the object of direct scrutiny when journalists, by applying them conscientiously, often inadvertently disguise their presence, let alone their impact; and when something goes awry, it is usually easier to blame the individual infractor, not the sacrosanct rules and routines that enable newsmaking.

This is not to suggest that the main problem of the news nowadays, as jeremiads have claimed, is that television now provides an oversimplified, overdramatized version of the news. One theme in [my analysis] is that technology itself is rarely as much of a problem compared to how it is used. Even in its current state, television's capabilities for presenting compelling and vivid evidence and breaking barriers of inattention are often greater than newspapers, which require previous interest and, often, previous knowledge. And the problem is the news as a whole, not just television news. Any biases attributable to individual modalities become less central when one recognizes there is no single "main source" from which Americans receive their news. The news habits of citizens are usually haphazard; important information is often derived from hearing the top-of-the-hour news summary on radio, scanning the headlines of the newsstand in front of the post office, or channel surfing on television. Thus, ABC News's proclamation, "More people get their news from ABC than from any other source," may be less a tribute to ABC than a commentary on the fragmentary news habits of American citizens.

Rather than bemoan this fragmentary approach, we should instead be impressed, not only at the capacities of citizens for creatively assembling political impressions of their own, but also at the way in which this reliance on a variety of news sources can alleviate the problems of relying on a single biased outlet. But this apparent willingness on the part of the public to consult multiple news outlets is vitiated by the considerable homogeneity in the news, a direct effect of the difficulties that news organizations have in figuring out just what is and isn't news. In particular, profit-oriented news organizations (and even to a lesser extent, their nonprofit counterparts) seek advertisers to whom they will sell access to their audiences. This economic imperative nurtures "production values" shared by almost all news outlets. The corresponding consensus on routines of newsmaking that exist across news organizations in order to crank out a predictable regular product pushes only toward certain political possibilities and away from others that are foreclosed.

Nor should we quickly decry the increasing media-mindedness of American political actors. Publicizing one's activities can be, and occasionally is, a powerful way to maintain official accountability, to ensure that the issues being addressed within political institutions correspond to the concerns of the public, and to bring the public into the democratic debates and deliberations in Washington. The problem is not that political actors have to "go public." Instead, the dilemma stems from the costs imposed on going public: namely that they must incorporate notions of newsworthiness and thereby particular politics not only into their communication strategies but into the very criteria for decisions and actions.

The governmental news media in the United States present a twofold problem. One is the *capacity* of the news media to perform the role that has devolved on it. Journalists are not well trained, nor are news organizations well equipped, to help weigh problems, set political agendas, examine alternatives, and study implementation. Journalistic criteria of importance and interest simply may or may not have much to do with societal concerns of politics and policy making. I have argued that the work of journalists favors news that is easily and regularly gathered, that is timely, terse, simply described, concrete, dramatic, colorful, and visualizable. So, to the extent that journalism organizes politics and wields power in the American political system, it directs attention: toward episodic outcroppings rather than continuing conditions; toward issues that fade quickly in public consciousness as newspersons begin to assume that the audience is getting as bored as they are with the same old concerns; and away from abstract complexity toward simple if not simplistic renderings of problems, policies, and alternatives.

Another problem, at least equally important, is that of *accountability*. If . . . journalists end up wielding political influence, one can only wonder: Who elected them? And to whom are journalists responsible? Newspersons will rightly contend that they are answerable to their audiences. But on what grounds? As in other areas of capitalism, one can easily doubt that consumers gravitate toward the better mousetrap. Instead, the public makes such choices shaped by how a product is marketed, whether oligopolies provide openings for innovation, and how investors react to new or old products.

Although journalists claim that they are acting as the "surrogate" for their audience, research has consistently found that they know little about their audiences and are even less interested. Avoiding this information may be rational for reporters, given how they already feel considerable direct pressure from superiors, colleagues, and sources. By paying less attention to the public, they can devote their energies to satisfying (or at least working on not upsetting) those immediate actors. Beyond opting out of the news, ways for citizens to hold the news media accountable are few. Newspapers may reprint corrections, but these far more often refer to errors of fact (e.g., the wrong middle initial) rather than of judgment. Even when news organizations do admit to the latter, such admissions tend to leave the routines and rules of newsworthiness intact and shift blame to individual lapses in conscientiously applying the rules, or, even more conveniently, to sources or the audience. Letters to the editor may be routinely solicited and reprinted, but similar rules of newsworthiness by which the news was selected seem to apply in cutting out which letters to reprint. Even the recent rise of the "ombudsman" in news organizations does not accomplish much, given that most ombudsmen see their position as a form of public relations for newspapers, explaining journalistic work to audiences, not an office to remind their colleagues of the demands and needs of the citizenry.

Contemporary news organizations are primarily oriented toward their audiences, not as citizens but as consumers. The most prominent audiences for the news are advertisers. Advertisers, not readers, after all, provide the bulk of the income and profit to news organizations. In an increasingly consolidating and profit-minded media industry, such profits become ever more central. How powerful the readers and viewers of the news can be under such circumstances is open to question. Mass circulation may simply be too expensive for news organizations, as compared to targeting a smaller, more affluent audience. The classic examples remain the mass circulation photo-weeklies such as *Life* and *Look* that continued to attract large readerships in the 1960s, but whose advertisers had increasingly gravitated toward television as the best way to sell their products, leading to the weeklies' paradoxical demise at the height of their popularity. Similar processes may be at work with metropolitan newspapers, who are often all too happy to see their circulation decline, if it trims costs of distribution without limiting the advertisers' interest in reaching readers with greater disposable income.

If the American political system has become increasingly dependent on the news media, not merely to communicate with the American people but to communicate among elites and activists and to help in the very process of government, it has empowered an institution that is neither well-designed to do so nor effectively politically accountable. Political actors have become ever more conscious of the need to make news, and they have become skilled at it as well, but, as sketched above, the demands of the news do not match the needs of a polity.

Walter Lippmann, the author of the following selection, was the dean of American journalism. He established the standards and defined the boundaries of journalism that guided his profession. In the following selection he stresses the subjective and interpretive side of most news. The press is an important political actor, but the press alone cannot shoulder the burdens of democracy. Responsible political institutions produce responsible news. Journalism by its very nature highlights "episodes, incidents, and eruptions." The press reports short-term incidents, but government requires long-term solutions. Journalistic realities cannot define democratic ideals.

Walter Lippmann (1889–1974) set the standard for all journalists to follow. Reporters should give the facts, not their opinions. The media should inform but not influence the electorate. His book *Public Opinion* (1922), from which the reading below is taken, was perhaps his most influential work.

Lippmann's arguments are:

1. Newspapers do not watch all the world, but only selected parts of it.
2. The news should consist of facts, not opinions.
3. Good stories require a factual basis, and therefore not all events can be accurately reported.

4. "The news does not tell you how the seed is germinating in the ground, but it may tell you when the first sprout breaks through the surface."
5. Good reporting always requires a good factual record.
6. News and truth are not the same thing because news is objective and truth subjective.
7. Self-governing peoples must rely upon themselves, not the media, and create institutions of knowledge and fact-gathering to make informed and responsible policy choices.

8

Walter Lippmann

PUBLIC OPINION

★★★

THE NATURE OF NEWS

All the reporters in the world working all the hours of the day could not witness all the happenings in the world. There are not a great many reporters. And none of them has the power to be in more than one place at a time. Reporters are not clairvoyant, they do not gaze into a crystal ball and see the world at will, they are not assisted by thought-transference. Yet the range of subjects these comparatively few men manage to cover would be a miracle indeed, if it were not a standardized routine.

Newspapers do not try to keep an eye on all mankind. They have watchers stationed at certain places, like Police Headquarters, the Coroner's Office, the County Clerk's Office, City Hall, the White House, the Senate, House of Representatives, and so forth. They watch, or rather in the majority of cases they belong to associations which employ men who watch "a comparatively small number of places where it is made known when the life of anyone . . . departs from ordinary paths, or when events worth telling about occur. For example, John Smith, let it be supposed, becomes a broker. For ten years he pursues the even tenor of his way and except for his customers and his friends no one gives him a thought. To the newspapers he is as if he were not. But in the eleventh year he suffers heavy losses and, at last, his resources all gone, summons his lawyer and arranges for the making of an assignment. The lawyer posts off to the County Clerk's office, and a clerk there makes the necessary entries in the official docket. Here in step the newspapers. While the clerk is writing Smith's business obituary a reporter glances over his shoulder and a few minutes later the reporters know Smith's troubles and are as well informed concerning his business status as they would be had they kept a reporter at his door every day for over ten years."

When Mr. Given says that the newspapers know "Smith's troubles" and "his business status," he does not mean that they know them as Smith knows them, or as Mr. Arnold Bennett would know them if he had made Smith the hero of a three volume novel. The newspapers know only "in a few minutes" the bald facts which are recorded in the County Clerk's Office. That overt act "uncovers" the news about Smith. Whether the news will be followed up or not is another matter. The point is that before a series of events become news they have usually to make themselves noticeable in some more or less overt act. Generally too, in a crudely overt act. Smith's friends may have known for years that he was taking risks, rumors may even have reached the financial editor if Smith's friends were talkative. But apart from the fact that none of this could be published because it would be libel, there is in these rumors nothing definite on which to peg a story. Something definite must occur that has unmistakable form. It may be the act of going into bankruptcy, it may be a fire, a collision, an assault, a riot, an arrest, a denunciation, the introduction of a bill, a speech, a vote, a meeting, the expressed opinion of a well known citizen, an editorial in a newspaper, a sale, a wage-schedule, a price change, the proposal to build a bridge. . . . There must be a manifestation. The course of events must assume a certain definable shape, and until it is in a phase where some aspect is an accomplished fact, news does not separate itself from the ocean of possible truth.

Naturally there is room for wide difference of opinion as to when events have a shape that can be reported. A good journalist will find news oftener than a hack. If he sees a building with a dangerous list, he does not have to wait until it falls into the street in order to recognize news. It was a great reporter who guessed the name of the next Indian Viceroy when he heard that Lord So-and-So was inquiring about climates. There are lucky shots but the number of men who can make them is small. Usually it is the stereotyped shape assumed by an event at an obvious place that uncovers the run of the news. The most obvious place is where people's affairs touch public authority. De minimis non curat lex. It is at these places that marriages, births, deaths, contracts, failures, arrivals, departures, lawsuits, disorders, epidemics and calamities are made known.

In the first instance, therefore, the news is not a mirror of social conditions, but the report of an aspect that has obtruded itself. The news does not tell you how the seed is germinating in the ground, but it may tell you when the first sprout breaks through the surface. It may even tell you what somebody says is happening to the seed under ground. It may tell you that the sprout did not come up at the time it was expected. The more points, then, at which any happening can be fixed, objectified, measured, named, the more points there are at which news can occur.

So, if some day a legislature, having exhausted all other ways of improving mankind, should forbid the scoring of baseball games, it might still be possible to play some sort of game in which the umpire decided according to his own sense of fair play how long the game should last, when each team should go to bat, and who should be regarded as the winner. If that game were reported in the newspapers it would consist of a record of the umpire's decisions, plus the reporter's impression of the hoots and cheers of the crowd, plus at best a vague account of how certain men, who had no specified position on the field moved around for a few hours on an unmarked piece of sod. The more you try to imagine the logic of so absurd a predicament, the more clear it becomes that for the purposes of newsgathering, (let alone the purposes of playing the game) it is impossible to do much without an apparatus and rules for naming, scoring, recording. Because that machinery is far from perfect, the umpire's life is often a distracted one. Many crucial plays he has to judge by eye. The last vestige of dispute could be taken out of the game, as it has been taken but of chess when people obey the rules, if somebody thought it worth his while to photograph every play. It was the moving pictures which finally settled a real doubt in many reporters' minds, owing to the slowness of the human eye, as to just what blow of Dempsey's knocked out Carpentier.

Wherever there is a good machinery of record, the modern news service works with great precision. There is one on the stock exchange, and the news of price movements is flashed over tickers with dependable accuracy. There is a machinery for election returns, and when the counting and tabulating are well done, the result of a national election is usually known on the night of the election. In civilized communities deaths, births, marriages and divorces are recorded, and are known accurately except where there is concealment or neglect. The machinery exists for some, and only some, aspects of industry and government, in varying degrees of precision for securities, money and staples, bank clearances, realty transactions, wage scales. It exists for imports and exports because they pass through a custom house and can be directly recorded. It exists in nothing like the same degree for internal trade, and especially for trade over the counter.

It will be found, I think, that there is a very direct relation between the certainty of news and the system of record. If you call to mind the topics which form the principal indictment by reformers against the press, you find they are subjects in which the newspaper occupies the position of the umpire in the unscored baseball game. All news about states of mind is of this character: so are all descriptions of personalities, of sincerity, aspiration, motive, intention, of mass feeling, of national feeling, of public opinion, the policies of foreign governments. So is much news about what is going to happen. So are questions turning on private profit, private income, wages, working conditions, the efficiency of labor, educational opportunity, unemployment, monotony, health, discrimination, unfairness, restraint of trade, waste, "backward peoples," conservatism, imperialism, radicalism, liberty, honor, righteousness. All involve data that are at best spasmodically recorded. The data may be hidden because of a censorship or a tradition of privacy, they may not exist because nobody thinks record important, because he thinks it red tape, or because nobody has yet invented an objective system of measurement. Then the news on these subjects is bound to be debatable, when it is not wholly neglected. The events which are not scored are reported either as personal and conventional opinions, or they are not news. They do not take shape until somebody protests, or somebody investigates, or somebody publicly, in the etymological meaning of the word, makes an *issue* of them. . . .

NEWS, TRUTH, AND A CONCLUSION

As we begin to make more and more exact studies of the press, much will depend upon the hypothesis we hold. If we assume . . . that news and truth are two words for the same thing, we shall, I believe, arrive nowhere. . . .

The hypothesis, which seems to me the most fertile, is that news and truth are not the same thing, and must be clearly distinguished. The function of news is to signalize an event, the function of truth is to bring to light the hidden facts, to set them into relation with each other, and make a picture of reality on which men can act. Only at those points, where social conditions take recognizable and measurable shape, do the body of truth and the body of news coincide. That is a comparatively small part of the whole field of human interest. In this sector, and only in this sector, the tests of the news are sufficiently exact to make the charges of perversion or suppression more than a partisan judgment. There is no defense, no extenuation, no excuse whatever, for stating six times that Lenin is dead, when the only information the paper possesses is a report that he is dead from a source repeatedly shown to be unreliable. The news, in that instance, is not "Lenin Dead" but "Helsingfors Says Lenin is Dead." And a newspaper can be asked to take the responsibility of not making Lenin more dead than the source of the news is reliable; if there is one subject on which editors are most responsible it is in their judgment of the reliability of the source. But when it comes to dealing, for example, with stories of what the Russian people want, no such test exists.

The absence of these exact tests accounts, I think, for the character of the profession, as no other explanation does. There is a very small body of exact knowledge, which it requires no outstanding ability or training to deal with. The rest is in the journalist's own discretion. Once he departs from the region where it is definitely recorded at the County Clerk's office that John Smith has gone into bankruptcy, all fixed standards disappear. The story of why John Smith failed, his human frailties, the analysis of the economic conditions on which he was shipwrecked, all of this can be told in a hundred different ways. There is no discipline in applied psychology, as there is a discipline in medicine, engineering, or even law, which has authority to direct the journalist's mind when he passes from the news to the vague realm of truth. There are no canons to direct his own mind, and no canons that coerce the reader's judgment or the publisher's. His version of the truth is only his version. How can he demonstrate the truth as he sees it? He cannot demonstrate it, any more than Mr. Sinclair Lewis can demonstrate that he has told the whole truth about Main Street. And the more he understands his own weaknesses, the more ready he is to admit that where there is no objective test, his own opinion is in some vital measure constructed out of his own stereotypes, according to his own code, and by the urgency of his own interest. He knows that he is seeing the world through subjective lenses. He cannot deny that he too is, as Shelley remarked, a dome of many-colored glass which stains the white radiance of eternity.

And by this knowledge his assurance is tempered. He may have all kinds of moral courage, and sometimes has, but he lacks that sustaining conviction of a certain technic which finally freed the physical sciences from theological control. It was the gradual development of an irrefragable method that gave the physicist his intellectual freedom as against all the powers of the world. His proofs were so clear, his evidence so sharply superior to tradition, that he broke away finally from all control. But the journalist has no such support in his own conscience or in fact. The control exercised over him by the opinions of his employers and his readers, is not the control of truth by prejudice, but of one opinion by another opinion that it is not demonstrably less true. Between Judge Gary's assertion that the unions will destroy American institutions, and Mr. Gomper's assertion that they are agencies of the rights of man, the choice has, in large measure, to be governed by the will to believe.

The task of deflating these controversies, and reducing them to a point where they can be reported as news, is not a task which the reporter can perform. It is possible and necessary for journalists to bring home to people the uncertain character of the truth on which their opinions are founded, and by criticism and agitation to prod social science into making more usable formulations of social facts, and to prod statesmen into establishing more visible institutions. The press, in other words, can fight for the extension of reportable truth. But as social truth is organized today, the press is not constituted to furnish from one edition to the next the amount of knowledge which the democratic theory of public opinion demands. This is not due to the Brass Check, as the quality of news in radical papers shows, but to the fact that the press deals with a society in which the governing forces are so imperfectly recorded. The theory that the press can itself record those forces is false. It can normally record only what has been recorded for it by the working of institutions. Everything else is argument and opinion, and fluctuates with the vicissitudes, the self-consciousness, and the courage of the human mind.

If the press is not so universally wicked, nor so deeply conspiring, . . . it is very much more frail than the democratic theory has as yet admitted. It is too frail to carry the whole burden of popular sovereignty, to supply spontaneously the truth which democrats hoped was inborn. And when we expect it to supply such a body of truth we employ a misleading standard of judgment. We misunderstand the limited nature of news, the illimitable complexity of society; we overestimate our own endurance, public spirit, and all-round competence. We suppose an appetite for uninteresting truths which is not discovered by any honest analysis of our own tastes.

If the newspapers, then, are to be charged with the duty of translating the whole public life of mankind, so that every adult can arrive at an opinion on every moot topic, they fail, they are bound to fail, in any future one can conceive they will continue to fail. It is not possible to assume that a world, carried on by division of labor and distribution of authority, can be governed by universal opinions in the whole population. Unconsciously the theory sets up the single reader as theoretically omnicompetent, and puts upon the press the burden of accomplishing whatever representative government, industrial organization, and diplomacy have failed to accomplish. Acting upon everybody for thirty minutes in twenty-four hours, the press is asked to create a mystical force called Public Opinion that will take up the slack in public institutions. The press has often mistakenly pretended that it could do just that. It has at great moral cost to itself, encouraged a democracy, still bound to its original premises, to expect newspapers to supply spontaneously for every organ of government, for every social problem, the machinery of information which these do not normally supply themselves. Institutions, having failed to furnish themselves with instruments of knowledge, have become a bundle of "problems," which the population as a whole, reading the press as a whole, is supposed to solve.

The press, in other words, has come to be regarded as an organ of direct democracy, charged on a much wider scale, and from day to day, with the function often attributed to the initiative, referendum, and recall. The Court of Public Opinion, open day and night, is to lay down the law for everything all the time. It is not workable. And when you consider the nature of news, it is not even thinkable. For the news, as we have seen, is precise in proportion to the precision with which the event is recorded. Unless the event is capable of being named, measured, given shape, made specific, it either fails to take on the character of news, or it is subject to the accidents and prejudices of observation.

Therefore, on the whole, the quality of the news about modern society is an index of its social organization. The better the institutions, the more all interests concerned are formally represented, the more issues are disentangled, the more objective criteria are introduced, the more perfectly an affair can be presented as news. At its best the press is a servant and guardian of institutions; at its worst it is a means by which a few exploit social disorganization to their own ends. In the degree to which institutions fail to function, the unscrupulous journalist can fish in troubled waters, and the conscientious one must gamble with uncertainties.

The press is no substitute for institutions. It is like the beam of a searchlight that moves restlessly about, bringing one episode and then another out of darkness into vision. Men cannot do the work of the world by this light alone. They cannot govern society by episodes, incidents, and eruptions. It is only when they work by a steady light of their own, that the press, when it is turned upon them, reveals a situation intelligible enough for a popular decision. The trouble lies deeper than the press, and so does the remedy. It lies in social organization based on a system of analysis and record, and in all the corollaries of that principle; in the abandonment of the theory of the omnicompetent citizen, in the decentralization of decision, in the coordination of decision by comparable record and analysis. If at the centers of management there is a running audit, which makes work intelligible to those who do it, and those who superintend it, issues when they arise are not the mere collisions of the blind. Then, too, the news is uncovered for the press by a system of intelligence that is also a check upon the press.

That is the radical way. For the troubles of the press, like the troubles of representative government, be it territorial or functional, like the troubles of industry, be it capitalist, cooperative, or communist, go back to a common source: to the failure of self-governing people to transcend their casual experience and their prejudice, by inventing, creating, and organizing a machinery of knowledge. It is because they are compelled to act without a reliable picture of the world, that governments, schools, newspapers and churches make such small headway against the more obvious failings of democracy, against violent prejudice, apathy, preference for the curious trivial as against the dull important, and the hunger for sideshows and three legged calves. This is the primary defect of popular government, a defect inherent in its traditions, and all its other defects can, I believe, be traced to this one.

Public journalism is a movement that has attempted to reshape the media in a way that makes it a responsible part of the democratic process. Public journalism seeks to highlight the long-term issues of concern to the community, rather then stressing episodic events that may be entertaining but do not inform public policy.

The following selection discusses the possibilities of public journalism within the context of political and media reality.

James Fallows has had a distinguished career in American journalism, including posts as Editor-in-Chief of the *Atlantic Monthly* and of *U.S. News and World Report.* He is a major player in the Washington media world.

Fallows' arguments in the following reading are:

1. The media invented "public journalism" to elevate its status.
2. Public journalism focuses more on issues than on the political gain as an end in itself. The goal is to inform the electorate so that it can make appropriate public policy choices. Reporters practicing public journalism cover campaigns and elections from the voters', rather than the candidates', points of view.
3. Critics of public journalism charge that it violates Walter Lippmann's maxim that reporters should stick to the facts pure and simple. They should not inject themselves or their organizations into politics in an attempt to improve upon democracy.
4. Criticism of public journalism has come entirely from within rather than without the media, as the general public seems to approve of the new approach.
5. Journalists have a clear choice to make: whether to continue their contemporary practice of entertaining the public, or to engage it in an ongoing democratic process.

9

James Fallows

Breaking the News

★★★

"Public Journalism":
An Attempt to Connect the Media with the Public

During the U.S. military's darkest moments just after the Vietnam War, a group of officers and analysts undertook a "military reform" movement. Rather than papering over the deep problems that the Vietnam years had revealed, and rather than searching for external sources of blame, this group attempted to locate the internal problems that had weakened the military so that the problems could be faced and solved. The "military reformers'" record of success was not perfect, but at their instigation the U.S. military coped with more of its fundamental difficulties than any other American institution has.

Since the early 1990s, a group of journalistic reformers has launched a similar attempt to cope with the basic weaknesses of their institution. As was the case with the military reformers, their efforts have been scorned by some of the most powerful leaders of the current establishment. As with the military reformers, they do not have the complete or satisfying answer to all of today's journalistic problems. But, like the military reformers, they are more right than wrong. At a minimum their ideas point the way to a media establishment that is less intensely scorned than today's is.

Those involved in the "public journalism" (sometimes called "civic journalism") movement stress its cooperative, collaborative nature. . . .

In 1991 the fledgling [public journalism] movement got an important boost when David Broder of the *Washington Post*, probably the best-respected political reporter of his time, gave a lecture in California implicitly endorsing their approach. His statement was seen as significant not simply because of his personal stature but also because he had had contact with the public-journalism advocates and had come to a conclusion like theirs on his own.

In a speech sponsored by the Riverside, California *Press-Enterprise* and the University of California at Riverside, Broder said that coverage of public affairs had become a cynical and pointless insiders' game. Political consultants—rather than candidates—had come to have a dominant role in politics, Broder said. And these hired guns, "these new political bosses, have become for those of us in political journalism not only our best sources but, in many cases, our best friends."

The two groups got along because they both loved the operating details of politics, Broder said. They felt a distance from the slightly comic, sweating candidates who had to give speeches and raise money and submit themselves to the voters' will. For these poor candidates, Broder said, election day really was a judgment day. But for the reporters and consultants, no matter what the results of the election, they could play the game over and over again.

There was a more disturbing similarity between the groups, Broder said. "We both disclaim any responsibility for the consequences of elections."

> Let me say again, for emphasis: We disclaim ANY responsibility for the consequences of elections. Consultants will tell you they are hired to produce victory on Election Day. Reporters will tell you that we are hired to cover campaigns. . . . I've often said to our White House reporters, "My job is to deliver these turkeys; after they're in office, they're your responsibility."
>
> What this means in less facetious terms is that a very large percentage of the information that the American people get about politics comes from people who disclaim any responsibility for the consequences of our politics.

After spending nearly four decades in this activity, Broder said, he felt uneasy about the consequences of his life's work. By concentrating on the operations of politics and disdaining the results, reporters "have colluded with the campaign consultants to produce the kind of politics which is turning off the American people." By the early 1970s—the time of movies like *The Candidate* and books like *The Selling of the President*—journalists began to realize that the most important part of a political campaign was the ads a candidate put on radio and television:

> So we began to focus on the ads, and we began to write about them. We began to write about the people who made the ads, the campaign consultants and media advisers and pollsters. We wrote about them so often that I think we have turned some

of them into political celebrities in their own right. We have helped to make them both famous and rich.

In all of this, we forgot about the people who were the consumers of these ads, those who had the message pushed at them, willingly or not, every time they turned on their radio or television set. We forgot our obligation as journalists to help them cope with this mass of political propaganda coming their way.

The line Broder had drawn—between accepting and ignoring the consequences of what reporters wrote—was to be the main dividing line between the public journalism movement and the "mainstream" press. Even before this speech, Broder had written a column issuing a similar challenge to journalists. "It is time for us in the world's freest press to become activists," he wrote in 1990, "not on behalf of a particular party or politician, but on behalf of the process of self-government."

Toward the end of advancing this kind of "activism," Broder laid out in his speech recommendations for future campaign coverage that would pay less attention to tactical maneuvers and more to the connection between the campaign and real national problems. One specific suggestion, which seems obvious now but had rarely been done before Broder proposed it, was that reporters cover campaign ads not from the candidates' point of view but from the voters'. That is, instead of emphasizing what each campaign was trying to accomplish with the ads—how they were exploiting their opponents' vulnerabilities, which interest groups they were trying to peel off, and how—the reporters should examine how truthful and realistic the advertisements were. One immediate effect of Broder's recommendation was the rapid spread of "Ad Watch"-type coverage in campaign coverage, in which correspondents examined political ads for smears and misrepresentations.

Public Journalism in Practice

Through meetings coordinated by Jay Rosen's Project on Public Life and the Press (which is based at New York University and funded by the Knight Foundation), public journalism became a "movement" by 1993. Its main base of support was in regional newspapers and some broadcast stations, usually working in partnership with the papers. By 1995 more than 170 newspapers had taken part in some activity tracked by Rosen's center. A conference in the spring of 1995 included representatives from papers or broadcast stations in California, Mississippi, Virginia, Wisconsin, Florida, Minnesota, Pennsylvania, Massachusetts, New Jersey, Maine, and elsewhere. Several books now exist chronicling these efforts.

Editors and reporters at these news organizations attempted to produce coverage that would make people feel reconnected to the public life of their community. The goal was not to promote one political party or one vision of economic or social policy, any more than *Sports Illustrated* coverage, while promoting interest in sports as a whole, is intended to promote one team. But, as Buzz Merritt put in an editorial before the Kansas gubernatorial elections in 1990, his paper would have "a strong bias: we believe the voters are entitled to have the candidates talk about the issues in depth."

The best-known project in public journalism's short history is probably the *Charlotte Observer*'s approach to covering the North Carolina elections in 1992. The paper's editors, who had carefully studied Broder's proposals and Merritt's 1990 election coverage in Wichita, didn't want their coverage to be driven by the issues that each candidate thought would be tactically useful in the election. Instead, they began an elaborate effort to determine what issues the state's people believed were most important, and what other issues might have the greatest impact on the state's future welfare even though the public was not yet fully aware of them. The paper commissioned a poll of more than a thousand area residents (not merely subscribers) to ask their views about the public issues that concerned them most. The poll was not a yes-or-no survey but involved extensive discussions to explore the reasons behind the respondents' views. After the initial polling, the *Observer* arranged for five hundred residents to serve as an ongoing citizens' advisory panel to the paper through the election season.

Based on the issues that emerged from the polls and panel discussions, as well as from efforts by the paper's reporters and editors to judge the trends that would affect the state, the paper drew up lists of topics about which the public expected answers from the candidates. These citizen-generated issues were not the same as the ones on which many of the candidates had planned to run. For instance, the citizen panels showed a widespread concern about environmental problems caused by Charlotte's rapid growth. Politicians had not planned to emphasize this theme, but the paper decided to push for statements on this and the other issues the citizen panels had recommended. At the same time, it ran fewer stories about advertising strategies, about horse-race-style opinion polls, and about other traditional campaign techniques.

The moment of truth for this new approach came early in the campaign season, and it involved a question that a newspaper did *not* ask. After the citizens' panel had stressed its interest in environmental issues (among other concerns), the *Observer* prepared a big grid to run in the newspaper, showing each candidate's position on the questions the panel had raised. At the time, the long-time Democratic officeholder Terry Sanford was running for the Senate. The *Observer*'s editor, Rich Opel, has described what happened next:

> Voters are intensely interested in the environment. . . . So our reporters went out to senatorial candidates and said, "Here are the voters' questions." Terry Sanford, the incumbent senator, called me up from Washington and said, "Rich, I have these questions from your reporter and I'm not going to talk about the environment until the general election." This was the primary. I said, "Well, the voters want to know about the environment now, Terry." He said, "Well, that's not the way I have my campaign structured." I said, "Fine, I will run the questions and I will leave a space under it for you to answer. If you choose not to, we will just say, 'Would not respond' or we will leave it blank." We ended the conversation. In about ten days he sent the answers down.

Most political reporters for most newspapers know how they would instinctively respond when a candidate told them he was delaying discussion of an issue. "That's interesting," they would say. "What's the thinking behind that?" Like a campaign consultant, the reporter would be instantly engaged in figuring out why the issue would be useless against other Democrats in the primaries but would be useful against Republicans in the general election. By responding as proxies for the public rather than as consultants' manqués, the reporters evoked the discussion their readers wanted to hear.

"This is not a way of being 'tough' on a candidate for its own sake, but of using toughness in service of certain public values," Jay Rosen has said of the Charlotte project. "It is also a way of adding some civility, since there are rewards to balance the penalties that dominate today's campaigns. In normal campaign coverage, candidates get praised and criticized, but on the basis of what values? In this case the paper said: *here* are the issues the public wants to hear about. We'll judge you on whether you respond to these views." Most newspapers, he said, also judge candidates by a set of values—but never lay out clearly for the reader or the candidate exactly what those values are. (In practice, they are usually tactical values—" handling" issues well, and so forth.) . . .

There are scores of other examples from scores of other cities. Some have been more successful than others in sustaining public involvement and improving public debate. In the most successful efforts, editors and reporters have listened carefully to public concerns—but have balanced what they learned that way with their own best judgment about the issues of greatest long-term significance to their readers. The editors and news directors who have launched these projects seem unanimous in one finding: that a public-journalism emphasis has drawn far *less* criticism from the public than their normal coverage has, and that it has attracted far *more* praise, interest, follow-up community activity, and other indicators that the journalists are on the right track.

Complaints from the Media Establishment

There has, however, been one important source of backlash against the public-journalism approach. It has come from the editors of the country's largest and most influential newspapers. Leonard Downie, executive editor of the *Washington Post*, has said the movement's basic premise is "completely wrong." Max Frankel, the former executive editor of the *New York Times*, has expressed a similar hostility—as have others, including William F. Woo, editor of the *St. Louis Post-Dispatch*.

The crux of their unhappiness lies with the concept of "objectivity." One of public journalism's basic claims is that journalists should stop kidding themselves about their ability to remain detached from and objective about public life. Journalists are not like scientists, observing the behavior of fruit flies but not influencing what the flies might do. They inescapably change the reality of whatever they are observing by whether and how they choose to write about it.

From the nearly infinite array of events, dramas, tragedies, and successes occurring in the world each day, newspaper editors and broadcast producers must define a tiny sample as "the news." The conventions of choosing "the news" are so familiar, and so much of the process happens by learned and ingrained habits, that it is easy for journalists to forget that the result reflects *decisions*, rather than some kind of neutral scientific truth.

At the national level, the daily public-affairs news concentrates heavily on what the president said and did that day; how well- or badly organized his staff seems to be; whether he is moving ahead or falling behind in his struggle against opponents from the other party; and who is using what tactics to get ready for the next presidential race. Each time the chairman of the Federal Reserve opens his mouth, he usually gets on the front page of the newspaper and on the evening network news. Each month, when the government releases its report on unemployment rates and consumer-price increases, papers and networks treat this as a genuine news event. Each summer when the leaders of industrialized nations hold their G-7 meeting, the news gives us a few minutes of prime ministers and presidents discussing their latest economic disputes. When the local school board selects a new superintendent of schools, that announcement, and the comments of the new superintendent, are played prominently in the local news.

A case could be made that some or all of these events are really the most important "news" that a broad readership needs each day. But you could just as easily make a case that most of these official, often ceremonial events should be overlooked and that a whole different category of human activity deserves coverage as "news." Instead of telling us what Newt Gingrich will do to block Bill Clinton's spending plans for education, the "news" might involve the way parochial schools work and ask whether their standard of discipline is possible in public schools. Instead of describing rivalries on the White House staff, the "news" could treat the presidency the way it does the scientific establishment, judging it mainly by public pronouncements and not looking too far behind the veil. The simplest daily reminder that the news is the result of countless judgment calls, rather than some abstract truth, is a comparison of the front page of the *Wall Street Journal* with that of almost any other major newspaper. The "news" that dominates four-fifths of most front pages is confined, in the *Journal*, to two little columns of news summary. (Here is an alarming fact: Those two columns represent more words than a half-hour TV news show would, if written out.) The rest of the front page represents the *Journal's* attempt to explain what is interesting and important about the world, though it may not be at the top of the breaking "news." The two great journalistic organizations that illustrate how creatively the "news" could be defined are in fact the *Journal's* news (not editorial) sections and National Public Radio's news staff. Each of them covers the breaking news but does so in a summary fashion, so it can put its energy, space, and professional pride into reports that are not driven by the latest official pronouncement.

"It's absolutely correct to say that there are objectively occurring events," says Cole Campbell, of the *Virginian-Pilot*. "Speeches are made, volcanoes erupt, trees fall. But *news* is not a scientifically observable event. News is a choice, an extraction process, saying that one event is more meaningful than another event. The very act of saying that means making judgments that are based on values and based on frames."

It might seem that in making this point, Campbell and his colleagues had "discovered" a principle that most people figure out when they are in high school. There is no such thing as "just the news," and that's why editors are both necessary and powerful. But the public-journalism advocates have pushed this obvious-seeming point toward a conclusion that has angered many other editors. They have argued that the way modern journalists *choose* to present the news increases the chance that citizens will feel unhappy, powerless, betrayed by, and angry about their political system. And because the most powerful journalistic organs are unwilling to admit that they've made this choice, Rosen says, it is almost impossible for them to change.

"I couldn't disagree more with that view of newspaper journalism," Leonard Downie of the *Washington Post* has said in discussing the public-journalism theory that reporters should be actively biased in favor of encouraging the community to be involved in politics:

I think our job is to report the news. To come as near as we can to giving people the truth, recognizing that the truth is multifaceted and that it changes from time to time as we learn more. I know that is what we do at the *Washington Post*. I know there are times when individual feelings among reporters and editors may cause them to want to take a side. We work very hard here to try to drive that out of our work.

Downie says that this approach is hard on his reporters, who in an attempt to suppress their personal feelings about an issue must "pretend to be less fully human than they really are." (Downie himself takes this belief to such an extreme that he *refuses to vote* in elections, feeling that this would make him too involved in the political process.) He admits that the newspaper's claim of "objectivity" is not convincing to many readers, who believe that the paper has its own angle on many stories. But he says that wavering even for a moment from the pursuit of "objectivity" would be disastrous.

> Where I am most bothered is when a newspaper uses its news columns—not its editorial page or its publisher—to achieve specific outcomes in the community. That is what I think is wrong, and very wrong. That line is very bright, and very sharp, and extremely dangerous. It is being manipulated by academics who are risking the terrible prostitution of our profession. Telling political candidates that they must come to a newspaper's forum, or that they must discuss certain issues—that is very dangerous stuff. That is not our role. There are plenty of institutions in every community to do this sort of thing. If newspapers are lax in covering these activities—if we are guilty only of covering crime and horse-race politics, then we should do our job better. We shouldn't change our job.

This defense of pure, detached "objectivity" drives many public-journalism advocates crazy. Rosen, Merritt, Campbell, and others say that when papers and TV stations have taken a more "engaged," less "objective" approach, they virtually never receive complaints from their readers or viewers. "*All* of the resistance to public journalism has come from other journalists, not from the public or politicians," Jay Rosen has said. "The resistance is always in the name of the community, but it is hard to find anyone in the community who objects." In its several years of public-journalism projects, the *Virginian Pilot* has received one hostile letter to the editor, claiming that its new approach to the community's problems meant abandoning the old standard of objectivity. But that letter came from a retired newspaper editor; the paper says it has received no similar complaints from readers without a professional axe to grind.

"I think Len Downie is right when he says that public journalism is an 'ideology,'" says Cole Campbell. "There are *two* ideologies, and he is unself-conscious about the ideology that drives his kind of journalism.

> The ideology of mainstream journalism is, When there is conflict, there is news. When there is no conflict, there's no news. That is ideological. It is out of touch with how people experience life.

Buzz Merritt elaborated on this point in *Public Journalism and Public Life*: "It is interesting that journalism's binding axiom of objectivity allows, even requires, unlimited toughness as a tool as well as a credo, yet it rejects *purposefulness*—having a motivation beyond mere exposure—as unprofessional. Without purposefulness, toughness is mere self-indulgence."

The Hidden Consensus

Beneath the apparent gulf that separates the public-journalism advocates from their elite critics is a broader ground of hopeful consensus. Although Leonard Downie objects vehemently to public journalism in theory, he has said that he respects most of the actual journalistic projects that have been done in its name. "The notion that in political campaigns you should shift some of your resources away from covering consultants and toward reporting the issues voters are primarily interested in—that is simply an evolution of good political journalism," he said.

> These are not new ways of reporting. Using public opinion surveys to find out what people think about their own communities, doing solutions reporting to see what things are working in solving societal problems—this is all part of what I would see as normal newspaper reporting.

But why, Downie asks, call this "public journalism"? Why not just call it "good journalism" and try to do more of it?

Other editors who have been on the warpath against the public-journalism concept, including William Woo of the St. Louis Post-Dispatch and Howard Schneider of Newsday, have also said there is "nothing new" in the concept of public-spirited reporting. It's what papers should have been doing all along.

The public-journalism advocates might take this as a sign that they are winning the battle. In the 1970s and early 1980s, the military reformers in the Pentagon knew that the tide had turned their way when their opponents began saying that there was "nothing new" in the reformers' analysis. After all, its principles had been in circulation since the time of Douglas MacArthur, or Robert E. Lee, or for that matter Genghis Khan.

The rancor surrounding the public-journalism debate actually seems to arise from two misunderstandings. One concerns the nature of journalism's "involvement" in public life. When Leonard Downie and Max Frankel hear that term, they seem to imagine drumbeating campaigns by a newspaper on behalf of a particular candidate or a specific action-plan for a community. What the editors who have put public journalism into effect mean is "just good journalism"—that is, making people care about the issues that affect their lives, and helping them see how they can play a part in resolving those issues.

And when big-paper editors hear that the public journalists want to "listen" to the public and be "guided" by its concerns, the editors imagine something that they dread. This sounds all too similar to pure "user-driven" journalism, in which the marketing department surveys readers to find out what they're interested in, and the editors give them only that. This version of public journalism sounds like an invitation to abandon all critical judgment and turn the paper into a pure "feel good" advertising sheet. It misrepresents the best conception of public journalism, which is that editors and reporters will continue to exercise their judgment about issues, as they claim to now, but will pay more attention than today's elite journalists do to the impact of their work on the health of democracy.

"I think the people who make this criticism have not looked closely enough at what public interest journalism is doing," William Kovach, of the Nieman Foundation, said in 1995. "Papers are using surveys, but they are very careful surveys; they're doing a lot of work in neighborhoods. It's not a politically designed opinion poll to take a snap judgment." The editors who have undertaken public-journalism projects say they are using their best reportorial skills to determine not what people want to hear but what issues concern them most, and then applying that knowledge in their coverage.

Leonard Downie is right: This approach is "just good journalism." The real questions it raises are not hair-splitting quarrels about what it should be called but the practical work of implementation.

JOURNALISM IN THE PUBLIC SPIRIT

Today's journalists can choose: Do they want merely to entertain the public or to engage it? If they want to entertain, they will keep doing what they have done for the last generation. Concentrating on conflict and spectacle, building up celebrities and tearing them down, presenting a crisis or issue with the volume turned all the way up, only to drop that issue and turn to the next emergency. They will make themselves the center of attention, as they exchange one-liners as if public life were a parlor game and make fun of the gaffes and imperfections of anyone in public life. They will view their berths as opportunities for personal aggrandizement and enrichment, trading on the power of their celebrity. And while they do these things, they will be constantly more hated and constantly less useful to the public whose attention they are trying to attract. In the long run, real celebrities—singers, quarterbacks, movie stars—will crowd them off the stage. Public life will become more sour and embittered, and American democracy will be even less successful in addressing the nation's economic, social, and moral concerns.

But if journalists should choose to engage the public, they will begin a long series of experiments and decisions to see how journalism might better serve its fundamental purpose, that of making democratic self-government possible. They could start with the example set by public journalism and work on the obvious problems and limits of that model.

The author of the following selection is the most widely-read Washington journalist in the country. He points out the complexities of journalism, the realities of reporting that often distance reporters from their subjects. Sometimes, however, reporters seek a more active role in the political process and become, wittingly or unwittingly, allies of politicians who want to manage the news for their own personal goals. Journalistic integrity is not always easily maintained. Political reporters are prone to conflicts of interest as they seek to advance their careers through access to power.

Regardless of the many journalistic pitfalls, Broder concludes that "a good newspaper is a citizen's best resource for exercising his rights and responsibilities in this Republic. It provides the broadest and, on occasion, deepest look into the affairs of the society and its government."

Called the "high priest of political journalism" *Washington Post* correspondent David S. Broder won the Pulitzer Prize in May 1973 for distinguished commentary. He is a frequent commentator on NBC's "Meet the Press" and the public television show "Washington Week in Review."

Broder's arguments in the next reading are:

1. The journalistic ideal requires reporters to seek the truth at almost all costs. Journalists sometimes put friendships and even families second as they pursue good stories.
2. Journalists never know as much as they should, and are inherently political outsiders.
3. The media's incentive to deliver startling information to the public conflicts with deliberate and thoughtful political coverage.
4. Politicians and reporters create conflict-of-interest problems when they seek to use each other for personal gain in their respective careers.
5. The public should be as critical of the newspapers it reads as of the politicians it elects. An informed public is the best guarantee of a responsible press.

10

David S. Broder

BEHIND THE FRONT PAGE

A JOURNALIST'S VALUES

Most sensible people will avoid journalism as a career. The job's abundant rewards are matched with its costs and risks. At the extreme, you can be shot at and killed, as so many war correspondents have been; you can be threatened and ostracized, as so many reporters were during the civil rights struggle.

Most of us face only an occasional angry citizen, cop, or government official, telling us to get the hell out of his sight—or else. But a journalist's life is inherently disrupted and disorganized. We work too hard and we play too hard. And we tend to die before our time.

The job is tougher on our families than on us. Divorce rates are high, and those who stay married still must contend with missed dinners, missed weekends, missed vacations. The strains arise because as journalists we put the pursuit and publication of news first. We feel the tug of family ties; of friendships; of ethnic, religious, racial, and national loyalties; and of our partisan, political, and social views. But we define ourselves by our calling, and we resolve most of our conflicts by making that goal uppermost.

Often that makes us do things that are less than admirable. In 1972, for example, at a restaurant in New Hampshire, I ran into a man who had been one of my closest friends in college and our early years in Washington. I asked what he was doing there. He was a Washington lawyer who represented Japanese companies. He and several other lawyers and lobbyists had volunteered to help the Democratic presidential primary campaign of House Ways and Means Committee Chairman Wilbur Mills. As we talked, something in my expression made him stop suddenly and say, "You're not going to write about this, are you?" I recognized the problem. He had greeted me as a friend, not a reporter. He was not a politician and he had imposed no ground rules. He had answered my questions candidly but as a friend. Now he felt entrapped. I suppose I could have said, "Look, if you're uncomfortable about what you're doing, you better clear out. Just pay your check, get on the next plane, and I'll forget we even talked or that I saw you up here."

That's not what I did. "You're not an unknown person," I told him. "You are in a restaurant in Manchester, New Hampshire, the week before the primary, and there are other reporters here. You are taking a role in a campaign I'm covering. The fact that you and your friends are here to help Wilbur Mills is news in my book. It's going to be written about." He said, "You can't do that. The people at my table saw me talking with you. If you write this story, it's going to embarrass me with Mills. It's going to ruin everything." I said, "You should have thought about that before all of you came up here. There's no way you guys are going to be involved without people knowing about it."

I wrote the story and our friendship ended, as I knew it would. I am not sure I did the right thing. I can rationalize the betrayal of friendship on grounds that had I not written the story, another reporter would have. But it still doesn't ease the pinch of conscience.

The longer you are a journalist, the more such troubling incidents you experience, the more the glamour disappears and the more obvious the limitations of the work become. We journalists always deal with partial information and know less than we should. We never have as much time as we need. And yet we must display our ignorance and haste in the most obvious way—by signing or broadcasting stories read or watched by people who know a hell of a lot more about the subject than we do. And they are not shy about letting us know where we went wrong.

Most important of all, journalists are always inherently outsiders. When an individual or team or nation has a great moment of achievement, we are observers, not celebrants. When tragedies happen, when a child drowns, when a president is killed, when a whole city goes up in flames, instead of sharing the emotions, we record them.

It takes a peculiar and in some respects almost perverse personality to choose a role in life that automatically distances you from the most profound experiences of your friends, your neighbors, your city, or your nation. We are voyeurs, not participants. And the best of us—a Walter Cronkite describing the first manned landing on the moon or a presidential funeral procession, a Frank Johnston photographing Jonestown, a John Hersey writing about Hiroshima—have to be at our most disciplined and dispassionate when almost every human instinct impels us to give way to joy or pain.

Even when reporters have their values before them and their roles thought through, they can land in unexpected controversy, as my colleagues William Greider and Milton Coleman both discovered. Greider, then the *Post*'s assistant managing editor for national news, and David Stockman had struck up a friendship in the late 1970s when Stockman was a representative from Michigan. When President-elect Reagan appointed Stockman director of the Office of Management and Budget, Greider proposed that their regular meetings continue under rules acknowledging Stockman's change of status to one of the administration's three or four central figures.

Greider would tape-record the conversations, which would be off the record for the *Post*'s immediate use. When both agreed, Greider would mine the material for a "full and serious" *Atlantic* magazine account of what promised to be a fateful year of budget policy. The meetings began, over Saturday-morning breakfasts at the Hay-Adams hotel, and by the end of the 1981 session of Congress, the two had met eighteen times.

As Greider wrote in the introduction to the book version of his expanded article, *The Education of David Stockman and Other Americans:*

> At the outset, Stockman and I were participating in a fairly routine transaction of Washington, a form of submerged communication which takes place with utter regularity between selected members of the press and the highest officials of government. Our mutual motivation, despite our different interests, was crassly self-serving. It did not need to be spelled out between us. I would use him and he would use me. . . . I had established a valuable peephole on the inner policy debates of the new administration. And the young budget director had established a valuable connection with an important newspaper. I would get a jump on the unfolding strategies and decisions. He would be able to prod and influence the focus of our coverage, to communicate his views and positions under the cover of our "off the record" arrangement, to make known harsh assessments that a public official would not dare to voice in the more formal settings of a press conference, speech, or "on the record" interview. . . . He was using me and I was using him. I did say that it was crass.

The insights Greider gained from Stockman helped steer the *Post*'s coverage of the budget battle. At the breakfasts, he persuaded Stockman to allow some of his statements to be used immediately on a background basis, as the views of "administration officials" or "senior budget officials." Even off-the-record comments helped Greider manage our coverage. Many of us, who had our own back-channel communications with the budget director, knew about Greider's meetings with Stockman.

Stockman's deal with Greider was unique because, at some point, the off-the-record restriction would be erased in the interest of accurate history. Shortly before Labor Day in 1981, after Reagan had signed the first budget and tax bills into law, Greider told Stockman he thought it was time to write. As Greider later told me, "I held my breath, because if he had said, 'No, I've got to go back to these issues in 1982 and I don't want you to write yet,' I would have been bound by our agreement." Instead, Stockman agreed. Greider's only fear as he began to write was that he had no story to tell.

Columnists Joseph Kraft, Robert Novak, and George Will were also meeting regularly with Stockman during the first nine months of 1981, and Greider thought that most informed readers knew what he knew: that "administration officials" and "senior budget officials" were increasingly dismayed by both the President's and Congress's decisions on tax and budget matters. To say that he and Stockman were unprepared for the storm that broke would be an understatement. I remember telling Greider that I had received my copy of the *Atlantic* at home the previous night, had sat up late reading his article, and thought it was "a hell of a piece." He said that he didn't realize that subscribers had received it already, and that he had better let Stockman know. Later, he told me that when Stockman asked him if he thought it would cause any stir, Greider said it would be "a two-day flap at most."

He could not have been more wrong. The inflammatory quotes—"None of us really knows what's going on with all these numbers. . . . The defense numbers got out of control. . . . Kemp-Roth was always a Trojan horse to bring down the top rate. . . . Supply-side is trickle-down theory. . . . The hogs were really feeding"—read like time bombs set to blow up administration policy from within. The credibility of Reagan's unique policy mixture of deep tax rate cuts, steep defense increases, and reductions in some domestic spending was under increasing attack. Stockman's words to Greider seemed to cut the last thread of plausibility for that policy.

Stockman was summoned to the White House for a session with the President, but he was not fired—an interesting reflection on the nature of the Reagan presidency.

Greider later said two things had disturbed him. The first was that other journalists had sensationalized his careful, balanced account. Greider's story was a subtle tale of the disillusionment of a somewhat naive, perhaps idealistic young public servant, who tried to execute a policy based on consistent principles and found himself, for all his efforts, defending intellectually shabby and morally offensive decisions. Greider's article had been a brilliant case study in the difficulty of governing.

The press and television exerpted from that narrative the sensational quotes and turned Stockman into a heretic blurting inconvenient truths about administration policies. "Thus," Greider wrote months later, "I was confronted with a brief personal glimpse of the qualities in the news media that trouble its more thoughtful critics—the relentless factuality, the haste, the transient attention that obscures meaning even as the media deliver the daily blizzard of startling information."

Second, Greider belatedly discovered the penalties for violating the rules of clique journalism. As I noted, Greider wondered if he had a story, because he already had seen (and in some cases been a conduit for) many references to the doubts of an official he, as an insider, could clearly identify as Stockman. Greider wrote:

> By now, it should be clear why Stockman and I both offended the "rules." The appearance in print of the budget director's candid commentaries shocked sophisticated readers but they were not surprised by the substance of what he was saying. Those who had followed the coded dialogue, who had translated the news stories about "senior budget officials" or perhaps heard Stockman say the same things in private meetings, knew well enough where he stood. Still, it was shocking. The unvarnished private dialogue of government is supposed to remain private—and separate from the bland, reassuring rhetoric of the public discourse. By going public, he violated the privacy and prerogatives of that network and so did I. Publishing the raw version of reality automatically depreciates the value of every insider's knowledge. It also refutes the images of order and

progress conveyed by the daily news. These stories of doubts and misgivings and policy battles had, in fact, been printed in the newspapers, but clearly they were not told in a way that made much impression outside the inner circle. As a newspaper editor, thinking my submerged conversations were helping inform general readers, I was most troubled by my belated recognition that the messages were not getting through.

Greider's arrangement with Stockman was criticized by some colleagues at the *Post* and other Washington papers. Howell Raines of the *New York Times* said at a 1983 Poynter Institute conference that he could not "escape the nagging feeling that the real message of this book is that for a time a great newspaper and a group of hard-working journalists got trapped into holding out on their readers, at a critical point in the Reagan administration, information that could have tilted the political balance."

As Greider learned, there are built-in problems when an editor on a daily newspaper takes on a sideline assignment as a magazine writer and uses that assignment for access under special guidelines to an official his paper is covering. The *Post*'s daily coverage of Stockman benefited from Greider's access, and, as Hobart Rowen, the *Post*'s senior economics writer, pointed out at the Poynter conference, other reporters at the *Post* were not inhibited by Greider's "arrangement" from writing, clearly and emphatically, about the contradictions in the Reagan policy mix. Admittedly, those columns and analytical articles lacked the impact of Stockman's confessions to Greider. But I can't see how Stockman could have made such confessions, on the record, while the budget and tax bill were going through Congress in 1981. Greider got him on the record faster than any other journalist in Washington, and that feat deserved congratulations not censure. At every stage of the interviewing, he bargained with Stockman to modify the ground rules so Greider could share the maximum of what he was learning with readers. At the first opening, he told Stockman he wanted to use the direct quotes in the magazine piece. He did exactly what a responsible journalist must do: put his obligation to the readers first. . . .

Some in journalism believe they can have all of its privileges as well as all the pleasures of actively participating in the political world. The have-it-both-ways clan can cite as an example the most eminent journalist of the last generation, Walter Lippmann. At age twenty-five, while working for the *New Republic*, he drafted labor speeches for Theodore Roosevelt, and later had friendships with almost every President through John F. Kennedy. As Ronald Steel noted in his biography of Lippmann, Kennedy consulted and flattered the old columnist constantly. Ted Sorensen brought a draft of Kennedy's inaugural address to Lippmann's house and accepted some minor changes in the text, which Lippmann praised in his column as "a remarkably successful piece of self-expression." Steel noted that Lippmann hired a new assistant who had worked in the Kennedy campaign and was also well connected at the White House, and, in short time, the columnist "became one of the shining ornaments of the Kennedy Administration." Lippmann's extracurricular activities did not diminish the exceptional quality of his journalism. But now when the journalist's role is more visible and controversial, the eminence some achieve carries with it added responsibilities and ought not act as an excuse for special privilege. At least that's my view, though I readily concede the whole ethical dilemma of outside activities and associations is one each journalist must solve for himself.

I have generally avoided entertaining the politicians I write about or being wined and dined by them. A few years ago, when a Republican I had known for twenty years and become genuinely fond of decided to run for President, I told him, rather pompously, that our custom of pleasant private lunches and long conversations would have to be sacrificed to his ambitions and my job responsibilities. On the other hand, I participate uninhibitedly in the Gridiron Dinner, cavorting in satirical skits while my invited guests from the political and journalistic worlds mingle at an event which many critics consider the ultimate expression of coziness between Washington reporters and officials.

Still, even by my flexible yardstick, the political involvements of some journalists raise troubling questions. William F. Buckley, Jr., the columnist, editor, author, and television personality, founded the Young Americans for Freedom, which has become a recruiting and training ground for a whole generation of conservative politicians. He ran for mayor of New York and has a well-publicized friendship with President Reagan. Among Democrats, the most notable example may be Ben Wattenberg, a former Lyndon Johnson speechwriter, who in recent years has combined his newspaper column with an activist role as the leader of the Coalition for a Democratic Majority, which has battled rival factions for control of the party platform and provided forums and support for favored political candidates.

But the most visible of Lippmann's successors is George F. Will, probably the most influential journalist today and certainly the most versatile, with a vast television, magazine, newspaper, and lecture audience. Will has worked vigorously to erase the inhibitions many of us think go with our jobs. A staff aide for a Republican senator before taking up journalism, Will has made no secret of his personal relationship with contemporary politicians. After hosting a dinner party for Ronald Reagan in 1980 which formally introduced the President-elect to Washington's political and social aristocracy, he laid into the "confused moralists" of Washington, who he said had been spreading a "silly scrupulosity" about press-government relations. "We all have our peculiar tastes. Some people like Popsicles. Others like Gothic novels. I like politicians. . . . A journalist's duty is to see politicians steadily and see them whole. To have intelligent sympathy for them, it helps to know a few as friends. Most that I know are overworked and underpaid persons whose characters can stand comparison with the characters of the people they represent, and of journalists." Journalists "have particular professional duties," he said, "but they and politicians are part of the same process, the quest for the public good."

What he did not mention in that column was that "the quest for the public good" had led him, not just to give dinner to an "overworked and underpaid" politician named Ronald Reagan, but to assist the same Reagan, a couple months earlier, in preparing to debate Jimmy Carter.

Will was one of three conservative journalists invited to Wexford, an estate in Virginia, where Reagan was rehearsing for the most important event in the campaign. One of them, *New York Times* columnist William Safire, had the good sense to say no. Another, Pat Buchanan, Safire's former colleague in the Nixon White House, said yes, which did not surprise me, because he has always put his ideology ahead of anything else.

When Will agreed to prep Reagan for the debate, he made a great mistake and caused many of us who admire him great pain. His work was not secret. As he pointed out, photographers saw him going into Wexford with David Stockman, then a young congressman, who was playing Carter in the rehearsals. But almost three years later, when it developed that Stockman and others on the Reagan team had obtained certain papers prepared for Carter's use in the debate, people took a closer look at who had been doing what.

The *Wall Street Journal* started it with a July 1983 front-page story headlined, "Should a Newsman Be Active Participant in Partisan Politics?"

The story quoted Will's ABC News commentary on the debate: "I think his game plan worked well. I don't think he was particularly surprised." It then disclosed that Reagan aides had had Carter's preparation materials and that, because he had helped rehearse Reagan, Will knew this.

Jack Nelson, the Washington bureau chief of the *Los Angeles Times*, told the *Journal* Will's action was "outrageous." The story pointed out that while "the network mentioned on debate night that Mr. Will had 'met' with candidate Reagan the day before, there wasn't any suggestion that he had participated in the preparations." Will said he went to Wexford because "it's like being invited into the locker room for a sportswriter," but he conceded, "I probably wouldn't go down there again."

The *New York Daily News* dropped his column, saying he had broken faith with his readers, but later reinstated it. Other editors either defended Will or said his column was too valuable to lose—as, indeed, it is. But the furor was large enough that one Sunday in July Will defended what he had done in a long column in the *Post* and answered his colleagues' questions on ABC-TV's *This Week with David Brinkley*, where he is a panelist.

In addition to his earlier points—that his presence was not secret and that he was of minimal substantive help to Reagan—he argued that as a columnist he had more license than a straight news reporter and that his partisanship toward Reagan was, as he put it, not exactly a "state secret."

So, he concluded his column:

> To those who ask: Should you have accepted access to Wexford?, my reply is: I think so. It was a valuable chance to see certain gears and pulleys of the political backstage. . . . Would I accept a similar invitation again? Wild horses could not drag me. This, for three reasons. First, some of the questions now being raised seem to me to have merit. Second, it makes so many people anxious. Third, my relationship with ABC is now formal and different. Then I generally appeared in a semi-debate format with a more liberal person.

Will's defense bothered me. First, he said that had he been a regular ABC News employee (as he was by 1983), he would have felt more of a responsibility to stay out of the debate rehearsal. But that reasoning overlooks the readers of his columns for *Washington Post* Writers Group and *Newsweek* magazine. Second, Will is as much of a sports fan as I am—we both have it bad—and he knew full well that sportswriters are invited to the locker room after the game, not before. What Will accepted was an invitation to be with the coaches at the last secret practice before the big game.

Stockman's possession of some of Carter's debate materials almost compromised him. Will said he never wrote about them "because their origin was unknown and their importance was nil." Suppose their origin had been announced at Wexford and their importance recognized by everyone in the room. What would he have done then? Suppose someone had said, "Our Carter sources tell us that he is going to do such-and-such in his closing statement. How do you want to answer him?" Would he have reported that or kept silent?

In his *Post* apologia, Will said, "I did not write about what I saw at Wexford because to have done so would have violated an unspoken but nonetheless important understanding that there are times when a writer is allowed access to things that the writer should not turn into material for his writings."

As far as I could judge, when Will went to Wexford, he was already assigned to comment on the debate for ABC and he would certainly continue to write about the Reagan-Carter campaign. Yet he knowingly entered a situation where no matter what he learned his hands were tied journalistically. That is a pretty dumb position for any journalist to get into. . . .

Increasingly, ethical issues, such as conflict of interest, are being addressed in newsrooms across the country. According to a 1983 Ohio State University survey of 902 news organizations, three quarters had written policies on such matters as outside work and the acceptance of gifts by their reporters and editors. The scrutiny is needed because in the television era journalists have far greater opportunities to turn their prominence into money or influence. For instance, those with familiar faces or by-lines can get lecture fees that often dwarf what most of us think a good week's pay.

No official rules apply to the profession as a whole. The Society of Professional Journalists, Sigma Delta Chi, adopted a code of ethics in 1926 and updated it in 1973. It says secondary employment and political involvement "should be avoided if it compromises the integrity of journalists and their employers." The code is necessarily general and lacks any enforcement mechanism. Each news organization sets its own standards and each journalist decides how far he will operate within their borders. At the *Post*, the managing editor must be informed in advance and can veto any outside employment, from book contract to teaching invitation. This policy guards against any infringement on the daily demands on a journalist's time and protects against any potential embarrassment the paper could incur from a staff member's inappropriate sideline or free-lance work. . . .

There are no safe shortcuts. In my more than thirty years as a reporter, for five different organizations, I have learned that the only way to cover a story is to cover it: to spend as much time with the people as humanly possible, to ask as many questions as they will tolerate, and never to assume I know what is going on without asking.

For all the reasons I have described, we often fall short of the truth. Whether covering the campaign trail, the Congress, or the White House, defining a public figure's character or tracing a complex plot, we sometimes miss the mark—by some distance. The news we present is distorted by the limits of our skills, the principals' reluctance to share all they know, and the pressures of time and space.

Still, a good newspaper is a citizen's best resource for exercising his rights and responsibilities in this Republic. It provides the broadest and, on occasion, deepest look into the affairs of the society and its government. Books and magazines can provide more concepts, perspectives, and history, and television and radio can bring you closer to the actual event. But a good newspaper has both immediacy and perspective that foster the discussion and judgment so essential to the dialogue of democracy.

Dialogue is the key word because neither our government nor our press functions well without public involvement. Voters and newspaper readers—the same people, really—are ultimately as well served by their government and their press as they demand to be.

Walter Lippmann wrote, "The theory of a free press is that the truth will *emerge* from free reporting and free discussion, not that it will be presented perfectly and instantly in any one account." Eric Sevareid quoted those words in a 1967 address to the Massachusetts legislature, and added, "The ultimate burden must fall upon the individual citizen. If he wishes to be well informed he must read widely in the press and listen widely to the broadcasts. No one example of either can serve him more than very partially."

You cannot be passive about citizenship or about journalism. A good newspaper will reward you only so far as you are devoted to reading it critically.

The paper you read is shaped by unstated, implicit values and biases which you must recognize. I admit that the mirrors we use to reflect reality are inevitably flawed by our own presuppositions and prejudices. You must correct the "spin" those twists impart to what you read. The clues are there in all the subjective elements—phrasing, word selection, story placement, sourcing—that shape a particular reporter's or paper's version of the news.

With these worthwhile efforts, the half hour you spend with the paper will give you more than a new set of facts and opinions; it will open a new set of your own questions. Every good journalist reads the paper or watches television news with this in mind: Where does the story go next? What questions remain unanswered? What new puzzles are there now to be solved?

So should you. And when your paper fails to answer your questions, let them—or us—know. At its best, a newspaper is in constant conversation with its readers, and you have to hold up your end of the dialogue. . . .

CHAPTER 3

BUREAUCRACY
AND ADMINISTRATION

Why is Running a Government
Tougher than Running a Business?

Congress creates administrative departments and agencies to carry out legislative mandates. The sovereignty of the people resides in Congress. Congress represents the people and legislates in the public interest. Congress is the only constitutionally legitimate body with express authority to legislate, that is, make public policy.

The Constitution provides for three governmental branches. The most important branches were the Congress and the President. Interaction between the legislative and executive branches defined the Madisonian separation of powers and checks and balances system. Placing the executive branch directly under presidential control maintained the relatively simple tripartite constitutional symmetry.

The bureaucratic paradigm, from the constitutional standpoint, folds the bureaucracy into the executive branch and gives the President control over it. The President is Chief Executive and Chief Administrator, and these roles are one and the same.

Alexander Hamilton's interpretation of the Constitution makes the President imperial and consequently administrators become presidential deputies. The Madisonian model, which balances presidential and congressional powers, defines executive power narrowly. Madison would also define public administration as executive and part of the President's Article II responsibility to see that the laws are faithfully executed.

The Constitution, then, simply does not take account of the powerful and often independent administrative branch that began to take shape in the nineteenth century and became a reality with Franklin D. Roosevelt's administrative presidency in the 1930s. The following selection analyzes the role of the bureaucracy in our constitutional system.

Peter Woll is a political scientist who has written extensively on all aspects of American government. His anthology, *American Government: Readings and Cases,* 13th edition (New York: Longman, 1999), is used as a supplement or standard text in introductory American government courses in universities and colleges throughout the nation. The essential arguments of the following reading are:

1. Congress creates the administrative branch to carry out its mandates. Ultimately the power of government comes to rest in a semi-autonomous bureaucracy.
2. Flexible interpretations of the Constitution accommodate the bureaucracy within its framework, even though the constitutional system of separation of powers and checks and balances did not provide for a hybrid administrative branch.
3. The President, Congress, and the courts exercise important powers over the administrative branch. Maintaining accountability to the traditional branches of the government helps to make the bureaucracy constitutionally responsible.

11

Peter Woll

THE BUREAUCRACY:
THE CONSTITUTIONAL IDEAL AND THE REALITY

★★★

The administrative branch today stands at the very center of our governmental process; it is the keystone of the structure. And administrative agencies exercise legislative and judicial as well as executive functions—a fact that is often overlooked. . . .

How should we view American bureaucracy? Ultimately, the power of government comes to rest in the administrative branch. Agencies are given the responsibility of making concrete decisions carrying out vague policy initiated in Congress or by the President. The agencies can offer expert advice, closely attuned to the most interested pressure groups, and they often not only determine the policies that the legislature and executive recommends in the first place, but also decisively affect the policy-making process. Usually it is felt that the bureaucracy is politically "neutral," completely under the domination of the President, Congress, or the courts. We will see that this is not entirely the case, and that the President and Congress have only sporadic control over the administrative process.

The bureaucracy is a semi-autonomous branch of the government, often dominating Congress, exercising strong influence on the President, and only infrequently subject to review by the courts. If our constitutional democracy is to be fully analyzed, we must focus attention upon the administrative branch. . . . [T]he problem of administrative responsibility is, how can we control the [political power] of the administrative branch? In order to approach an understanding of this difficult problem, it is necessary to appreciate the nature of the administrative process and how it interacts with other branches of the government and with the general public. It is also important to understand the nature of our constitutional system, and the political context within which agencies function.

CONSTITUTIONAL DEMOCRACY AND BUREAUCRATIC POWER

We operate within the framework of a constitutional democracy. This means, first, that the government is to be limited by the separation of powers and Bill of Rights. Another component of the system, federalism, is designed in theory to provide states with a certain amount of authority when it is not implied at the national level. Our separation of powers, the system of checks and balances, and the federal system, help to explain some of the differences between administrative organization here and in other countries. But the Constitution does not explicitly provide for the administrative branch, which has become a new fourth branch of government. This raises the question of how to control the bureaucracy when there are no clear constitutional limits upon it. The second aspect of our system, democracy, is of course implied in the Constitution itself, but has expanded greatly since it was adopted. We are confronted, very broadly speaking, first with the problem of constitutional limitation, and secondly with the problem of democratic participation in the activities of the bureaucracy. The bureaucracy must be accommodated within the framework of our system of constitutional democracy. This is the crux of the problem of administrative reponsibility.

Even though the Constitution does not explicitly provide for the bureaucracy, it has had a profound impact upon the structure, functions, and general place that the bureaucracy occupies in government. The administrative process was incorporated into the constitutional system under the heading of "The Executive Branch." But the concept of "administration" at the time of the adoption of the Constitution was a very simple one, involving the "mere execution" of "executive details," to use the phrases of Hamilton in *The Federalist*. The idea, at that time, was simply that the President as Chief Executive would be able to control the executive branch in carrying out the mandates of Congress. In *Federalist 72*, after defining administration in this very narrow way, Hamilton stated:

> . . . The persons, therefore, to whose immediate management the different administrative matters are committed ought to be considered as Assistants or Deputies of the Chief Magistrate, and on this account, they ought to derive their offices from his appointment, at least from his nomination, and ought to be subject to his superintendence.

It was clear that Hamilton felt the President would be responsible for administrative action as long as he was in office. This fact later turned up in what can be called the "presidential supremacy" school of thought, which held and still holds that the President is *constitutionally* responsible for the administrative branch, and that Congress should delegate to him all necessary authority for this purpose. Nevertheless, whatever the framers of the Constitution might have planned if they could have foreseen the nature of bureaucratic development, the fact is that the system they constructed in many ways supported bureaucratic organization and functions independent of the

President. The role they assigned to Congress in relation to administration assured this result, as did the general position of Congress in the governmental system as a check or balance to the power of the President. Congress has a great deal of authority over the administrative process.

If we compare the powers of Congress and the President over the bureaucracy it becomes clear that they both have important constitutional responsibility. Congress retains primary control over the organization of the bureaucracy. It alone creates and destroys agencies, and determines whether they are to be located within the executive branch or outside it. This has enabled Congress to create a large number of *independent* agencies beyond presidential control. Congress has the authority to control appropriations and may thus exercise a great deal of power over the administrative arm, although increasingly the Bureau of the Budget and the President have the initial, and more often than not the final say over the budget. Congress also has the authority to define the jurisdiction of agencies. Finally, the Constitution gives to the legislature the power to interfere in presidential appointments, which must be "by and with the advice and consent of the Senate."

Congress may extend the sharing of the appointive power when it sets up new agencies. It may delegate to the President pervasive authority to control the bureaucracy. But one of the most important elements of the separation of powers is the electoral system, which gives to Congress a constituency which is different from and even conflicting with that of the President. This means that Congress often decides to set up agencies beyond presidential purview. Only rarely will it grant the President any kind of final authority to structure the bureaucracy. During World War II, on the basis of the War Powers Act, the President had the authority to reorganize the administrative branch. Today he has the same authority, provided that Congress does not veto presidential proposals within a certain time limit. In refusing to give the President permanent reorganization authority, Congress is jealously guarding one of its important prerogatives.

Turning to the constitutional authority of the President over the bureaucracy, it is somewhat puzzling to see that it gives him a relatively small role. He appoints certain officials by and with the advice and consent of the Senate. He has directive power over agencies that are placed within his jurisdiction by Congress. His control over patronage, once so important, has diminished sharply under the merit system. The President is Commander-in-Chief of all military forces, which puts him in a controlling position over the Defense Department and agencies involved in military matters. In the area of international relations, the President is by constitutional authority the "Chief Diplomat," to use Rossiter's phrase. This means that he appoints Ambassadors (by and with the advice and consent of the Senate), and generally directs national activities in the international arena—a crucially important executive function. But regardless of the apparent intentions of some of the framers of the Constitution as expressed by Hamilton in *The Federalist*, and in spite of the predominance of the Presidency in military and foreign affairs, the fact remains that we seek in vain for explicit constitutional authorization for the President to be "Chief Administrator."

This is not to say that the President does not have an important responsibility to act as Chief of the bureaucracy, merely that there is no constitutional mandate for this. As our system evolved, the President was given more and more responsibility until he became, in practice, Chief Administrator. At the same time the constitutional system has often impeded progress in this direction. The President's Committee on Administrative Management in 1937, and later the Hoover Commissions of 1949 and 1955, called upon Congress to initiate a series of reforms increasing presidential authority over the administrative branch. It was felt that this was necessary to make democracy work. The President is the only official elected nationally, and if the administration is to be held democratically accountable, he alone can stand as its representative. But meaningful control from the White House requires that the President have a comprehensive program which encompasses the activities of the bureaucracy. He must be informed as to what they are doing, and be able to control them. He must understand the complex responsibilities of the bureaucracy. Moreover, he must be able to call on sufficient political support to balance the support which the agencies draw from private clientele groups and congressional committees. This has frequently proven a difficult and often impossible task for the President. He may have the *authority* to control the bureaucracy in many areas, but not enough *power*.

On the basis of the Constitution, Congress feels it quite proper that when it delegates legislative authority to administrative agencies it can relatively often place these groups outside the control of the President. For example, in the case of the Interstate Commerce Commission, Congress had delegated final authority to that agency to control railroad mergers and other aspects of transportation activity, without giving the President the right to veto. The President might have felt that a particular merger was undesirable because it was in violation of the antitrust laws, but the Interstate Commerce Commission was likely to feel differently. In such a situation, the President could do nothing because he did not have the *legal authority* to take any action. If he could muster enough political support to exercise influence over the ICC, he would be able to control it, but the absence of legal authority was an important factor in such cases and diminished presidential power. Moreover, the ICC drew strong support from the railroad industry, which was able to counterbalance the political support possessed by the President and other groups that wished to control it. Analogous situations exist with respect to other regulatory agencies.

Besides the problem of congressional and presidential control over the bureaucracy, there is the question of judicial review of administrative decisions. The rule of law is a central element in our Constitution. The rule of law means that decisions judicial in nature should be handled by common law courts, because of their expertise in rendering due process of law. When administrative agencies engage in adjudication their decisions should be subject to judicial review—at least, they should if one supports the idea of the supremacy of law. Judicial decisions are supposed to be rendered on an independent and impartial basis, through the use of tested procedures, in order to arrive at the accurate determination of the truth. Administrative adjudication should not be subject to presidential or congressional control, which would mean political determination of decisions that should be rendered in an objective manner. The idea of the rule of law, derived from the common law and adopted within the framework of our constitutional system, in theory limits legislative and executive control over the bureaucracy.

The nature of our constitutional system poses very serious difficulties to the development of a system of administrative responsibility. The Constitution postulates that the functions of government must be separated into different branches with differing constituencies and separate authority. The idea is that the departments should oppose each other, thereby preventing the arbitrary exercise of political power. Any combination of functions was considered to lead inevitably to arbitrary government. This is a debatable point, but the result of the Constitution is quite clear. The administrative process, on the other hand, often combines various functions of government in the same hands. Attempts are made, of course, to separate those who exercise judicial functions from those in the prosecuting arms of the agencies. But the fact remains that there is a far greater combination of functions in the administrative process than can be accommodated by strict adherence to the Constitution.

It has often been proposed, as a means of alleviating what may be considered the bad effects of combined powers in administrative agencies, to draw a line of control from the original branches of the government to those parts of the bureaucracy exercising similar functions. Congress would control the legislative activities of the agencies, the President the executive aspects, and the courts the judicial functions. This would maintain the symmetry of the constitutional system. But this solution is not feasible, because other parts of the Constitution, giving different authority to these three branches, make symmetrical control of this kind almost impossible. The three branches of the government are not willing to give up whatever powers they may have over administrative agencies. For example, Congress is not willing to give the President complete control over all executive functions, nor to give the courts the authority to review all the decisions of the agencies. At present, judicial review takes place only if Congress authorizes it, except in those rare instances where constitutional issues are involved.

Another aspect of the problem of control is reflected in the apparent paradox that the three branches do not always use to the fullest extent their authority to regulate the bureaucracy, even though they wish to retain their power to do so. The courts, for example, have exercised considerable self-restraint in their review of administrative decisions. They are not willing to use all their power over the bureaucracy. Similarly, both Congress and the President will often limit their dealings with the administrative branch for political and practical reasons.

In the final analysis, we are left with a bureaucratic system that has been fragmented by the Constitution, and in which administrative discretion is inevitable. The bureaucracy reflects the general fragmentation of our political system. It is often the battleground for the three branches of government, and for outside pressure groups which seek to control it for their own purposes.

THE RISE OF THE ADMINISTRATIVE PROCESS: THE REALITY

What has caused the development of this large administrative branch which exercises all the functions of government, usually within the same agency? The reasons for the rise of the bureaucracy can be largely explained by observing how the transfer of legislative, executive, and judicial functions has occurred from the primary branches of the government.

Administrative agencies exercise legislative power because Congress and the President are unable and unwilling to cope with all the legislative problems of the nation.

The President is "Chief Legislator." Congress is supposed to exercise the primary legislative function. But clearly, given the scope of modern government, it would be impossible for the President and Congress to deal on a continuous basis with the myriad legislative concerns that arise. The President's "program" is necessarily incomplete. It deals with major legislative problems which happen to be of interest to him and of concern to the nation at a particular time. Much of the President's program is formulated by the bureaucracy. In any event, it ultimately has to be carried out by administrative agencies, provided Congress approves.

For the most part Congress is concerned with formulating policy in very broad terms. It has neither the technical information nor the time to cope with the intricate phases of modern legislation. Moreover, it is often unwilling to deal with difficult political questions, for this would necessitate taking sides and alienating various segments of the public. It frequently passes on to the bureaucracy the burden of reconciling group conflict. The bureaucracy receives the unresolved disputes that come both to Congress and to the President, making it one of the most important political arms of the government. The concept of the bureaucracy as neutral is actually contrary to the facts.

Turning to the judicial arena, the development of administrative law has taken place because of the need for a more flexible mechanism for resolving cases and controversies arising under new welfare and regulatory statutes. The idea that the functions of government can be divided into legislative, executive, and judicial categories, and segregated into three separate branches of the government, is outdated because of the growth of a complex and interdependent economy requiring government regulation. Effective regulatory power often requires a combination of legislative and judicial functions.

Examples of the Development of Administrative Agencies. At the beginning of the republic, our bureaucracy was very small. It was quite capable of domination by the President, and at that time the President was the Chief Administrator in fact as well as in theory. No one then could conceive of the growth of a complex bureaucracy such as we know today, and it was only proper to feel that the activities of the executive branch would be, for the most part, politically neutral under the control of the President and Congress. The fact that the President was supposed to be politically neutral gave the concept of a neutral bureaucracy real meaning.

The original bureaucracy consisted of the War, Navy, State, and Treasury Departments, along with the office of Attorney General (the Department of Justice was created in 1870). These departments were extraordinarily small, and although distance and the difficulty of communications may have created some barriers to presidential domination over an agency such as the State Department, most agencies were easily subject to scrutiny by both Congress and the White House. This was the only time in American history when it was accurate to picture the administrative branch as a hierarchical structure with the President at the apex.

The development of administrative agencies after the Civil War resulted from public pressure which in turn reflected changing economic, social, and political conditions. For the most part agencies were created to deal with specific problems. The growth of the major departments reflected the expansion of government generally. The *laissez faire* ideal of a government remote from the community began to prove inadequate at the end of the nineteenth century. At this time, expanded powers were given to the Justice Department under the Sherman Act of 1890. This was necessary, it was felt, to deal with the rising restraints of trade and the growth of monopolies. In the regulatory area, the Interstate Commerce Commission was created in 1887 as the first national regulatory agency to supervise the railroad industry. The general expansion of the government was reflected in the establishment of the Justice Department in 1870, the Post Office Department in 1882, and the Department of Agriculture in 1889, succeeding the Commissioner of Agriculture, an office established in 1862. Present day bureaucracy has its roots in the latter part of the nineteenth century. But even then the administrative branch was fairly small and relatively powerless.

In examining the characteristics of nineteenth century bureaucracy, it can be seen that although the ideal of *laissez faire* had begun to tarnish, nevertheless it was still powerful and was reflected in the domination of big business interests within the governmental process. Although the frontier had receded significantly, it was still an important factor in absorbing excess energy and alleviating at least some of the grievances caused by economic interdependence. National communications were not highly developed. The integrative force of a strong Presidency was just beginning to be felt. The concept of the welfare state, which led to the vast expansion of the bureaucracy during the New Deal period, was unknown. Both theoretical and practical considerations militated against the creation at that time of a significant and pervasive administrative process. There was, it is true, a great deal of agitation and demand for government action to curb economic abuses. This was quite evident, for example, in the strong agitation of agricultural interests leading to the creation of the ICC. However, these protests were largely ineffective.

The real growth of the administrative process came in the twentieth century, when added powers were given to agencies which were already established, and new agencies were developed to expand government influence.

Expansion of the Bureaucracy in the Twentieth Century. The twentieth century saw the growth of a welfare philosophy of government, an enlargement of the problems created by the interdependence of economic groups, and the development of the country into a national community where the impact of activity in one area was felt in many others. There was increased political pressure for more government action which in turn required an expanded administrative process. Neither Congress, the Presidency, nor the judiciary could cope with the tremendous increase in the workload of government. Nor could they meet all the needs for innovation in the governmental process. Where a new type of adjudication was required to handle an increasing number of complex cases, the common law framework as well as the Constitution prevented the judiciary from embarking upon necessary programs and new procedures. Congress continued to work in modern times much as it had in the past, dealing with problems through a rather cumbersome hearing process.

It would be very difficult for Congress radically to change the legislative process because of constitutional as well as political limitations. These create obstacles to unity and continuity in the legislature. The courts too are constrained by the system. To take an example: suppose the judiciary decided to change the "case and controversy" rule, which requires that they adjudicate only cases properly brought before them involving concrete controversies. This would clearly violate Article 3 of the Constitution, and would be very difficult to bring about without a constitutional Amendment. These are the kinds of factors that led increasingly to the growth of bureaucracy. New forms of government were needed, and the administrative branch, which was not hampered by constitutional restrictions to the same degree as the original three branches, was able to fill this need.

Turning to some examples of agencies created in the twentieth century: the Federal Reserve Board, established in 1913 to stand at the head of a Federal Reserve system, was necessitated by changes in the banking industry which had resulted in a need for some kind of national control and standards. The Federal Trade Commission, created in 1914, was designed to expand the control of the national government over restraints of trade and deceptive business practices. The FTC reflects the need for a separate administrative agency with authority distinct from that of the courts and the Justice Department. This need indicated in part the failure of the Sherman Act of 1890 as it had been administered by the Justice Department through an unsympathetic judiciary. By 1920, the Federal Power Commission had been created, and in 1927 initial steps were taken to regulate the communications industry with the establishment of a Federal Radio Commission, which in 1934 was transformed into the Federal Communications Commission.

The proliferation of agencies during the New Deal can be seen in the Securities and Exchange Commission of 1933, the National Labor Relations Board of 1935, the Civil Aeronautics Board and Civil Aeronautics Administration (now the Federal Aviation Agency) created in 1937 and reorganized in 1958. New regulatory bureaus were created in the Department of Agriculture and other executive departments. Many New Deal agencies were created on the basis of presidential support rather than on the demands of private interests. This contrasted with the Interstate Commerce Commission which was created primarily because of strong agrarian demands for government control. The New Deal period was a time when President Roosevelt acted as a focal point for the expansion of the bureaucracy, and it was his ingenuity and power that often provided the balance of political support necessary for this purpose.

Since the New Deal period, there has been a notable expansion of bureaucratic power in the Defense Department, which has been put on a permanent basis since World War II and has strong political support from the armaments industry. Also an agency such as NASA reflects changing technology and subsequent innovations in governmental policy. NASA has now become one of our most important agencies, employing a large number of people and receiving huge appropriations.

Characteristics of Administrative Agencies

Administrative agencies are generally characterized by their size, the complexity of the decisions that they must make, specialization, and the combination of several governmental functions. Another characteristic of primary importance is the fact that no agency can exist without strong political support. All agencies have constituencies to which they are responsible. Their constituencies include congressional committees with which they negotiate appropriations and policy changes; the White House; the courts, which will review certain of their decisions provided the conditions of judicial review are met; and private groups. Administrative agencies operate within a highly charged political environment and this fact immediately distinguishes government bu-reaucracy from private business. The administrative process in government cannot be considered similar to that in business, except in a very limited range of activities. And insofar as their activities are not political, they are not particularly significant for the study of government.

The Problem of Administrative Responsibility

How do the agencies perform the tasks that have been assigned to them? Are they act-ing responsibly within the framework of our constitutional democracy? These ques-tions involve an analysis of administrative procedure and accountability. The bureau-cracy must be viewed as a political decision-making arena, and the appropriateness of particular decisions must be analyzed in terms of the goals that have been set for soci-ety and for government.

Management goals in the private sector are efficiency and bottom-line results. The myr-iad political constraints on public sector bureaucracies make the world of public man-agement entirely different. Politics defines government "efficiency." Political or govern-ment efficiency is measured by the ability to arrive at solutions that effectively compromise competing political interests. The following selection analyzes why govern-ment agencies cannot be run like a business.

James Q. Wilson is a prominent political scientist who has taught at the University of California, Los Angeles and Harvard University. He is widely known for his writings on the administrative state.

In the following reading his essential arguments are:

1. The ideals of accountability, equity, fiscal integrity, and efficiency confront different realities in the public and private sectors.
2. Bureaucracies should be judged differently in the public and private sectors.
3. Public bureaucracies operate within a framework of democratic values that support public participation, competitive bidding on contracts, and the need to maintain a reputation for integrity and fairness. How these values are accomplished defines public "efficiency."
4. The constitutional system of separation of powers and checks and balances also adds a dimension to the definition of governmental efficiency that the private sec-tor can ignore. Private sector efficiency requires the accumulation of all power in the same hands, but in the public sector that arrangement leads to a despotism and oppression that our constitutional democracy rejects in theory and practice.

12

James Q. Wilson

BUREAUCRACY:
WHAT GOVERNMENT AGENCIES DO
AND WHY THEY DO IT

★★★

On the morning of May 22, 1986, Donald Trump, the New York real estate developer, called one of his executives, Anthony Gliedman, into his office. They discussed the inability of the City of New York, despite six years of effort and the expenditure of nearly $13 million, to rebuild the ice-skating rink in Central Park. On May 28 Trump offered to take over the rink reconstruction, promising to do the job in less than six months. A week later Mayor Edward Koch accepted the offer and shortly thereafter the city appropriated $3 million on the understanding that Trump would have to pay for any cost overruns out of his own pocket. On October 28, the renovation was complete, over a month ahead of schedule and about $750,000 under budget. Two weeks later, skaters were using it.

For many readers it is obvious that private enterprise is more efficient than are public bureaucracies, and so they would file this story away as simply another illustration of what everyone already knows. But for other readers it is not so obvious what this story means; to them, business is greedy and unless watched like a hawk will fob off shoddy or overpriced goods on the American public, as when it sells the government $435 hammers and $3,000 coffeepots. Trump may have done a good job in this instance, but perhaps there is something about skating rinks or New York City government that gave him a comparative advantage; in any event, no larger lessons should be drawn from it.

Some lessons can be drawn, however, if one looks closely at the incentives and constraints facing Trump and the Department of Parks and Recreation. It becomes apparent that there is not one "bureaucracy problem" but several, and the solution to each in some degree is incompatible with the solution to every other. First there is the problem of accountability—getting agencies to serve agreed-upon goals. Second there is the problem of equity—treating all citizens fairly, which usually means treating them alike on the basis of clear rules known in advance. Third there is the problem of responsiveness—reacting reasonably to the special needs and circumstances of particular people. Fourth there is the problem of efficiency—obtaining the greatest output for a given level of resources. Finally there is the problem of fiscal integrity—assuring that public funds are spent prudently for public purposes. Donald Trump and Mayor Koch were situated differently with respect to most of these matters.

Accountability

The Mayor wanted the old skating rink refurbished, but he also wanted to minimize the cost of the fuel needed to operate the rink (the first effort to rebuild it occurred right after the Arab oil embargo and the attendant increase in energy prices). Trying to achieve both goals led city hall to select a new refrigeration system that as it turned out would not work properly. Trump came on the scene when only one goal dominated: get the rink rebuilt. He felt free to select the most reliable refrigeration system without worrying too much about energy costs.

Equity

The Parks and Recreation Department was required by law to give every contractor an equal chance to do the job. This meant it had to put every part of the job out to bid and to accept the lowest without much regard to the reputation or prior performance of the lowest bidder. Moreover, state law forbade city agencies from hiring a general contractor and letting him select the subcontractors; in fact, the law forbade the city from even discussing the project in advance with a general contractor who might later bid on it–that would have been collusion. Trump, by contrast, was free to locate the rink builder with the best reputation and give him the job.

Fiscal Integrity

To reduce the chance of corruption or sweetheart deals the law required Parks and Recreation to furnish complete, detailed plans to every contractor bidding on the job; any changes after that would require renegotiating the contract. No such law constrained Trump; he was free to give incomplete plans to his chosen contractor, hold him accountable for building a satisfactory rink, but allow him to work out the details as he went along.

Efficiency

When the Parks and Recreation Department spent over six years and $13 million and still could not reopen the rink, there was public criticism but no city official lost money. When Trump accepted a contract to do it, any cost overruns or delays would have come out of his pocket and any savings could have gone into his pocket (in this case, Trump agreed not to take a profit on the job).

Gliedman summarized the differences neatly: "The problem with government is that government can't say, 'yes' . . . there is nobody in government that can do that. There are fifteen or twenty people who have to agree. Government has to be slower. It has to safeguard the process."

INEFFICIENCY

The government can't say "yes." In other words, the government is constrained. Where do the constraints come from? From us.

Herbert Kaufman has explained red tape as being of our own making: "Every restraint and requirement originates in somebody's demand for it." Applied to the Central Park skating rink Kaufman's insight reminds us that civil-service reformers demanded that no city official benefit personally from building a project; that contractors demanded that all be given an equal chance to bid on every job; and that fiscal watchdogs demanded that all contract specifications be as detailed as possible. For each demand a procedure was established; viewed from the outside, those procedures are called red tape. To enforce each procedure a manager was appointed; those managers are called bureaucrats. No organized group demanded that all skating rinks be rebuilt as quickly as possible, no procedure existed to enforce that demand, and no manager was appointed to enforce it. The political process can more easily enforce compliance with constraints than the attainment of goals.

When we denounce bureaucracy for being inefficient we are saying something that is half true. Efficiency is a ratio of valued resources used to valued outputs produced. The smaller that ratio the more efficient the production. If the valued output is a rebuilt skating rink, then whatever process uses the fewest dollars or the least time to produce a satisfactory rink is the most efficient process. By this test Trump was more efficient than the Parks and Recreation Department.

But that is too narrow a view of the matter. The economic definition of efficiency (efficiency in the small, so to speak) assumes that there is only one valued output, the new rink. But government has many valued outputs, including a reputation for integrity, the confidence of the people, and the support of important interest groups. When we complain about skating rinks not being built on time we speak as if all we cared about were skating rinks. But when we complain that contracts were awarded without competitive bidding or in a way that allowed bureaucrats to line their pockets we acknowledge that we care about many things besides skating rinks; we care about the contextual goals—the constraints—that we want government to observe. A government that is slow to build rinks but is honest and accountable in its actions and properly responsive to worthy constituencies may be a very efficient government, *if* we measure efficiency in the large by taking into account *all* of the valued outputs.

Calling a government agency efficient when it is slow, cumbersome, and costly may seem perverse. But that is only because we lack any objective way for deciding how much money or time should be devoted to maintaining honest behavior, producing a fair allocation of benefits, and generating popular support as well as to achieving the main goal of the project. If we could measure these things, and if we agreed as to their value, then we would be in a position to judge the true efficiency of a government agency and decide when it is taking too much time or spending too much money achieving all that we expect of it. But we cannot measure these things nor do we agree about their relative importance, and so government always will appear to be inefficient compared to organizations that have fewer goals.

Put simply, the only way to decide whether an agency is truly inefficient is to decide which of the constraints affecting its action ought to be ignored or discounted. In fact that is what most debates about agency behavior are all about. In fighting crime are the police handcuffed? In educating children are teachers tied down by rules? In launching a space shuttle are we too concerned with safety? In building a dam do we worry excessively about endangered species? In running the Postal Service is it important to have many post offices close to where people live? In the case of the skating rink, was the requirement of competitive bidding for each contract on the basis of detailed specifications a reasonable one? Probably not. But if it were abandoned, the gain (the swifter completion of the rink) would have to be balanced against the costs (complaints from contractors who might lose business and the chance of collusion and corruption in some future projects).

Even allowing for all of these constraints, government agencies may still be inefficient. Indeed, given the fact that bureaucrats cannot (for the most part) benefit monetarily from their agencies' achievements, it would be surprising if they were not inefficient. Efficiency, in the large or the small, doesn't pay.

But some critics of government believe that inefficiency is obvious and vast. Many people remember the 1984 claim of the Grace Commission (officially, the President's Private Sector Survey on Cost Control) that it had identified over $400 billion in savings that could be made if only the federal government were managed properly. Though the commission did not say so, many people inferred that careless bureaucrats were wasting that amount of money. But hardly anybody remembers the study issued jointly by the General Accounting Office and the Congressional Budget Office in February 1984, one month after the Grace Commission report.

The GAO and CBO reviewed those Grace recommendations that accounted for about 90 percent of the projected savings, and after eliminating double-counting and recommendations for which no savings could be estimated, and other problems, concluded that the true savings would be less than one-third the claimed amount.

Of course, $100 billion is still a lot of money. But wait. It turns out that about 60 percent of this would require not management improvements but policy changes: for example, taxing welfare benefits, ending certain direct loan programs, adopting new rules to restrict Medicare benefits, restricting eligibility for retirement among federal civilian workers and military personnel, and selling the power produced by government-owned hydroelectric plants at the full market price.

That still leaves roughly $40 billion in management savings. But most of this would require either a new congressional policy (for example, hiring more Internal Revenue Service agents to collect delinquent taxes), some unspecified increase in "worker productivity," or buying more services from private suppliers. Setting aside the desirable goal of increasing productivity (for which no procedures were identified), it turns out that almost all of the projected savings would require Congress to alter the goals and constraints of public agencies. If there is a lot of waste (and it is not clear why the failure to tax welfare benefits or to hire more IRS agents should be called waste), it is congressionally directed waste.

Military procurement, of course, is the biggest source of stories about waste, fraud, and mismanagement. There cannot be a reader of this book who has not heard about the navy paying $435 for a hammer or the air force paying $3,000 for a coffeepot, and nobody, I suspect, believes Defense Department estimates of the cost of a new airplane or missile. If ever one needed evidence that bureaucracy is inefficient, the Pentagon supplies it.

Well, yes. But what kind of inefficiency? And why does it occur? To answer these questions one must approach the problem just as we approached the problem of fixing up a skating rink in New York City: We want to understand why the bureaucrats, all of whom are rational and most of whom want to go a good job, behave as they do.

To begin, let us forget about $435 hammers. They never existed. A member of Congress who did not understand (or did not want to understand) government accounting rules created a public stir. The $3,000 coffeepot existed, but it is not clear that it was overpriced.* But that does not mean there are no problems; in fact, the real problems are far more costly and intractable than inflated price tags on hammers and coffeemakers. They include sticking too long with new weapons of dubious value, taking forever to acquire even good weapons, and not inducing contractors to increase their efficiency. What follows is not a complete explanation of military procurement problems; it is only an analysis of the contribution bureaucratic systems make to those problems.

When the military buys a new weapons system—a bomber, submarine, or tank—it sets in motion a procurement bureaucracy comprised of two key actors, the military program manager and the civilian contract officer, who must cope with the contractor, the Pentagon hierarchy, and Congress. To understand how they behave we must understand how their tasks get defined, what incentives they have, and what constraints they face.

. . . In short, you can have less bureaucracy only if you have less government. Many, if not most, of the difficulties we experience in dealing with government agencies arise from the agencies being part of a fragmented and open political system. If an agency is to have a sense of mission, if constraints are to be minimized, if authority is to be decentralized, if officials are to be judged on the basis of the outputs they produce rather than the inputs they consume, then legislators, judges, and lobbyists will have to act against their own interests. They will have to say "no" to influential constituents, forgo the opportunity to expand their own influence, and take seriously the task of judging the organizational feasibility as well as the political popularity of a proposed new program. It is hard to imagine this happening, partly because politicians and judges have no incentive to make it happen and partly because there are certain tasks a democratic government must undertake even if they cannot be performed efficiently. The greatest mistake citizens can make when they complain of "the bureaucracy" is to suppose that their frustrations arise simply out of management problems; they do not—they arise out of governance problems.

---

*This is what happened: The navy ordered a package of maintenance equipment. One of the items was an inexpensive hammer; some of the others were very expensive test devices. Under the accounting rules then in effect, the supplier was allowed to allocate overhead costs in equal percentages to each item. This was simpler than trying to figure out how much overhead should be attributed to each individual item (in which case the difficult-to-make items would, of course, have accounted for more of the overhead than the easy-to-make ones such as a hammer). As a result, the bill showed the hammer as costing several hundred dollars in "overhead," for a total of $435. When a sailor unpacked the box, he found this bill and, not understanding the equal-allocation formula, called his congressman. A myth was born. See James Fairhall, "The Case for the $435 Hammer," *Washington Monthly* (January 1987): 47–52. The "coffeepot" did cost about $3,000, but it was purchased to make coffee for the more than three hundred soldiers who would be carried on a C-5A transport. Commercial airlines often pay that much for coffeemakers on their jumbo jets. See J. Ronald Fox, *The Defense Management Challenge* (Boston: Harvard Business School Press, 1988), 31.

BUREAUCRACY AND THE AMERICAN REGIME

The central feature of the American constitutional system—the separation of powers—exacerbates many of these problems. The governments of the United States were not designed to be efficient or powerful, but to be tolerable and malleable. Those who devised these arrangements always assumed that the federal government would exercise few and limited powers. As long as that assumption was correct (which it was for a century and a half) the quality of public administration was not a serious problem except in the minds of those reformers (Woodrow Wilson was probably the first) who desired to rationalize government in order to rationalize society. The founders knew that the separation of powers would make it so difficult to start a new program or to create a new agency that it was hardly necessary to think about how those agencies would be administered. As a result, the Constitution is virtually silent on what kind of administration we should have. At least until the Civil War thrust the problem on us, scarcely anyone in the country would have known what you were talking about if you spoke of the "problem of administration."

Matters were very different in much of Europe. Kings and princes long had ruled; when their authority was captured by parliaments, the tradition of ruling was already well established. From the first the ministers of the parliamentary regimes thought about the problems of administration because in those countries there was something to administer. The centralization of executive authority in the hands of a prime minister and the exclusion (by and large) of parliament from much say in executive affairs facilitated the process of controlling the administrative agencies and bending them to some central will. The constitutions of many European states easily could have been written by a school of management.

Today, the United States at every level has big and active governments. Some people worry that a constitutional system well-designed to preserve liberty when governments were small is poorly designed to implement policy now that governments are large. The contrast between how the United States and the nations of Western Europe manage environmental and industrial regulation . . . is illuminating: Here the separation of powers insures, if not causes, clumsy and adversarial regulation; there the unification of powers permits, if not causes, smooth and consensual regulation.

I am not convinced that the choice is that simple, however. It would take another book to judge the advantages and disadvantages of the separation of powers. The balance sheet on both sides of the ledger would contain many more entries than those that derive from a discussion of public administration. But even confining our attention to administration, there is more to be said for the American system than many of its critics admit.

America has a paradoxical bureaucracy unlike that found in almost any other advanced nation. The paradox is the existence in one set of institutions of two qualities ordinarily quite separate: the multiplication of rules and the opportunity for access. We have a system laden with rules; elsewhere that is a sure sign that the bureaucracy is aloof from the people, distant from their concerns, and preoccupied with the power and privileges of the bureaucrats—an elaborate, grinding machine that can crush the spirit of any who dare oppose it. We also have a system suffused with participation: advisory boards, citizen groups, neighborhood councils, congressional investigators, crusading journalists, and lawyers serving writs; elsewhere this popular involvement would be taken as evidence that the administrative system is no system at all, but a bungling, jerry-built contraption wallowing in inefficiency and shot through with corruption and favoritism.

That these two traits, rules and openness, could coexist would have astonished Max Weber and continues to astonish (or elude) many contemporary students of the subject. Public bureaucracy in this country is neither as rational and predictable as Weber hoped nor as crushing and mechanistic as he feared. It is rule-bound without being overpowering, participatory without being corrupt. This paradox exists partly because of the character and mores of the American people: They are too informal, spontaneous, and other-directed to be either neutral arbiters or passionless Gradgrinds. And partly it exists because of the nature of the regime: Our constitutional system, and above all the exceptional power enjoyed by the legislative branch, makes it impossible for us to have anything like a government by appointed experts but easy for individual citizens to obtain redress from the abuses of power. Anyone who wishes it otherwise would have to produce a wholly different regime, and curing the mischiefs of bureaucracy seems an inadequate reason for that. Parliamentary regimes that supply more consistent direction to their bureaucracies also supply more bureaucracy to their citizens. The fragmented American regime may produce chaotic government, but the coherent European regimes produce bigger governments.

In the meantime we live in a country that despite its baffling array of rules and regulations and the insatiable desire of some people to use government to rationalize society still makes it possible to get drinkable water instantly, put through a telephone call in seconds, deliver a letter in a day, and obtain a passport in a week. Our Social Security checks arrive on time. Some state prisons, and most of the federal ones, are reasonably decent and humane institutions. The great majority of Americans, cursing all the while, pay their taxes. One can stand on the deck of an aircraft carrier during night flight operations and watch two thousand nineteen-year-old boys faultlessly operate one of the most complex organizational systems ever created. There are not many places where all this happens. It is astonishing it can be made to happen at all.

Politics controls the beginning and end of the regulatory process. Congress creates regulatory agencies in response to political demands seeking government protection of special interests. Regulatory politics always involves the competing interests of those seeking an opposing regulation. Congress neatly extracts itself from having to resolve this conflict by delegating to administrative agencies the authority to make regulatory policies and resolve disputes. The enabling legislation that creates regulatory agencies does not define policies, but only offers vague guidelines for agencies to follow.

Regulatory agencies can no longer avoid resolving political conflict but must face it head on. The "merits" of regulatory policies are as much political as economic. The following selection explains why regulatory policies cannot be "objective" but must inevitably take into account competing goals and values, as well as facts.

Michael D. Reagan is a social scientist who has written extensively on government regulation and the economy.

He argues in the following selection:

1. Regulation is political and normative, requiring regulators to balance values with often conflicting political and economic interests.
2. The disciplines of economics, political science, and the physical sciences are relevant but not decisive in shaping regulatory policies.
3. Regulators have to accommodate economic competition and political conflict. Regulatory policies can not be linear because they require compromise. Regulatory paradigms always yield to political realities.

13

Michael D. Reagan

REGULATION IN PERSPECTIVE

★★★

Regulation is political. It is an activity of government, and it involves values, interests, conflicts, and the making of choices by persons concerned with constituencies and elections. It can, therefore, never be a simple application of microeconomic principles. There is, in short, a political rationality to be considered in evaluating regulatory policy . . .

The directions of policy can change quickly. Starting in the late 1970s under President Jimmy Carter, and continuing with a quickened pace under President Ronald Reagan, the politically most active part of the regulatory arena of government has been the question of deregulation. There has been more talk about removing regulations than about adding or maintaining them. Yet, in the years 1968–80, we had the strongest continuous extension of regulation since the 1930s, and perhaps in all of American experience. That twelve-year period saw the creation not only of the Environmental Protection Agency (EPA), to which new programs have been added as recently as the Superfund in 1980, but the Occupational Safety and Health Administration (OSHA), the National Highway Transportation Safety Administration (NHTSA), the Consumer Products Safety Commission (CPSC), and the Office of Surface Mining (OSM), plus a host of statutes establishing even more programs to be distributed among these and other agencies. To achieve an understanding of the political-economic dynamics of the intertwined, seemingly contradictory trends of deregulation and new regulation is a major objective of this [selection]. We will start with the most basic proposition: regulation is political.

REGULATION IS A POLITICAL PROCESS

In a classic study of business regulation, Marver H. Bernstein wrote that the "determination of regulatory goals does not result inevitably from the logical analysis of certain economic facts, nor is it automatically deduced from a set of propositions concerning the nature of the political state and the proper boundaries of political action in a democratic society." In light of the rise to prominence in regulatory affairs of highly complex scientific and technological dimensions—as in air and water pollution, or toxic and radiological waste disposal—we should add that regulatory goals cannot be deduced from scientific principles, either.

It is not that economics, political science, and the physical sciences are irrelevant to regulatory policy-making. Rather, they are not decisive in themselves. Why is that? Since most regulation is directed at business behavior, can we not simply apply microeconomics? While writings occasionally imply that one can make policy by economic analysis alone, the more sophisticated presentations make it clear that what economic analysis—and other technical frameworks—can do is to illuminate choices, not decide them. To illuminate a choice is to explore its consequences and implications, both for the intended goal and any side effects it may have. If one has three options laid out as means for reaching an objective, any analytic process that helps to forecast the costs and consequences of each of the three will be helpful in reaching a decision.

Beyond such analyses, however, there are always judgmental dimensions and value choices to be made, and these are not reducible to programmed analysis. Judgmental elements enter because all the facts necessary to complete an analytic model are rarely available, and for some dimensions the value of experience may be greater than that of any formal framework. Value choices have to be made because the important questions in regulatory affairs are not simply instrumental (i.e., how to achieve a clearly specified objective), but involve differences of view, interests, and criteria regarding what is to be accomplished, not simply how. Even the "how" questions are complicated by the interrelationships within our physical and social systems: the means that may give us the most of objective A may do so by reducing what we can have in terms of objective B. A good example is the conflict between automobile safety and fuel efficiency: smaller, lighter cars look good in EPA mileage ratings, but are much less crash-worthy than the lumbering giants of twenty years ago. Regulators of fuel efficiency requirements should be aware of related accident statistics, but such knowledge cannot possibly settle the trade-off question for them.

Thus, regulatory decisions are at least as much political as they are technical, with political here meaning concerned with the allocation of values in the society. To allocate values is to make choices among values; since there is rarely total consensus on the values to be given primacy, there is almost always conflict over the allocation decisions. The conflict involves competing ideas, individuals, and often organized interests claiming to represent various values. Politics implies a struggle to see who will decide, who will win the contest of values. As [John T. Woolley] puts it, "for whom policy is good or bad is what politics is all about." In a democratic society, the policy struggle basically takes the form of competing efforts to persuade those in a position to make the formal . . . allocation of values; and majoritarian politics (even a majority consisting of a coalition of minorities) means bargaining and compromise. As Daniel Bell has written, "politics is haggling, or else it is force." Rarely does one position get carried to full fruition, for coalition building in a political system as open and diversified as that of the United States necessarily means giving up some of B to get more of A, or modifying how one reaches A to do less damage to B. . . .

At this point, one might ask: wouldn't it be a better world if . . . decisions were made on the basis of objective analysis and technical expertise—"on the merits," so to speak? The difficulty with this method, however, is that the preconditions necessary for making decisions on the merits are rarely present in public affairs generally, and even more rarely in hotly contested matters of regulation.

Let's look behind the phrase, using two concrete illustrations. In an extensive study of the interplay of economic, technological, legal, and political factors in shaping and enforcing the Clean Air Act, [R. Shep] Melnick points out numerous anomalies in processes through which the EPA sets standards of allowable air pollutants. The legislation, he writes, "presents standard setting as a scientific investigation of the location of health effect 'thresholds'" a threshold being a concentration "at which sensitive individuals begin to suffer adverse health effects." This makes standard setting sound medical and scientific. But "few scientists now believe it is possible to identify non-zero health effect thresholds for most pollutants," and a congressional advocate of clean air programs admitted that the safe threshold concept was really "a necessary myth." Thus, asserts Melnick, "each time the EPA publishes or revises a standard, it must make a *policy choice* about what constitutes an 'acceptable' health risk. Standard setting is thus a political process, both in the sense that the EPA must make choices not dictated by medical evidence and in the sense that many political forces seek to influence its decision."

We should examine another example from broadcasting regulation. When the Federal Communications Commission (FCC) allocates a frequency for a new TV station, the statutory guidelines contained in the law that gives the agency its authority call for such decisions to be made in accordance with the "public interest, convenience and necessity." How is the FCC to make its decision on the merits? Would that mean awarding the broadcasting license to the applicant with the greatest experience, even if that firm has no roots in the community that the station is to serve? Or do the merits lie with an inexperienced group, but one with many local leaders among its board members? In fact, the FCC has made each of these criteria decisive, in different cases, but careful observers have assessed that fact as evidencing not choices on an objective, expert basis, but as rationalizations for choices made on grounds of political favoritism. Once a channel has been awarded, the FCC's problem at renewal time is greater: to compare the merits (performance) of the incumbent operator of the station with the merits (pledges of what it will do for the community) of the challenging applicant(s). Two FCC commissioners have called this problem "a riddle within an enigma within a conundrum," and that is not how one would describe a situation in which decisions could be made on the merits.

FCC frequency allocations provide little basis for quantitative evaluation. Perhaps policy decisions that can be run through a quantified analysis are more likely to be made on the merits? Perhaps, in some cases; yet the respected Congressional Research Service studied the fashionable quantitative approach known as cost-benefit analysis, and found that the single most significant determinant of the outcome of the cost-benefit analyses covered was the factor of who conducted the analysis: the results fit the preconceptions of the agency doing the analysis. In other words, political conflicts and questions of decision-making power seem to outweigh abstract merits.

The reason for this should now be apparent: to settle something on the merits presupposes agreement on what the merits are, which is the point of dispute in most public policy matters. Great national crises sometimes produce instant consensus on what matters most—as in World War II, or when the nation rallied to meet the challenge of Sputnik I in 1957. With such consensus, one can meaningfully contemplate deciding how to meet the objective on the basis of the merits; the goal is clear, as is its priority over other goals that may have to be partially dislodged or deferred. To decide on the merits, then, has a clear meaning: how to effectively reach an objective on which all agree to place overwhelming priority. Since such agreement hardly ever occurs, policy-making is almost always an exercise in political conflict, bargaining, and the search for acceptable tradeoffs among multiple worthy objectives. This is true of regulation, as of most areas of national policy-making, and it is a basic perspective that permeates this book, in conscious contrast with the many nonpolitical science studies of regulation that embrace the rationality of economic efficiency as the sole litmus test for assessing regulatory rule making.

To a political scientist, there is some irony, or at least a sense of *déjà vu*, in recalling that before we achieved some sophistication regarding the realities of policy-making we had an earlier period—that of the Progressive Movement, 1900–1914—in which it was thought that the politics could be taken out of policy-making, and neutral expertise enthroned in its place. The peculiar regulatory structure that we know as the independent regulatory commissions (IRCs) is even today a living residue of that heritage, one whose operations have been much criticized by the same observers who assume that their kind of formal analysis can successfully substitute for the political process.

We can provide yet additional context for the proposition that regulation is political, by noting that all public policy can be seen as a combination of goals plus facts plus values, putting this in the form of

$$P = G + F + V$$

We mean to show that there are three necessary components of any public policy, but that none of them is sufficient alone to determine policy.

Some examples will illustrate the insufficiency of each of these factors, despite a strong tendency for all of us to ignore their interdependency in practice—which leads to what we call "jumping to conclusions." First, take the fact that highway safety programs save lives at one-tenth the "per life saved" cost of OSHA's health standards programs. Does that tell us, by itself, that we should cut the OSHA programs because they are less cost-effective? No, it does not, because a different value choice might suggest that we should keep both programs, but add budget support to the highway program. Or, we should start with a value position and see if it settles what policy should be—as so often seems to be the case in everyday political discussions. For example, take the proposition that regardless of income, all Americans should (*should* indicates a value statement; *is* indicates a factual one) have access to good quality medical care; therefore, government should regulate physicians' fees. The "therefore" really doesn't follow as smoothly as that statement makes it appear, because there are, factually, other ways in which the same value can be served (e.g., by national health insurance that pays a doctor's usual fees). Thus, a fact needs to be considered in light of varying value positions, and a value can usually be served through more than one factual arrangement.

Even when we have both the facts and the values lined up, the policy result may not be objectively or nonpolitically determined. For instance, the Carter administration and its regulatory agency heads strongly endorsed environmental protection and health and safety values. The facts of air and water pollution were clear enough, as were a number of major threats to worker and consumer health and safety. Did this combination lead to an unambiguous policy of maximum regulatory effort through the OSHA and the EPA? No, especially in 1978–80. Why? Because an even higher value priority was placed on economic stabilization, and the overriding goal became that of dampening the then-raging inflationary fires. In that same time period, another notable conflict was between environmental regulation and energy policy: reducing oil imports versus air pollution if use of coal was increased. These cases illustrate the basic political fact of a multiplicity of goals and values to be served at any given time. This combines with the basic economic fact of limited resources to create a policy world of difficult choices.

It is rarely a simple case of good versus bad in policy; usually it is a matter of competing good things, an improved physical environment, and a stable economy being two of the more stable goals of our time. Not only does the number of goals mean that value priorities need to be selected simply because we can't do everything at once, but the policy-making situation is complicated further by the interconnectedness of goals, such that increased pursuit of one diminishes (contrary to the policy-maker's intent) what can be achieved of the other, as with our earlier example of auto fuel economy purchased at the expense of decreased auto safety.

Regulatory policy (as any other policy) results from an interplay of goals, facts, and values. None of these is unidimensional; all are multiple and competitive—and generally have predictable consequences for specific interests. In turn, these interests are diverse, they cannot always be maximized by the same policy direction, and they are often aggressively represented in the political process by organized, articulate groups. The result of these factors: policy-making is first and foremost a political enterprise—before, during, and after it is an exercise in economic or technologic analysis. . . .

Effective policy implementation requires good management. Using a hypothetical situation, the following selection analyzes the complex dimensions of public policy management and implementation. In the political process nothing is simple, and even management of such a seemingly simple policy as implementing an AIDS vaccination program is fraught with political dangers at every turn.

Martin A. Levin is a Professor of Politics at Brandeis University and an expert in public policy.

His major points in the following selection are:

1. Management matters in implementing policy initiatives. Constitutional prescriptions and political realities, however, have fragmented governmental institutions, making the efficient management of government programs difficult if not impossible.
2. Governmental division, political conflict, and private competition would very likely stymie the implementation of an AIDS vaccination program notwithstanding strong public support for it.
3. Once initial policy choices are made, the political realities of management always slow and can even defeat implementation.

14

Martin A. Levin

THE DAY AFTER AN AIDS VACCINE IS DISCOVERED: MANAGEMENT MATTERS

★★★

Imagine for a moment, if you will, that we pick up the newspaper tomorrow morning and read that a fully effective AIDS vaccine has been discovered. When this happens, everyone's response will be one of joy. We all would suppose this to be the happy ending to the long nightmare of AIDS. I want to suggest that, unfortunately, nothing could be further from the truth.

The discovery of an effective AIDS vaccine will not be the beginning of the end. It will only be the end of the beginning. This is because management matters—and management is not always a routine task. The same is true for many similar breakthroughs that I will refer to as point decisions—like deregulatory breakthroughs, or independence from colonial or totalitarian rule. In all these cases, freedom is only the beginning. We must tell this to our students and to practitioners.

The day after an AIDS vaccine is discovered will only usher in the next chapter of this ordeal. It will be the start of an even more difficult period: the implementation of the campaign to inoculate all Americans with an AIDS vaccine.

MANAGEMENT MATTERS

I predict the following scenario. This period will be marked by serious management problems and delays, during which time many Americans will continue to die of AIDS. Many billions will be spent on treating cases of AIDS that continue to develop after the discovery of a vaccine.

The management problems and delays will result from many serious conflicts: scientific controversy over the vaccine's effectiveness and safety; threats of lawsuits over side effects and demands of manufacturers calling for indemnification from them; professional and institutional timidity among health care providers; media sensationalization of rare cases. All these conflicts will discourage the public from embracing the vaccination program. A lack of leadership is likely because this is all so controversial, and because formal authority is so fragmented in the health care field. But even with the best of leadership, any vaccine program will find its implementation and management difficult because it will face a complex situation filled with booby traps—some benign, others less so. I will detail some of these traps.

But first I would note that my predictions are based on our general model of management problems . . . and the specific experience of the unsuccessful 1976 swine flu vaccination program. These conflicts and management problems occurred before because they are endemic to the process of implementing policy initiatives, for reasons that this [selection] explains. This is why management matters.

Scientific Controversy over Safety and Effectiveness

From the moment of discovery of an AIDS vaccine, even before the predictable production and distribution problems arise, controversy is likely to rage among scientists and professionals over its safety and effectiveness. The FDA will feel pressure from some groups, as it has in the past, to move the vaccine to market quickly. Others will try to delay authorization.

Threats of Lawsuits and Manufacturers' Requests for Indemnification

There will be threats of lawsuits, both by those who fear getting AIDS from the vaccine and by those who fear other side effects. Side effects are likely to be negligible. But fears will be widespread for several reasons, including the fact that there will be at least some negative side effects, as there typically are in any complex medical intervention.

Even more problematic, the manufacturers will want to be indemnified from these suits before they produce the vaccine. This indemnification will not occur automatically. There will be protracted conflicts. During this ensuing delay, more people will contract AIDS.

The dynamics of public relations may significantly complicate the vaccine's implementation. For example, drug and insurance companies will fear criticism and negative media coverage both for delaying the vaccine's release or for any later side effects. Companies might be moved to defend themselves by publicly emphasizing the vaccine's possible risks, which would undermine public confidence before it even hit the market.

Professional and Institutional Timidity and Conflict

Delays will arise not only from concern about the safety and wisdom of using a new vaccine, but also from professional and institutional timidity. Concern for individual careers may create incentives for not participating in a risky, large-scale inoculation program. Conversely, professional ambitions may result in competing approaches to inoculation aimed at building public reputations—which will in turn exacerbate conflict and delay.

For example, the goal of reinforcing awareness of preventative medicine and vaccinations underlay the push by the Center for Disease Control (CDC) and its head, Dr. David Sencer, for using the swine flu vaccine in an immediate, universal inoculation program in 1976. But a dozen years later, as New York City Health Commissioner at the beginning of the AIDS epidemic, Dr. Sencer strongly put the brakes on governmental responses to the new epidemic. He did not move to regulate bath houses, accurately suspected as playing a major role in transmitting the virus, lest he be criticized for too aggressive government action, as he had been after the swine flu scare. Many said that this delay significantly added to the spread of AIDS in New York.

The institutions administering the vaccine are very likely to disagree about how it should be done: Who should get it first? Should the first priority be the riskiest populations, such as gay men, members of minority communities, and IV drug users? Or should it go to those who can pay for it out of their own pocket or through insurance? Or should teenagers be given a high priority because of their potential sexual activity, and because our society generally wishes to give priority to the protection of children? If so, should minority teenagers be given priority? Should preadolescent children be given priority because they will be teenagers soon?

Who will pay for those who can't afford the vaccine? Who will compensate the institution for administering it to those who can't afford it? Who will ensure that everyone gets it? How will the workers who are administering the vaccine be protected? How will they be paid?

The pressures on these institutions will be increased because AIDS victims and their organizations, especially those in the gay and minority communities, probably will not want funds diverted from their treatment to this universal inoculation campaign. Such conflicts will create further institutional timidity and delays in implementing the program.

Media Sensationalism

The media will make a problematic situation worse by fueling public fears. Exceptional incidents, such as a health care worker becoming infected in the course of her duties, will inevitably occur, and the media will sensationalize them. Then, by repeating them frequently, they will make the atypical seem typical.

This is not hypothetical. The media constantly repeated the story of the Florida dentist who allegedly gave AIDS to his patients. They almost never explained that the risk of getting AIDS from health care providers was extremely remote.

Today we even have major problems implementing the inoculation of simple and noncontroversial vaccines, like measles and polio, in poor inner-city neighborhoods.

And there will be almost nothing about an AIDS vaccine that will be either simple or noncontroversial.

The Effects on a Fragile Public Consciousness

The public is likely to embrace the vaccination program slowly for many reasons, especially because people take their cues from professionals and thus will reflect their hesitancy and even resistance. Existing myths about AIDS and how it is transmitted will further heighten fears that will impede a vaccination program. In particular, people are likely to have irrational fear about the vaccine for their teenagers and children—just as now, when parents keep their children from going to school with an AIDS victim such as Ryan White.

The Difficulty of Management in Our Political System

Why will these conflicts and delays happen? First, because while management matters, it is also quite difficult, especially within our political system's fragmented structure of power and authority.

There's a second reason that these conflicts will be difficult to resolve: Most of the general public, as well as many in government, do not understand the importance of management. They do not appreciate the significance of implementation strategies for developing sound and effective public policy. They think the initial policy choice—the point decision—is sufficient. Instead, I argue that the discovery is only the beginning.

A Major Management Problem

The absence of political support for an AIDS vaccination program will also make these conflicts difficult to resolve—but this won't make it any less of management problem. Rather, the absence of political support will make it more of a management problem than it ordinarily would be. It will turn the typically routine implementation of inoculating people with a vaccine, as it was with the polio vaccine, into a major management problem, as was the case with the swine flu vaccine. This is because management is broader than the process of implementation. Management is not a value-free process. It is a political endeavor concerned with ends as well as means. Policy is always being made in the management process. Policy is created by carrying out line decisions, as well as in choosing point decisions. . . .

In the preceding selection, Martin A. Levin argues that management decisions and the behavior of diverse interests affect the implementation of what seem to be even the best, and simplest, of public policy initiatives. In this selection, Sandra Thurman, head of the White House Office on National AIDS Policy, discusses how politics and the availability of numerous options complicate policymaking on AIDS. The selection is taken from an interview with Thurman, conducted on June 5, 1998, by Steve Roberts on *The Diane Rehm Show,* produced by public radio station WAMU at American University in Washington, D.C., and distributed by National Public Radio. A key feature of this interview is Thurman's political discussion of the different goals and reasoning that can bring AIDS policy and national drug control policy into conflict, emblematic of the factors that need to be considered by government officials when they design and implement policies. Also interesting is Thurman's discussion of how her career and beliefs relate to her role in government. While our ideals encourage us to believe that good ideas solve difficult problems, Levin and Thurman illustrate the reality of how competing viewpoints and interests can complicate implementation of even the brightest ideas. The selection was adapted and transcribed by Eric J. Broxmeyer.

The major points of this interview are:

1. Government officials face heavy pressure when they are at the head of an office involved with contentious issues.
2. Political compromises and the differing interests of government agencies and officials complicate the effort to establish and implement policy.
3. Thurman's background in politics has helped her promote and implement public policy in the highly political environment of the White House. Good ideas are not enough: they must be shepherded through the system by people with astute political sensibilities.
4. Echoing the point made in the previous selection by Martin A. Levin, Thurman notes that managing AIDS policy was in many ways easier in the past, when there were fewer policy options available.

15

Sandra Thurman

THE POLITICS OF AIDS

★★★

STEVE ROBERTS: From WAMU in Washington, I'm Steve Roberts, sitting in today for Diane Rehm. When AIDS patient and activist Steve Michael died last week, he left behind instructions for an unusual funeral. He wanted to keep working for the cause even after his death from AIDS, so yesterday 200 protesters marched to the White House with Steve Michael's casket to demand action from President Clinton's administration. The open casket on Pennsylvania Avenue was yet another reminder that the deadly virus is still making its way through the American population. Sandy Thurman doesn't get much chance to forget about the problem, it's her job. Sandy Thurman is head of the White House Office on National AIDS Policy and faces the complex medical, social and political problems of AIDS every day. She's here with me in the studio to talk about her work, she's our guest in Diane's regular series, of women at work. This is our June installment and, Sandy Thurman, thanks so much for being with us.

SANDRA THURMAN: Thanks for having me.

STEVE ROBERTS: . . . Let me start with a simple question: what's the hardest thing about your job?

SANDRA THURMAN: I think the hardest thing about the job is the complexity and the size of this issue and how fast it's growing. I mean the harder we work, the bigger the issue gets.

STEVE ROBERTS: In what sense?

SANDRA THURMAN: Well, we have increasing numbers of people living with AIDS around the world, increasing numbers of people becoming infected every day. In fact, just last December, we found out from the UN AIDS program that the epidemic was moving about twice as fast as we had originally thought. So we have almost thirty million people infected worldwide and, here, in the United States, the epidemic is moving into increasingly difficult to reach populations: women, people of color, young people. Over 50 percent of our new infections in this country are in people under 25 years of age. So, as hard as we work, you know, we're still way behind.

STEVE ROBERTS: But there has been news in recent months that the rate of infection has slowed down. Is that right?

SANDRA THURMAN: The rate of infection hasn't slowed down. There's some, you know, maybe, small drop in rates of infection. The rate of AIDS cases have declined dramatically and the rates of AIDS deaths have declined dramatically, but the rates of HIV infection, in fact, have not, so that's an area of great concern to us.

STEVE ROBERTS: And what explains the drop in the development of full-blown AIDS cases or in death? Is this largely attributable to the new medications that are on the market?

SANDRA THURMAN: Yes, absolutely, largely attributable, because of the new medications that people are able to access in this country, which, of course, they can't in other parts of the world.

STEVE ROBERTS: As I mentioned in the introduction, Sandy Thurman, you're at the epicenter of a very emotional issue.

SANDRA THURMAN: Oh, yes.

STEVE ROBERTS: Yesterday, just one more example of that. I must say we scheduled this interview long before we knew . . . that we were going to have a demonstration in front of the White House, but it does highlight that point. And, at that funeral, or that demonstration, one of the speakers called Bill Clinton a "murdering liar." You're sitting there in the White House in charge of his policy on this issue. What's your reaction when someone says that?

SANDRA THURMAN: Well, I mean, the reaction is . . . is what it's always been around this issue. People are very, very frustrated by the fact that we're looking at a life-threatening disease that we can't do anything about . . . or very much about. And, in seventeen years, we've made a lot of progress in treatment. We have very little progress toward a cure, we're hoping to make some progress toward a vaccine, but this has always been an emotional issue for people and it continues to be. And, you know, the President has been very committed to this issue since the beginning, since his first campaigns, and has really helped us develop a real policy that has increased funding dramatically. We've tripled funding since 1993 for care and treatment of people with AIDS in this country. We've increased the budget for drugs that are helping people live longer and better lives by over 450 percent just since 1996. We've increased the budget for research by over 50 percent. So, we've done a lot, but, no matter how much we do in an epidemic like this, it's never going to be enough. And, Steve Michael's funeral, I think, points out to us that while we have great news, on the one hand, with people living better and longer lives as a result of these great new therapies, people are still dying of this disease and we can't forget that. And that's why it's so important, why Steve's message is so important.

STEVE ROBERTS: And there also is a counter argument. There are people who would look at the figures that you just recited and say that this is too much. That this is to some extent a zero sum game, that money spent on AIDS is not spent on breast cancer, or diabetes, or Parkinson's, or many other diseases. We've had programs . . . shows on *The Diane Rehm Show*, on this issue . . . how do you answer that point of view, that because of the kind of demonstrations we say yesterday, that AIDS actually gets *more* attention than it deserves?

SANDRA THURMAN: Well, I don't think that it gets more attention than it deserves. In fact, I think that it's comparing apples and oranges. Certainly, we don't want to take money away from cancer research or Alzheimer's research to put into AIDS research. I think the trick for us in this country where we have resources to bring to bear to fight all kinds of diseases is that we have to do that. And, we're seeing support from Congress and from the administration to dramatically increase the spending on the National Institutes of Health to do this very kind of research. You know, AIDS is a new disease, cancer is not new, Alzheimer's is not new, AIDS is fairly new, seventeen years old. And, it's a contagious disease, and it's spreading not only here in the United States but around the world at dramatic rates. So, I think we have to look at this as a crisis and put the resources into HIV and AIDS research that not only will help us stop this epidemic and this disease, but will also help us fighting other diseases.

STEVE ROBERTS: In terms of this emotional swirl that comes, that seems to be swirling around your office and the whole debate . . . the other issue, public policy, which of course has been in the news in recent weeks, was the decision by the administration on the issue of federal funding for needle exchange programs, widely anticipated in the AIDS community, widely anticipated that Secretary Shalala would announce that as a result of the scientific findings, that federal money would go into these programs. The last-minute decision change announced that, yes, the President agreed that the science was on the side of needle exchange programs but did not provide the funding: a political compromise, obviously. What was your reaction to that pullback?

SANDRA THURMAN: Well, obviously, I think that all of my colleagues know I was greatly disappointed with that decision. I have, as a person who ran a community-based AIDS service organization for years, and have worked on the frontlines of this epidemic, always been a supporter of needle exchange programs. And, so, certainly I would have liked to have seen the federal government provide funding. But, on the other hand, I realize that this is a very hot political issue for people and, what the President and many of his advisors didn't want to do, was politicize this issue any more than it was already politicized. So, I think it was sort of a 50 percent win for us that we were able to say that the science does indeed work and give the local communities across the country who have needle exchange programs the opportunity to use the imprimatur of the science of the federal government to say, yes, these programs do work and advocate, help them advocate at the state level, the local level, to get these programs supported there. This dialogue will continue. This is certainly not the end of our discussion about needle exchange, particularly when we look at the fact that 50 percent of all new infections, more than 50 percent, are a result of IV drug use.

STEVE ROBERTS: Why did you lose that battle?

SANDRA THURMAN: Why did I lose that battle? Well, you know, I fought as hard as I could, and I lost. I think that there was a lot of concern in Congress, a lot of pressure brought to bear by very conservative members of Congress. I think there was some concern inside other parts of the administration regarding . . .

STEVE ROBERTS: Mainly the Office of Drug Policy?

SANDRA THURMAN: Sure, well, the Office of Drug Policy, and other offices as well. You know, people who are responsible for explaining to the American public why it is that we are going to spend money on giving clean needles to people who are injecting drugs. And it's not easy to explain to people why needle exchange programs work. It's not an easy sell, it's hard to put in a sound bite that helps people understand it readily. And, I think, one of the things that we don't do in this country is understand drug use, or addiction in general. I think we understand a little bit about alcoholism, but we have a long way to go with our understanding of addiction, in particularly with injection drugs. So, I think it just points to several places where we have some real educating to do.

STEVE ROBERTS: . . . [I]t is a tough thing to explain. And within the White House Council, Barry McCaffrey, former General Barry McCaffrey, [who] heads the Drug Policy Office, was very outspoken in saying this is the wrong message for this administration to be sending. Whatever the science says, if you put federal money behind needle exchange programs, you are not only, in effect, saying we approve of drug use, but even encouraging it in some ways. And this was the wrong public health message. How did you argue with that argument within the White House?

SANDRA THURMAN: Well, I mean, we talked about it at length. I mean, again, I think the science speaks for itself. What we do know is that we can take the opportunity of a needle exchange program to take a dirty needle off the streets, away from the addict, and to give them a clean needle. And, in that process, make contact with some of our hardest to reach populations in this country, hard-core drug addicts—most of whom are not young people, most of whom are middle-aged, in fact—and use that exchange as an opportunity to build a relationship that helps us get these people into drug treatment. I mean, the bottom line here, and Barry McCaffrey and I happen to agree on this, that we have to get people off of drugs in this country. Certainly, that's our goal. And we share that goal. But you can't get people into treatment unless you build relationships of trust and these folks, who are using injection drugs, for the most part are some of the most disenfranchised people in this country. So, you know, I regret that we've missed an opportunity to build those relationships and get people into the treatment they need. On the other hand, I mean, there is a real challenge about drug treatment. We only have one slot available, one drug treatment slot available, for every ten addicts, or people who are using drugs, who need treatment. So we've got to advocate on that side of the fence, too.

STEVE ROBERTS: . . . You were quoted recently in the *Washington Post* profile of you, saying that no one likes to see you coming. Now I find that hard to believe.

SANDRA THURMAN: Well, thank you.

STEVE ROBERTS: You seem like a very nice person. But, why . . . and you said in fact that the issues that you deal with, and the choices that you force people to make and confront, make your colleagues very cranky, I think you were quoted. Now, why is that, why doesn't anybody want to see you coming?

SANDRA THURMAN: Well, because I talk about the things that no one wants to talk about. I talk about sex . . . and I talk about money, and I talk about drugs, and I talk about death, you know, all kinds of things that make people really uncomfortable. And then if we want to push it to the dinner table conversation, I can talk about religion and the reason we haven't had the kind of response that we need to in this country from the religious community in this epidemic. . . . Of all the subjects that people try to avoid in polite conversations, they all fall in my bailiwick. So, that's why they hate to see me coming.

STEVE ROBERTS: And do you find that your perch within the White House, as mentioned earlier, was created by President Clinton, in part to have a place where these subjects were discussed, and to have an advocate like you, but it's been . . . there's been a high turnover there—I think you're the fourth. Is it partly because it is such a tough job and you are so unpopular with your colleagues that people don't stay in this job very long?

SANDRA THURMAN: Well, I think a couple of things. I think that it depends on the personality of the person who holds this job. One of the advantages I think I have over my predecessors, who were very capable and very smart, is that I grew up in politics. It's not that I've done public health, but I've also done politics. The White House is a political machine, certainly we do policy there, but if you don't understand how to move the policy inside a political system, it's very, very hard to be heard and very hard to be effective. So I think one of the reasons that there was such high turnover is, number one, because it is a very difficult job. But, number two, is because people who didn't have political experience couldn't get done what they felt like they needed to get done. So everybody was unhappy. They were unhappy and our colleagues were unhappy as well. I think I'm in a little different position this time.

STEVE ROBERTS: Well, you in fact boast that you're a fourth-generation political activist, and we were talking in the first hour, actually, about some of the places where it seems that there's a resurgent confidence in professional politicians, as opposed to amateurs, in elected office. Talk a bit about your background and how you had this political background you mentioned to me, that your mother, and my mother-in-law, Lindy Boggs, are old, old friends from Democratic politics . . .

SANDRA THURMAN: Right, that's correct, yes.

STEVE ROBERTS: . . . And let's talk about how you came to this—I know there are two strains in your background, this political strain and the public health strain—talk first about the political background.

SANDRA THURMAN: Well, I have sort of an interesting background. I am a fourth-generation advocate. My grandmother worked very hard to get prisoners out of balls and chains and out of the cages that they were kept in on roadside gangs in Georgia many years ago. My great-grandmother was a big advocate of education for children of all races, equal education, which is kind of unusual for a woman at the turn of the century. And my mother was an activist on behalf of women, and was chairman of the Democratic Party in Georgia for many years and on the Democratic National Committee, and actually headed . . . my first political campaign as a child was the Kennedy campaign, John Kennedy's campaign, that Mother chaired in Georgia. And so I grew up watching how politics worked and watching how you can use your relationships and you can use your access to get things done that mattered. So, in between doing public health, I would take time off, as I did in the Clinton campaign in 1992, to work in political campaigns. Because again, while I prefer to do the work on the front lines, having done that, I understand that if policies don't reflect the needs of those on the front lines, and there's a gap in between, then nothing really happens. So then I sort of seized on that experience to move into this arena, the policy arena, to get some work done.

STEVE ROBERTS: But, also, there's an interesting set of experiences that brought you to this particular issue. As you mentioned, there's a long strain of different things that the women in your family, and it's striking that all of your forebears in politics were women, was that a reinforcement, that is, unusual lineage, particularly in the South?

SANDRA THURMAN: Well, yes, it was a great reinforcement. I mean, what great role models to have. And to sort of grow up in the South during the time of the civil rights movement. And to have people in my house like Martin Luther King, Jr. and like Daddy King, his father . . . who I always admired so, to watch how people could really effect change, particularly in the South and with women, was kind of unusual and I think that has given me the confidence and the ability, and probably the sense of humor, to take a job like this and really find great opportunities for fun and growth in this.

STEVE ROBERTS: As I said, there's also a fascinating story about how you came to focus on the AIDS epidemic and AIDS issues as the core of your interest as an advocate, as a political advocate. It all started with your former husband, who was, I think, a lawyer in Atlanta, taking a turn in his career: talk about what happened.

SANDRA THURMAN: Well, it was interesting, he was practicing law. In fact, we had met when he was living in Washington, clerking at the U.S. Supreme Court, and then went on to practice law . . . trial law, and was getting bored. The travel schedule was very difficult and he started investing in bars. And, one of the bars that he invested in, and built, was a gay bar in Atlanta. And we hired a wonderful man to run the bar for us, who was one of our first friends, and one of the earliest people in Atlanta to die of AIDS. And we were both devastated. As a result of that, I started working in the AIDS community. I had background in hospice. I had kept my father at home when he died when I was in my twenties, and learned about hospice and studied with Elizabeth Kübler-Ross, so I had some understanding about issues relative to death and dying and taking care of people at home. And, in those early days, you couldn't find anyone to help you care for someone at home. There was no one to give respite care. People were very, very afraid in the early '80s of AIDS, and so I started volunteering and taking care of my friends and then teaching friends how to take care of their loved ones who were sick. One thing led to another and I wound up in the AIDS business. . . .
    . . . And it was hard, because during those early years my husband and I lost probably ten of our closest friends. I mean, these were the people that we were working

with, you know, my husband's employees. And it was very, very difficult for us both, and so we wanted to find a way to respond. And so it changed my career.

STEVE ROBERTS: . . . [I]n general, it takes enormous resiliency and resources to keep going in that world, doesn't it?

SANDRA THURMAN: It does. It does. It was very, very difficult and that's one of the reasons why I came off on the front lines of HIV and AIDS some five years ago to go to work at the Carter Center and work on policy issues for awhile. Because I began to see myself, and many professionals who work in the helping professions find this, began to see myself showing symptoms of burnout that I was monitoring in all of our staff. But when I looked in the mirror and saw that there were symptoms in myself, I thought . . . hmm . . . I need to take a break, which isn't unusual. But it is hard and, in those early days, we had no therapies, so there was nothing we could do for people except to help them die with dignity and grace. And that was the only thing we had.

The unusual, I think, or the odd thing about that, from where I sit today, is that managing the epidemic was much easier in the days when we could almost do nothing than it is today. I mean, the issues and the policies and the challenges that we face today are much more complex, and in many ways, much more difficult to deal with than plain old death and dying, which is what we had to do in the early days. You know, we had no choices . . . there wasn't really anything we could do back then. And life, in many ways, was simpler, although extraordinarily painful.

CHAPTER 4

THE SEPARATION OF POWERS

How Independent Is the Judiciary?

The Constitution is the supreme law of the land, our fundamental law which the Supreme Court interprets in individual cases and controversies. Within the Constitution's framework the Court may also interpret and apply natural and common law principles. The Constitution binds both Congress and the states. Congress gave to the Supreme Court the power to exercise judicial review over state action in the Judiciary Act of 1789. The Supreme Court independently assumed the power of judicial review over Congress.

The Supreme Court interprets and applies fundamental law in exercising judicial review. However, as the following selection describes, the Supreme Court's role as interpreter of a higher law may clash with another American ideal: popular sovereignty.

Robert G. McCloskey was one the country's outstanding authorities on the Supreme Court and the judicial system. His work, *The American Supreme Court,* is a classic. He taught in the Government Department at Harvard University.

McCloskey's major points in the following selection are:

1. The Founding Fathers had no blueprint for the Supreme Court to emerge as one of the most powerful institutions in government.

2. The Constitution does not clearly state the Supreme Court's authority to review congressional or state legislative actions. The Constitution, however, does not preclude such review.

3. A potential conflict exists between the Declaration of Independence's fundamental principle of "consent of the governed," and the Constitution's embodiment of a higher law. The former supports popular government, the latter limits it. Congress and the President, the "political" institutions of government, represent popular sovereignty. The Supreme Court through judicial review applies constitutional limits to popular will.

4. The Supreme Court "blends orthodox judicial functions with policymaking functions in a complex mixture." Politics defines the outer boundaries of judicial power. Within those boundaries the extraordinary power the Supreme Court has assumed derives from constitutional ambiguities and the resulting lack of consensus on what the Constitution means. The Supreme Court became the final arbiter of the Constitution by default.

16

Robert G. McCloskey

THE AMERICAN SUPREME COURT

THE GENESIS AND NATURE OF JUDICIAL POWER

On June 21, 1788, when the convention of New Hampshire voted 57 to 46 to approve the proposed national constitution, the requirement of nine ratifying states was fulfilled and the United States of America sprang into legal being. Opportunity for instant creation of this magnitude occurs only in fiction and law, and the delegates did not underrate their historic moment. They were careful to specify that it came at one o'clock in the afternoon, for they feared that Virginia might act that very evening and claim a share in the honor. They need not have worried. The Virginians were in for three more days of oratory, mostly by Patrick Henry, before their state's proud name could be added to the list.

Fifteen months later, President Washington accomplished another of these portentous juridical feats by signing the Judiciary Act of 1789, which was to be called many years afterward "probably the most important and the most satisfactory Act ever passed by Congress." The latter-day eulogist was himself a Supreme Court justice, and his good opinion of a law that made him one of the most august figures in the nation is not surprising; a long roll of eminent statesmen since 1789 could be called to testify on the other side. But hardly one of them would dispute his opinion that the Act was extremely important, for it not only established the far-flung system of federal courts but boldly defined their jurisdiction, and especially that of the Supreme Court, in such a way that the states, Congress, and the President could be held subject to judicial authority.

. . . [T]hey would not have known much about the prospects of their Court and the Constitution, for the very good reason that so little about either had been firmly decided. . . .

No one quite knew, for example, what was meant when the Constitution endowed Congress with power "to regulate commerce among foreign nations, and among the several states"; or to make all laws "necessary and proper" for carrying out the national government's other powers; or when it was asserted that the Constitution as well as laws and treaties made by the nation were "the supreme law of the land." . . .

As for the Supreme Court, its future was even more uncertain. The Constitution has comparatively little to say about the Court or the federal judiciary in general. The "judicial power of the United States," whatever it may be, is vested in the Supreme Court and in such other courts as Congress may establish. But the composition of the Court, including the number of its members, is left for congressional decision; and, while federal judges cannot be removed except by impeachment, there is nothing to prevent Congress from creating additional judgeships whenever it chooses. Furthermore, although the judicial power "extends" to a variety of cases described in Article III, section 2, the second paragraph of that section significantly qualifies what the first seems to have granted, and gives Congress power to control the Supreme Court's jurisdiction over appeals from lower courts. Since the cases that reach the Court directly without first being heard in other courts are comparatively minor in quantity or importance, this legislative authority over appeals (over the "appellate jurisdiction") is a license for Congress to decide whether the Supreme Court will be a significant or a peripheral factor in American government.

Most important of all, the Constitution makes no explicit statement about the nature of the Court's power even when a case admittedly falls within its jurisdiction. Some of the uncertainties outlined above were resolved, temporarily at any rate, by the passage of the Judiciary Act. Its famous Section 25 gave the Supreme Court power to reverse or affirm state court decisions which had denied claims based on the federal Constitution, treaties, or laws. This meant that such cases could be reached by the Supreme Court through its appellate jurisdiction. But suppose a state court had denied such a claim under the federal Constitution and the Supreme Court of the United States reversed on the ground that the state court's interpretation of the Constitution was in error. And suppose further that the state court obstinately continued to insist upon its own interpretation. Was there anything in the Constitution to guarantee that the Supreme Court's opinion would prevail, that the Supreme Court's authority was superior to state courts? Or suppose, to carry the matter a step further, that the state court had held a federal law invalid as conflicting with the *national* Constitution and the Supreme Court *agreed* with this holding, thus asserting its authority to overthrow an act of Congress. Does the Constitution make it *clear* that the Court has this final authority of "judicial review" over national legislative enactments?

The answer to both questions is a fairly solid "no." As for state decisions it has been argued that the "supreme law of the land" clause and the clause extending the judicial power to cases arising under the Constitution do make it clear that the Supreme Court was intended to be pre-eminent on questions of constitutional interpretation. If the Constitution is supreme and the Supreme Court has jurisdiction over cases involving the Constitution, then it follows that the Court's word on such matters is paramount over all others—so the argument runs. But in the first place this reasoning is not unassailable, for as defenders of states' rights were later passionately to insist, the fact that the Constitution is supreme does not settle the question of who decides what the Constitution means. And in the second place enthusiasts for judicial review have never quite been able to explain why so formidable a power was granted by implication rather than by flat statement. As for judicial review of congressional acts, the support in the language of the Constitution was even more suppositious, and arguments for the authority derived solely from that language seem inevitably to beg the question.

None of this is to say that the framers of the Constitution would have been surprised to see the Supreme Court exercising the power of judicial review in some form, both as against the states and as against Congress. Indeed there is ample evidence that most of them who had thought about it expected that the Court would do so, however distressing it is that they failed to make their expectations explicit. But neither the framers nor the ratifying state conventions (whose views are in some ways more relevant to the issue) had any general understanding about the particular form that the judicial review would take and the role that the Supreme Court would therefore assume. . . .

In short, neither the words of the Constitution nor the provable intent of those who framed and ratified it justified in 1790 any certitude about the scope or finality of the Court's power to superintend either the states or Congress. The most that can be said is that language and intent did not *preclude* the Court from becoming the puissant tribunal of later history. . . .

[T]he Constitution was potentially the convergence point for all the ideas about fundamental law that had been current in America since the colonization period. Of course the notion of a law-above-government, a "higher" law, was well known throughout the Western world, but the colonists had given it a special domestic cast, infusing it with interpretations drawn from their own unique experience. While most Europeans thought of higher law as exercising a moral restraint on government, they did not argue that this moral limit was legally enforceable, that it was positive law, practically binding the governors. Even before the Revolutionary controversy, Americans had found it easy to assume that it was just that, for their own legislatures had long been literally bound by "higher law" in such forms as the colonial charters and decisions of the British Privy Council. . . .

[T]he Declaration of Independence [, though,] had founded just government on the "consent of the governed"; the next and natural step was to regard the people as not only a consenting but a willing entity and to declare, as Jefferson later said, that "the will of the majority is in all cases to prevail." . . .

Yet plainly that concept conflicted with the doctrine of fundamental law which was also, and concurrently, treasured by Americans. Popular sovereignty suggests *will*; fundamental law suggests *limit*. The one idea conjures up the vision of an active, positive state; the other idea emphasizes the negative, restrictive side of the political problem. It may be possible to harmonize these seeming opposites by logical sleight of hand, by arguing that the doctrines of popular sovereignty and fundamental law were fused in the Constitution, which was a popularly willed limitation. But it seems unlikely that Americans in general achieved such a synthesis and far more probable, considering our later political history, that most of them retained the two ideas side by side. This propensity to hold contradictory ideas simultaneously is one of the most significant qualities of the American political mind at all stages of national history, and it helps substantially in explaining the rise to power of the United States Supreme Court.

For with their political hearts thus divided between the will of the people and the rule of law, Americans were naturally receptive to the development of institutions that reflected each of these values separately. The legislature with its power to initiate programs and policies, to respond to the expressed interest of the public, embodied the doctrine of popular sovereignty. The courts, generally supposed to be without will . . . generally revered as impartial and independent, fell heir almost by default to the guardianship of the fundamental law. It did not avail for . . . enemies of the judicial power to insist that a single department could exercise *both* the willing and the limiting functions. The bifurcation of the two values in the American mind impellingly suggested that the functions should be similarly separated. And the devotion of Americans to both popular sovereignty and fundamental law insured public support for the institution that represented each of them.

Consequences for American Constitutionalism

This dualism of the American mind, symbolized on the one hand by "political" institutions like the Congress and the Presidency and on the other hand by the Court and the Constitution, helps account for a good deal that seems baffling in later history. In logical terms it might appear strange that the nation should resoundingly approve the New Deal in 1936 and a few months later stoutly defend against attack the Supreme Court that had cut the heart from the New Deal program. But the paradox is related as branch to root to the historic dualism between popular sovereignty and the doctrine of fundamental law that developed with the birth throes of the American political system. The separation of the two ideas in the American mind had been emphasized by intervening events: strong-minded judges had added new arguments for the Court's constitutional prerogative; congressmen and presidents, busy with more pressing concerns, had been content except for fitful rebellious impulses to let those arguments go unchallenged; and the cake of custom had hardened over the original disjunction. But it was made possible at the outset by our native tendency to harbor conflicting ideas without trying, or caring, to resolve them.

The United States began its history, then, with a Constitution that posed more questions than it answered and with a Supreme Court whose birthright was most uncertain. The temper of the times and the deep-seated inclinations of the American political character favored the future of both these institutions and at the same time prescribed their limits and helped determine their nature. American devotion to the principle of fundamental law gave the Constitution its odor of sanctity, and the American bent for evading contradictions by assigning values to separate compartments allowed the Supreme Court to assume the priestly mantle. But like most successes, in politics and elsewhere, this one had a price. The failure to resolve the conflict between popular sovereignty and fundamental law perhaps saved the latter principle, but by the same token it left the former intact. And this meant that the fundamental law could be enforced only within delicately defined boundaries, that constitutional law though not simply the creature of the popular will nevertheless had always to reckon with it, that the mandates of the Supreme Court must be shaped with an eye not only to legal right and wrong, but with an eye to what popular opinion would tolerate.

We have seen, then, that the Constitution makers postponed some of the most vital questions confronting them, that the Constitution and the Supreme Court inherited the quasi-religious symbolic quality attached to the doctrine of "higher law," but that the dogmas of popular sovereignty also continued to survive and flourish and therefore influence constitutionalism. The consequences of all this were several. For one thing the Constitution itself could not become the certain and immutable code of governmental conduct that some of its latter-day idolators imagined it to be. Conceived in ambiguity as well as liberty, it could never escape that legacy. The framers had said in effect: with respect to certain questions, some of them very momentous, the Constitution means whatever the circumstances of the future will allow it to mean. But since those circumstances were almost sure to vary, the result was that alterability became the law of the Constitution's being: it might mean one thing in 1855, something else in 1905, and something still different in 1955, depending upon what circumstances, including popular expectations, warranted.

To be sure, as the years went on there was a certain accumulation of fairly well-fixed interpretations, and the picture of a constitutional system in eternal flux should not be overdrawn. . . . Nevertheless only a very bold constitutional scholar would declare that he *knows* how the commerce clause or the due process clauses will be understood by the next generation. And when we count up the clauses whose past is variable and whose future is uncertain they far exceed in significance if not in number their more stable fellows.

The Court's Constitutional Powers and Duties

As for the Supreme Court, its nature has also been heavily and permanently influenced by the factors just described. As might be expected, any description of the judicial function in America is shot through with paradoxes. To begin with, the observer confronts the fact that the Court does inherit a responsibility for helping to guide the nation, especially with respect to those long-term "value questions" that are so vital to the maintenance of a just political order. A good many gallons of ink have been spilled over the issue of whether such a heavy assignment should have devolved on the judiciary. John Marshall, "the great Chief Justice," has been accused of seizing the bitter cup all too gladly and thus setting a pattern of usurpation for future judges to follow. Insofar as this indictment rests on the supposed "intent of the framers," it suffers from the weakness already remarked: that so few of the framers had any clear views one way or another about the subject.

On the other hand, insofar as the charge is that the nation was unwise to delegate this duty to the judges (or allow them to assume it), it may be right, but is also perilously near to irrelevance. For this amounts to saying that America was unwise to be the nation that it was. The American mind conceived a dichotomy between the willed law of legislative enactment and the discovered or pronounced law of the Constitution, and "judicial review" was, as we have seen, one result. The fallacy of making such a distinction may be palpable enough from our modern perspective, but the fact remains that it was not palpable to Marshall's generation, and nothing very helpful is accomplished by arguing that it should have been.

Nor is it much more profitable to urge that the Court should now put off the responsibility it once so eagerly took up, even if it be conceded that the original arrogation was unwise. Historical accident and bad logic may explain the inception of judicial review, but by now the American nation has lived with the consequences for more than 150 years. Our courts and, even more important, our legislatures have been shaped by the understanding that the judiciary will help in charting the path of governmental policy. A rough division of labor has developed from that understanding, for it is assumed that the legislature can focus largely on the task of "interest representation," while passing on to the courts a substantial share of the responsibility for considering the long-term constitutional questions that continually arise. Appearances may be deceptive. Congressmen may self-righteously insist that they serve both the Constitutional Tradition and their Constituents, but the needs of these two masters seem to coincide with remarkable invariability; and it is fair to infer that interests and pressures play the larger part in the legislative process.

Surely this is no indictment of that process, for the American tradition respects, as has been said, the will of today's popular majority, and interests must therefore be paid due heed. But the American tradition also sets great store, as we have also seen, by the set of values associated with the "rule of law," which history has rightly or wrongly consigned in heavy part to the judiciary. In a world of abstractions, one might argue that this historic division, since it defies good sense, ought to be obliterated. But in the world that history has given us, the almost certain result would be that pure calculation of interest-group pressures defined the course of government in the United States. It is too much to ask that a legislative process as interest-dominated as ours abjure its traditions at this late date and take on the functions of a high court as well. Yet until it does, the judiciary must accept its own traditional responsibility, lest the very idea of limited government be lost. Critics may legitimately debate whether the Court should play a greater or lesser part in directing the ship of state. That it must play some part is the penalty of its heritage.

The Conditions of Judicial Control

Yet once this is said, it must immediately be added—or reiterated—that the tradition which transmits this power to the Court likewise prescribes the conditions of its exercise. The nation expects the judges to aid in deciding policy questions, but the nation is prone, with sublime inconsistency, to grow fiercely resentful if the aid becomes repression, if the judges bypass certain ill-marked but nevertheless quite real boundaries, two of which merit special consideration.

In the first place, there are the limitations implied by the fact that the Supreme Court is expected to be both a "court" in the orthodox sense of the word and something very much more as well. A full account of the confusions fostered by this seeming contradiction would almost involve a recapitulation of Supreme Court history. Legions of judges and their devotees have believed, or professed to believe, that constitutional law was a technical mystery revealing itself in terms of unmistakable precision to those who had the key, that the Constitution was the record and the judges merely the impartial phonograph that played it, a group of men who somehow managed to stop being men when they put on their robes and would not dream of letting their subjective value judgments affect their understanding of the Constitution. No court was ever like this, no system of law was ever so sure a guide to its interpreters. And the myth of a perfect judiciary perfectly administering a perfect Constitution was therefore deeply impaired in the twentieth century by writers who pointed out what some perceptive observers had always known—that judges are mortal. Like senators and presidents, it was said, judges may have prejudices, and those prejudices may affect their understanding of the Constitution. In fact, the critics went on, the American Supreme Court, so far from merely and imperturbably reflecting eternal constitutional verities, is a willing, policy-making, *political* body.

All this was perfectly true as far as it went, and it provided a useful antidote to previous oversimplifications. But the trouble was that it tended to foster an oversimplification of its own: "legal realists," impressed by the discovery that the Supreme Court was more than a court, were sometimes prone to treat it as if it were not a court at all, as if its "courthood" were a pure façade for political functions indistinguishable from those performed by the legislature. Such a view bypasses everything that is really interesting about the institution and obscures, as much as the discredited old mythology ever did, its true nature.

For the fascinating thing about the Supreme Court has been that it blends orthodox judicial functions with policy-making functions in a complex mixture. And the Court's power is accounted for by the fact that the mixture is maintained in nice balance; but the fact that it *must* be maintained in such a balance accounts for the limitations of that power. The Court's claim on the American mind derives from the myth of an impartial, judicious tribunal whose duty it is to preserve our sense of continuity with the fundamental law. Because that law was initially stated in ambiguous terms, it has been the duty of the Court to make "policy decisions" about it, that is, to decide what it means in the circumstances existing when the question is presented. But though the judges do enter this realm of policy-making, they enter with their robes on, and they can never (or at any rate seldom) take them off; they are both empowered and restricted by their "courtly" attributes.

They cannot, for example, even decide a question unless it is presented in the form of a "case" between two or more interested parties; and the Supreme Court early, and wisely, held that to render "advisory opinions" even to the President would be incongruous with the judicial function. Sometimes the Court is criticized for leaning over backward to find technical and, to a layman, unduly "legalistic" reasons for leaving important constitutional questions unsettled. Often the drag of precedent inhibits the judges from revising constitutional principles as quickly as might be desirable. And finally there are whole large areas of constitutional determination which the Court deliberately and rather consistently leaves alone (for example, the issue of whether a state has "a republican form of government," Art. IV, sec. 4) on the grounds that the questions therein raised are not appropriate for judicial determination.

Any individual decision along any of these lines may well be subject to criticism, for the judges of the Supreme Court, being [human], can err. But it is the greatest of nonsense to generalize the criticism into impatience with the Court's "legalistic" demeanor as such, since the logical conclusion of such a criticism is to align the judicial power squarely with the legislative power and to erase the differentiation of function that is the Court's basis for being. And it is also wrong to suppose that the Court's insistence on such attributes of judiciality is a mere pose, designed to hoodwink the public without hampering the judges. . . . The judges have usually known what students have sometimes not known—that their tribunal must be a court, as well as seem one, if it is to retain its power. The idea of fundamental law as a force in its own right, distinguishable from today's popular will, can only be maintained by a pattern of Court behavior that emphasizes the separation. If departures from that pattern are too frequent and too extreme, the emphasis will be lost and the idea itself will be imperiled.

One consequence, then, of the Supreme Court's peculiar origins is this necessity that it perform legislative (or quasi-legislative) tasks with judicial tools, which is roughly akin to the assignment of playing baseball with a billiard cue. But its problems do not end there. A second result, as has already been intimated, is the need for the judges to reckon, in making rules and guiding policy, with the imperatives of public opinion no matter how impeccably "judicial" is the method by which the rules are arrived at. This is not to say that the Court should consult the latest bulletins on the popular climate and shape its judgments accordingly. But it is to say that public concurrence sets an outer boundary for judicial policy-making; that judicial ideas of the good society can never be too far removed from the popular ideas. The Republic might have been dedicated at the outset to the principle of pure popular sovereignty, and in that event the Supreme Court would have inherited only the important but secondary responsibility of statutory interpretation. On the other hand, it is imaginatively, though not perhaps practically, conceivable to establish a governmental system in which the fundamental law absolutely controls the public will, and in such a system the Court might enjoy utter independence. But America, as we have seen, chose neither of these worlds, but tried to have the best of them both: the upshot is that the Court, while sometimes checking or at any rate modifying the popular will, is itself in turn checked or modified.

America has thus had two sovereigns, but this somewhat outlandish arrangement has been maintained only because each of the partners has known the meaning of self-restraint. In the critical literature of the past generation or two, one has read much about judicial tyranny, and the vision of a populace bent on social reform but shackled by an unfeeling Court's despotism seems to have beguiled more than one observer. In truth the Supreme Court has seldom, if ever, flatly and for very long resisted a really unmistakable wave of public sentiment. It has worked with the premise that constitutional law, like politics itself, is a science of the possible.

The Contours of Court History

There is a final point, which is at the same time very much like a summary of the discussion so far. We have seen that both the meaning of the Constitution and the nature of the Supreme Court's authority were left in doubt by the framers, that circumstances nonetheless conspired to favor the early growth of both constitutionalism and judicial power, but that those same circumstances also helped to set the terms within which these institutions would develop. The Constitution became a symbol of American patriotic devotion, but a symbol whose continued force depended on its continued flexibility in the face of shifting national needs. The Supreme Court became a venerated institution, half judicial tribunal and half political preceptor, sensitive but not subservient to popular expectations, obliged by its tradition to share the duties of statesmanship, but equally obliged to be alert that its share did not exceed its capacities.

The history of the Court and its treatment of the Constitution can be broadly understood as an endless search for a position in American government that is appropriate to these conditions imposed by its genesis. The quest is laden with difficulties because the paradoxes of the Court's existence can only be reconciled, even temporarily, by the most delicate balancing of judgments. It is unending because every such tentative reconciliation is sure to be disturbed ultimately by the relentless course of history, and every such major disturbance sends the judges forth on another chapter in their odyssey.

. . . The Court's greatest successes have been achieved when it has operated near the margins rather than in the center of political controversy, when it has nudged and gently tugged the nation, instead of trying to rule it.

. . . It is true that such a judicial policy calls for rather extraordinary talents of character and intelligence. The Court must alter its own perspectives as history's perspectives are altered, yet must not move so fast that the idea of continuity is lost. It must allow government some leeway to act either wisely or foolishly, yet must not become so acquiescent that the concept of constitutional limit is revealed as an illusion. This requires judges who possess what a great poet called "negative capability"—who can resist the natural human tendency to push an idea to what seems its logical extreme, to have done with half-measures and uncertainties. It requires judges who can practice the arts of discrimination without losing the light of reason and getting lost in a welter of *ad hoc*, pragmatic judgments. For it is part of the glory and strength of the American constitutional tradition that it assumes the possibility of being rational about the state and its powers and limits.

The Constitution in Article III gives Congress the authority not only to create courts "inferior" to the Supreme Court but also the power to define the appellate jurisdiction of the federal judiciary. Additionally, Congress controls appropriations for the judiciary and is limited only by the constitutional stipulation that the compensation of federal judges can not be reduced.

The following selection analyzes how the political reality of congressional meddling in judicial affairs can make the achievement of the ideal of fair and efficient administration of justice difficult.

Robert A. Katzmann, formerly Walsh Professor of Government and Professor of Law at Georgetown University, was appointed to the Second Circuit Court of Appeals in 1999. Katzmann has written extensively on the courts and the judicial process.

His major points in the following selection are:

1. Under the separation of powers and checks and balances system no branch was to have the incentive or the means to encroach upon coordinate branches.
2. Judicial independence is a fundamental constitutional principle.
3. The checks and balances system gives Congress the authority to confirm judicial appointments. Congress has politicized the confirmation process in an attempt to sway prospective judicial interpretation of statutory law.
4. Congress has also used its constitutional authority to control the appellate jurisdiction of the courts to influence them.
5. Congress legitimately can and reasonably should criticize the courts, but it must be careful not to chill judicial independence.

17

Robert A. Katzmann

COURTS, CONGRESS, AND THE CHALLENGES OF GOVERNANCE

★★★

Governance in the United States is a process of interaction among institutions—legislative, executive, and judicial—with separate and sometimes clashing structures, purposes, and interests. The Founders envisioned that constructive tension among those governmental institutions would not only preserve liberty but would also promote the public good. No branch was to encroach upon the prerogatives of the others, yet in some sense each was dependent upon the others for its sustenance and vitality. And that interdependence would contribute to an informed and deliberative process. Governance, then, is premised on each institution's respect for and knowledge of the others and on a continuing dialogue that produces shared understanding and comity.

. . . [O]ne key link in the chain is that between the federal judiciary and Congress. This relationship shapes the administration of justice in critical ways. What is at issue in part is the integrity of political institutions: the judiciary needs to function in an environment respectful of its core values and mission, with the requisite resources; and the legislative branch seeks a judicial system that faithfully interprets its laws and efficiently discharges justice. But a goal even greater than the well-being of particular branches of government is at stake: the preservation of the means by which justice is dispensed fairly and efficiently.

A host of issues presses upon the nerves of the relationship: the prospect of an ever rising caseload; federalization of the law; resource constraints; concerns about the confirmation process; increasing legislative scrutiny of judicial decisionmaking and the administration of justice; and debates about how the courts should interpret legislation.

An illustrative pattern of court-legislature interaction reveals the sources of the tension. Congress passes laws increasing the judiciary's work in such highly charged areas as criminal justice. The courts lament that resources have not kept pace with these expanded duties to ensure the prompt and fair resolution of cases. Some in Congress respond that, especially at a time of large national budget deficits, courts need to manage their operations more efficiently, and that Congress should more closely monitor how the judiciary administers justice in an effort to strengthen accountability. For some in the judicial branch, such congressional examination could impinge upon judicial autonomy. As the plot thickens, some members of Congress sharply criticize judges for particular decisions, asserting that they misunderstand, indeed sometimes distort, the meaning of the law. In reaction, Congress may even enact legislation curbing judicial discretion. Defenders of the judiciary maintain that the legislators often pass vague statutes with little guidance about their meaning (particularly in areas in which they do not want to take political heat), leave the controversy to the courts to resolve, and then blame the judiciary for decisions rendered. At times, the severity of the legislative critique heightens judges' concerns about threats to judicial independence.

If the strains are to be eased, then it is imperative to understand the nature of the relationship between the branches, and each branch must understand the other. . . .

Institutional Ties

The formal institutional ties between the federal courts and Congress are clear enough. In the exercise of its authority to advise and consent, the Senate confirms or rejects the president's judicial nominees. Congress creates judgeships; determines the structure, jurisdiction, procedures (both civil and criminal), and substantive law of the federal courts; passes laws affecting such disparate areas as judicial discipline and sentencing policy; and sets appropriations and compensation. The legislative branch adds to the judiciary's responsibilities whenever it enacts laws that result in court cases arising under the statutes.

For their part, courts affect Congress whenever they construe the meaning of statutes. The task is a formidable one in the twentieth century, an age that has produced an "orgy of statute making." . . . The New Deal reinforced the importance of legislation, as statutes changed from their generally more limited character to major programmatic laws widely affecting public policy in virtually every sector of daily life. Because the character of the laws has altered, so too have the opportunities and frequency with which the judiciary has had to interpret legislative meaning with often wide-ranging policy effects. Legislation that is vague, ambiguous, contradictory, or technically complex frequently spawns litigation, leading to the judicial role. Indeed, in virtually every area of public policy—such as civil rights, redistricting, disability, environment, business, and criminal justice—the federal courts have been called upon to discern legislative meaning.

In a system of interdependence, the Founders sought to create a zone of judicial independence in resolving cases: "There is no liberty, if the power of judging be not separated from the legislative and executive powers." That independence required that judges be insulated from public pressure, free to make unpopular decisions. To secure that independence, the Constitution provides for lifetime tenure and prohibits reductions in compensation.

But judicial independence in a system of interdependent responsibilities is not without friction. From the outset, in the confirmation process, the Senate must learn enough about nominees to evaluate their fitness. At the same time, any exchanges between senators and nominees, in the give and take of the hearing, must preserve the integrity of the judicial process; care must be taken that particular cases not be prejudged and that impartiality be maintained. More broadly, and apart from the confirmation process, Congress has a legitimate interest in the administration of justice; the judiciary, for its part, is concerned with ensuring that it retains discretion in managing its affairs, to the degree necessary to preserve judicial independence. As a participant in statutory decisionmaking, the courts' legitimacy will rest in large measure on their understanding of how Congress works and their capacity to interpret legislation consistent with legislative meaning.

At bottom, good governance, as it relates to judicial-legislative relations, depends upon at least four ingredients: a sensible way to choose judges, the bedrock of the courts; a proper attention to the manner in which courts interpret statutes; the development of mechanisms to transmit to Congress judicial opinions identifying perceived problems in statutes; and a process of communications between the courts and Congress to ensure both branches' institutional well-being and the fair and efficient administration of justice.

Problems

In the view of many observers, these elements are lacking or in need of repair or attention. The confirmation process, according to some, has become politicized in ways that threaten the independence of the judiciary. But for others the problem is that nominees are not sufficiently forthcoming in the confirmation hearings and thus hinder the Senate in its deliberations. Difficulties are compounded by a lack of shared understanding and agreement about the appropriate roles of the branches in the appointment and confirmation process. Issues abound: Should the Senate exercise an independent, coequal role, or one of deference in the exercise of advice and consent? What criteria are appropriate in examining nominees? Can the Senate legitimately inquire into the judge's conception of the judicial role or into the values and judicial philosophy that might help motivate the judge's decisionmaking? In the confirmation hearing, what kinds of questions are appropriate to ask of nominees and what kinds of answers are responsive yet faithful to norms of judicial independence? How has the process changed over time? What are the roles of interest groups, media advertising, and the media generally? What sorts of changes, if any, might be useful?

The question of how judges should interpret statutes has sparked much discussion because different approaches can lead to different outcomes. How, for example, should judges interpret an ambiguous statute? Should they confine their inquiry to the words of the statute and the statutory framework? Or should they look for guidance in the legislative history—such as committee reports and floor colloquies—in the effort to understand congressional meaning? Justice Antonin Scalia, for one, has criticized those who resort to "that last hope of lost interpretive causes, that St. Jude . . . of statutory construction, legislative history," arguing that such materials are illegitimate for a number of reasons, not the least of which that they are not formally part of the law or voted upon by the legislators. In response, Justice David Souter commented that "the shrine, however, is well peopled (though it has room for one more) and its congregation has included such noted elders as Mr. Justice Frankfurter." And then, quoting Frankfurter, he continued: "A statute, like other living organisms, derives significance and sustenance from its environment, from which it cannot be severed without being mutilated. . . . The meaning of such a statute cannot be gained by confining inquiry within its four corners."

From the congressional side, concern about how judges interpret legislation—whether the courts do not necessarily do what Congress intended—has led to hearings specifically devoted to the judicial construction of statutes. At the confirmation hearings themselves, senators routinely question nominees about the way they approach statutes, making clear their displeasure with methods that disregard legislative history. Indeed, the "Scalia" question has become a predictable part of the hearing. As Senator Herbert H. Kohl, Democrat of Wisconsin, asked Ruth Bader Ginsburg: "So I take it you don't feel safe on the same island, you don't see yourself on the same island of legislative intent as Justice Scalia?"

Participants much involved in judicial-legislative relations have pointed to problems of communication and understanding. Chief Justice William H. Rehnquist stated: "Congress, understandably concerned with the increasing traffic [in] drugs and the violence resulting from the use of guns, has legislated again and again to make what once were only state crimes federal offenses. . . . All of this means that in talking about the future of the federal courts, we must understand that Congress will probably continue to enact new legislation which provides new causes of action for litigants on the civil side of the docket, and new federal crimes to be prosecuted on the criminal side of the federal docket." Yet, as the Judicial Conference of the United States' *Long Range Plan for the Federal Courts* has noted: "The regrettable reality is that [sizable budgetary] increases have not kept pace with the volume and costs of additional tasks that the courts have assumed under new congressional mandates. Insufficient resources are ultimately a threat to judicial branch independence." Former Representative Neal Smith, Democrat of Iowa, longtime chair of the House Appropriations Subcommittee, which handles the judiciary's budget, put it this way:

The courts do not have many advocates in Congress. They do not have a constituency. Congress continues to pass more and more laws that require the courts to assume jurisdiction of more cases and add to their workload. Congress is eager to authorize more judges, but when it comes to paying for them, the members of Congress do not think that is a very high priority.

In perhaps the strongest formulation, Judge Frank M. Coffin, then chair of the U.S. Judicial Conference Committee on the Judicial Branch (and a former legislator), remarked a decade ago: "The judiciary and Congress not only do not communicate with each other on their most basic concerns; they do not know how they may properly do so. . . . The condition we describe, if not an acute crisis, is that of a chronic, debilitating fever." Judge James L. Buckley (a former U.S. senator) similarly observed: "It is self-evident that these two institutions will impact on one another in a dozen different ways. Yet, for whatever strange reason, each institution tends to be miserably unacquainted with the problems faced by the other."

Abner J. Mikva, the former chief judge of the U.S. Court of Appeals for the D.C. Circuit (and once a member of Congress), commented that the difficulty "as often as not is the unawareness that the legislative branch and the judicial branch have of each other's game rules." Judge Deanell Reece Tacha, another chair of the U.S. Judicial Conference Committee on the Judicial Branch, lamented that "the complexities of the law-making and law-interpreting tasks in the third century of this republic cry out for systematic dialogue between those who make and those who interpret legislation." Justice Shirley S. Abrahamson of the Wisconsin Supreme Court and her coauthor described the working relationship of judges and legislators as "atonal, if not dissonant."

Robert W. Kastenmeier, longtime chair of the Subcommittee on Courts, Civil Liberties, and Administration of Justice of the House Judiciary Committee, and his counsel, Michael J. Remington, wrote that "as participants in the legislative process, we are struck by the simple fact that few in Congress know much about or pay attention to the third branch of government." For his part, Senator Joseph R. Biden Jr., Democrat of Delaware, then chair of the Judiciary Committee, called for a change in "the rhetoric we [judges and legislators] use with one another publicly and privately." He continued, "Some of . . . you [judges] find [it] offensive, and you should, as you read about congressmen and senators who find it politically expedient to use judges, their salaries, their independence, their life tenure, all of which are important, . . . for their own political gain. . . . Some of us [find it offensive when we] read . . . [in] return comments about 'those politicians'. . . . We both have to start talking with one another in ways differently than we have the last ten years." Senator Charles E. Grassley, Republican of Iowa, wondered if "maybe there is an arrogance about judges" who objected to a questionnaire he disseminated to the judiciary delving into its work ways.

These commentaries suggest that issues of communication and understanding are well worth exploring. . . .

Opening Doors

Communication between courts and Congress will not eliminate tensions rooted in different institutional roles. But, at the very least, it can break down those groundless fears and suspicions that distance spawns. The multiplicity of circumstances and the interplay of a host of variables affecting judicial-congressional interaction suggest the peril of prescribing absolute rules governing communication—a series of "thou shalts" and "thou shalt nots." Rather than promulgate strict rules, the better course may be to weigh the advantages and disadvantages, costs and benefits, of different types of communication and to monitor and assess the effects of such exchanges. The presumption in favor of expanding contact under appropriate conditions and continuing discussion among judges and legislators could have the practical effect of promoting not only the good faith upon which governance depends, but also the effective workings of government the Founders envisioned.

WHAT LIES AHEAD

In Jonathan Swift's *A Tale of a Tub*, a father gives each of his sons a new coat. "You are to understand," instructed the father, "that these coats have two virtues contained in them: one is, that with good wearing, they will last you fresh and sound as long as you live; the other is, that they will grow in the same proportion with your bodies, lengthening and widening of themselves, so as to be always fit." The Constitution, our coat of governance, has served us as well; it has protected and nurtured the body politic, even as we have stretched and grown. It has weathered storms and proved remarkably resilient against the elements. The court-Congress weave, of supple tension, has been a critical part of the cloth. The climate today is challenging: expanding caseloads under budgetary constraints, federalization of civil and criminal laws, and heightened scrutiny of the administration of justice and of judges. The task at hand is to understand the sources of the strain so that the weavers can attend to the fabric of court-Congress relations.

Sources of the Strain

In the normal course, as Congress enacts laws to address societal problems, it is inevitable that such legislation will result in court cases. Through the federalization of criminal and civil justice, the jurisdiction and caseload of the federal courts will expand. Vesting the judiciary with added responsibilities, without a concomitant increase in resources, could hinder the administration of justice.

At the same time that Congress expects the judiciary to do more, its scrutiny of the courts is likely to become more intense. Not so many years ago, the judicial budget was considerably less than that of the Congress; today, it is greater (more than $3 billion), although still less than one-fifth of 1 percent of the entire federal budget. In an era when Congress is under pressure to tighten its own belt, and less funding is available for government programs generally, it is not surprising that how the judiciary manages its affairs would be more closely examined. Congressional review is likely to take the form of greater oversight, especially where the costs are highly visible and measurable (courthouse construction and space use generally are thus prime targets).

Moreover, Congress will insist that the courts be ever more attentive to cost containment and more accountable to the legislative branch.

A related source of strain has to do with judicial salaries, which as of early 1997 had not been adjusted for inflation since 1993. Some members of Congress have indicated that they will not support such adjustments for themselves or for judges until the federal budget is in balance. But the judiciary's concern is that a continuing erosion in compensation will affect the capacity to attract and retain judges of the highest quality. . . .

Because the judiciary is an important participant in the shaping of public policy, the congressional presence will continue to be felt in the judicial confirmation process. In major cases affecting the interpretation of statutes, Congress will be watchful as well. On matters of policy, such as criminal justice, the legislative branch will actively monitor court decisions; for example, Congress will continue to press on with efforts to contain discretion in sentencing and prison litigation.

Efforts to strip the courts of jurisdiction are not new, as Walter F. Murphy's account of the 1950s reminds us. Such attempts have recurred throughout the ensuing decades; indeed, in 1982, two opponents of such attempts, Senator Daniel Patrick Moynihan and Richard K. Eaton, warned of a "constitutional crisis." Evidence that Congress will from time to time seek to limit access to federal courts is recent legislation restricting suits by death row inmates, class actions in certain immigration cases, and class action litigation funded by the Legal Services Corporation. Judicial reaction to such measures is likely to vary; in the case of changes in habeas suits, for example, the legislation generated both support and opposition among individual judges.

Some legislators' criticism of the judiciary for the decisions of individual judges, long a part of the political landscape, will almost certainly continue. But the irony today is that some of the attacks are just as likely to emanate from those dissatisfied with the way judges are discharging their *expanded* duties in such sensitive areas as crime and drugs. For defenders of the judiciary, such expressions risk making the courts a political football. In this view, Congress, unable to definitively address a problem itself, passes ambiguous legislation, leaves it to the judiciary to interpret, and then blames judges for the decisions made. The upshot of these criticisms may well be more frequent calls for judicial discipline or even impeachment.

Judicial Responses

For the judiciary, greater responsibilities will lead to an intensification of the ongoing efforts to develop procedures for the more efficient disposition of large numbers of cases. . . .

Expanding jurisdiction and judgeships will intensify debate about such other fundamental issues as the role of the federal courts and the number of federal judges. The federal courts are part of a dual system, in which responsibility is shared with the state courts. Although the federal and state courts are not entirely separate and independent, judicial federalism has historically meant that each would have a distinct character. The federal courts would be of limited jurisdiction in keeping with the "constitutional principle that the national government is a government of delegated powers in which the residual power remains in the states." . . .

Today, the federal judiciary's concern with the impact of federalization has led both Chief Justice William H. Rehnquist and the Long Range Planning Committee of the Judicial Conference to reiterate the courts' support for limited jurisdiction and "against further expansion of federal jurisdiction into areas which have been previously the province of state courts enforcing state laws." . . .

Shared Responsibility

If one thing is certain, it is that the judiciary cannot unilaterally resolve any of these issues; the role of Congress is pivotal. The constitutional Framers intended that the branches of government, each with differing perspectives, would through "separateness but interdependence" contribute to sound decisions. For the judiciary and Congress, this means a shared appreciation of each other's obligations, of respect for judicial independence and the legitimate prerogatives of the legislative branch.

Judicial independence is a term not easily defined. Indeed, the task for those who would seek to preserve it will be to define the term so that it is more than an abstract ideal. The challenge is to devise a framework so that the constituent elements of judicial independence can be concretely identified and applied. At a basic level, judicial independence means that judges can make decisions free of political retribution; that resources exist to ensure that justice can be dispensed fairly and efficiently; and that within reasonable limits and with appropriate accountability, the judiciary has the discretion to manage its own affairs. The term thus encompasses at least two components: that of "decisional" autonomy in adjudicating cases, and "institutional" autonomy in administering the work of the judiciary as a coequal branch.

From the judges' perspective, the challenge for the Congress is to express disagreement without chilling judicial independence; to engage in oversight without micromanagement, as both Senator Paul Simon and Chief Justice Rehnquist have put it. Reasoned criticisms of judicial decisions and of the administration of justice are useful and valuable; but excesses in rhetoric and political attacks can heighten insecurity about legislative intentions.

Appreciation of the legislative role recognizes that Congress has important responsibility—constitutionally assigned—in such matters as appropriations, compensation, confirmation, structure, and procedure. Legislative oversight of the courts can help ensure judicial accountability. Moreover, as public officials sworn to uphold the Constitution, senators and representatives have an independent duty to interpret it.

From the congressional perspective, the challenge for the judiciary is to understand that not every disagreement is a threat to independence; that inquiry into how the judiciary spends its money or time is not a hostile act. In a strong defense of an independent judiciary, Representative Eleanor Holmes Norton, Democrat of the District of Columbia, remarked: "Some people would say . . . you are in the Congress. When you ask [judges] questions, people may think you are trying to intimidate them.

I do not think so. I think that if we are appropriating article 3 courts every year that we have a right to know something about their activities. I leave a very large space for criticism and inquiry."

The courts probably can lessen their concerns about congressional micromanagement to the extent they continue to find ways to strengthen internal mechanisms of accountability. Judge Michael M. Mihm, a member of the executive committee of the Judicial Conference, commented: "I think Congress has every right to very carefully scrutinize everything that we do, from our purchasing processes, to personnel, to the question of what work we're performing. . . . I think most people in the judiciary would accept, without question, that almost everything we do can be done more efficiently, and at lower cost." Chief Judge Richard S. Arnold, the chair of the budget committee of the Judicial Conference, put the issue in context:

> We have seen in the last few years a great increase in the interest level of Congress in the details of our operations, and that poses an opportunity and a problem. The opportunity is for us judges to realize that we work for the people, just as the members of Congress do, and if somebody, some taxpayer, even a taxpayer who's a member of Congress, wants to know what we are doing, they have a right to know. By the same token, there can be instances in which congressional interest becomes excessive. We hope that does not occur, and I have to say that in the time I've been budget chair I have never had an experience where some member of Congress has said to me, "We're not going to give you your money this year because we don't like your decisions."

Congress recognized the importance of funding the judiciary when, amidst a budget stalemate that led to government shutdowns, it appropriated funds for the entire fiscal year. Such is the degree of expansion in the judicial workload that over time such increases have not kept pace with the courts' stated needs.

"Still a Good Coat"

The full use of the methods of communication discussed earlier . . . could do much to facilitate a dialogue between the courts and the Congress. Through the coordinated efforts of the various parts of the federal judiciary—the Judicial Conference, the Administrative Office of the U.S. Courts, the Federal Judicial Center—and of the Congress, deliberative discussions about the challenges facing the judiciary will continue. But differences in perspectives, grounded in differing institutional responsibilities and priorities, will also persist. There are likely to be continued disagreements about federalization, the role and size of the judiciary, resources, and congressional oversight.

Ultimately, the vitality of judicial-congressional relations, indeed, of the first and third branches themselves, depends upon the understanding and support of the citizenry. If, as Learned Hand once declared, "liberty lies in the hearts of men and women," it thrives when the people dedicate their energies to the institutions of democratic life. And thus it behooves educators, political leaders, community groups, and the media to engage the public in a continuing discussion about the need to maintain effective government and to work to sustain its structures. We owe it to our students, from their earliest years, to teach them about the link between civic responsibility and government. The task is greater than ever in an era of increasing public doubts about the efficacy of our institutions.

And, as part of that discussion, we would do well to remind ourselves that what Benjamin N. Cardozo wrote about the common law applies to the fabric of court-Congress relations: "Even now with all the wear and tear, it is still a good coat. . . . Let us make it over as reverently as our fathers [and mothers] made it for us, and hand it down to our descendants." That we can do if we recognize that even the sturdiest coat has threads in danger of unraveling, but with proper attention and goodwill the tailors of governance can preserve it for the generations to come.

Ideally, the Supreme Court is the final arbiter of the constitutional and statutory issues it addresses. In reality, however, as the following selection makes clear, a Supreme Court decision is only the starting point in a long and complicated process of policymaking.

Lawrence Baum is a political scientist who writes about the Supreme Court.

He argues in the following selection:

1. The Supreme Court is political because its power to make important decisions inevitably draws it into a political vortex. The litigation that ends up in the Supreme Court reflects politics by other means. The politicization of the confirmation process also reflects the political power of the courts.
2. Courts make public policy through legal interpretation of constitutional and statutory law.
3. The relatively small number of cases the Supreme Court decides, judicial self-restraint, and the policymaking power of other governmental branches limit judicial power.
4. Another limit on the Supreme Court's power is the need for implementation of its decisions. Implementation is an imperfect process that can dilute a Supreme Court decision. Difficulties in achieving desegregation of public education after *Brown v. Board of Education* in 1954 illustrate the implementation problem. The failure of police, prosecutors, and even judges to carry out *Miranda* warnings also illustrates how an unambiguous Supreme Court decision is circumvented.

18

Lawrence Baum

A Perspective on the Court

★★★

The Court in Law and Politics

The Supreme Court as a Legal Institution. The Supreme Court is, first of all, a court—the highest court in the federal judicial system. Like other courts, it has a specified *jurisdiction*, the power to hear and decide particular kinds of cases. And, like other courts, it can decide legal issues only in those cases that are brought to it. Although the Supreme Court differs from every other court in the United States, its behavior and its position in the political system are influenced by the fact that it *is* a court.

Perhaps most important, the Supreme Court makes decisions within a legal framework. While Congress simply writes new law, the policy choices that the Court faces are framed as interpretations of existing law. In this respect the Court operates within a constraint from which legislators are free.

In another respect, however, the Supreme Court's identity as a court reduces the constraints on it. The widespread belief that courts should be insulated from the political process has given the Court a certain degree of actual insulation. The lifetime appointments of Supreme Court justices allow them some freedom from concerns about approval by political leaders and voters. Justices usually stay out of partisan politics, because open involvement in partisan activity is perceived as inappropriate. And because direct contact between lobbyists and justices is generally deemed unacceptable, interest group activity in the Court is basically restricted to the formal channels of legal argument.

The Supreme Court as a Political Institution. The insulation of the Supreme Court from politics should not be exaggerated. People sometimes speak of courts as if they are, or at least ought to be, "nonpolitical." In a literal sense, of course, this is impossible: as part of government, courts are political institutions by definition. What people really mean when they refer to courts as nonpolitical is that courts are separate from the political process and that their decisions are unaffected by nonlegal considerations. This is also impossible—for courts in general and certainly for the Supreme Court.

The Court is political chiefly because it makes important decisions on major issues; people care about those decisions and want to influence them. As a result, appointments to the Court are frequently the subject of political battles. Similarly, interest groups bring cases and present arguments to the Court in an effort to affect what it does. Because members of Congress pay attention to the Court's decisions and hold powers over the Court, the justices may take Congress into account when they decide cases. And their own political values affect the votes they cast and the opinions they write in the Court's decisions.

Thus the Supreme Court should be viewed as both a legal institution and a political institution. What it does and how it operates are influenced by both the political process and the legal system. This ambiguous position makes the Court more complex in some ways than most political institutions; it also makes the Court an interesting case study in political behavior.

The Court as a Policy Maker

This [reading] is concerned with the Supreme Court in general, but I give particular emphasis to the Court's role in the making of public policy—the authoritative rules by which government institutions seek to influence the operation of government and to shape society as a whole. Legislation to provide subsidies for wheat farmers, a judge's ruling in an auto accident case, and a Supreme Court decision laying down rules to govern police procedure are all examples of public policy. The Court may be viewed as part of a policy-making system that includes lower courts as well as the other branches of government.

Policy Making through Legal Interpretation. As I have noted, the Supreme Court makes public policy by interpreting provisions of law. Issues of public policy come to the Court in the form of legal questions that the Court is empowered to resolve. In this respect the Court's policy making differs fundamentally in form from that of Congress.

The Court does not face legal questions in the abstract. Rather, it addresses these questions in the process of settling specific controversies between parties (sometimes called litigants) that bring cases to it. In a sense, then, every decision by the Court has three aspects: it is a judgment about the specific dispute brought to it, an interpretation of the legal issues in that dispute, and a position on the policy questions that are raised by the legal issues.

These three aspects can be illustrated with the Court's decision in a 1996 case, *Board of County Commissioners v. Umbehr*. Keen Umbehr, owner of a waste hauling business, held a contract with a Kansas county to dispose of solid waste. Umbehr strongly criticized the county governing board at its meetings and in local newspapers, and he once ran unsuccessfully for a seat on the Board. In 1991 the Board voted to terminate his contract with the county. A year later he sued the Board in federal court, claiming that it had terminated his contract in retaliation for his criticism in violation of his free speech rights under the First and Fourteenth Amendments to the Constitution. The federal district court in Kansas held that as an independent contractor, Umbehr did not have the same free speech rights that a government employee possesses; on that basis, the court ruled that his claim against the Board need not be considered. The court of appeals for the Tenth Circuit reversed the district court's decision. The Supreme Court accepted the Board's petition to hear the case, and it reached a decision.

With regard to the specific dispute in the case, the Court affirmed the court of appeals decision and sent the case back—*remanded* it—to that court for further action. That action likely would be a further remand to the district court for the trial that Umbehr originally had been denied. He might ultimately win or lose the case, but the Supreme Court's decision meant that he had a chance to win.

With regard to the legal issue in the *Umbehr* case, the Court held that the First and Fourteenth Amendments protected contractors from government retaliation for exercise of their free speech rights, though that protection had to be balanced against the interests of a government body that makes a contract. That rule became applicable to any other cases in which contractors alleged that their contracts had been terminated in retaliation for what they said or wrote.

Finally, the *Umbehr* decision constituted a significant expansion of free speech rights. In recent years the Court has taken a mixed position in cases involving freedom of expression, interpreting those rights broadly in some decisions but adopting narrower interpretations in others. Its protection of the rights of government contractors shifted the balance a little in favor of a broad reading of the First Amendment, though future decisions would tell more about where the current Court draws the line between free speech and government interests that may weigh against it.

The Court's Significance in Policy Making. Through its individual decisions and lines of decisions, the Supreme Court contributes a great deal to government policy on a variety of important issues. The Court's assumption of this role has been facilitated by several circumstances. For one thing, as the French observer Alexis de Tocqueville noted more than a century ago, "scarcely any political question arises in the United States that is not resolved, sooner or later, into a judicial question." One reason that policy disputes tend to reach the courts is the existence of a written Constitution whose provisions offer a basis for challenging the legality of government actions.

Because so many policy questions come to the courts, the Supreme Court has the opportunity to rule on a large number that are significant. Moreover, during much of its history the Court has welcomed that opportunity, first insisting on its supremacy as legal arbiter and later making frequent use of its chances to rule on major issues. By doing so, it has made itself the subject of considerable criticism, not only for its specific rulings but for its general activism as a policy maker. The term *judicial activism* is sometimes used to indicate disapproval. "Basically," according to Joel Grossman, "judicial activism is what the other guy does that you don't like." Negative connotations aside, the term can have many meanings. But its key element is that a court makes significant changes in public policy, particularly in policies established by other institutions. In this sense the Court has engaged in a great deal of activism, and not everyone agrees that its activism is legitimate or wise.

At the same time, the Court's role in policy making is limited by three conditions. First, the Court can do only so much with the relatively few decisions that it makes in a year. In the 1993 through 1996 terms, the Court issued decisions with full opinions in fewer than 90 cases each year. In deciding such a small number of cases, the Court addresses only a select group of policy issues. Inevitably, there are whole fields of policy that it barely touches. Even in the areas in which the Court does act, it can deal with only a limited number of the issues that exist at a given time.

Second, the Court exercises considerable judicial restraint, which is the avoidance of activism. This behavior stems in part from judges' training in a legal tradition that emphasizes the value of restraint, and in part from a desire to avoid controversy and attacks on the Court. Judicial restraint is reflected in the Court's refusal to hear some important and controversial cases, such as the legal challenges brought against U.S. participation in the war in Vietnam. It is also reflected in the frequent—though not consistent—practice of deciding cases on relatively narrow grounds where possible.

Third, even a highly activist Court is limited in its impact by the actions of other policy makers. The Court is seldom the final government institution to deal with the policy issues that it addresses. Its rulings usually must be implemented by lower court judges and administrators, who often retain considerable discretion about how they will put a Supreme Court decision into effect. The impact of a decision concerning police searches for evidence depends largely on how police officers react to it. Congress and the president influence the ways in which the Court's decisions are carried out, and they can overcome its interpretations of federal statutes simply by amending those statutes. In this way Congress has superseded several of the Court's interpretations of civil rights law in recent years. There may be a considerable difference between what the Court rules on an issue and the public policy that ultimately results from government actions on that issue.

For these reasons, those who see the Supreme Court as the dominant force in the U.S. government almost surely are wrong. But if not dominant, the Court is a very important policy maker. Certainly the extent of its role is extraordinary for a court. . . .

The Supreme Court is the highest interpreter of federal law, and people often think of it as the final arbiter of the issues it addresses. But . . . this image of the Court is misleading. It is more useful to think of the Court as one of many institutions that participate in a fluid process of policy making.

Often the Court's decisions decide only one aspect of an issue or offer general guidelines that other policy makers have to fill in. Even when the Court seems to rule decisively on an issue, other institutions may limit the impact of that ruling or negate it altogether. Congress and the president can write a new statute to override the Court's interpretation of an old one. Congress and the states can amend the Constitution to overcome a constitutional decision. Judges and administrators can choose not to carry out a Supreme Court policy fully. And the Court's ultimate impact on society is mediated by the actions of other institutions in and out of government. The Court may influence the strength of the labor movement or the status of women, but so do many other forces—including some that are likely to be far more powerful than the Court. . . .

IMPLEMENTATION OF SUPREME COURT POLICIES

More important than the outcome of a case for the litigants are the broader effects of the legal rules that the Supreme Court lays down in its opinions. Like statutes or presidential orders, these rules have to be implemented—put into effect—by administrators and judges. Judges' task is to apply the Court's interpretations of law whenever they are relevant to a case. For administrators, ranging from cabinet officers to police officers, the task is to follow the requirements that the Court creates for the way they carry out their work.

The responses of judges and administrators to the Court's rules of law can be examined in terms of their compliance and noncompliance with these rules. But the Court's decisions may evoke responses ranging from complete rejection to enthusiastic acceptance and extension, and the concept of compliance does not capture all the possible variations.

The Effectiveness of Implementation

Implementation is an imperfect process. People sometimes assume that when Congress enacts a statute, other policy makers automatically do what is required to make the statute effective. In reality, implementation of statutes is far from automatic. Indeed, congressional policies frequently fail to achieve their objectives because they are carried out poorly. The same is true of Supreme Court decisions: judges and administrators do not necessarily carry them out fully, so they may create a gap between the Court's goals and the actual results.

This does not mean that implementation always works badly. Any policy maker is likely to have a mixed record in getting its policies put into effect. This certainly is true of the Supreme Court. Some of the Court's decisions are carried out more effectively than others, and specific decisions are implemented better in some places or situations than in others.

On the whole, the Court seems to achieve considerable success in getting its policies carried out by lower courts, especially appellate courts. When the Court takes a new doctrinal position, judges generally do their best to follow its lead. One example is *Employment Division v. Smith* (1990), in which the Court narrowed constitutional protection for religious practices that conflict with federal and state laws. After the Court's decision, lower courts ruled in favor of those practices considerably less often. Even on issues as controversial as abortion, judges usually apply the Supreme Court's rulings as well as they can.

Certainly outright refusal to follow the Court's doctrines is unusual. . . . More common is what might be called implicit noncompliance, in which a court purports to follow the Supreme Court's lead but actually evades the implications of the Court's rulings for the case in question. To take one example, lower federal courts have engaged in some implicit noncompliance with the Court's decisions on the administration of public welfare programs.

Implementation problems seem more common among administrators than among judges. Problems at the federal level are illustrated by the long period in which the Patent and Trademark Office failed to carry out Supreme Court rulings on the standards to be used in awarding or denying patents to applicants. At the state level, major examples include . . . school desegregation and police investigations, to be considered shortly.

There have also been widespread implementation problems on procedural matters in state trial courts, which resemble administrative agencies in some respects.

Many courts have complied only in part with several of the Warren and Burger Court decisions on criminal procedure, such as the ruling that juvenile defendants are entitled to basic procedural rights. The Court's decision in *Tate v. Short* (1971), holding that an indigent person cannot be sentenced to jail because of inability to pay a fine, has been subverted by judges who fail to inquire into a defendant's ability to pay.

Two Case Studies of Implementation

School Desegregation. Before the Supreme Court's 1954 decision in *Brown v. Board of Education*, separate schools for black and white students existed throughout the Deep South and in most districts of border states such as Oklahoma and Maryland. The Court's decision required that these dual school systems be eliminated. Full desegregation in the border states took time, but considerable compliance with the Court's ruling came within a few years. In contrast, policies in the Deep South changed very slowly. As late as 1964-1965, there was no Deep South state in which even 10 percent of the black students went to school with any white students—a minimal definition of desegregation. This resistance requires a closer look.

Judges and school officials in the Deep South responded to the *Brown* decision in an atmosphere hostile to desegregation. Visible opinion among white citizens was strongly opposed to desegregation; the opinion of black citizens was far less important because a large proportion of them were prevented from voting. Throughout the South, public officials encouraged resistance to the Supreme Court. In 1956, ninety-six southern members of Congress signed a "Southern Manifesto" that attacked the *Brown* decision. Governors and legislatures expressed a strong distaste for desegregation and took official action to prevent it. Governor Orval Faubus of Arkansas, for instance, intervened to block desegregation in Little Rock in 1957.

In this atmosphere school officials generally sought to maintain the status quo. Most administrators personally favored segregation and did everything possible to preserve it. Those administrators who wanted to comply with the Court's ruling were deterred from doing so by pressure from state officials and local citizens.

In places where the schools did not act on their own, parents could file suits in the federal district courts to challenge the continuation of segregated systems. In many districts no suits ever were brought; one reason was fear of retaliation.

Even where suits were brought, their success was hardly guaranteed. In its second decision in *Brown* in 1955, the Supreme Court gave federal district judges substantial freedom to determine the appropriate schedule for desegregation in a school district. Many judges themselves disagreed with the *Brown* decision, and all felt local pressure to proceed slowly if at all. As a result, few demanded speedy desegregation of the schools, and many supported school officials in resisting change. In Dallas, for instance, two district judges struggled mightily to maintain segregation.

Some judges did support the Court wholeheartedly, but they found it difficult to overcome delaying tactics by school administrators and elected officials. In New Orleans, Judge J. Skelly Wright worked hard to bring about desegregation, but the Louisiana governor and legislature fought his efforts with considerable success.

After a long period of resistance, officials in the southern states began to comply. In the second decade after *Brown*, most dual school systems in the South were finally dismantled. Although school segregation was not eliminated altogether, the proportion of black students attending school with whites increased tremendously, as shown in the Table.

The initial and key impetus for this change came from Congress. The Civil Rights Act of 1964 allowed federal funds to be withheld from institutions that practiced racial discrimination. In carrying out that provision, the Department of Health, Education, and Welfare required that schools make a "good-faith start" toward desegregation in order to receive federal aid. Faced with a threat to important financial interests, school officials felt some compulsion to go along. The 1964 act also allowed the Justice Department to bring desegregation suits where local residents were unable to do so, and this provision greatly increased the potential for litigation against school districts that refused to change their policies. This congressional action was reinforced by the Court, whose decisions in 1968 and 1969 demanded effective desegregation without further delay.

In the 1970s the Court turned its attention to the North. In many northern cities, a combination of housing patterns and school board policies had created a situation in which white and nonwhite students generally went to different schools. In a Denver case, *Keyes v. School District No. 1* (1973), the Court held that segregation caused by government in such cities violated the Fourteenth Amendment and required a remedy. In a series of decisions over the next decade, the Court spelled out rules with which to identify constitutional problems and to devise remedies for northern-style segregation.

On the whole, federal district judges in the North supported the Court more than their southern counterparts. Many were willing to order sweeping remedies for segregation in the face of strong local opposition to those remedies, particularly bus-

TABLE

Percentage of Black Elementary and Secondary Students Going to School with Any Whites, in Eleven Southern States, 1954–1973

School year	Percentage	School year	Percentage
1954–1955	0.001	1964–1965	2.25
1956–1957	0.14	1966–1967	15.9
1958–1959	0.13	1968–1969	32.0
1960–1961	0.16	1970–1971	85.6
1962–1963	0.45	1972–1973	91.3

Sources: Southern Education Reporting Service, *A Statistical Summary, State by State, of School Segregation-Desegregation in the Southern and Border Area from 1954 to the Present* (Nashville: Southern Education Reporting Service, 1967) (for 1954–1967); U.S. Bureau of the Census, *Statistical Abstract of the United States* (Washington, D.C.: Government Printing Office, 1971 and 1975) (for 1968–1973).

Note: The states are Alabama, Arkansas, Florida, Georgia, Louisiana, Mississippi, North Carolina, South Carolina, Tennessee, Texas, and Virginia.

ing. One judge ordered the imposition of higher property taxes to pay for school improvements that might facilitate desegregation in Kansas City. Another held a city in New York State and some of its council members in contempt for failing to approve new public housing for a similar purpose. Ironically, the Court found some of these remedies *too* sweeping.

Few northern school districts took significant steps to eliminate segregation until they were faced with a court order or pressure from federal administrators. For the most part, however, northern districts complied with desegregation orders rather than resisting. Compliance was increased by the willingness of some district judges to supervise school desegregation directly and closely.

Congress did not support northern desegregation. Beginning in 1968 it enacted several legal provisions to prohibit federal agencies from taking action to require school busing for desegregation, and it took some limited and ineffective steps to limit the issuance of busing orders by federal courts. Presidents differed in their use of litigation and financial pressure to support desegregation. The Reagan administration sought to restrict the scope of court-imposed remedies for segregation.

The record of implementation in school desegregation is complex. In the Deep South, the Court's decisions ultimately were implemented, but only with considerable help from the other two branches. In the border states, the Court achieved substantial change even before receiving outside assistance. In the North, the Court was able to bring about major changes in school practices despite some opposition from the other branches.

Police Investigation. The Warren Court imposed substantial procedural requirements on the police in two areas of criminal investigation, issuing a landmark decision in each. In search and seizure, *Mapp v. Ohio* (1961) extended to the states the "exclusionary rule," under which evidence illegally seized by the police cannot be used against a defendant in court. The *Mapp* decision thus provided an incentive for police to follow rules for legal searches that the Court established in other decisions. In the area of interrogation, *Miranda v. Arizona* (1966) required that suspects be given a series of warnings before police questioning if their statements were to be used as evidence. How have judges and police officers responded to those rules?

Lower court responses to *Mapp* and *Miranda* have been mixed. Some state supreme courts criticized the decisions and interpreted them narrowly. At the trial level, many judges who sympathize with the police are reluctant to exclude evidence from trials on the basis of Supreme Court rules. But some lower court judges have applied the Court's rulings vigorously.

While the basic rules of *Mapp* and *Miranda* remain standing, the Burger and Rehnquist Courts have narrowed their protections of suspects. Many lower courts have followed this new direction enthusiastically. But some state supreme courts that support the rulings of the 1960s have found a legitimate means to establish broader protections of procedural rights by declaring that rights denied by the Court under the U.S. Constitution are protected independently by state constitutions. The most important example concerns the Court's ruling in *United States v. Leon* (1984). In *Leon*, the Court held that evidence seized on the basis of a search warrant that had been improperly issued could be used in court if the officers engaging in the search had a "good faith" belief that the warrant was justified. At least nine state supreme courts have held that there is no good faith exception to the search rules in their own constitutions.

Inevitably, *Mapp* and *Miranda* were unpopular in the law enforcement community. Most police officers want maximum freedom for their investigative activities and resent court decisions that impose constraints on them. But they also want their evidence to stand up in court. The result has been a complex pattern of police behavior.

In the case of police questioning, it appears that literal compliance with the *Miranda* rules gradually has become standard practice. For instance, a scholar who observed nearly two hundred interrogations in three California cities in the 1990s found no instances in which detectives were required to provide *Miranda* warnings and failed to do so.

Despite the warnings, most suspects waive their rights and answer questions. One reason is that police officers structure the situation to induce a waiver. One common approach is exemplified by this statement from a detective to a suspect:

> In order for me to talk to you specifically about the injury with [the victim], I need to advise you of your rights. It's a formality. I'm sure you've watched television with the cop shows right and you hear them say their rights and so you can probably recite this better than I can, but it's something I need to do and we can get this out of the way before we talk about what's happened.

Officers sometimes continue to question suspects who have invoked their right to remain silent or to wait for a lawyer. Civil rights lawyers in 1995 presented an excerpt from a training manual used in Los Angeles and Santa Monica in which detectives were encouraged to undertake this practice. Although information obtained through such questioning cannot be admitted directly in court, under a 1971 Supreme Court decision that evidence can be used to impeach a defendant's testimony.

This noncompliance indicates that police officers find *Miranda* to be a hindrance despite the high rate of waivers by suspects. But the Court's ruling serves them well in other respects. Most suspects are still willing to talk, and departments that have suspects sign a form in which they waive their *Miranda* rights have a very strong defense against claims of improper practices.

By threatening that evidence would be excluded from court proceedings, *Mapp* gave police officers an incentive to comply with the body of judicial rules for searches and seizures. Prior to that time, according to one scholar, officers "*systematically* ignored the requirements of the Fourth Amendment because there was no reason to pay attention to it." In effect, then, *Mapp* was an effort to bring about a revolution in police practices.

In those terms, *Mapp* has been partially successful. It produced significant changes in police behavior, including a substantial increase in the use of search warrants in some departments. It appears, as we would expect, that *Mapp*'s effects have increased over time as police adjusted to it. Sociologist Jerome Skolnick observed police search practices in one large city in the 1960s and then in the 1980s, and he concluded that compliance with legal rules "improved significantly."

But compliance is far from perfect. Studies indicate that in a relatively small but significant number of cases, prosecutors drop charges because of illegally seized evidence or judges grant motions to suppress illegal evidence. Such actions occur most often in cases involving "search-intensive" crimes such as drug offenses. Some non-compliance is inadvertent, reflecting the complexity and ambiguity of the body of rules that police are asked to follow in searches and seizures. According to one judge, "the law is so muddy that the police can't find out what they are allowed to do even if they wanted to." Intentional noncompliance reflects the conflict that police officers often perceive: if they follow the applicable legal rules, they cannot obtain evidence that they see as critical. . . .

Summary. The Supreme Court's policies are implemented more effectively in some settings than in others. Judges generally carry out the Court's policies more fully than administrators because communication of decisions to judges is relatively good, most judges accord the Court considerable authority, and their self-interest is less likely to conflict with the implementation of decisions. For some of the same reasons, federal judges and administrators are probably better implementers of decisions than are their state counterparts. The Court's decisions are communicated to them more effectively, and its authority and sanctions affect them more directly.

On the whole, the Court's policies are implemented fairly well, but the gap between the rules of law that the Court establishes and the actions taken by judges and administrators is often considerable. To a degree, this gap reflects the Court's weaknesses as a policy maker, in that it can exert little control over the implementation process. Most important, the sanctions that it can apply to disobedient officials are relatively weak compared with those available to Congress or the president. But more striking than this difference is the similarity in the basic positions of Court, Congress, and president: each proclaims policies that have uncertain and often unhappy fates in the implementation process.

Conclusion: The Court, Public Policy, and Society

It is now possible to reach some general conclusions about the role of the Supreme Court as a public policy maker. . . . [T]hat role is fundamentally limited in some respects but still quite important.

The most obvious limitation on the Court's role is that it addresses only a small number of issues. In many policy areas, the Court rarely makes decisions. To take the most important example, the Court is a minor participant in the making of foreign policy. And it plays only a small part in many fields of significant judicial activity, such as contract law and family relations.

Even in its areas of specialization, the Court intervenes in the policy-making process only in limited ways. It makes decisions on a small sample of the issues that affect the rights of criminal defendants or freedom of expression. And the Court has been cautious about substituting its judgment for that of Congress and the president.

When the Court does intervene, its impact is often reduced by the actions of other institutions and individuals. A ruling that public schools must eliminate organized prayers does not guarantee that those observances will disappear. Efforts to broaden freedom of expression may be stymied by conditions in society that the Court cannot influence.

These limitations must be balanced against the Court's considerable strengths. Certainly a great many Supreme Court decisions have significant direct effects. Antitrust decisions determine whether companies can merge. School desegregation decisions determine the schools that students attend. Interpretations of the Voting Rights Act shape the course of local politics. The effects of capital punishment decisions are literally matters of life and death for some people.

The Court also helps to shape political and social change. Its partial opposition to government regulation of private business was ultimately overcome, but the Court slowed a fundamental change in the role of government. If *Roe v. Wade* was not as consequential as most people think, it *has* been the focus of a major national debate and struggle for more than two decades. The Court's decisions have not brought about racial equality, even in conjunction with other forces, but they have helped to spur changes in race relations.

As the examples of abortion and civil rights suggest, the Court is perhaps most important in creating conditions for action by others. . . .

In September of 1953, President Eisenhower nominated California Governor Earl Warren for the Chief Justiceship of the Supreme Court. Warren presided over a Supreme Court that made many controversial decisions from 1953–1969. Eisenhower thought that Warren would encourage judicial restraint, and was surprised to find that the Warren Court set out to be one of the most active in history with its decision in *Brown v. Board of Education* in 1954. The Warren Court continued after its *Brown* decision to seek actively the implementation of desegregation. In other areas it "nationalized" most of the provisions of the Bill of Rights, and shocked the nation in *Engel v. Vitale* (1962) when it held that prayers in public schools constituted an unconstitutional establishment of religion prohibited by the First and Fourteenth Amendments.

Chief Justice Warren confronted a sharply divided court in his first year. Liberal Justices Hugo Black and William O. Douglas opposed conservative Justices Felix Frankfurter and Robert Jackson. The four other Justices fluctuated between the two sides, making it difficult to achieve a majority—let alone unanimity—on such important issues as school desegregation, which the Court had taken up the year before Warren's appointment.

Warren's strong leadership eventually produced a unanimous decision in *Brown v. Board of Education*, holding that segregation in public education violated the Fourteenth Amendment's equal protection clause.

In the following selection, Chief Justice Warren describes the complicated dimensions of Supreme Court decisionmaking, and the political realities that can delay and impede implementation of Supreme Court decisions.

Chief Justice Warren's major conclusions about Supreme Court decisionmaking in the following selection are:

1. The Supreme Court seeks to maintain its credibility and the public's respect as it renders its often momentous opinions, as in *Brown v. Board of Education* in 1954.
2. Because of the importance of the *Brown* decision, the Court sought unanimity to enhance its credibility and prevent obstruction.
3. While opponents of the *Brown* decision delayed its implementation for many years, the case began a process to achieve equal rights in education and other fields.
4. The Supreme Court was the triggering force in ending segregation, but it needed the support of Presidents Kennedy and Johnson to implement its *Brown* decision.

19

Earl Warren

THE SUPREME COURT YEARS

★★★

The day of my induction as Chief Justice of the United States was for me at once the most awesome and the loneliest day of my public career. . . . I approached the high office with a reverential regard and with a profound recognition of my unpreparedness to assume its obligations in such an abrupt manner.

It was completely different from the other offices I had held. Before becoming a district attorney, I had had four years of grooming in that office and had definite ideas as to how it could be improved. On becoming state attorney general, I had many years' background of law enforcement locally, statewide, and nationally. I also knew county government and its relation to the state, and felt prepared to plunge into both the civil and criminal aspects of the job. As governor, my experience in these earlier positions had acquainted me with many of the problems of the state and with ways of tackling them in the best interest of the public. I also knew the personalities involved and the atmosphere in which I must work, and while I did not feel that I had answers to all the issues of growth and war that confronted me, I had a solid background of experience for approaching them.

With the Chief Justiceship, it was quite different. I was not acquainted with Washington or even with members of the Supreme Court.

. . . In a matter of hours after first coming to the Court, I learned more about the important cases previously mentioned to me by some of its members. They called for a full Court at the opening of the term and were lumped as the school desegregation cases.

There were five of them, from Kansas, Virginia, South Carolina, Delaware, and the District of Columbia. While the latter was in a somewhat different setting because it did not involve a state law, they all involved the so-called "separate but equal" doctrine as established by the Supreme Court in the case of *Plessy v. Ferguson* (1896). That decision declined to prohibit separate railroad accommodations for blacks and whites. It sought to justify racial segregation for almost every movement or gathering so long as "separate but equal" facilities were provided and became known as the "Jim Crow" doctrine. The central issue in each of these school cases was:

> Does segregation of children in public schools solely on the basis of race, even though the physical facilities and other "tangible" factors may be equal, deprive the children of the minority group of equal educational opportunities?

The five cases had been argued during the 1952 term before I came to the Court but had not been decided and had been put over for reargument, with a set of specific questions for discussion.

The United States Government . . . argued as a friend of the Court in favor of the positions maintained by the black students' lawyers. The first case was argued December 7, 1953, and it was easy to understand why the Court felt it necessary to have a full complement of justices. The case had been first argued exactly a year before, and failure to reach an agreement had caused resubmission for argument. This would normally indicate a difference of opinion within the Court but without any knowledge by the outside world as to the degree or nature of the disagreement. In these circumstances, there is always the danger of an evenly divided four-to-four Court if any member is absent or disqualifies himself, which means the decision of the Court below is affirmed without opinion from the Supreme Court and without any precedential value.

Some of the cases under review had been decided against the black petitioners in the lower courts on the authority of the much eroded "separate but equal" doctrine of *Plessy v. Ferguson.*

To have affirmed these cases without decision and with the mere statement that it was being done by an equally divided Court, if such had been the case, would have aborted the judicial process and resulted in public frustration and disrespect for the Court. The Court was thoroughly conscious of the importance of the decision to be arrived at and the impact it would have on the nation. With this went realization of the necessity for secrecy in our deliberations and for achieving unity, if possible.

. . . [Many] people wonder . . . why we do not have open hearings on our discussions as Congress is supposed to do. But if one stops to think about the consequences of open hearings, it is easy to understand the necessity for such secrecy. Many Court decisions have a strong impact on the economy of the nation, or at least some part of it. Because, as a rule, the Court deals only with the facts of the given case, such reverberations might not even be known to us in our complex and conglomerate economy. If premature word were to escape from the Conference Room as to the outcome of a case, dire results might follow. Those with the unauthorized information might prosper greatly while the uninformed might be bankrupted. Some of our cases radically affect the stock market. For instance, when the Court in an antitrust case dissolved the existing relationship between the giant General Motors and Du Pont companies, the stock market was markedly affected, and if someone had been allowed to have advance notice of the decision, he could have made an enormous but illegitimate profit at the expense of the uninformed. The same result could occur in the divestiture of large bank mergers or international conglomerates, as in recent federal actions involving the International Telephone and Telegraph Company. Although this security was a matter of constant concern, I can say with great relief that there never was a leak during my sixteen years on the Court. In fact, I only heard of one suspicion of a security breakdown in the years immediately preceding mine, and it turned out not to be a leak but rather a case of someone's correctly guessing the outcome of a case after psychoanalyzing the members of the Court from their past decisions in related matters.

. . . To return to our method of handling the school segregation cases, we were all impressed with their importance and the desirability of achieving unanimity if possible. Realizing that when a person once announces he has reached a conclusion it is more difficult for him to change his thinking, we decided that we would dispense with our usual custom of formally expressing our individual views at the first conference and would confine ourselves for a time to informal discussion of the briefs, the arguments made at the hearing, and our own independent research on each conference day, reserving our final opinions until the discussions were concluded.

We followed this plan until the following February, when it was agreed that we were ready to vote. On the first vote, we unanimously agreed that the "separate but equal" doctrine had no place in public education. The question then arose as to how this view should be written—as a *per curiam* (by the Court) or as a signed, individualized opinion. We decided that it would carry more force if done through a signed opinion, and, at the suggestion of some of the Justices, it was thought that it should bear the signature of the Chief Justice. I consented to this, and then the importance of secrecy was discussed. We agreed that only my law clerks should be involved, and that any writing between my office and those of the other Justices would be delivered to the Justices personally. This practice was followed throughout and this was the only time it was required in my years on the Court. It was not done because of suspicion of anyone, but because of the sensitiveness of the school segregation matter and the prying for inside information that surrounded the cases. It was thought wise to confine our communications to the fewest possible people as a matter of security. Headway being made in conference was discussed informally from time to time, and on occasion I would visit with Mr. Justice Jackson, who was confined to the hospital, to inform him of our progress. Finally, at our conference on May 15, we agreed to announce our opinion the following Monday, subject to the approval of Mr. Justice Jackson, who was still recuperating from a heart attack which had incapacitated him for some time. I went to the hospital early Monday morning, May 17, and showed the Justice a copy of the proposed opinion as it was to be released. He agreed to it, and to my alarm insisted on attending the Court that day in order to demonstrate our solidarity. I suggested that it was unnecessary, but he insisted, and was there at the appointed time.

It was a momentous courtroom event and, unlike many other such events, it has not lost that character to this day. . . .

There was another side to the coin in these five segregation cases, which all raised the same central issue and four of which are compendiously referred to as *Brown v. Board of Education of Topeka* (1954). In the *Brown* decision, we decided only that the practice of segregating children in public schools solely because of their race was unconstitutional. This left other questions to be answered. For instance, could plaintiffs bring court actions as *class* actions for all who were similarly situated or should persons actually joining in the action be entitled to relief only for themselves? What court should determine the decree in each case? For what reason could there or could there not be any delay in obeying the Court's mandate and to what extent? All such questions we continued until the next term, inviting the United States and all states affected by our decision to file briefs and argue if they desired to do so.

These cases, postponed because of the death of Mr. Justice Jackson, which left an eight-man Court, came on for argument from April 11 to 14, 1955, with the newly appointed Mr. Justice John M. Harlan in attendance.

. . . The principal arguments on this phase of the case, as well as in the original proceeding, were made by John W. Davis for the states and Thurgood Marshall, now an Associate Justice of the Supreme Court of the United States, for the plaintiffs' side. The arguments, for me at least, took a strange course. One might expect, as I did, that the lawyers representing black school children would appeal to the emotions of the Court based upon their many years of oppression, and that the states would hold to strictly legal matters. More nearly the opposite developed. Thurgood Marshall made no emotional appeal, and argued the legal issues in a rational manner as cold as steel. On the other hand, states' attorney Davis, a great advocate and orator, former Democratic candidate for the presidency of the United States, displayed a great deal of emotion, and on more than one occasion broke down and took a few moments to compose himself.

Again the Court was unanimous in its decision of May 31, 1955, reaffirming its earlier opinion of May 17, 1954, by asserting the fundamental principle that any kind of racial discrimination in public education is unconstitutional, and that all provisions of federal, state, or local law requiring or permitting such discrimination must yield to this principle. Recognizing that because full application of these constitutional principles might require solution of a wide variety of local school desegregation problems, school authorities were given the primary responsibility for elucidating, assessing, and solving such problems. However, it was stipulated that courts would ultimately have to consider whether the action of school authorities constituted implementation in good faith of the governing constitutional principles.

We discussed at great length in conference whether the Supreme Court should make the factual determinations in such cases or whether they should be left to the courts below, deciding finally to leave them to the latter, subject, of course, to our review, because they were getting closer to the problems involved, and were in a better position to engage meaningfully in the fact-finding process. As guidelines for them, we directed that neither local law nor custom should be permitted to interfere with the establishment of an integrated school system, and that the process of achieving it should be carried out with "all deliberate speed"—a phrase which has been much discussed by those who are of the opinion that desegregation has not proceeded with as much celerity as might have been expected. These people argued that the Supreme Court should merely have directed the school districts to admit Brown and the other plaintiffs to the schools to which they sought admission, in the belief this would have quickly ended the litigation. This theory, however, overlooks the complexity of our federal system, the time it takes controversial litigation to proceed through the hierarchy of courts to the Supreme Court, the fact that the administration of the public school system is a state and local function so long as it does not contravene constitutional principles, that each state has its own system with different relationships between state and local government and that the relationship can be changed at will by the state government if there should be a determination to bypass or defeat the decision of the Supreme Court. Evidence that such evasion would occur came immediately in some of the resolutions and laws initiated by certain states. In this, they were encouraged by the so-called Southern Manifesto, signed by over a hundred Southern representatives and senators in the Congress of the United States. It urged all such states to defy the Supreme Court decision as being against their way of life and their "good" race relations, and to use "all lawful means" to make the decision ineffective. So reinforcing was this Manifesto to Southern defiance that the doctrine of "Nullification"—first advanced by John C. Calhoun of South Carolina, discredited more than a century before and made forever inapplicable by the Civil War Amendments—was revived by Southern governors, legislators, and candidates there for public office. The doctrine, in simple terms, argued that states have the right to declare null and void and to set aside in practice any law of the federal government which violates their voluntary compact embodied in the United States Constitution. The doctrine, of course, did not prevail, but the delay and bitterness occasioned by it caused inestimable damage to the extension of equal rights to citizens of every race, color, or creed as mandated by the Fourteenth Amendment.

With courage drawn from this profession of faith in white supremacy by practically every Southern member of Congress, together with oft-repeated congressional speeches and statements to the effect that no nine honest men could possibly have come to the conclusion reached by the Court in *Brown* v. *Board of Education*, excited and racist-minded public officials and candidates for office proposed and enacted every obstacle they could devise to thwart the Court's decision. This was aggravated by the fact that no word of support for the decision emanated from the White House. The most that came from high officials in the Administration was to the effect that they could not be blamed for anything done to enforce desegregation in education because it was the Supreme Court, not the Administration, that determined desegregation to be the law, and the Executive Branch of the government is required to enforce the law as interpreted by the Supreme Court. Bernard Shanley, the personal counsel of the President, in an effort to allay Southern animosity against the Administration, was reported in the press to have said in a speech that the *Brown* case had set race relations in the South back by a quarter of a century. The aphorism (dear to the hearts of those who are insensitive to the rights of minority groups) that discrimination cannot be eliminated by laws, but only by the hearts of people, also emanated from the White House.

A few years later, Governor George Wallace was emboldened to stand at the entrance to the University of Alabama, and, in the face of the Deputy Attorney General of the United States, who had read to him the order of a United States district judge directing the university to admit a black student, shout in defiance, "Segregation in the past, segregation today, segregation forever."

The Court expected some resistance from the South. But I doubt if any of us expected as much as we got. Nor did I believe that there would develop in the Republican Party, which freed the slaves through the Civil War and the Thirteenth Amendment and granted them all the attributes of citizenship through the Fourteenth and Fifteen Amendments, a Southern strategy which had for its purpose a restriction of such rights in order to capture the electors of those states and achieve the presidency. I, for one, thought it would be wonderful if, by the time of the centennial of the Fourteenth Amendment (1968), the principle of desegregation in *Brown v. Board of Education* could be a reality throughout the land. And I still believe that much of our racial strife could have been avoided if President Eisenhower had at least observed that our country is dedicated to the principle that . . .

> We hold these Truths to be self-evident, that all Men are created equal, that they are endowed by their Creator with certain unalienable Rights, that among these are Life, Liberty and the Pursuit of Happiness . . . (Declaration of Independence)

With his popularity, if Eisenhower had said that black children were still being discriminated against long after the adoption of the Thirteenth, Fourteenth, and Fifteenth Amendments, that the Supreme Court of the land had now declared it unconstitutional to continue such cruel practices, and that it should be the duty of every good citizen to help rectify more than eighty years of wrongdoing by honoring that decision—if he had said something to this effect, we would have been relieved, in my opinion, of many of the racial problems which have continued to plague us. But he never even stated that he thought the decision was right until after he had left the White House.

I have always believed that President Eisenhower resented our decision in *Brown v. Board of Education* and its progeny. Influencing this belief, among other things, is an incident that occurred shortly before the opinion was announced. The President had a program for discussing problems with groups of people at occasional White House dinners. When the *Brown* case was under submission, he invited me to one of them. I wondered why I should be invited because the dinners were political in nature, and there was no place for me in such discussions. But one does not often decline an invitation from the President to the White House, and I accepted. There were several people present at this particular one. I was the ranking guest, and as such sat at the right of the President and within speaking distance of John W. Davis, the counsel for the segregation states. During the dinner, the President went to considerable lengths to tell me what a great man Mr. Davis was. At the conclusion of the meal, in accordance with custom, we filed out of the dining room to another room where coffee and an after-dinner drink were served. The President, of course, precedes, and on this occasion he took me by the arm, and, as we walked along, speaking of the Southern states in the segregation cases, he said, "These are not bad people. All they are concerned about is to see that their sweet little girls are not required to sit in school alongside some big overgrown Negroes."

Fortunately, by that time, others had filed into the room, so it was not necessary for me to reply. Shortly thereafter the *Brown* case was decided, and with it went our cordial relations. While Nina and I were occasionally invited to the White House after the decision for protocol reasons when some foreign dignitary was being entertained or were invited to some foreign embassy for a reciprocal honoring of the President, I can recall few conversations that went beyond a polite "Good evening, Mr. President" and "Good evening, Mr. Chief Justice."

Some Southern states, and Northern areas as well, have used every conceivable device to thwart the principle of the *Brown* case, and they have been successful in preventing full compliance or even that degree of compliance sufficient to create good will between the races. Because of these drawbacks, some people are of the belief that the Court's decree was a failure, but the fact is that real progress has been made. However, the tragedy of the situation is that because of the resistance die-hard segregationists have made, advances have come about only after torrid litigation or after federal legislation which has emphasized the unfairness of the white supremacy theory to the point that deep bitterness against whites is felt by all minority groups—blacks, Chicanos, Puerto Ricans, Asians, and American Indians. That, too, can be remedied whenever we all realize the importance of the Thirteenth, Fourteenth, and Fifteenth Amendments to the Constitution in granting absolute equality of citizenship to "*Everyone* born or naturalized in the United States . . ."

. . . Many people despair as to the integrative effectiveness of *Brown* v. *Board of Education* because it has not been a complete success. They fail to recognize the great impact it has made in educational and other fields and in its stimulation of Congress to legislate for equal rights.

All of the various segregation case decisions went hand-in-hand with the principle of *Brown* v. *Board of Education*. Those decisions related not only to blacks but equally to all racial groups that were discriminated against. In fact, I reported a case of jury discrimination against Mexican-Americans, now styled Chicanos, two weeks before the *Brown* case in *Hernandez* v. *Texas* (1954). In that case, the defendant had been convicted of murder over his protest that people of his class had been systematically excluded from jury service as far back as anyone could remember. Fourteen per cent of the population of the county had Latin names, yet the state stipulated that:

> . . . for the last twenty-five years there is no record of any person with a Mexican or Latin American surname having served on a jury commission, grand jury or petit jury in Jackson County.

The state contended that this and other acts of discrimination did not violate the Constitution because the Fourteenth Amendment bore only on the relationship between blacks and whites. We hold that it applied to "any delineated class" and reversed the conviction. And so it must go with any such cases. They apply to any class that is singled out for discrimination. Most of our cases have involved blacks, but that is because there are more of them; they are more widespread and have been the most discriminated against.

Tortuous as school desegregation has been, the effect the *Brown* case had on various apartheid practices was stupendous. The federal courts made meaningful many spin-offs from it and with minor exceptions those courts met every test in following the Supreme Court. I have no doubt that when history appraises this difficult era, the real heroes to emerge will be the federal district judges and the judges of the Circuit Courts of Appeals in the southern and border states. . . .

The reason I speak in such high praise of the Southern federal judges is that we of the Supreme Court merely *declared* the constitutional principle prohibiting segregation because of the race. We left those judges the job of *implementing* it in a region where three centuries of slavery and invidious segregation had case-hardened a way of life that permitted no deviation from the theory of white supremacy. District and circuit courts were the closest to the problem and knew the changes that could reasonably be made to accomplish the desired result. Faced with violent criticism in some places, they responded nobly. I have been told by some judges involved that on their visits home after some of their decisions, friends of many years, on seeing them approaching, would deliberately and obviously cross to the other side of the street to avoid greeting them. Not only they but their families were often humiliated in a variety of ways.

I recall one incident at a Judicial Council Meeting of the Fourth Circuit where the judges, in executive session, were reporting on conditions within their jurisdiction. One of the newly appointed district judges said, in substance, "After my decision in a recent school desegregation case, one of the statesmen of our region said in a public speech that, before having any evidence in the case, I sat down with the Negro plaintiffs and wrote the judgment which I ultimately rendered in their favor. Now, if I had done that, it was something for which I should be impeached. But, of course, I did no such thing. I am not asking this council to do anything in the matter, but you all have had more experience than I, and I would like to know if you have any advice for me."

There was silence for a few moments, and finally Judge Morris A. Soper of the Court of Appeals said, "It wouldn't make any difference to me whether the son-of-a-bitch is a statesman or not. I would seek him out and tell him in public that he is a goddamn liar."

That ended the matter peremptorily. I feel sure Judge Soper would have done just that. He was then over eighty years of age, and was as vigorous as a man many years his junior. He was from a former slave state which was completely conditioned to the Southern culture, as was the younger judge who asked the question, and it was difficult for him personally to accept some of the changes brought about by the *Brown* decision. On the other hand, as a federal judge, he accepted the legal interpretation of the Supreme Court. He did so without deviation, and I am sure the accusation that a judge conspired with one of the parties to prejudge a case was so abhorrent to him that he would not have let it go unchallenged.

Although the courts were the triggering force in destroying the old "separate but equal" fallacy, Presidents Kennedy and Johnson and the Congress are entitled to a fair share of credit for making meaningful the rights guaranteed by the Civil War Constitutional Amendments. In this connection, it must be remembered that in a number of early historic cases the Supreme Court narrowly interpreted those Amendments and eventually announced the "separate but equal" doctrine of *Plessy* v. *Ferguson*. That was used to open the door to all manner of discriminations, without leaving an opportunity to prevent them. In 1957, Lyndon Johnson, then the majority leader of the Senate, sponsored and had passed the first Civil Rights Bill in many decades. It was not an omnibus bill, but it pointed the way toward the public accommodation and voting rights bills that were later sponsored by President Kennedy and carried on to passage by President Johnson after Kennedy's assassination. . . .

Chapter 5

The Separation of Church and State

Must Public Duty Replace Private Belief?

The Supreme Court has decried the Constitution's requirement of a wall of separation between church and state. The wall is not impenetrable. The Court held, in *Lemon v. Kurtzman,* 403 U.S. 602 (1971), that a congressional or state statute can survive the prohibitions of the First Amendment's establishment clause if it passes a three-pronged test: first, a statute "must have a secular legislative purpose; second, its principal or primary effect must be one that neither advances nor inhibits religion; finally, the statute must not foster 'an excessive government entanglement with religion.'" The Supreme Court in the *Lemon* test attempted to compromise constitutional requirements for the separation of church and state with political demands for various forms of state support for religions.

Ironically, the framers of the First Amendment's establishment and free exercise of religion clauses intended for them to prevent the establishment of a *national* religion. States were to be left free to establish their own religions and to restrict the free exercise of religions.

The Supreme Court "nationalized" the First Amendment free exercise clause in *Cantwell v. Connecticut* (1941) and the establishment clause in *Everson v. Board of Education* (1947), as part of the "liberty" protected by the Fourteenth Amendment's due process clause. Essentially, the Court found that liberty of expression included religious beliefs, which states could not abridge or advance without proving a compelling governmental interest. Constitutional doctrine prohibits governmental interference with religious pluralism. Government cannot "establish" one religion over another, nor promote a particular religion's beliefs.

The constitutional ideal of a religiously neutral government seems to be clear and un-challengeable. However, in the real political world religious organizations have always been part of the galaxy of special interests that make demands on governments to promote their causes. While the First Amendment protects religious beliefs as part of freedom of ex-pression, our political culture proclaims that religious beliefs should remain part of private, not public, discourse. Secular, not religious, concerns should dictate public policies.

The following selection is from a speech by former New York governor Mario Cuomo, once considered a leading candidate for the Democratic presidential nomina-tion. Cuomo presents his view of the connection between religion and politics. He argues that public officials who hold strong religious beliefs must respect the realities of the re-ligious and political pluralism of the broader community they serve.

Mario Cuomo was governor of New York from 1983–1994. He ran for governor after losing a race for mayor of New York City to Ed Koch in 1977. As governor he became a leading spokesman for the liberal core of the Democratic Party. He electrified Democratic delegates to the presidential nominating convention with his 1992 keynote speech. He debated running for the presidency in 1988 and 1992, but declined, citing his responsi-bilities as governor.

A devout Catholic, Cuomo argues in the following reading:

1. The constitutional separation between church and state does not require an ab-solute separation between religion and politics.
2. Politicians should continue to adhere to their religious beliefs, but must not impose them upon others. Above all, political leaders must uphold the Constitution and the freedoms it protects, which include religious freedom.
3. Religious values have an important place in public life, not as absolutes but as argu-ments for particular public policies. The separation of church and state must be pre-served, but religious beliefs and public life cannot and should not be separated.

20

Mario Cuomo

RELIGIOUS BELIEF AND PUBLIC MORALITY: A CATHOLIC GOVERNOR'S PERSPECTIVE

I would like to begin by drawing your attention to the title of this lecture: "Religious Belief and Public Morality: A Catholic Governor's Perspective." I was not invited to speak on church and state generally. Certainly not Mondale vs. Reagan. The subject assigned is difficult enough. I will not try to do more than I've been asked.

It's not easy to stay contained. Certainly, although everybody talks about a wall of separation between church and state, I've seen religious leaders scale that wall with all the dexterity of Olympic athletes. In fact, I've seen so many candidates in churches and synagogues that I think we should change election day from Tuesdays to Saturdays and Sundays.

I am honored by this invitation, but the record shows that I am not the first governor of New York to appear at an event involving Notre Dame. One of my great predecessors, Al Smith, went to the Army-Notre Dame football game each time it was played in New York.

His fellow Catholics expected Smith to sit with Notre Dame; protocol required him to sit with Army because it was the home team. Protocol prevailed. But not without Smith noting the dual demands on his affections. "I'll take my seat with Army," he said, "but I commend my soul to Notre Dame!"

Today I'm happy to have no such problem: Both my seat and my soul are with Notre Dame. And as long as Father McBrien doesn't invite me back to sit with him at the Notre Dame-St. John's basketball game, I'm confident my loyalties will remain undivided.

In a sense, it's a question of loyalty that Father McBrien has asked me here today to discuss. Specifically, must politics and religion in America divide our loyalties? Does the "separation between church and state" imply separation between religion and politics? Between morality and government? Are these different propositions? Even more specifically, what is the relationship of my Catholicism to my politics? Where does the one end and other begin? Or are the two divided at all? And if they're not, should they be?

Hard questions.

No wonder most of us in public life—at least until recently—preferred to stay away from them, heeding the biblical advice that if "hounded and pursued in one city," we should flee to another.

Now, however, I think that it is too late to flee. The questions are all around us, and answers are coming from every quarter. Some of them have been simplistic, most of them fragmentary and a few, spoken with a purely political intent, demagogic.

There has been confusion and compounding of confusion, a blurring of the issue, entangling it in personalities and election strategies instead of clarifying it for Catholics, as well as others.

Today I would like to try to help correct that.

I can offer you no final truths, complete and unchallengeable. But it's possible this one effort will provoke other efforts—both in support and contradiction of my position—that will help all of us understand our differences and perhaps even discover some basic agreement.

In the end, I'm convinced we will all benefit if suspicion is replaced by discussion, innuendo by dialogue; if the emphasis in our debate turns from a search for talismanic criteria and neat but simplistic answers to an honest—more intelligent—attempt at describing the role religion has in our public affairs and the limits placed on that role.

And if we do it right—if we're not afraid of the truth even when the truth is complex—this debate, by clarification, can bring relief to untold numbers of confused— even anguished—Catholics, as well as to many others who want only to make our already great democracy even stronger than it is.

I believe the recent discussion in my own state has already produced some clearer definition. In early summer an impression was created in some quarters that official church spokespeople would ask Catholics to vote for or against candidates on the basis of their political position on the abortion issue. I was one of those given that impression. Thanks to the dialogue that ensued over the summer—only partially reported by the media—we learned that the impression was not accurate.

Confusion had presented an opportunity for clarification, and we seized it. Now all of us are saying one thing—in chorus—reiterating the statement of the National Conference of Catholic Bishops that they will not "take positions for or against political candidates" and that their stand on specific issues would not be perceived "as an expression of political partisanship."

Of course the bishops will teach—they must—more and more vigorously and more and more extensively. But they have said they will not use the power of their position, and the great respect it receives from all Catholics, to give an imprimatur to individual politicians or parties.

Not that they couldn't if they wished to—some religious leaders do; some are doing it at this very moment.

Not that it would be a sin if they did—God doesn't insist on political neutrality. But because it is the judgment of the bishops, and most of us Catholic lay people, that it is not wise for prelates and politicians to be tied too closely together.

I think that getting this consensus was an extraordinarily useful achievement.

Now, with some trepidation, I take up your gracious invitation to continue the dialogue in the hope that it will lead to still further clarification.

Let me begin this part of the effort by underscoring the obvious. I do not speak as a theologian; I do not have that competence. I do not speak as a philosopher; to suggest that I could would be to set a new record for false pride. I don't presume to speak as a "good" person except in the ontological sense of that word. My principal credential is that I serve in a position that forces me to wrestle with the problems you've come here to study and debate.

I am by training a lawyer and by practice a politician. Both professions make me suspect in many quarters, including among some of my own coreligionists. Maybe there's no better illustration of the public perception of how politicians unite their faith and their profession than the story they tell in New York about "Fishhooks" McCarthy, a famous Democratic leader on the Lower East Side and right-hand man to Al Smith.

"Fishhooks," the story goes, was devout. So devout that every morning on his way to Tammany Hall to do his political work, he stopped into St. James Church on Oliver Street in downtown Manhattan, fell on his knees and whispered the same simple prayer: "Oh, Lord, give me health and strength. We'll steal the rest."

"Fishhooks" notwithstanding, I speak here as a politician. And also as a Catholic, a lay person baptized and raised in the pre-Vatican II church, educated in Catholic schools, attached to the church first by birth, then by choice, now by love. An old-fashioned Catholic who sins, regrets, struggles, worries, gets confused and most of the time feels better after confession.

The Catholic Church is my spiritual home. My heart is there and my hope.

There is, of course, more to being a Catholic than a sense of spiritual and emotional resonance. Catholicism is a religion of the head as well as the heart, and to be a Catholic is to say "I believe" to the essential core of dogmas that distinguishes our faith.

The acceptance of this faith requires a lifelong struggle to understand it more fully and to live it more truly, to translate truth into experience, to practice as well as to believe.

That's not easy: Applying religious belief to everyday life often presents challenges.

It's always been that way. It certainly is today. The America of the late twentieth century is a consumer society, filled with endless distractions, where faith is more often dismissed than challenged, where the ethnic and other loyalties that once fastened us to our religion seem to be weakening.

In addition to all the weaknesses, dilemmas and temptations that impede every pilgrim's progress, the Catholic who holds political office in a pluralistic democracy—who is elected to serve Jews and Moslems, atheists and Protestants, as well as Catholics—bears special responsibility. He or she undertakes to help create conditions under which all can live with a maximum of dignity and with a reasonable degree of freedom; where everyone who chooses may hold beliefs different from specifically Catholic ones—sometimes contradictory to them; where the laws protect people's rights to divorce, to use birth control and even to choose abortion.

In fact, Catholic public officials take an oath to preserve the Constitution that guarantees this freedom. And they do so gladly. Not because they love what others do with their freedom, but because they realize that in guaranteeing freedom for all, they guarantee our right to be Catholics: our right to pray, to use the sacraments, to refuse birth control devices, to reject abortion, not to divorce and remarry if we believe it to be wrong.

The Catholic public official lives the political truth most Catholics through most of American history have accepted and insisted on: the truth that to assure our freedom we must allow others the same freedom, even if occasionally it produces conduct by them which we would hold to be sinful.

I protect my right to be a Catholic by preserving your right to believe as a Jew, a Protestant or nonbeliever, or as anything else you choose.

We know that the price of seeking to force our beliefs on others is that they might some day force theirs on us.

This freedom is the fundamental strength of our unique experiment in government. In the complex interplay of forces and considerations that go into the making of our laws and politics, its preservation must be a pervasive and dominant concern.

But insistence on freedom is easier to accept as a general proposition than in its applications to specific situations. There are other valid general principles firmly embedded in our Constitution which, operating at the same time, create interesting and occasionally troubling problems. Thus the same amendment of the Constitution that forbids the establishment of a state church affirms my legal right to argue that my religious belief would serve well as an article of our universal public morality. I may use the prescribed processes of government—the legislative and executive and judicial processes—to convince my fellow citizens—Jews and Protestants and Buddhists and nonbelievers—that what I propose is as beneficial for them as I believe it is for me; that it is not just parochial or narrowly sectarian but fulfills a human desire for order, peace, justice, kindness, love, any of the values most of us agree are desirable even apart from their specific religious base or context.

I am free to argue for a governmental policy for a nuclear freeze, not just to avoid sin but because I think my democracy should regard it as a desirable goal.

I can, if I wish, argue that the state should not fund the use of contraceptives devices, not because the pope demands it, but because I think that the whole community—for the good of the whole community—should not sever sex from an openness to the creation of life.

And surely I can, if so inclined, demand some kind of law against abortion, not because my bishops say it is wrong, but because I think that the whole community, regardless of its religious beliefs, should agree on the importance of protecting life—including life in the womb, which is at the very least potentially human and should not be extinguished casually.

No law prevents us from advocating any of these things: I am free to do so.

So are the bishops. And so is Rev. Falwell.

In fact, the Constitution guarantees my right to try. And theirs. And his.

But should I? Is it helpful? Is it essential to human dignity? Does it promote harmony and understanding? Or does it divide us so fundamentally that it threatens our ability to function as a pluralistic community?

When should I argue to make my religious value your morality? My rule of conduct your limitation?

What are the rules and policies that should influence the exercise of this right to argue and promote?

I believe I have a salvific mission as a Catholic. Does that mean I am in conscience required to do everything I can as governor to translate all my religious values into the laws and regulations of the state of New York or the United States? Or be branded a hypocrite if I don't?

As a Catholic, I respect the teaching authority of the bishops.

But must I agree with everything in the bishops' pastoral letter on peace and fight to include it in party platforms?

And will I have to do the same for the forthcoming pastoral on economics even if I am an unrepentant supply-sider?

Must I, having heard the pope renew the church's ban on birth control devices, veto the funding of contraceptive programs for non-Catholics or dissenting Catholics in my state?

I accept the church's teaching on abortion. Must I insist you do? By law? By denying you Medicaid funding? By a constitutional amendment? If so, which one? Would that be the best way to avoid abortions or to prevent them?

These are only some of the questions for Catholics. People with other religious beliefs face similar problems.

Let me try some answers.

Almost all Americans accept some religious values as a part of our public life. We are a religious people, many of us descended from ancestors who came here expressly to live their religious faith free from coercion or repression. But we are also a people of many religions, with no established church, who hold different beliefs on many matters.

Our public morality, then—moral standards we maintain for everyone, not just the ones we insist on in our private lives—depends on a consensus view of right and wrong. The values derived from religious belief will not—and should not—be accepted as part of the public morality unless they are shared by the pluralistic community at large, by consensus.

That values happen to be religious values does not deny them acceptability as a part of this consensus. But it does not require their acceptability, either.

The agnostics who joined the civil rights struggle were not deterred because that crusade's values had been nurtured and sustained in black Christian churches. Those on the political left are not perturbed today by the religious bias of the clergy and lay people who join them in the protest against the arms race and hunger and exploitation.

The arguments start when religious values are used to support positions which would impose on other people restrictions they find unacceptable. Some people do object to Catholic demands for an end to abortion, seeing it as a violation of the separation of church and state. And some others, while they have no compunction about invoking the authority of the Catholic bishops in regard to birth control and abortion, might reject out of hand their teaching on war and peace and social policy.

Ultimately, therefore, the question whether or not we admit religious values into our public affairs is too broad to yield a single answer. Yes, we create our public morality through consensus, and in this country that consensus reflects to some extent religious values of a great majority of Americans. But no, all religiously based values don't have an *a priori* place in our public morality.

The community must decide if what is being proposed would be better left to private discretion than public policy; whether it restricts freedoms and if so to what end, to whose benefit; whether it will produce a good or bad result; whether overall it will help the community or merely divide it.

The right answers to these questions can be elusive. Some of the wrong answers, on the other hand, are quite clear. For example, there are those who say there is a simple answer to all these questions; they say that by history and practice of our people we were intended to be—and should be—a Christian country in law.

But where would that leave the nonbelievers? And whose Christianity would be law, yours or mine?

This "Christian-nation" argument should concern—even frighten—two groups: non-Christians and thinking Christians.

I believe it does.

I think it's already apparent that a good part of this nation understands—if only instinctively—that anything which seems to suggest that God favors a political party or the establishment of a state church is wrong and dangerous.

Way down deep the American people are afraid of an entangling relationship between formal religions—or whole bodies of religious belief—and government. Apart from constitutional law and religious doctrine, there is a sense that tells us it's wrong to presume to speak for God or to claim God's sanction of our particular legislation and his rejection of all other positions. Most of us are offended when we see religion being trivialized by its appearance in political throwaway pamphlets.

The American people need no course in philosophy or political science or church history to know that God should not be made into a celestial party chairman.

To most of us, the manipulative invoking of religion to advance a politician or a party is frightening and divisive. The American people will tolerate religious leaders taking positions for or against candidates, although I think the Catholic bishops are right in avoiding that position. But the American people are leery about large religious organizations, powerful churches or synagogue groups engaging in such activities—again, not as a matter of law or doctrine, but because our innate wisdom and democratic instinct teach us these things are dangerous.

Today there are a number of issues involving life and death that raise questions of public morality. They are also questions of concern to most religions. Pick up a newspaper and you are almost certain to find a bitter controversy over any one of them: Baby Jane Doe, the right to die, artificial insemination, embryos in vitro, abortion, birth control—not to mention nuclear war and the shadow it throws across all existence.

Some of these issues touch the most intimate recesses of our lives, our roles as someone's mother or child or husband; some affect women in a unique way. But they are also public questions, for all of us.

Put aside what God expects—assume if you like there is no God—then the greatest thing still left to us is life. Even a radically secular world must struggle with the questions of when life begins, under what circumstances it can be ended, when it must be protected, by what authority; it too must decide what protection to extend to the helpless and the dying, to the aged and the unborn, to life in all its phases.

As a Catholic I have accepted certain answers as the right ones for myself and my family and because I have, they have influenced me in special ways, as Matilda's husband, as a father of five children, as a son who stood next to his own father's deathbed trying to decide if the tubes and needles no longer served a purpose.

As a governor, however, I am involved in defining policies that determine other people's rights in these same areas of life and death. Abortion is one of these issues, and while it is one issue among many, it is one of the most controversial and affects me in a special way as a Catholic public official.

So let me spend some time considering it.

I should start, I believe, by noting that the Catholic Church's actions with respect to the interplay of religious values and public policy make clear that there is no inflexible moral principle which determines what our political conduct should be. For example, on divorce and birth control, without changing its moral teaching the church abides the civil law as it now stands, thereby accepting—without making much of a point of it—that in our pluralistic society we are not required to insist that all our religious values be the law of the land.

Abortion is treated differently.

Of course there are differences both in degree and quality between abortion and some of the other religious positions the church takes: Abortion is a "matter of life and death," and degree counts. But the differences in approach reveal a truth, I think, that is not well enough perceived by Catholics and therefore still further complicates the process for us. That is, while we always owe our bishops' words respectful atten-tion and careful consideration, the question whether to engage the political system in a struggle to have it adopt certain articles of our belief as part of public morality is not a matter of doctrine: It is a matter of prudential political judgment.

Recently, Michael Novak put it succinctly: "Religious judgment and political judgment are both needed," he wrote. "But they are not identical."

My church and my conscience require me to believe certain things about divorce, birth control and abortion. My church does not order me—under pain of sin or expul-sion—to pursue my salvific mission according to a precisely defined political plan.

As a Catholic I accept the church's teaching authority. While in the past some Catholic theologians may appear to have disagreed on the morality of some abortions (it wasn't, I think, until 1869 that excommunication was attached to all abortions without distinction), and while some theologians still do, I accept the bishops' posi-tion that abortion is to be avoided.

As Catholics my wife and I were enjoined never to use abortion to destroy the life we created, and we never have. We thought church doctrine was clear on this, and—more than that—both of us felt it in full agreement with what our hearts and our con-sciences told us. For me, life or fetal life in the womb should be protected, even if five of nine justices of the Supreme Court and my neighbor disagree with me. A fetus is different from an appendix or a set of tonsils. At the very least, even if the argument is made by some scientists or some theologians that in the early stages of fetal develop-ment we can't discern human life, the full potential of human life is indisputably there. That—to my less subtle mind—by itself should demand respect, caution, in-deed—reverence.

But not everyone in our society agrees with me and Matilda.

And those who don't—those who endorse legalized abortions—aren't a ruthless, callous alliance of anti-Christians determined to overthrow our moral standards. In many cases the proponents of legal abortion are the very people who have worked with Catholics to realize the goals of social justice set out in papal encyclicals: the American Lutheran Church, the Central Conference of American Rabbis, the Presby-terian Church in the United States, B'nai B'rith Women, the Women of the Episco-pal Church. These are just a few of the religious organizations that don't share the church's position on abortion.

Certainly we should not be forced to mold Catholic morality to conform to dis-agreement by non-Catholics however sincere or severe their disagreement. Our bish-ops should be teachers, not pollsters. They should not change what we Catholics be-lieve in order to ease our consciences or please our friends or protect the church from criticism.

But if the breadth, intensity and sincerity of opposition to church teaching shouldn't be allowed to shape our Catholic morality, it can't help but determine our ability—our realistic, political ability—to translate our Catholic morality into civil law, a law not for the believers who don't need it but for the disbelievers who reject it.

And it is here, in our attempt to find a political answer to abortion—an answer be-yond our private observance of Catholic morality—that we encounter controversy within and without the church over how and in what degree to press the case that our morality should be everybody else's, and to what effect.

I repeat, there is no church teaching that mandates the best political course for making our belief everyone's rule, for spreading this part of our Catholicism. There is neither an encyclical nor a catechism that spells out a political strategy for achieving legislative goals.

And so the Catholic trying to make moral and prudent judgments in the political realm must discern which, if any, of the actions one could take would be best.

This latitude of judgment is not something new in the church, not a development that has arisen only with the abortion issue. Take, for example, the question of slavery. It has been argued that the failure to endorse a legal ban on abortions is equivalent to refusing to support the cause of abolition before the Civil War. This analogy has been advanced by the bishops of my own state.

But the truth of the matter is, few if any Catholic bishops spoke for abolition in the years before the Civil War. It wasn't, I believe, that the bishops endorsed the idea of some humans owning and exploiting other humans; Pope Gregory XVI in 1840 had condemned the slave trade. Instead it was a practical political judgment that the bishops made. They weren't hypocrites; they were realists. At the time Catholics were a small minority, mostly immigrants, despised by much of the population, often vilified and the object of sporadic violence. In the face of a public controversy that aroused tremendous passions and threatened to break the country apart, the bishops made a pragmatic decision. They believed their opinion would not change people's minds. Moreover they knew that there were Southern Catholics, even some priests, who owned slaves. They concluded that under the circumstances arguing for a constitutional amendment against slavery would do more harm than good, so they were silent. As they have been generally in recent years on the question of birth control. And as the church has been on even more controversial issues in the past, even ones that dealt with life and death.

What is relevant to this discussion is that the bishops were making judgments about translating Catholic teachings into public policy, not about the moral validity of the teachings. In so doing they grappled with the unique political complexities of their time. The decision they made to remain silent on a constitutional amendment to abolish slavery or on the repeal of the Fugitive Slave Law wasn't a mark of their moral indifference; it was a measured attempt to balance moral truths against political realities. Their decision reflected their sense of complexity, not their diffidence. As history reveals, Lincoln behaved with similar discretion.

The parallel I want to draw here is not between or among what we Catholics believe to be moral wrongs. It is in the Catholic response to those wrongs. Church teaching on slavery and abortion is clear. But in the application of those teachings—the exact way we translate them into action, the specific laws we propose, the exact legal sanctions we seek—there was and is no one, clear, absolute route that the church says, as a matter of doctrine, we must follow.

The bishops' pastoral letter "The Challenge of Peace" speaks directly to this point. "We recognize," the bishops wrote, "that the church's teaching authority does not carry the same force when it deals with technical solutions involving particular means as it does when it speaks of principles or ends. People may agree in abhorring an injustice, for instance, yet sincerely disagree as to what practical approach will achieve justice. Religious groups are as entitled as others to their opinion in such cases, but they should not claim that their opinions are the only ones that people of good will may hold."

With regard to abortion, the American bishops have had to weigh Catholic moral teaching against the fact of a pluralistic country where our view is in the minority, acknowledging that what is ideally desirable isn't always feasible, that there can be different political approaches to abortion besides unyielding adherence to an absolute prohibition.

This is in the American Catholic tradition of political realism. In supporting or opposing specific legislation the church in this country has never retreated into a moral fundamentalism that will settle for nothing less than total acceptance of its views.

Indeed, the bishops have already confronted the fact that an absolute ban on abortion doesn't have the support necessary to be placed in our Constitution. In 1981 they put aside earlier efforts to describe a law they could accept and get passed, and supported the Hatch Amendment instead.

Some Catholics felt the bishops had gone too far with that action, some not far enough. Such judgments were not a rejection of the bishops' teaching authority: The bishops even disagreed among themselves. Catholics are allowed to disagree on these technical political questions without having to confess.

Respectfully and after careful consideration of the position and arguments of the bishops, I have concluded that the approach of a constitutional amendment is not the best way for us to seek to deal with abortion.

I believe that legal interdicting of abortion by either the federal government or the individual states is not a plausible possibility and even if it could be obtained, it wouldn't work. Given present attitudes, it would be Prohibition revisited, legislating what couldn't be enforced and in the process creating a disrespect for law in general. And as much as I admire the bishops' hope that a constitutional amendment against abortion would be the basis for a full, new bill of rights for mothers and children, I disagree that this would be the result.

I believe that, more likely, a constitutional prohibition would allow people to ignore the causes of many abortions instead of addressing them, much the way the death penalty is used to escape dealing more fundamentally and more rationally with the problem of violent crime.

Other legal options that have been proposed are, in my view, equally ineffective. The Hatch Amendment, by returning the question of abortion to the states, would have given us a checkerboard of permissive and restrictive jurisdictions. In some cases people might have been forced to go elsewhere to have abortions, and that might have eased a few consciences, but it wouldn't have done what the church wants to do—it wouldn't have created a deep-seated respect for life. Abortions would have gone on, millions of them.

Nor would a denial of Medicaid funding for abortion achieve our objectives. Given *Roe v. Wade*, it would be nothing more than an attempt to do indirectly what the law says cannot be done directly; worse, it would do it in a way that would burden only the already disadvantaged. Removing funding from the Medicaid program would not prevent the rich and middle classes from having abortions. It would not even assure that the disadvantaged wouldn't have them; it would only impose financial burdens on poor women who want abortions.

Apart from that unevenness, there is a more basic question. Medicaid is designed to deal with health and medical needs. But the arguments for the cutoff of Medicaid abortion funds are not related to those needs. They are moral arguments. If we assume health and medical needs exist, our personal view of morality ought not to be considered a relevant basis for discrimination.

We must keep in mind always that we are a nation of laws—when we like those laws and when we don't.

The Supreme Court has established a woman's constitutional right to abortion. The Congress has decided the federal government should not provide federal funding in the Medicaid program for abortion. That, of course, does not bind states in the allocation of their own state funds. Under the law, the individual states need not follow the federal lead, and in New York I believe we cannot follow that lead. The equal protection clause in New York's Constitution has been interpreted by the courts as a standard of fairness that would preclude us from denying only the poor—indirectly, by a cutoff of funds—the practical use of the constitutional right given by *Roe v. Wade*.

In the end, even if after a long and divisive struggle we were able to remove all Medicaid funding for abortion and restore the law to what it was—if we could put most abortions out of our sight, return them to the backrooms where they were performed for so long—I don't believe our responsibility as Catholics would be any closer to being fulfilled than it is now, with abortion guaranteed by law as a woman's right.

The hard truth is that abortion isn't a failure of government. No agency or department of government forces women to have abortions, but abortion goes on. Catholics, the statistics show, support the right to abortion in equal proportion to the rest of the population. Despite the teaching in our homes and schools and pulpits, despite the sermons and pleadings of parents and priests and prelates, despite all the effort at defining our opposition to the sin of abortion, collectively we Catholics apparently believe—and perhaps act—little differently from those who don't share our commitment.

Are we asking government to make criminal what we believe to be sinful because we ourselves can't stop committing the sin?

The failure here is not Caesar's. This failure is our failure, the failure of the entire people of God.

Nobody has expressed this better than a bishop in my own state, Joseph Sullivan, a man who works with the poor in New York City, is resolutely opposed to abortion and argues, with his fellow bishops, for a change of law. "The major problem the church has is internal," the bishop said last month in reference to abortion. "How do we teach? As much as I think we're responsible for advocating public-policy issues, our primary responsibility is to teach our own people. We haven't done that. We're asking politicians to do what we haven't done effectively ourselves."

I agree with the bishop. I think our moral and social mission as Catholics must begin with the wisdom contained in the words "Physician, heal thyself." Unless we Catholics educate ourselves better to the values that define—and can ennoble—our lives, following those teachings better than we do now, unless we set an example that is clear and compelling, then we will never convince this society to change the civil laws to protect what we preach is precious human life.

Better than any law or rule or threat of punishment would be the moving strength of our own good example, demonstrating our lack of hypocrisy, proving the beauty and worth of our instruction.

We must work to find ways to avoid abortions without otherwise violating our faith. We should provide funds and opportunity for young women to bring their child to term, knowing both of them will be taken care of if that is necessary; we should teach our young men better than we do now their responsibilities in creating and caring for human life.

It is this duty of the church to teach through its practice of love that Pope John Paul II has proclaimed so magnificently to all peoples. "The church," he wrote in *Redemptor hominis* (1979), "which has no weapons at her disposal apart from those of the Spirit, of the word and of love, cannot renounce her proclamation of 'the word . . . in season and out of season.' For this reason she does not cease to implore . . . everybody in the name of God and in the name of man: Do not kill! Do not prepare destruction and extermination for each other! Think of your brothers and sisters who are suffering hunger and misery! Respect each one's dignity and freedom!"

The weapons of the word and of love are already available to us: We need no statute to provide them.

I am not implying that we should stand by and pretend indifference to whether a woman takes a pregnancy to its conclusion or aborts it. I believe we should in all cases try to teach a respect for life. And I believe with regard to abortion that, despite *Roe v. Wade*, we can, in practical ways. Here, in fact, it seems to me that all of us can agree.

Without lessening their insistence on a woman's right to an abortion, the people who call themselves "prochoice" can support the development of government programs that present an impoverished mother with the full range of support she needs to bear and raise her children, to have a real choice. Without dropping their campaign to ban abortion, those who gather under the banner of "prolife" can join in developing and enacting a legislative bill of rights for mothers and children, as the bishops have already proposed.

While we argue over abortion, the U.S. infant-mortality rate places us sixteenth among the nations of the world. Thousands of infants die each year because of inadequate medical care. Some are born with birth defects that, with proper treatment, could be prevented. Some are stunted in their physical and mental growth because of improper nutrition.

If we want to prove our regard for life in the womb, for the helpless infant—if we care about women having real choices in their lives and not being driven to abortions by a sense of helplessness and despair about the future of their child—then there is work enough for all of us. Lifetimes of it.

In New York, we have put in place a number of programs to begin this work, assisting women in giving birth to healthy babies. This year we doubled Medicaid funding to private-care physicians for prenatal and delivery services.

The state already spends $20 million a year for prenatal care in outpatient clinics and for inpatient hospital care.

One program in particular we believe holds a great deal of promise. It's called "New Avenues to Dignity," and it seeks to provide a teen-age mother with the special service she needs to continue with her education, to train for a job, to become capable of standing on her own, to provide for herself and the child she is bringing into the world.

My dissent, then, from the contention that we can have effective and enforceable legal prohibitions on abortion is by no means an argument for religious quietism, for accepting the world's wrongs because that is our fate as "the poor banished children of Eve."

Let me make another point.

Abortion has a unique significance but not a preemptive significance.

Apart from the question of the efficacy of using legal weapons to make people stop having abortions, we know our Christian responsibility doesn't end with any one law or amendment. That it doesn't end with abortion. Because it involves life and death, abortion will always be a central concern of Catholics. But so will nuclear weapons. And hunger and homelessness and joblessness, all the forces diminishing human life and threatening to destroy it. The "seamless garment" that Cardinal Bernardin has spoken of is a challenge to all Catholics in public office, conservatives as well as liberals.

We cannot justify our aspiration to goodness simply on the basis of the vigor of our demand for an elusive and questionable civil law declaring what we already know, that abortion is wrong.

Approval or rejection of legal restrictions on abortion should not be the exclusive litmus test of Catholic loyalty. We should understand that whether abortion is outlawed or not, our work has barely begun: the work of creating a society where the right to life doesn't end at the moment of birth; where an infant isn't helped into a world that doesn't care if it's fed properly, housed decently, educated adequately; where the blind or retarded child isn't condemned to exist rather than empowered to live.

The bishops stated this duty clearly in 1974 in their statement to the Senate subcommittee considering a proposed amendment to restrict abortions. They maintained such an amendment could not be seen as an end in itself. "We do not see a constitutional amendment as the final product of our commitment or of our legislative activity," they said. "It is instead the constitutional base on which to provide support and assistance to pregnant women and their unborn children. This would include nutritional, prenatal, childbirth and postnatal care for the mother, and also nutritional and pediatric care for the child through the first year of life. . . . We believe that all of these should be available as a matter of right to all pregnant women and their children."

The bishops reaffirmed that view in 1976, in 1980 and again this year when the U.S. Catholic Conference asked Catholics to judge candidates on a wide range of issues—on abortion, yes; but also on food policy, the arms race, human rights, education, social justice and military expenditures.

The bishops have been consistently "prolife" in the full meaning of that term, and I respect them for that.

The problems created by the matter of abortion are complex and confounding. Nothing is clearer to me than my inadequacy to find compelling solutions to all of their moral, legal and social implications. I—and many others like me—are eager for enlightenment, eager to learn new and better ways to manifest respect for the deep reverence for life that is our religion and our instinct. I hope that this public attempt to describe the problems as I understand them will give impetus to the dialogue in the

Catholic community and beyond, a dialogue which could show me a better wisdom than I've been able to find so far.

It would be tragic if we let that dialogue become a prolonged, divisive argument that destroys or impairs our ability to practice any part of the morality given us in the Sermon on the Mount, to touch, heal and affirm the human life that surrounds us.

We Catholic citizens of the richest, most powerful nation that has ever existed are like the stewards made responsible over a great household: From those to whom so much has been given, much shall be required. It is worth repeating that ours is not a faith that encourages its believers to stand apart from the world, seeking their salvation alone, separate from the salvation of those around them.

We speak of ourselves as a body. We come together in worship as companions, in the ancient sense of that word, those who break bread together and who are obliged by the commitment we share to help one another, everywhere, in all we do and in the process to help the whole human family. We see our mission to be "the completion of the work of creation."

This is difficult work today. It presents us with many hard choices.

The Catholic Church has come of age in America. The ghetto walls are gone, our religion no longer a badge of irredeemable foreignness. This newfound status is both an opportunity and a temptation. If we choose, we can give in to the temptation to become more and more assimilated into a larger, blander culture, abandoning the practice of the specific values that made us different, worshiping whatever gods the marketplace has to sell while we seek to rationalize our own laxity by urging the political system to legislate on others a morality we no longer practice ourselves.

Or we can remember where we come from, the journey of two millennia, clinging to our personal faith, to its insistence on constancy and service and on hope. We can live and practice the morality Christ gave us, maintaining his truth in this world, struggling to embody his love, practicing it especially where that love is most needed, among the poor and the weak and the dispossessed. Not just by trying to make laws for others to live by, but by living the laws already written for us by God, in our hearts and our minds.

We can be fully Catholic: proudly, totally at ease with ourselves, a people in the world, transforming it, a light to this nation. Appealing to the best in our people, not the worst. Persuading not coercing. Leading people to truth by love. And still, all the while, respecting and enjoying our unique pluralistic democracy. And we can do it even as politicians.

The author of the following selection argues that religion and democratic politics are not incompatible. He attacks Cuomo's position in the preceding selection that religious beliefs are a legitimate part of public discussion only insofar as they do not conflict with community consensus. Thiemann argues that political beliefs should be an important part of the public discussion that leads to a consensus on important issues of public policy. Religion has always been an important part of our polity, and neither the Supreme Court nor contemporary politics should ignore the legitimacy of religious expression in the public realm.

Ronald F. Thiemann is a Professor at the Harvard Divinity School.

The points he makes in the following selection are:

1. The Constitution supports religious freedom in the private sphere, but also allows religious values to be part of public discourse.
2. Religious values should be an important component of public consensus in a pluralistic democracy.
3. Religious values in public discussion should be given the greatest weight when they conform to the values of constitutional democracy. Political pluralism accepts diversity, and religious beliefs in the public realm should follow suit.
4. "Church" and "state," as in the separation of church and state, cannot be simply defined. What constitutes church and state in modern life is highly complex on both sides of the equation.
5. The Supreme Court should rethink its establishment clause and free exercise clause doctrines to support a greater role for religious belief in public life.

21

Ronald F. Thiemann

RELIGION IN PUBLIC LIFE: A DILEMMA FOR DEMOCRACY

RELIGION, VALUES, AND PUBLIC DECISION-MAKING

Should the personal religious beliefs of politicians influence their role as public officials? When the personal beliefs of a public official conflict with the policies he or she is charged to administer how should this dilemma be resolved? What role, if any, should the particular moral principles of a religious community play in the formation of policies in a pluralistic democracy?

On September 13, 1984, at the height of the controversy surrounding religion's place in public life, Governor Mario Cuomo of New York addressed the Department of Theology at the University of Notre Dame on the topic "Religious Belief and Public Morality." In a courageous but controversial address, Governor Cuomo, a Roman Catholic layman, spoke to the issue of abortion and his responsibilities as a Catholic public official. Just three months earlier John Cardinal O'Connor, Archbishop of New York, had indicated publicly that the church could exercise disciplinary measures, including the ban of excommunication, against public officials who failed to conduct themselves in accord with Catholic moral teaching. Since Geraldine Ferraro, a Catholic laywoman and supporter of abortion rights, was then a candidate for vice president, Cuomo's speech had significant political and religious implications.

Cuomo begins his address by describing the dual responsibility demanded of the religiously committed public official. On the one hand, the politician is a loyal child of the church, committed "to the essential core of dogmas that distinguishes our faith" and engaged in "a lifelong struggle to understand [that faith] more fully and to live it more truly." On the other hand, as an office holder in a pluralistic democracy "he or she undertakes to help create conditions under which *all* can live with a maximum of dignity and with a reasonable degree of freedom; where everyone who chooses may hold beliefs different from specifically Catholic ones—sometimes contradictory to them."

The freedom inherent in the constitutional tradition allows religiously motivated arguments to enter the public sphere as long as they are "not just parochial or narrowly sectarian but fulfill a human desire for order, peace, justice, kindness, love, any of the values most of us agree are desirable even apart from their specific religious base or context." Acknowledging his own personal belief that "the whole community . . . should agree on the importance of protecting life—including life in the womb," Cuomo then asks, "When should I argue to make my religious value your morality? . . . What are the rules and policies that should influence the exercise of this right to argue and promote?" In his answer to those questions Cuomo appeals to the notion of communal consensus.

> Our public morality then—the moral standards we maintain for everyone, not just the ones we insist on in our private lives—depends on a *consensus view of right and wrong.* The values derived from religious belief will not—and should not—be accepted as part of the public morality unless they are shared by the pluralistic community at large, by consensus (italics added).

Having made this point about moral consensus, Cuomo then immediately asserts that the problems with religion in public life begin when "religious values are used to support positions which would impose on other people restrictions they find unacceptable." "The community must decide if what is being proposed would be better left to private discretion than public policy; whether it restricts freedom, and if so to what end, to whose benefit."

While Cuomo's position is nuanced and subtle, his line of reasoning still presents some genuine difficulties. The argument seems to go like this: Our constitutionally guaranteed freedom allows the use of religious arguments in the public realm as long as those arguments appeal to values embraced by a significant portion of our pluralistic population. Purely sectarian arguments, that is, arguments that can only appeal to religious grounds, have no place in the persuasive forum of a constitutional democracy. Moreover, those values that guide public morality are established by a "consensus view of right and wrong" and religious values are appropriate only *insofar* as they "are shared by the pluralistic community at large." The use of religious arguments to impose restrictions on the freedom of others is particularly reprehensible and is unacceptable in a democracy.

But surely there is an element of circularity in this position. Religious arguments are welcomed in public debate as long as they are already accepted by communal consensus. But how then can religious arguments ever play a role in *forming* that consensus? It appears that religiously based arguments are acceptable only after they are no longer relevant to one of the most basic forms of political debate, the discussion which seeks to shape a consensus about our public morality. Ironically, Cuomo's argument eliminates religious argumentation from the very sphere in which its expertise would seem most relevant, the formation of communal values. On Cuomo's interpretation, it appears that religious arguments against slavery would have been unacceptable as long as the legal and political consensus supported slavery. Consequently, religious arguments cannot function to overturn a consensus that religious people find morally objectionable. Moreover, any religious argument which functions to restrict the freedom of others is, on Cuomo's reading, inappropriate in a pluralistic democracy. But surely some moral arguments ought to be used to restrict the freedom of others if that freedom violates a value that the community ought to hold dear. Arguments against slavery, in favor of minority civil rights, and in support of equal opportunity for women are designed to overturn a political and moral consensus through the use of moral persuasion. It is odd, indeed, for religious arguments to be eliminated from such vital moral debate simply because they begin from religious premises.

The instability of Cuomo's position becomes even more obvious when he applies it to his own role as a public official motivated by religious convictions. "As a Catholic," Cuomo admits that he accepts the church's teachings on abortion "as the right ones for myself and my family. . . . As a governor, however, I am involved in defining policies that determine *other* people's rights in these same areas of life and death." The question of whether one's personal religious beliefs should become the basis for public policy is "not a matter of doctrine; it is a matter of prudential political judgment." Since the Catholic position on abortion "is in the minority," "political realism" dictates that a legal prohibition of abortion is not appropriate, given the lack of consensus on this issue among the general populace.

Cuomo then proceeds to offer an eloquent account of the steps Catholics might realistically take to offer support to those women and children, particularly among the poor, who are victimized by current social policies.

> We should understand that whether abortion is outlawed or not, our work has barely begun: the work of creating a society where the right to life doesn't end at the moment of birth; where an infant isn't helped into a world that doesn't care if it's fed properly, housed decently, educated adequately; where the blind or retarded child isn't condemned to exist rather than empowered to live.

"We can be fully Catholic," Cuomo concludes, "leading people to truth by love. And still, all the while, respecting and enjoying our unique pluralistic democracy. And we can do it even as politicians."

Cuomo's final remarks are an important reminder of the inadequacy of slogans like "pro-life" and "pro-choice" to capture the complexity of ethical reflection in the formation of social policies. And yet the moral distinctions he seeks to draw between private and public, between personal conviction and political judgment remain troubling. It is striking that Cuomo never subjects the "Catholic position on abortion" to careful scrutiny. He simply acknowledges that as a loyal Catholic he accepts the church's teaching. But on what grounds? By appeal to what moral principles? Cuomo gives the impression that he accepts the teaching simply because it is taught by the Catholic hierarchy, but that is a surprising position for one so well versed in moral reasoning to adopt. The subtlety Cuomo demonstrates in applying Christian moral principles to questions of social policy for the poor (or in another context on the issue of capital punishment) is lacking when it comes to the issue of abortion. Here he seems content to accept a teaching in his private or personal behavior but to disregard it in his public or political behavior. But since this teaching asserts that abortion is the taking of innocent life, it is difficult to imagine that a morally sensitive person could accept that moral verdict in the private realm but somehow disregard it in the public realm. Garry Wills certainly seems correct when in a review of the Governor's Notre Dame speech he asserts "that Cuomo claims to believe the Church's teaching on abortion, but acts as if he does not."

Cuomo has two escape routes available, if he wishes to avoid Wills's critique: he can develop the moral components of his political argument into a critique of the reasoning of the Catholic bishops, or he can apply the moral reasoning of the bishops to the public realm and thereby revise the political position he has taken. But as long as he keeps the two positions separated by an appeal to privacy, or moral consensus, or political prudence, he will appear to be entrapped in a contradictory position. Thus we look in vain to one of the most articulate of American politicians for clarity on the vexing problem of the relation between religiously motivated convictions and the development of public policies.

This review . . . illustrates the confusion that characterizes our current reflection on the place of religion in American public life. Our corporate bewilderment on these matters is so deep and pervasive that it yields incoherent decisions and contradictory policies. This tangled web of issues has created a knot so snarled that it resists the efforts of our best public figures to untie it.

DEBUNKING THE MYTHS ABOUT RELIGION

Efforts to define a proper role for public religion in America have been impeded by the widespread acceptance of certain fundamental misunderstandings about the nature and function of religious belief and practice. These "myths" about religion often distort the thinking of even the most sophisticated contemporary analysts. The debate concerning religion's proper role in society cannot proceed with clarity until these misleading myths are debunked.

Myth: *"Religious belief is inherently irrational or nonrational; therefore religious warrants can never meet appropriate standards of publicity."*

The assumption that religious belief is irrational or nonrational is widely held among adherents and critics of religion alike. The commonplace distinction between faith and reason often leads both parties in the debate to develop this distinction into an absolute dichotomy. Too often religious apologists seek to defend their beliefs by defining faith as an independent or autonomous sphere wholly insulated from external scrutiny or critique. In so doing, they hope to provide a protected space within which religious belief and practice can develop and flourish without outside interference. To some extent, the notion of the "wall of separation between church and state," particularly as it was conceived by Roger Williams, relies on this familiar but misguided attempt to separate religion from those "alien" forces that might dilute or defile it. Critics of religion often seize upon this religious self-definition as evidence that such beliefs and practices can never meet standard criteria of publicity. Accepting the believers' claim to "privacy" at face value, they develop arguments designed to exclude all matters of faith from public discussion. . . .

It is a mistake for believers or nonbelievers to treat faith as a private enclave immune from inquiry or critique. . . .

As long as criteria of publicity are not explicitly designed to exclude religion from public discussion, religious beliefs are capable of meeting primary public standards of accessibility. It does not follow, however, that all religious warrants should be accorded the same welcome in public debate. The important issue is not whether an argument appeals to a religious warrant; the issue is whether the warrant, religious or not, is compatible with the basic values of our constitutional democracy. Arguments that appeal to racist ideologies or to doctrines of religious persecution are incompatible with basic democratic values. We should not seek to preclude these arguments from the public sphere; that strategy could easily lead to a violation of free speech. Instead, we should seek to educate the citizenry regarding the fundamental values of democracy, so that when they encounter such arguments they will reject them. The point is that we cannot by philosophical or political fiat decide in advance which arguments we will accept in the public sphere. Rather, we must learn to understand and evaluate all arguments that seek a public hearing.

The foregoing analysis does not imply that the values of constitutional democracy must be the final arbiter of the validity of all beliefs, including religious ones. Rather, the argument proposes that within the public realm the values of liberty, equality, and mutual respect function as the ideals toward which our political actions should strive. . . .

Myth: "*Religious beliefs, particularly those that make claims to truth, are not compatible with democracy's fundamental value of tolerance or mutual respect and should therefore be prohibited from the public realm.*"

This criticism has considerable historical evidence to support it. . . . [L]iberal political theory arose in part as a response to the terror unleashed in Europe by the post-Reformation religious wars. The founders of the American republic feared the link between religion and self-interest and sought to defend the new nation against the threat of religious factionalism. Historically religion's role in exacerbating tensions in the quarrelsome debates over slavery and prohibition is clearly evident. Contemporary examples abound—one thinks especially of the issues of abortion and homosexuality—to document the deeply divisive role religion can play in public life. On the face of it, then, this criticism seems less like a myth than a well-established historical conclusion.

My point is not to dispute the historical evidence establishing religion's divisive role in public life but to dispute the theological contention that religion must play such a role because its claims to truth are inevitably absolute. The mythology of religious absolutism has often dominated the self-understanding of communities of faith and has thereby contributed to religion's bellicose place in political history. My theoretical defense of public religion will be of little effect unless religious communities reform their views of faith's contribution to a pluralistic society. . . .

As long as the "myth of absoluteness" dominates the self-understanding of religious communities, they cannot be confident participants in a pluralistic society. . . .

Fundamental to the philosophical acceptance of pluralism is the conviction that we have no self-evident, incorrigible means of establishing the truth of our assertions. . . .

BEYOND THE WALL OF SEPARATION: THE ROLE OF THE COURTS

The time has now come to indicate the significance of my discussion of public religion and democratic values for the decision-making process in the nation's courts. Though I have sought to be an informed critic of the judiciary, I am acutely aware that I write as a theologian, not as a constitutional scholar or a jurist. Nonetheless, I believe that my attempt to clarify the proper public role of religion does have consequences for the judicial branch's treatment of religion. I will highlight four issues: (1) the anachronistic categories of church and state; (2) the limited significance of the notion of "separation"; (3) the need to return to fundamental constitutional values; and (4) the necessity of developing a consistent conceptual framework within which to consider both religion clauses.

Even if the courts had not embarked upon their confusing conceptual journey in the aftermath of the *Everson* decision, the very categories of "church" and "state" would force a reconsideration of first amendment adjudication. Given the rapid increase in religious diversity within the United States, the term "church" is simply not sufficient to refer to the varieties of religious practice in our country. Moreover, by privileging the Christian term for religious community, the courts give the unfortunate impression that they define religion through the perspective of Christianity. That impression would not be so serious had the court's actions not reinforced that view. Two recent cases raise particular concern.

In 1986, the Supreme Court upheld a lower court decision prohibiting Captain Simcha Goldman, an Orthodox Jew, from wearing a yarmulke while on duty in a health clinic in which he served. In writing for the majority, Justice Rehnquist stated that the standard military uniform encourages "the subordination of the desires and interests of the individual to the needs of the service." In this characterization, the wearing of the yarmulke is identified not as an aspect of required religious practice but of mere individual desire and interest. Consequently, the religious dimension of the case was simply side-stepped, and the Court rendered its opinion by supporting the need of the military for a uniform dress code. The irony is that the Court thus avoided altogether the religious question and refused to treat this case as one of free exercise.

Had they taken more seriously the wearing of the yarmulke as a matter of required Orthodox religious practice and applied the "compelling governmental interest" test, the case undoubtedly would have been decided otherwise. Had the question of religious obligation been considered, it is difficult to imagine that the Court could have sustained a judgment that the state had a compelling governmental interest. Surely the wearing of a yarmulke is a significant religious practice and deserved the protection of the first amendment guarantee of freedom of religion. The fact that minority religious practice received this discriminatory ruling is of particular concern.

An even more troubling free exercise case is *Employment Division* v. *Smith,* 1990. In this case, the Supreme Court upheld Oregon's denial of unemployment compensation sought when two employees were dismissed from their jobs for using a controlled substance, peyote, in a native American religious ritual. Here the majority explicitly rejected the common "compelling interest" criterion, arguing that such a standard "would be courting anarchy," because it "would open the prospect of constitutionally required religious exemptions from civic obligations of almost every conceivable kind." What the Court failed to acknowledge is that religious exemptions are essential precisely for those minority faiths that the free exercise and nonestablishment clauses are designed primarily to protect. The "compelling interest" criterion is crucial for the protection of the rights of minority religions that are unlikely to fare well in a legislative context in which majority rule holds sway. It is important to remember that when alcohol was officially a "controlled substance" during the Prohibition era, the sacramental use of wine was specifically exempted from the ordinance. Had it not been, it is inconceivable to imagine that the Court would not have acted to exempt a practice so central to the faith of the majority religion. Why should a minority religious practice not be similarly protected?

Clearly, these cases are influenced by factors more complicated than the mere use of the term "church," but that word does serve as a symbolic reminder that the notions of church and state have become dangerously outmoded. The Court must engage in much more sophisticated analysis of the relation between religious belief and practice and the long regulative arm of the government. "Church" no longer suffices to describe the religious reality of America, and "state" does not capture the complexity of the government's extensive net of welfare regulations.

The notion of separation is similarly outmoded. At best the idea of separation identifies a single aspect of the relationship between religion and government, namely, that neither institution should exercise final authority over the values, beliefs, and practices of the other. But "separation" is surely an odd word to use to make that important point. Independence of authority is necessary precisely because religion and government are deeply intertwined in so many ways. The interdependence of these two complex realities requires that the issue of independent authority be stated explicitly. Given the significant confusion that the notion of separation—and its associated concepts of neutrality and accommodation—has introduced into judicial reasoning, it is surely time to jettison it.

The courts need to engage in a fundamental reconsideration of the criteria for religion clause adjudication, focusing on the basic constitutional values of freedom, equality, and equal respect. The judicial branch needs to sit again at the feet of Madison and reassert his fundamental insight that both religion clauses are designed to defend religious freedom. Madison's presentation clearly shows that the free exercise and nonestablishment clauses are both grounded in an argument regarding freedom of conscience. Both clauses are designed to defend religious freedom in its individual and corporate expressions. If both clauses are concerned with religious freedom, then the attempt by the Supreme Court to develop independent traditions of adjudication for the free exercise and nonestablishment clauses is virtually doomed to failure.

More important, the Court needs to develop a conceptual framework that will take us beyond the judicial and cultural impasses created by the notion of the "separation of church and state." The religion clauses are designed to protect the freedom of religion in its individual and communal expressions and to prohibit the state from favoring any particular form of religious belief or practice. The clauses are not designed to prohibit religious individuals or communities of faith from entering into the pluralistic conversation that constitutes a liberal democracy. The Court's reasoning has been undermined by the conceptual burden imposed by the unwieldy notions of neutrality, separation, and accommodation. The Court should forgo further tinkering with the problematic "Lemon test" and should return to the fundamental values that undergird the entire constitutional tradition and the First Amendment in particular: freedom, equality, and toleration. Four principles should guide the Court's reconsideration of religion clause adjudication. First, religious freedom should be protected as a fundamental right to be constrained only if there is a compelling governmental interest at stake. Religious freedom and diversity constitute no threat in a pluralistic democracy. Second, religious traditions should be dealt with equally under the law. Government should not give preference to any one tradition, particularly the majority tradition of the nation. But this principle does not justify the "secular purpose" criterion, or prohibit government from supporting initiatives that allow for the equal flourishing of diverse religious practices. Third, if religion is to play a larger role in American public life, the courts must take special care to note whether apparent "facially neutral" regulations actually create an unfair burden for religious communities. Communities of faith contribute to public life in part by offering their adherents alternative modes of meaning and interpretation to the dominant secular culture. If that unique contribution is to be maintained, then the ability of these communities to practice their faith freely becomes especially important. Fourth, minority religions are particularly vulnerable to the "tyranny of the majority," and their freedoms must be guarded with especial care. This principle becomes even more important as religious diversity increases within America.

If the courts were to return to these fundamental values and principles, the disturbing trend toward restricting minority religious practice would certainly be reversed. Establishment adjudication, on the other hand, would probably not change significantly; however, the reasoning offered for such decisions would improve dramatically. Prayer in public school would still be prohibited because such prayer inevitably constrains the religious freedom of some students. Moments of silence could be approved, since each individual could freely engage in some form of reflection, meditation, or even daydreaming during this uncoerced period of time. Governments should be permitted to provide parochial schools with the same type of aid offered to nonreligious private schools, as long as such aid does not directly contribute to the advancement of the religious subject matter taught in the school. Additionally, governments would be prohibited from sponsoring religious observances of any kind, though they should take no steps to constrain the ability of communities of faith to display their own symbols on religious holidays. If the courts refocus their attention on the basic values and principles, they may not introduce dramatic new changes in establishment law, but their decisions and opinions could be reasoned with greater clarity and could achieve broader public accessibility. If the courts dismantle the tortured legacy of post-*Everson* adjudication and embark on a new appropriation of Madisonian reasoning they might contribute to the clarification of religion's proper role in public life. And that would be a gift not just to communities of faith but also to our common pluralistic democracy.

American politics and rhetoric dismiss religious beliefs as largely irrational and sometimes dangerous dogma, the author of the following reading argues. But, the author continues, religious beliefs matter to a large segment of the community. Religious adherence should not be ridiculed or excluded from politics, but rather should be respected as an important part of the democratic political process.

Stephen L. Carter is one of America's foremost scholars in matters of religion, morals, public life, and constitutional law. He is a Professor of Law at Yale University.

Here, Carter explains some of the reasons why discussing religion in American public life is so difficult.

His main points are:

1. Americans have tried, perhaps too hard, to isolate religion and matters of belief from the realm of public debate and government. This forces people to act sometimes as though their religion is unimportant.
2. The language we use to discuss religion is important.
3. When people act publicly as though their faith *does* matter, they risk ridicule and punishment.
4. Religions and faiths are increasingly seen not as the fundamentals upon which many base their lives, but rather as passing and changeable fads.

22

Stephen L. Carter

THE CULTURE OF DISBELIEF

★★★

Contemporary American politics faces few greater dilemmas than deciding how to deal with the resurgence of religious belief. On the one hand, American ideology cherishes religion, as it does all matters of private conscience, which is why we justly celebrate a strong tradition against state interference with private religious choice. At the same time, many political leaders, commentators, scholars, and voters are coming to view any religious element in public moral discourse as a tool of the radical right for reshaping American society. But the effort to banish religion for politics' sake has led us astray: In our sensible zeal to keep religion from dominating our politics, we have created a political and legal culture that presses the religiously faithful to be other than themselves, to act publicly, and sometimes privately as well, as though their faith does not matter to them.

Recently, a national magazine devoted its cover story to an investigation of prayer: how many people pray, how often, why, how, and for what. A few weeks later came the inevitable letter from a disgruntled reader, wanting to know why so much space had been dedicated to such nonsense.

Statistically, the letter writer was in the minority: by the magazine's figures, better than nine out of ten Americans believe in God and some four out of five pray regularly. Politically and culturally, however, the writer was in the American mainstream, for those who do pray regularly—indeed, those who believe in God—are encouraged to keep it a secret, and often a shameful one at that. Aside from the ritual appeals to God that are expected of our politicians, for Americans to take their religions seriously, to treat them as ordained rather than chosen, is to risk assignment to the lunatic fringe.

Yet religion matters to people, and matters a lot. Surveys indicate that Americans are far more likely to believe in God and to attend worship services regularly than any other people in the Western world. True, nobody prays on prime-time television unless religion is a part of the plot, but strong majorities of citizens tell pollsters that their religious beliefs are of great importance to them in their daily lives. Even though some popular histories wrongly assert the contrary, the best evidence is that this deep religiosity has always been a facet of the American character and that it has grown consistently through the nation's history. And today, to the frustration of many opinion leaders in both the legal and political cultures, religion, as a moral force and perhaps a political one too, is surging. Unfortunately, in our public life, we prefer to pretend that it is not.

Consider the following events:

- When Hillary Rodham Clinton was seen wearing a cross around her neck at some of the public events surrounding her husband's inauguration as President of the United States, many observers were aghast, and one television commentator asked whether it was appropriate for the First Lady to display so openly a religious symbol. But if the First Lady can't do it, then certainly the President can't do it, which would bar from ever holding the office an Orthodox Jew under a religious compulsion to wear a yarmulke.

- Back in the mid-1980s, the magazine *Sojourners*—published by politically liberal Christian evangelicals—found itself in the unaccustomed position of defending the conservative evangelist Pat Robertson against secular liberals who, a writer in the magazine sighed, "see[m] to consider Robertson a dangerous neanderthal because he happens to believe that God can heal diseases." The point is that the editors of *Sojourners*, who are no great admirers of Robertson, also believe that God can heal diseases. So do tens of millions of Americans. But they are not supposed to say so.

- In the early 1980s, the state of New York adopted legislation that, in effect, requires an Orthodox Jewish husband seeking a civil divorce to give his wife a *get*—a religious divorce—without which she cannot remarry under Jewish law. Civil libertarians attacked the statute as unconstitutional. Said one critic, the "barriers to remarriage erected by religious law . . . only exist in the minds of those who believe in the religion." If the barriers are religious, it seems, then they are not real barriers, they are "only" in the woman's mind—perhaps even a figment of the imagination.

- When the Supreme Court of the United States, ostensibly the final refuge of religious freedom, struck down a Connecticut statute requiring employers to make efforts to allow their employees to observe the sabbath, one Justice observed that the sabbath should not be singled out because all employees would like to have "the right to select the day of the week in which to refrain from labor." Sounds good, except that, as one scholar has noted, "It would come as some surprise to a devout Jew to find that he has 'selected the day of the week in which to refrain from labor,' since the Jewish people have been under the impression for some 3,000 years that this choice was made by God." If the sabbath is just another day off, then religious choice is essentially arbitrary and unimportant; so if one sabbath day is inconvenient, the religiously devout employee can just choose another.

- When President Ronald Reagan told religious broadcasters in 1983 that all the laws passed since biblical times "have not improved on the Ten Commandments one bit," which might once have been considered a pardonable piece of rhetorical license, he was excoriated by political pundits, including one who charged angrily that Reagan was giving "short shrift to the secular laws and institutions that a president is charged with protecting." And as for the millions of Americans who consider the Ten Commandments the fundaments on which they build their lives, well, they are no doubt subversive of these same institutions.

These examples share a common rhetoric that refuses to accept the notion that rational, public-spirited people can take religion seriously. It might be argued that such cases as these involve threats to the separation of church and state, the durable and vital doctrine that shields our public institutions from religious domination and our religious institutions from government domination. I am a great supporter of the separation of church and state, . . . but that is not what these examples are about.

What matters about these examples is the *language* chosen to make the points. In each example, as in many more that I shall discuss, one sees a trend in our political and legal cultures toward treating religious beliefs as arbitrary and unimportant, a trend supported by a rhetoric that implies that there is something wrong with religious devotion. More and more, our culture seems to take the position that believing deeply in the tenets of one's faith represents a kind of mystical irrationality, something that thoughtful, public-spirited American citizens would do better to avoid. If you must worship your God, the lesson runs, at least have the courtesy to disbelieve in the power of prayer; if you must observe your sabbath, have the good sense to understand that it is just like any other day off from work.

The rhetoric matters. A few years ago, my wife and I were startled by a teaser for a story on a network news program, which asked what was meant to be a provocative question: "When is a church more than just a place of worship?" For those to whom worship is significant, the subtle arrangement of words is arresting: *more than* suggests that what follows ("just a place of worship") is somewhere well down the scale of interesting or useful human activities, and certainly that whatever the story is about is *more than* worship; and *just*—suggests that what follows ("place of worship") is rather small potatoes.

A friend tells the story of how he showed his résumé to an executive search consultant—in the jargon, a corporate headhunter—who told him crisply that if he was serious about moving ahead in the business world, he should remove from the résumé any mention of his involvement with a social welfare organization that was connected with a church, but not one of the genteel mainstream denominations. Otherwise, she explained, a potential employer might think him a religious fanatic.

How did we reach this disturbing pass, when our culture teaches that religion is not to be taken seriously, even by those who profess to believe in it? Some observers suggest that the key moment was the Enlightenment, when the Western tradition sought to sever the link between religion and authority. One of the playwright Tom Stoppard's characters observes that there came "a calendar date—*a moment*—when the onus of proof passed from the atheist to the believer, when, quite suddenly, the noes had it." To which the philosopher Jeffrey Stout appends the following comment: "if so, it was not a matter of majority rule." Maybe not—but a strong undercurrent of contemporary American politics holds that religion must be kept in its proper place and, still more, in proper perspective. There are, we are taught by our opinion leaders, religious matters and important matters, and disaster arises when we confuse the two. Rationality, it seems, consists in getting one's priorities straight. (Ignore your religious law and marry at leisure.) Small wonder, then, that we have recently been treated to a book, coauthored by two therapists, one of them an ordained minister, arguing that those who would put aside, say, the needs of their families in order to serve their religions are suffering from a malady the authors call "toxic faith"—for no normal person, evidently, would sacrifice the things that most of us hold dear just because of a belief that God so intended it. (One wonders how the authors would have judged the toxicity of the faith of Jesus, Moses, or Mohammed.)

We are trying, here in America, to strike an awkward but necessary balance, one that seems more and more difficult with each passing year. On the one hand, a magnificent respect for freedom of conscience, including the freedom of religious belief, runs deep in our political ideology. On the other hand, our understandable fear of religious domination of politics presses us, in our public personas, to be wary of those who take their religion too seriously. This public balance reflects our private selves. We are one of the most religious nations on earth, in the sense that we have a deeply religious citizenry; but we are also perhaps the most zealous in guarding our public institutions against explicit religious influences. One result is that we often ask our citizens to split their public and private selves, telling them in effect that it is fine to be religious in private, but there is something askew when those private beliefs become the basis for public action.

We teach college freshmen that the Protestant Reformation began the process of freeing the church from the state, thus creating the possibility of a powerful independent moral force in society. As defenders of the separation of church and state have argued for centuries, autonomous religions play a vital role as free critics of the institutions of secular society. But our public culture more and more prefers religion as something without political significance, less an independent moral force than a quietly irrelevant moralizer, never heard, rarely seen. "[T]he public sphere," writes the theologian Martin Marty, "does not welcome explicit Reformed witness—or any other particularized Christian witness." Or, for that matter, any religious witness at all.

Religions that most need protection seem to receive it least. Contemporary America is not likely to enact legislation aimed at curbing the mainstream Protestant, Roman Catholic, or Jewish faiths. But Native Americans, having once been hounded from their lands, are now hounded from their religions, with the complicity of a Supreme Court untroubled when sacred lands are taken for road building or when Native Americans under a bona fide religious compulsion to use peyote in their rituals are punished under state antidrug regulations. (Imagine the brouhaha if New York City were to try to take St. Patrick's Cathedral by eminent domain to build a new convention center, or if Kansas, a dry state, were to outlaw the religious use of wine.) And airports, backed by the Supreme Court, are happy to restrict solicitation by devotees of Krishna Consciousness, which travelers, including this one, find irritating. (Picture the response should the airports try to regulate the wearing of crucifixes or yarmulkes on similar grounds of irritation.)

The problem goes well beyond our society's treatment of those who simply want freedom to worship in ways that most Americans find troubling. An analogous difficulty is posed by those whose religious convictions move them to action in the public arena. Too often, our rhetoric treats the religious impulse to public action as presumptively wicked—indeed, as necessarily oppressive. But this is historically bizarre. Every time people whose vision of God's will moves them to oppose abortion rights are excoriated for purportedly trying to impose their religious views on others, equal calumny is implicitly heaped upon the mass protest wing of the civil rights movement, which was openly and unashamedly religious in its appeals as it worked to impose its moral vision on, for example, those who would rather segregate their restaurants. . . .

THE PRICE OF FAITH

When citizens do act in their public selves as though their faith matters, they risk not only ridicule, but actual punishment. In Colorado, a public school teacher was ordered by his superiors, on pain of disciplinary action, to remove his personal Bible from his desk where students might see it. He was forbidden to read it silently when his students were involved in other activities. He was also told to take away books on Christianity he had added to the classroom library, although books on Native American religious traditions, as well as on the occult, were allowed to remain. A federal appeals court upheld the instruction, explaining that the teacher could not be allowed to create a religious atmosphere in the classroom, which, it seems, might happen if the students knew he was a Christian. One wonders what the school, and the courts, might do if, as many Christians do, the teacher came to school on Ash Wednesday with ashes in the shape of a cross imposed on his forehead—would he be required to wash them off? He just might. Early in 1993, a judge required a prosecutor arguing a case on Ash Wednesday to clean the ashes from his forehead, lest the jury be influenced by its knowledge of the prosecutor's religiosity.

Or suppose a Jewish teacher were to wear a yarmulke in the classroom. If the school district tried to stop him, it would apparently be acting within its authority. In 1986, after a Jewish Air Force officer was disciplined for wearing a yarmulke while on duty, in violation of a military rule against wearing headgear indoors, the Supreme Court shrugged: "The desirability of dress regulations in the military is decided by the appropriate military officials," the justices explained, "and they are under no constitutional mandate to abandon their considered professional judgment." The Congress quickly enacted legislation permitting the wearing of religious apparel while in uniform as long as "the wearing of the item would [not] interfere with the performance of the member's military duties," and—interesting caveat!—as long as the item is "neat and conservative." Those whose faiths require them to wear dreadlocks and turbans, one supposes, need not apply to serve their country, unless they are prepared to change religions.

Consider the matter of religious holidays. One Connecticut town recently warned Jewish students in its public schools that they would be charged with *six* absences if they missed two days instead of the officially allocated one for Yom Kippur, the holiest observance in the Jewish calendar. And Alan Dershowitz of Harvard Law School, in his controversial book *Chutzpah*, castigates Harry Edwards, a Berkeley sociologist, for scheduling an examination on Yom Kippur, when most Jewish students would be absent. According to Dershowitz's account, Edwards answered criticism by saying: "That's how I'm going to operate. If the students don't like it, they can drop the class." For Dershowitz, this was evidence that "Jewish students [are] second-class citizens in Professor Edwards's classes." Edwards has heatedly denied Dershowitz's description of events, but even if it is accurate, it is possible that Dershowitz has identified the right crime and the wrong villain. The attitude that Dershowitz describes, if it exists, might reflect less a personal prejudice against Jewish students than the society's broader prejudice against religious devotion, a prejudice that masquerades as "neutrality." If Edwards really dared his students to choose between their religion and their grade, and if that meant that he was treating them as second-class citizens, he was still doing no more than the courts have allowed all levels of government to do to one religious group after another—Jews, Christians, Muslims, Sikhs, it matters not at all. The consistent message of modern American society is that whenever the demands of one's religion conflict with what one has to do to get ahead, one is expected to ignore the religious demands and act . . . well . . . *rationally.*

Consider Jehovah's Witnesses, who believe that a blood transfusion from one human being to another violates the biblical prohibition on ingesting blood. To accept the transfusion, many Witnesses believe, is to lose, perhaps forever, the possibility of salvation. As the Witnesses understand God's law, moreover, the issue is not whether the blood transfusion is given against the recipient's will, but whether the recipient is, at the time of the transfusion, actively protesting. This is the reason that Jehovah's Witnesses sometimes try to impede the physical access of medical personnel to an unconscious Witness: lack of consciousness is no defense. This is also the reason that Witnesses try to make the decisions on behalf of their children: a child cannot be trusted to protest adequately.

The machinery of law has not been particularly impressed with these arguments. There are many cases in which the courts have allowed or ordered transfusions to save the lives of unconscious Witnesses, even though the patient might have indicated a desire while conscious not to be transfused. The machinery of modern medicine has not been impressed, either, except with the possibility that the Witnesses have gone off the deep end; at least one hospital's protocol apparently requires doctors to refer protesting Witnesses to psychiatrists. Although the formal text of this requirement states as the reason the need to be sure that the Witness knows what he or she is doing, the subtext is a suspicion that the patient was not acting rationally in rejecting medical advice for religious reasons. After all, there is no protocol for packing *consenting* patients off to see the psychiatrist. But then, patients who consent to blood transfusions are presumably acting rationally. Perhaps, with a bit of gentle persuasion, the dissenting Witness can be made to act rationally too—even if it means giving up an important tenet of the religion.

And therein lies the trouble. In contemporary American culture, the religions are more and more treated as just passing beliefs—almost as fads, older, stuffier, less liberal versions of so-called New Age—rather than as the fundaments upon which the devout build their lives. (The noes have it!) And if religions *are* fundamental, well, too bad—at least if they're the *wrong* fundaments—if they're inconvenient, give them up! If you can't remarry because you have the wrong religious belief, well, hey, believe something else! If you can't take your exam because of a Holy Day, get a new Holy Day! If the government decides to destroy your sacred lands, just make some other lands sacred! If you must go to work on your sabbath, it's no big deal! It's just a day off! Pick a different one! If you can't have a blood transfusion because you think God forbids it, no problem! Get a new God! And through all of this trivializing rhetoric runs the subtle but unmistakable message: pray if you like, worship if you must, but whatever you do, do not on any account take your religion seriously. . . .

Nowhere is the debate over separation of church and state more heated than in abortion politics. The Catholic church and Protestant fundamentalists strongly oppose abortion on religious grounds. Pro-choice advocates argue that the abortion issue is not religious, but a matter of a woman's civil right to privacy.

The reality of American politics is that in the final analysis judges are the high priests of our political system. The Constitution is the higher law, and the Supreme Court its interpreter and guardian. Laurence Tribe argues that judges have the power and the obligation to define our constitutional rights and liberties, and in the process limit governmental power. The Constitution and the Supreme Court stand above both democratic politics and religious beliefs.

Laurence H. Tribe is a constitutional scholar at Harvard University. Here, his main points are:

1. The abortion issue is about many things, including constitutional limits and the interaction of the judiciary and other political forces. To argue that the courts should not decide a question because it is somehow "political" does not tell us how other actors should reach decisions, and it ignores the fact that, at some point, the judiciary will inevitably be involved.
2. We should remember that the *Roe* decision itself was a compromise.
3. Critics argue that the Court overstepped its proper bounds in the *Roe* decision. The Supreme Court, however, acts in an "undemocratic" way whenever it acts to strike down a law as unconstitutional. This is the reality of our judiciary's role in the constitutional system.

23

Laurence H. Tribe

ABORTION: THE CLASH OF ABSOLUTES

★★★

FINDING ABORTION RIGHTS IN THE CONSTITUTION

Because the abortion question is so difficult and may be approached in so many ways, it should be no surprise that the approach taken by the U.S. Supreme Court generates continuing controversy. It would be foolish to expect any judicial approach to the abortion question to be uncontroversial; if that test were applied, every answer to the question would be wrong. But neither difficulty nor controversy can justify letting the Court's decision in *Roe* escape critical examination. Was that decision legally defensible? We address that issue next, exploring some of the implications of deciding the constitutional question in different ways.

We should be clear at the outset that the abortion issue poses constitutional problems not simply for judges but for every federal, state, or local official who must at some point address the issue. Each such official is required to take an oath to uphold the Constitution of the United States. Even if the Supreme Court were someday to conclude that judges have no business enforcing constitutional limitations in the abortion area, that conclusion would not relieve other public officials of the burden of deciding what they believe those limitations are. In deciding what laws to vote for or against or what enforcement measures to take, public officials cannot properly avoid considering what they believe the Constitution allows or requires them to do.

Those who either defend or attack the constitutional analysis contained in *Roe v. Wade* purely in terms of the role judges should or should not play in our system of government are therefore missing much of what is at stake. Of course, *Roe v. Wade* involved, in part, the question of what the judicial role should be. But that is only part of what it involved. It involved as well the question of what protection, if any, the Constitution, as a document addressed to all officials, extends either to a woman who wishes to terminate her pregnancy or to the fetus, or to both. To say that the abortion question should be resolved, in whole or in part, by officials other than judges tells us nothing about how those officials should resolve it.

In addition, it is an illusion to imagine that all aspects of the abortion issue could possibly be left to officials outside the judicial system. However tempting it might be for judges to throw up their hands and say that the whole matter should be resolved "politically," a little thought should make clear that judges must, at a minimum, set the outer boundaries of political power in this area.

Suppose, for example, that the Constitution is interpreted so as to give each state broad latitude in deciding which abortions to permit and which to prohibit. Judges would still have to decide whether or not a state could pass a law that would force a woman to save a viable fetus when that would require delivery by caesarean section. Judges would still have to decide whether or not a state could constitutionally force a woman to abort one fetus in order to save its twin if the medical circumstances were such that only one could live. Judges would still have to decide whether or not a state could impose financial pressures designed to force a woman on welfare to abort a fetus that would be born with severe genetic defects and whose survival after birth would require a large commitment of public resources.

Whatever a court might conclude about government's power over normal pregnancy, it could hardly avoid determining the limits of government power over an ovum that has been fertilized in a test tube. May the government require that such a fertilized ovum be preserved for future implantation? May the government require that such an ovum be frozen until its fate has been agreed upon? May the sperm donor be given an enforceable veto over the woman's decision to discard the ovum after its test tube fertilization? May the government enforce her promise to have the fertilized ovum implanted in her uterus? May it enforce her promise to have it implanted in another woman? If state officials refuse to enforce such promises, are they violating any rights of the persons to whom those promises were made?

Courts simply cannot avoid deciding, in the multitude of cases spawned by the newest technologies and the oldest human desires, *who* will be permitted to decide *what*: the woman, the man, a doctor, a hospital, or the state?

WAS ROE RIGHTLY DECIDED?

For all the talk of possible future compromises, it must not be forgotten that *Roe* itself represented a compromise. The Supreme Court in *Roe v. Wade* had heard arguments that the woman's right to decide for herself whether, when, and why to terminate a pregnancy is absolute. The Court's conclusion was unequivocal: "With this we do not agree." Thus, the Court in *Roe* and in the decisions that followed it upheld the validity of government regulations requiring that all abortions be performed by licensed physicians, government regulations to protect the health of women in second-trimester abortions and beyond, and government regulations to protect the unborn from abortions that are not needed to protect the woman's life or health once the fetus is "viable" (i.e., can survive outside the woman).

Still, no judicial ruling since segregated public schools were held unconstitutional by *Brown v. Board of Education* has generated anything resembling the degree of criticism and even outright violence triggered by *Roe v. Wade*. Criticism of the decision, and particularly of its result, has led to a revolution in constitutional law that may have profound consequences for all Americans, a revolution touching the full range of our rights. It has already led to a radical transformation in the role of the American judiciary.

The "Judicial Restraint" Objection

One unexpected consequence of *Roe v. Wade* was the growth of a veritable cottage industry promoting judicial restraint. The epithet "judicial activism," the foe of supposed champions of restraint, is most often used to describe the work of the Supreme Court of the 1950s and 1960s under Chief Justice Earl Warren. But *Roe*, sometimes derided as an example of unparalleled judicial activism, was decided by the Court under the leadership of conservative Chief Justice Warren Burger. Indeed, the decision in *Roe* was written by Nixon appointee Harry Blackmun and was joined by conservative jurists Potter Stewart and Lewis Powell as well as by Chief Justice Burger, who was appointed by President Nixon precisely to fulfill a campaign promise to change the activist complexion of the federal judiciary.

People have undertaken to criticize *Roe*, in every aspect and from every angle, as *illegitimate* judicial activism, and the sheer volume of the attack seems to have lent it legitimacy. Are these criticisms convincing?

"Legislators and Not Judges Should Decide"

The simplest argument against *Roe*, an argument that has gained considerable credence and that has great resonance in a nation devoted to principles of democracy, criticizes *Roe* as antidemocratic. The issue of abortion rights, the reasoning goes, should be returned to Congress and to state and local legislators for decision in a democratic way by the legislative process. How sound is that argument?

Our system of government, of course, neither offers us nor threatens us with *absolute* democracy, in the style, say, of ancient Athens, where it is said that each citizen cast one vote on all matters, or in the style of the New England town meeting. Ours is a republican form of government, in which the votes of citizens are used primarily to select legislatures and executives, which themselves select judges whose role it is to ensure that the government does not violate basic rights or otherwise upset the fundamental agreements underlying our governmental institutions. The whole *point* of an independent judiciary is to be "antidemocratic," to preserve from transient majorities those human rights and other principles to which our legal and political system is committed. Without this role there would be nothing to stop a bare majority of our citizens from deciding tomorrow that the minority should be enslaved or required to give up its belongings for the greater good of the greater number. This elementary civics lesson is forgotten or ignored by those who would leave *every* issue of individual rights that was a matter of moral controversy to be decided *solely* by the legislative and executive branches. And in the end, most of these critics do not seriously attempt to deny that the federal judiciary, and ultimately the Supreme Court of the United States, is empowered to invalidate legislation, although duly enacted by the democratically elected representatives of the people, if it runs afoul of the Constitution.

In particular, the protections of the first eight amendments to the Constitution—the "Bill of Rights" (guaranteeing freedom of speech and of religion, the right to bear arms, and so forth)—and of the Fourteenth Amendment, adopted after the Civil War, which guarantees all persons equal protection of the laws and prohibits deprivations of life, liberty, or property without due process of law, insulate certain aspects of individual behavior from governmental intrusion and provide norms for government action that no legislature can contravene, although the exact bounds of these rights may be open to debate.

Should a legislature, through the democratic process, enact a law that transgresses the guarantees contained in the Constitution, the federal courts have not merely the power but the obligation to strike that law down. Indeed, the Constitution provides for unelected judges, appointed by the President and confirmed by the Senate, who serve for life and whose salary cannot be diminished, precisely to prevent them from making decisions based on the popular will, however formally and democratically expressed.

This power of judicial review and invalidation was first exercised by the Supreme Court to strike down an act of Congress in an opinion written by the great chief justice John Marshall in the case of *Marbury v. Madison* in 1803. There a disappointed office seeker named William Marbury, who had been named to a federal post by President John Adams, sued Secretary of State James Madison for refusing to deliver his commission of office when the administration of President Adams was replaced by that of President Thomas Jefferson. The Supreme Court, after saying that Madison and the new President were acting lawlessly, pronounced itself powerless to award Marbury the judicial relief he sought, explaining that the act of Congress which supposedly empowered it to hear Marbury's suit against Madison violated the Constitution's provision defining the Court's jurisdiction to try cases. Writing for the Court, Chief Justice Marshall held that much as the Court would like to rely on that act of Congress, its duty to obey the Constitution required it to strike that act down. Striking down a law as unconstitutional is "undemocratic," in the sense that no simple majority acting through the legislative process can overcome a ruling of the Supreme Court holding a law invalid. But it is a cornerstone of our system of government.

As Justice Robert Jackson wrote in 1943 in an opinion for the Court holding that children cannot be punished by public authorities for refusing to take part in a school's compulsory flag salute ceremony, the "very purpose of a Bill of Rights was to withdraw certain subjects from the vicissitudes of political controversy, to place them beyond the reach of majorities and officials and to establish them as legal principles to be applied by the courts. One's right to life, liberty, and property, to free speech, a free press, freedom of worship and assembly, and other fundamental rights may not be submitted to vote; they depend on the outcome of no elections."

Every time a court holds that a duly enacted law violates the Constitution, it behaves in what might be described as an antidemocratic way. But this does not make the court's action a usurpation of power. The antidemocratic nature of *Roe* provides no decisive evidence of its illegitimacy—provided we agree, as nearly everyone does, that the Constitution itself has sufficiently democratic roots to count as an enduring basis for a government of, by, and for the people. The question remains, though: Can *Roe* find support in the Constitution?

"The Right to Privacy Is Not in the Constitution's Text"

A second basis for objection to *Roe* is that it protects a right, the right to privacy, that appears nowhere in the text of the Constitution. The Court, it is said, in a naked power grab and on the strength of nothing more than personal disagreement with the outcome of the legislative process, illegitimately carved out an area and put it beyond the reach of the democratic, political branches of government. If true, the charge would be grave indeed; the Supreme Court's only warrant to override the outcome of politically democratic processes is the agreement of "We the People," as the Constitution's preamble calls those in whose name it is ordained.

Judge Robert Bork, in his 1989 book *The Tempting of America*, could find in the Court's opinion "not one line of explanation, not one sentence that qualifies as legal argument." In the years since *Roe*, according to Bork, "no one, however pro-abortion, has ever thought of an argument that even remotely begins to justify *Roe v. Wade* as a constitutional decision. . . . There is no room for argument," writes Bork, "about the conclusion that the decision was the assumption of illegitimate judicial power and usurpation of the democratic authority of the American people."

What may surprise some, given the certitude with which Judge Bork and a number of others pronounce that *Roe v. Wade* was constitutionally illegitimate, is how many lawyers and law professors throughout the country believe the Supreme Court's decision in that case was entirely correct as a legal matter. For example, a friend of the court brief was filed in the *Webster* case "on behalf of 885 American law professors . . . who believe that the right of a woman to choose whether or not to bear a child, as delineated . . . in *Roe v. Wade*, is an essential component of constitutional liberty and privacy commanding reaffirmation by [the Supreme] Court." Similarly, the American Bar Association in February 1990 approved a resolution expressing the ABA's recognition that "the fundamental rights of privacy and equality guaranteed by the United States Constitution" encompass "the decision to terminate [a] pregnancy."

Now, of course, nearly a thousand law professors and the nation's leading organization of lawyers could certainly be wrong on a matter of law. But how plausible is it that all of them would fail to recognize as blatant a legal blunder as some say the Court made in *Roe*? To understand what separates the vast majority of lawyers and legal scholars from those who continue to insist that no honest and professionally competent attorney or academic could possibly agree with *Roe*, we need to look more closely at what *Roe's* most strident critics claim.

On the most simplistic level, of course, the critics are correct. The word "privacy" is not in the text of the Constitution. But the guarantees of the Constitution are not like itemized deductions. The Constitution contains broad provisions whose meaning requires judicial interpretation. Interpretation, in turn, requires judgment.

One of the most important of these broad provisions, contained in the Fourteenth Amendment, reads: "No State shall . . . deprive any person of life, liberty, or property, without due process of law." It is the guarantee of "liberty" contained in the due process clause, sometimes also called the liberty clause, of the Fourteenth Amendment that provides protection of our rights from infringement by the state governments. And the word "liberty" simply is not self-defining. . . .

CHAPTER 6

CAMPAIGN FINANCE

Why Is A Free Country So Expensive?

An abiding belief in American political culture is that money and politics go together and money corrupts the political process. Taking money out of politics is somewhat akin to taking politics out of politics, an idealistic but futile endeavor. The pursuit of power defines politics, and reform politics is no exception. Political reformers seek shifts in the balance of power in their favor. Naturally, political reformers proclaim their goals are in the national interest. Campaign finance reform, as all other reform movements, seeks shifts in the balance of political power. The public interest manifesto of campaign finance reformers masks individual and group pursuit of political power.

The following selection casts campaign finance practices as the political villain that undermines an idealized democratic process.

Greg D. Kubiak wrote *The Gilded Dome* based on his experiences as a legislative assistant to a United States senator from 1983 to 1990. Kubiak's main points are:

1. Campaign finance reform offers the best vehicle by which to examine the operations of Congress and the interests and ethics of individual members. This is because members are deeply and personally interested in campaign finance.
2. Money is the "mother's milk" of politics, and large donations carry the risk of what Kubiak sees as undue influence and unfair access. However, money is a necessary and unavoidable part of getting elected.
3. A kind of sport develops: donors want access, and politicians want to raise ever more money. Suggestions for reform of the campaign finance system need to look at ethics as well as the competition involved in the political system.
4. "'[P]olitics permeates all that we do." Campaign finance reform illustrates many of the dynamics that make changing laws and regulations so difficult.

24

Greg D. Kubiak

THE GILDED DOME

★★★

Many of us have the perception that members of Congress represent us by casting votes on the chamber floors, working in committee hearings on various issues, and protecting "truth, liberty, and the American way" through stirring oratory, much the way James Stewart did in the film *Mr. Smith Goes to Washington.* Yet underneath the pleasing and concealing [Capitol] dome, a very different world exists.

WE THE PEOPLE

Perhaps the most basic principle within our system of government—a principle that has kept the United States functioning through civil and world wars, economic depressions, and various government scandals—is that each branch of government has oversight and constraints placed on it by another branch. Moveover, the citizens of the United States theoretically have the ultimate say in government because we have the power to vote.

Yet what oversight do we as electors of the government exercise beyond our vote? Who really has the most say in not just how members of Congress vote but what they vote on? Who sets the legislative agenda? Congress? Political consultants? Lobbyists? The Democratic and Republican party leaders? Political action committees? The people? These are valid questions for every citizen of a democratic society, not just students of civics and political science or political activists.

As a holder of a bachelor's degree in political science, I read the texts, heard the lectures, and examined the constructs of the legislative process. As a legislative assistant to a U.S. senator, I saw a much different world in which that process works. I saw the use and abuse of legislative rules, the importance of legislative leadership, and the power of individual motivation. These traits relate more to human psychology than they do to civics. . . .

Like any element of society, Congress must be governed by rules. When those rules get broken, bent, or outdated, they should be exposed and changed. Everyone who is affected by decisions made by Congress has an interest in how Congress makes its decisions. . . .

When we read about congressional action in the newspapers or hear on the evening news about a bill being passed, we get a false impression of the legislative branch of our federal government. Not all of its work can be neatly packaged in ninety seconds on the networks or in a five-paragraph news wire story. While I do not intend to bash Congress for its collective inability to get results on issues of importance to the everyday lives of citizens, it is important to realize that congressional action does not equal a democratic product. In fact, most congressional action is best defined by volumes of bills introduced, speeches made, press conferences held, studies commissioned, investigations launched, or action threatened. Surprisingly little of Congress's valuable energy is used to generate actual legislation that gets enacted.

In the 101st Congress, from the beginning of 1989 through adjournment in October 1990, a total of 11,824 bills and resolutions were introduced in the House and Senate. That works out to almost twenty-one bills each day that each branch of the Congress was in session. However, in 1989, only 240 of those measures became law, 410 in 1990. The rules of Congress purposely slow down the path of some bills on their way to the law books. Most bills do require thoughtful consideration, and, I believe for the most part, we can thank our forefathers for a legislative system that operates very slowly.

To isolate behavior and get the truest sense of how the process works, what single issue offers the most incisive view of how Congress really operates? I assert that there is one legislative issue that not only affects the deep, personal interest of nearly every senator but also stands as an illustration of the ethical character of the institution itself—campaign finance reform. It is one issue on which all members believe themselves to be experts.

Senate and House candidates must abide by the laws governing campaign finance. Voters are limited to selecting candidates who campaign within those legal and financial boundaries. Citizens are affected by elected officials who accept our votes and public trusts. All of us, then, should look beneath the gilded dome covering our Congress and review the outdated legal and ethical boundaries governing our electoral process.

MONEY: THE MOTHER'S MILK OF POLITICS

In 1992, members of the U.S. Senate received an annual salary of just over $125,000. Yet the cost of running a successful race for election to that body averaged $4 million. Senators running for reelection must raise roughly $12,000 each week during each year of their six-year term to amass an adequate campaign war chest. To the average American, such funds must surely seem extravagant and such a fund-raising capacity, exhaustive.

Even after being adjusted for inflation, the four Senate election (six-year) cycles between 1982 and 1988 saw an increase in the cost of winning a seat in the US. Senate—from 51 percent to 166 percent. In other words, when the seven elections from 1976 to 1988 were calculated by what the winning candidate spent (in 1976 dollars) to get elected, the results were as follows: the 1982 elections cost 100 percent more than in 1976; the 1984 elections cost 51 percent more than the 1978 elections; the 1986 elections cost 166 percent more than the 1980 elections; and the 1988 elections cost 54 percent more than 1982 spending.

Moreover, money follows power. On February 11, 1986, the *Wall Street Journal* ran a story entitled "Some Ways and Means Members Saw a Surge in Contributions during Tax Overhaul Battle." The piece, written by Brooks Jackson and Jeff Birnbaum, looked at individuals on the tax-writing committee, such as Rep. Wyche Fowler (D-Ga.). Fowler, who had only a 27 percent approval score from the pro-business barometer of the U.S. Chamber of Commerce (and, conversely, a 67% approval from the AFL-CIO), raised over $57,000 in one day from Texas contributors affiliated with Quintana Petroleum Corporation of Houston at an event arranged by a Washington business lobbyist. Interested in tax provisions favorable to the drilling industry, Fowler, like others, received immense financial support from interests unaccustomed to contributing to liberal Democrats. (Over 40% of Fowler's 1985 receipts in his bid to unseat Sen. Mack Mattingly [R] in the 1986 race came from PACs.) Then Congressman Judd Gregg (R-N.H.) told the *Wall Street Journal* that being on a prestigious, influential committee was "like night and day, being on the Science Committee before and being on Ways and Means now," in terms of raising money.

Indeed, ABC's "20/20" reported in the midst of the markup of that tax bill that then Senate Finance Committee Chairman Bob Packwood (R-Ore.) was the top recipient of political action committee (PAC) money the previous year. Out of $966,016 in PAC money, $344,326 came from the insurance industry, $105,700 came from the banking/finance industry, and another $93,565 came from labor unions; all had a substantial stake in the tax bill.

A public interest lobbyist, Fred Wertheimer of Common Cause, told "20/20,"

> The system legalizes buying influence. . . . When I give you, a member of Congress, a substantial amount of money, we both know that you've accepted money from me and you know I have something in mind. . . . They [PACs] are buying a lot more than access. But even if that was all they were buying, what kind of system do we have, where you get access to your representative if you can put up a bunch of money?

People with money are ready, if not eager, to fill with money the outstretched hands of incumbents who come to them months, even years, before their elections. PACs are the most obvious, visible, and powerful force in providing money. And they do it for a reason.

In a 1985 interview about PACs, Tom Baker of the National Association of Home Builders, one of the largest such committees, told CBS News why contributions to incumbents were good investments. "We want access. We want to be able to get in the door and be heard."

But newspaper columnist Mark Shields reverses the view-finder. In a 1991 column, he explained that PACs are not the principal villain in the corrupt system. "PACs . . . are frequently victims of legalized extortion at the hands of incumbents who sit on congressional committees, the decisions of which can directly affect the fate, fortune, and future of the PAC's membership. Failure to contribute carries with it the risk of loss of access to the fundraiser/lawmaker and no chance to please your members' taste."

PACs, which numbered 4,170 in 1990, became "the ultimate whipping boy in the debate over reform," according to a May 1990 advertisement in the *National Journal*. The ad, placed by the National Association of Business PACs (NABPAC), was part of a public campaign to remind Congress and the public that—a result of a previous reform bill—PACs "have stimulated millions of Americans to become involved in our political system."

PACs cover a wide range of occupational and special interests, a spectrum beyond the categories of animal, vegetable, and mineral. There are committees for avocado farmers, Native Americans, rum distillers, Walt Disney employees, right-to-life advocates, sellers of Avon products, Ohio psychologists, and Veterans of Foreign Wars. Individually, they represent no threat to democracy.

But what has been their collective effect on congressional behavior and electoral competition? Whereas in the 1974 election cycle, PAC contributions only made up about 17 percent of a House member's receipts, twelve years later that figure doubled to 34 percent. The actual dollar amount contributions of PACs to Congress grew from $12.5 million in 1974 to $149.9 million in 1990, nearly a 1,200 percent increase.

Such facts might not indicate cause for major concern to those who believe an open system of government must allow for political activism in the form of financial assistance. However, if the system is truly "open," why is the staggeringly disproportionate share of that $149.9 million—a ratio of 11 to 1—going to incumbents?

The answer lies in the fact that special, monied interests—PACs, lobbyists, political fundraisers, and wealthy individuals—want "more than just good government" in return for their contribution, as a Senate leader once said. Some may want an appointment, say, ten minutes with the senator, to discuss a tax provision. Some may want a vote against a nomination in the committee of a senator. Some may just want an "insurance policy" of sorts, the ability to see the member of Congress when they need him or her. People who give a $25 donation to a political candidate's bean supper fund-raising event may want "good government." However, people who write a $1,000 check to a congressman's campaign committee probably want access.

Over the course of several years as a Senate aide, I came to discover that for many in Congress, raising money is seen as a sport. The strategy, the hunt, the catch, and the victory are immensely enjoyable, as though it were sportfishing or a baseball game. . . .

One Hill office implemented a systematically coded rolodex for a senator to keep track of lobbyists and organizations with PACs to denote who or which were contributors to the senator's reelection efforts. With such a system, it would be far easier to decide who would receive an appointment with the senator when such requests were made.

Still other staffers were instructed to make lists of interest groups and PACs that could best be targeted for requests for contributions and honoraria. Such an activity is a common occurrence in many, if not most, Hill offices, despite the broad ethics and campaign laws that restrict political activity in congressional offices.

Such examples, only a scratch on the surface, expose a system in need of analysis at the least and massive overhaul at the most. The words of retiring senators decrying the "money chase" for campaign dollars may roll off the ears of voters as the protests of old-fashioned politicians exiting an electronically sophisticated world. But increasingly, Congress and the citizens it represents, believe something must be done to clean up the system.

CAMPAIGN FINANCE REFORM

Campaign finance reform (CFR) was debated in the Senate from 1985 to 1992. This debate encompassed discussions on PAC reform, spending limits, public financing, "soft money," independent expenditures, and a constitutional amendment limiting campaign spending. No one segment of the congressional election finance system could be isolated to represent the problems in the law.

The Senate realized that if it changed the law dealing with PACs, it would have to address the increasing practice of informally organizing wealthy individuals to contribute to elections. If it disallowed contributions by PACs to candidates, they might increasingly utilize their First Amendment rights to engage in "independent expenditures." Or if the Senate did not constrain newly discovered loopholes in political party finances, money deterred through spending limits could be funneled through national parties to affect federal elections.

This explains the "pop-up" theory in the study of campaign finance. The assumption is that if one stops the flow of political money through one legal avenue, it will find a way to flow through another and pop up somewhere else.

If years of staffing the battle of campaign finance reform taught me one thing, it was that it must be viewed as more than a one-dimensional issue. Some senators saw it as a purely partisan debate. Republicans assumed Democrats wanted only to strengthen their hold on control of Congress with revision of the law. For some, that was true. Democrats assumed Republican resistance was to preserve individual seats in Congress. For some, that was true.

Several opponents of campaign spending limits, a ban on political action committees, and other reforms argued that millions and millions of dollars each year are spent to market such consumer items as bottled water, cosmetics, and dog food. So why worry about how much is spent on something as important as democracy? Still others contended that the volume of money from disclosed, limited sources was a healthy, free-enterprise show of political support for a candidate. They pointed out repeatedly that arbitrary limits on political access gained with money was an imposition of the government over the governed and that competition would thus be stifled. . . .

A balanced view of this issue would recognize that reform of the campaign finance system must be considered from both an ethical and a competitive standpoint. . . .

At issue, therefore, is not just how much it costs to run for the Senate but from whom the money comes. After fruitless years of filibuster, posturing, ethics investigations, and behind-the-scenes negotiations, Congress eventually passed a reform bill, only after they felt certain it would be vetoed. The underlying rationale that is given by political analysts as to why campaign reform has not yet been passed is simple: what incentive do those who vote on it have to change it, if that same system put them in office?

PERSONAL AND SPECIAL INTERESTS

Each of the one hundred members of the Senate, with the occasional exception of one or two appointed to fill a vacancy because of death or resignation, is elected by the people of his or her state after a long and exhausting campaign. This has been the case since the adoption of the 17th amendment in 1913, which provides for direct election by the people. While most candidates leave the day-to-day operations of a campaign to consultants, fund-raisers, paid campaign staff, and volunteers, it is safe to say that they consider themselves to be virtual experts in the field, due to their personal interest in their own career.

Proponents of campaign finance reform, in their own way, have said, "Congress is becoming a 'closed shop' company and needs some healthy competition." The argument went that through government intervention, Congress would be more accessible to the common citizen and thus a more responsive institution. Yet the jobs and the livelihood of members of Congress would be in jeopardy if changes in campaign finance laws were made. Senators seemed to be saying, "If I got elected, everything must be fine." Like any person, a senator has a natural, special interest in keeping his or her job.

Congress does not fare well in any political analysis of the public's opinion of their own member's performance. Pollsters and political scientists constantly recite this fact. But it tells us nothing. The collective stalemate so common to Congress is typical in any committee or organization in which human nature prevails in a search for consensus over confrontation. Congress is no exception. Further, electors of public officials are reluctant to admit to electing a bad or weak officeholder, as such a misjudgment reflects poorly on the voter. In 1960, despite the historically narrow margin of victory John Kennedy had in that election, a much larger number of voters polled months later said they voted for the president.

The persistent low level of public esteem for Congress seems to revolve around money, ethics, and the constant campaign. The candidacy of Ross Perot and the appeal of Bill Clinton for "change" in Washington uniquely connected with 1992 voters. So any serious review of the systemic problems afflicting Congress must look at our officeholders' relationship to money. Any effort to reform congressional campaigns must contend with special and personal interests.

These interests are not just those of members of Congress and candidates for office. They are the interests of the PACs we assume will be curtailed by new rules of the game and broadcasters expected to abide by new political advertising rules. Those who will be affected most significantly will be the voters, who are expected to get a clearer picture of politics from any new set of rules. Still, no one takes those rules more seriously and more personally than the officeholders, who typically want to be reelected.

In their defense, some Hill veterans probably feel like a tenured college professor who is told that a new faculty member will be interviewed and possibly placed in the professor's job, upsetting the established tradition of job security. While Congress was never meant to be a tenured position, anyone would be leery of new rules that bolster competitors.

Sen. William Proxmire (D-Wisc.), who retired from the Senate at the end of 1988, was long noted not only for his "golden fleece awards" aimed at government waste but also for his "myth of the day" floor statements. One such speech was delivered on September 26, 1986, on campaign finance reform.

The myth was clearly stated: "We dare not tamper with the campaign finance laws because of the law of unintended consequences." In keeping with his style of asking rhetorical questions on the Senate floor, Proxmire inquired, "What are the real reasons that Congress refuses to reform campaign financing? I believe there are two:

political advantage and incumbency." He continued, "Every change must pass Congress, which is, by definition, composed of incumbents. And incumbents are leery of any change which might benefit a challenger. . . . The people are ahead of the politicians. The people believe that the present system is little better than legalized influence peddling. They are right. We should be representing the people and not a political party or an incumbent."

In an interview after his retirement from the Senate, I asked Proxmire if he felt special interest money could be linked to the costly multibillion-dollar savings and loans bailout. He told me, "I am convinced that PAC contributions and individual contributions of savings and loan officials persuaded members of the Banking Committee in the Senate, which I chaired, to support weaker regulation responsible for the S&L debacle."

Clearly, if you believe that big campaign money affects government policy and government policy affects taxpayers, then it is in the interest of all taxpayers that the rules affecting big campaign money be changed. Otherwise, taxpayers will continue to pay for big policy mistakes like the S&L bailout.

MOTIVATION TO CHANGE

In stinging oratory about the conduct of Senate Democrats after the controversial nomination of Robert Bork to the Supreme Court, Republican Sen. Alan Simpson of Wyoming charged in a speech on the Senate floor that the Congress only responds to the symbols of "emotion, fear, guilt, or racism." In his disgust for the special interest campaign against Bork, Simpson argued that it is these four devices that push the Congress to act. His point, broadly interpreted, is that Congress wrongfully acts on variable winds of popular will, which can be misguided, instead of exercising their balanced judgments.

In a short but action-filled five years on Capitol Hill, it was also my observation that Congress rarely acts on a national issue until and unless it is surrounded by public outcry, emotion, or fear. It is my further observation that "special interests," in many forms and through numerous avenues, run the Congress to a larger degree than ever before and in a way that is unhealthy for a democratic form of government. . . .

POLITICS PERMEATES ALL WE DO

"[P]olitics" permeates all that we do. It is not limited to presidential and city council campaigns but exists in all professional and personal settings.

Politics surrounds the simplest of social exchanges and everyday quid pro quos. It is seen when a young associate with a downtown law firm—who is a frequent racquetball partner with a senior attorney—gets an office with a window while a more senior associate does not. It occurs when the son of athletic boosters gets more playing time on the basketball court than he might if his parents were not club donors.

Politics is the science of actions of politic persons who use shrewd, expedient, discreet, or delicate actions or words to influence or accomplish their ends. Often employed in perhaps unintentional schemes to gain influence, while not in the form of a direct bribe, is money. The story of campaign finance reform illustrates the resistance of changing the law and the money it regulates, as well as power and the human behavior that clings to it. The influence of money is one issue. The pursuit of it is quite another.

Congressman Barney Frank, a Massachusetts Democrat and maverick reformer, said, "We're the only people in the world who are expected to accept thousands and thousands of dollars and not be influenced by them." But the motivation to have financial security in a campaign speaks to another human reality. Money in election campaigns and society-at-large is viewed as a factor of success. Money for a campaign is perceived as an essential means to a desirable end—being an elected member of Congress.

Thus, those whose names we face in the voting booth in a biennial ritual of democracy are our most vital link to government. The rules that regulate whom we choose in that process are perhaps the most essential and elemental to our democracy. If they are flawed in design or practice, our government will bear those scars. If we the people are ignorant of those flaws, we must educate ourselves and work to effect change. The notion of "term limitations" in the Constitution jumps the gun on a people's right to choose. Political debate and competition have always been the saving grace of democracy. If we see a nonresponsive attitude from elected officials, we have the tools to discharge them from their duties without limiting our future choices with the immovable pillar of a constitutional amendment.

We can accept that politics will surely permeate the discussions on what role money plays in who is elected and how they perform when they are in office. We can accept that money's role in the electoral process is a given that affects ethical behavior and competitive realities. But more than just political speeches, press accounts, and public interest studies, a process occurs in the debate of how to change those rules. It begins in the long, dark corridors of the Capitol. . . .

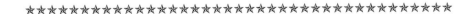

Fundraising is the overriding reality of political campaigning. Media and polling costs, and the political consulting firms that put them together, are expanding year by year.

The following selection analyzes the connection between money and politics, and describes how the realities of political fundraising affect Congress. Featured in this piece is Tony Coelho, who now heads Vice President Gore's 2000 presidential campaign.

Brooks Jackson is an award-winning journalist who has worked for the Associated Press, CNN, and the *Wall Street Journal*. Jackson's major points are:

1. Both parties use sophisticated techniques to raise money, even if some of these methods can prove embarrassingly unsuccessful.

2. The ethic guiding politicians in fundraising is one in which a quid pro quo cannot be explicitly mentioned. This creates a fine line between having access and influence, on the one hand, and entitlement to special favors, on the other.
3. The influence of money means that voters risk having their influence on their representatives usurped by that of big-money donors.

25

Brooks Jackson

Honest Graft

★★★

[Congressman Tony] Coelho's access peddling, like much of what he did at the Democratic campaign committee, began as imitation of techniques first invented by Republicans. The GOP had been marketing contacts with its own most powerful policymakers since capturing the White House and the Senate in 1980. The Republican National Committee's "Eagles" club cost $10,000 a year, and entitled members to meet with Cabinet officers, Senate committee chairmen, and even the President himself. Business lobbyists who gave $5,000 in PAC funds to President Reagan's reelection effort in 1984 became members of a "Presidential Forum" and were promised face-to-face meetings with administration officials on taxes, trade policy, and military spending, among other subjects, plus special privileges at the party's national convention. The limit-skirting "bundling party" staged by the Republican congressional committee, at which PAC managers posed for pictures with the President after donating $20,000 to GOP House candidates, was only a variation of this access-peddling game.

During 1986 the administration was pushing a massive rewrite of the tax code, making its tax experts particularly valuable as fund-raising agents. As the debate on reform heated up, Secretary of the Treasury James Baker traveled around the country giving briefings in return for campaign donations. One such session had to be canceled when a too blatant invitation attracted unwanted publicity; it specifically solicited corporate funds for the Georgia state GOP. Corporate money was legal in Georgia politics but not at the federal level, and this solicitation was too reminiscent of the illegal corporate funds donated to the 1972 Nixon campaign that were uncovered as part of the Watergate scandals. Worse, the Georgia GOP advertised Baker's presentation as a "tax seminar" for businessmen from the Atlanta area, emphasizing the connection between tax legislation and campaign money.

Both parties took such embarrassments in stride. Selling access to the powerful produced too much money for them to fret about appearances. "The Republicans had their Eagles, and they were damned successful," said Michael Fraioli, staff director of the Speaker's Club. "What have the Democrats got? We didn't have the President of the United States, but we had the Speaker of the House."

Coelho said he wanted to move the party away from reliance on big donors and he put great stock in small gifts raised through computer-addressed letters. He said he envisioned a financially secure party organization, more influential with its candidates than any PAC or moneyed interest and itself beholden only to a mass of rank-and-file members who sent in small donations through the mail.

"Direct mail is fabulous right now," Coelho said. "It's going to be over 50 percent of our money, gross." He predicted rapid future growth in these small donations, with no strings attached. "We've got to go to 90 percent, that's where I wish. If I had the stamina I'd stay another two years, because I think in two more years you could move it to 80 percent or more."

But Coelho's dream wasn't coming true. Prospecting for new givers through the mail was expensive and only marginally productive. Coelho tried harder than any other Democrat to raise small donations from rank-and-file citizens, but ultimately he failed to build anything close to the broad base of donors enjoyed by the Republicans.

The reason was simple: the best-educated, highest-income groups of liberal and progressive Americans weren't buying what Coelho and the Democrats were selling. They gave instead to groups like Common Cause and People for the American Way. In 1986 Common Cause claimed 279,000 dues-paying members, while Coelho had 260,000 donors. Common Cause received $10.6 million in 1986, far more than the campaign committee realized from all sources.

Democrats often tried to excuse their failure to attract more financial support from ordinary citizens by saying Democrats were poor, Republicans were rich. But that alibi was inadequate, despite the obvious truth that the richest Americans tended to be Republicans and the poorest were overwhelmingly Democratic. The fact was that millions of well-heeled Democrats and political independents sympathized with the party's noblest themes—compassion, peace, and fairness—but withheld donations.

Extensive polling in 1987 by the Gallup Organization for the Times Mirror Company found two sizable groups of upper-middle-class, politically sophisticated Americans who tended to vote Democratic but who gave little to the party. Among a group it called "60's Democrats"—well-educated people who favored government spending on social programs and strongly identified with peace, civil rights, and environmental movements—51 percent had incomes exceeding $30,000 a year but only 11 percent said they had given money to a political party committee. Another group, called "Seculars"—non-religious people favoring cuts in military spending and opposing both school prayer and legal restrictions on abortions—naturally recoiled from Reagan-style Republicanism and sympathized with Democrats. Of the "Seculars," 49 percent had incomes over $30,000 but only 8 percent gave to a party committee. By contrast, the highest levels of party giving were reported by a Republican group called "Enterprisers." Of that group, 24 percent reported giving to a party committee. And while it was the most affluent segment in the study, with 61 percent reporting incomes exceeding $30,000 annually, it was outnumbered by the other two upper-middle-class groups, which leaned toward the Democrats. "Enterprisers" made up 10 percent of the population, while "60's Democrats" and "Seculars" together constituted 16 percent.

Coelho's direct-mail targets were largely aging pensioners worried about the future. A marketing analysis conducted for his committee in 1985 showed that nearly two-thirds of its donors were over age fifty-five, and 37 percent were retired. To appeal to them Coelho used the names of Speaker O'Neill and Florida Rep. Claude Pepper, who was born in 1900 and was the oldest member of Congress. Like many other direct-mail promoters, Coelho played on his donors' fears; a letter sent in early 1985 said, "A MOVE IN CONGRESS TO SLASH MEDICARE BENEFITS COULD COME QUICKLY," and asked for donations to the campaign committee to "stop Republicans from cutting aid." The committee sent out 1.3 million copies of that letter, carrying O'Neill's signature. It pulled in nearly twice as many new donors as the experts had expected. But O'Neill withdrew the use of his name on the grounds that the letter was causing needless alarm among the elderly. Coelho later sent more copies bearing his own signature instead, but Coelho lacked the Speaker's appeal and the response was unsatisfactory. Committee officials estimated that with O'Neill's name the committee would have gained 6,500 additional new donors and $350,000.

Kathryn Smiley, Coelho's direct-mail expert, said the marketing study showed what she knew instinctively about her donors anyway: "They don't own recreational vehicles. They don't go cross-country skiing." Families with children generally didn't give; "I have nothing to sell to them."

The party got relatively little support from issue-oriented liberals. Once, Coelho insisted on sending a fund-raising letter stressing the issue of military waste, but it cost more to produce and mail than it brought in. He couldn't find any Democrat to sign the letter who was seen as able to do anything about the problem, so he signed the letter himself. "I felt that defense waste was an excellent issue for us," Coelho said, "but it just bombed." . . .

A curious kind of ambivalence pervaded Washington. Everybody knew that lobbyists gave money to buy access and, whether indirectly or overtly, to gain some influence over legislation. So the more money lawmakers took, the more most of them professed to dislike it.

Coelho's ethical code was common among lawmakers. Doing official favors for donors was permitted. The unforgivable sin was to make the connection explicit. Coelho told a story that illustrated the point.

"I had a guy who paid to join the Speaker's Club, $5,000," Coelho said. "He joined, and then he had a problem with the government. He brought it to my attention. I brought it to Billy Ford's attention." Ford, of Michigan, was chairman of the Post Office and Civil Service Committee. "They went into it, checked it out, and tried to help him and so forth. . . . It was a complaint against the government in regards to harassment or something. I can't remember all the details. I hope they did a good job. The bottom line was they couldn't do anything for him. So I told him this."

The way Coelho told the story, the donor then overstepped the line. "He said, 'You know, I gave you my $5,000. I expect better treatment than that.'

"I said, 'That's the end of the conversation. . . . You brought up the wrong subject.'"

Undaunted, the donor showed up at a Speaker's Club reception at which O'Neill was present for the unveiling of his portrait. As the donor attempted to speak to O'Neill, Coelho called in several plainclothes Capitol policemen. "Everywhere he went, they were right with him," Coelho said. "So he came up to me and he said, 'Listen, I am insulted that you are doing that.' And I said, 'You are not going to discuss any of these activities. You can go to anybody you want, say what you want to anybody, but you're not going to do it here. We're going to kick you out. You're not invited. You crashed in. I'll let you stay in here; you crashed in. But you say one damn word, you're out.'"

For Coelho, putting the official machinery of the House of Representatives to work on behalf of a $5,000 donor was no more out of line than giving him fancy luggage tags. He said he became offended only when the donor suggested an explicit entitlement to official favors. "There is a fine line," Coelho explained. "I don't mind [donors] bringing up that they have a problem [with the government]. But don't ever try to create the impression with me, or ever say it—if you say it, it's all over—that your money has bought you something. It hasn't. There's a real delicate line there, and it's hard for people to understand how we do it."

The embittered donor told the story a bit differently. Theodore Gianoutsos was by his own description an eccentric gadfly and outspoken Democrat who in 1983 had been fired by the Reagan administration from a job at the Department of the Interior, allegedly for disrespect. His wife, Françoise, had also been laid off from a federal job at the Office of Personnel Management. The two were avid hunters who wanted to will their modest estate to the government to promote the proper use of firearms and to protect endangered birds of prey. They had haunted the Capitol for years, personally lobbying for the establishment of a National Fish and Wildlife Foundation to receive their bequest.

Though hardly wealthy—they lived in a rented, one-story brick house in a working-class Washington suburb with their two hunting dogs—the couple had given thousands of dollars to Democratic candidates and party organizations since 1980, including $4,825 to the Democratic National Committee and $12,755 to Coelho's committee. In early 1984, when their wildlife foundation bill was stalled in the Senate, the Gianoutsoses asked Coelho for help. "I have absolutely no influence over there," Coelho told them. "If you were a member over there, Ted, we could set you up and you could talk to those people."

Theodore Gianoutsos recalled, "It was absolutely clear to me he wanted more money. We were asking for nothing, and he wanted more." The bill passed anyway and became law in March 1984.

The split with Coelho occurred when the Gianoutsoses pressed too ardently for congressional help regarding the loss of their jobs. They once secured an audience with O'Neill by buttonholing him at a Speaker's Club golf outing. "You've been saying your door is always open," Theodore said. "I'll see you in twenty-four hours," O'Neill replied. After hearing them, however, O'Neill declined to do anything officially. "You ought to get a lawyer," he said. The meeting was in June 1984, but the couple persisted for months. In August they sent a handwritten letter saying, "We did expect a lot of you, because we have always believed in you. . . . WHERE THE HELL ARE YOU NOW, MR. SPEAKER?" Coelho finally tossed them out of the Speaker's Club in October, after the incident at the unveiling of O'Neill's portrait. He said in a letter, "Under the circumstances, I think it is best that we return your dues." Enclosed was a check for $3,825, the installments they had paid during 1984.

Coelho didn't see anything wrong with helping Gianoutsos officially, at least up to a point, because congressmen did favors for constituents all the time. Indeed, they saw that as the most rewarding part of their job. Few elections were won by voting for wise national policies; political survival depended much more on constituent service, lobbying for federal grants for the local college, working to salvage the weapons system produced at the local plant, or writing letters to regulatory agencies about a local businessman's complaint.

Increasingly . . . House members were acting as ombudsmen not only for their constituents but also for their donors. Those who gave money came to be a second constituency, one not envisioned by the drafters of the Constitution. Coelho interceded for a donor from another state just as naturally as he would have for a businessman from Modesto, in his own district. One was entitled to help by virtue of residence, the other by virtue of his currency.

The rising tide of special-interest money was changing the balance of power between voters and donors, between lawmakers' constitutional constituents and their cash constituents. Voters retained the ultimate power to defeat a lawmaker at the polls on election day. But reaching those voters required ever-larger sums of money to buy advertising, postage, opinion polling, computers, and other paraphernalia of modern political campaigns. So donors gained importance at the expense of the electorate. This amounted to a de facto amendment to the Constitution. The constitutional change was ratified, in effect, by the forces of economics and technology, without a vote and without much general appreciation of what was at stake.

Voters still prevailed on any issue if enough of them knew about it and cared strongly enough. But they typically made their judgments based on a wide variety of factors, and most didn't pay close attention until the closing weeks of a political campaign. Donors meanwhile exercised their power to give or to withhold money continuously, as lawmakers stepped up fund-raising from an election-year chore to an annual affair. And when the donors were PACs or professional lobbyists, they paid very close attention to how each member voted, even on obscure amendments in otherwise unwatched subcommittees. The power of the voters was supreme, but infrequently exercised and motivated by diffuse factors. The power of cash constituents was crisply focused, vigilantly exercised, and growing. . . .

Too often, moneyed interests prevail by blocking legislation they don't want. Consider housing. . . . Homeless people and unskilled, jobless youths crowd our cities. Yet the AFL-CIO, financial backbone of the Democratic party, insists on applying Depression-era regulations to federally subsidized housing, pushing up labor costs and reducing the number of apartments that can be built for the poor. Real-estate developers, a rich source of money for both parties, look for subsidies and tax write-offs as the price for building any such housing at all. The obvious becomes unthinkable: Congress dare not consider training jobless ghetto youths in the construction trades and employing them directly at low but decent wages to build no-frills apartments for low-income renters and buyers. Such a direct program would produce more and cheaper housing units than at present and in the bargain create productive citizens from among the tax-eating welfare class. But it would infuriate moneyed interests.

The psychological, even subconscious effect of money is to chill initiatives that donors don't want. As a practical matter, the outcome is the same as if votes had been sold outright. The effect on national policy and well-being are the same. But Coelho says, "One is morally wrong, in effect. The other is legally wrong. There's a big difference." He sees himself as a law abiding player in an immoral system.

TOWARD REAL REFORM

Nearly everyone complains that something is wrong with the American political system. Liberals see a Congress bought by business interests, while PAC managers complain they are being shaken down by money-hungry legislators. Lawmakers detest the rising cost of campaigning, the inconvenience and indignity of asking for money, and the criticism they endure for accepting it. Democrats envy the Republican party's financial strength and decry the sinister influence of big money and expensive political technology while trying to get as much of both for themselves as possible. Republicans, betrayed by the business PACs they nourished, seethe at their inability to dislodge Democratic incumbents. Critics of various leanings deplore lawmakers who use their office to help themselves or moneyed benefactors. Liberal and conservative commentators alike are calling the system "corrupt."

The problem isn't corruption; it is more serious than that. If unprincipled buying and selling of official favors was at fault, then the solution would be simple; honest legislators would refuse to participate, and prosecutors or voters would deal with the rest. To be sure, corruption does exist; it is hard to imagine any other community of 535 souls where felonies are so often proven. But those illegalities are only symptoms of the underlying sickness.

The true predicament is that perverse incentives twist the behavior of ordinary legislators. The system of money-based elections and lobbying rewards those who cater to well-funded interests, both by keeping them in office and by allowing them to enrich themselves while they serve. It also punishes those who challenge the status quo. . . . And it bends even the best of intentions, like Tony Coelho's priestly instincts, toward the courtship of moneyed cliques. As Coelho himself says, "the process buys you out." The system doesn't require bad motives to produce bad government.

America is becoming a special-interest nation where money is displacing votes. Congress commands less and less support among the electorate as it panders increasingly to groups with money, yet its members cling to office like barnacles on the hull of a broken-down steamer.

Voters seem to sense their diminished influence. The more money the politicians spend, ostensibly to get supporters to the polls, the more people just stay home. In 1986 only 33.4 percent of those old enough to cast ballots actually did so for House candidates, the lowest turnout since 1930. Congressional candidates spent a record $450 million in the 1986 elections, not counting additional millions in both hard and soft money raised by political parties and the independent electioneering of PACs. That represented an increase of 20 percent over the previous election and a rise of 131 percent from 1978. But the money served mostly to protect incumbents, especially in the House, where sitting members outspent challengers three to one.

The inverse relationship between spending and turnout doesn't mean that too much money is being spent: quite the opposite. In races where both incumbents and challengers spend freely, turnout generally goes up, for the obvious reason that voters are more aware of the contest and the candidates. The problem is that the outcome of most races is being determined in advance, largely because fewer challengers can raise the ever-larger sums necessary to mount a credible campaign. Fifty-one House members had no opposition at all in the 1986 election, and more than 98 percent of the incumbents who ran were re-elected. For too many constituents, voting is becoming a waste of time.

Parties are losing their competition with the growing influence of special interests. Coelho's energetic "party-building" efforts have actually encouraged House Democrats to become more reliant on special-interest money. The campaign committee gets its own funds increasingly from lobbyists, PACs, and businessmen, and committee officials constantly push candidates to raise PAC money for themselves. House Democrats are drawing nearly half their re-election funds from PACs and a minuscule portion from the party. More than ever, members of Congress are political freebooters, financially beholden not to their party but to scores of favor-seeking groups.

Some political scientists are using the term "ungovernable" to describe such a society, marked by the increasing power of narrow factions. As cash-based constituencies proliferate, lawmakers are tugged and hauled in all directions. Defending particular spending programs, tax breaks, and permissive economic regulations keeps needed campaign funds flowing. But such measures collectively contribute to intractable federal budget deficits and a malfunctioning economy.

Individual lawmakers manage to escape their share of the blame for deficits and economic calamities. They win re-election regularly by attending ribbon-cuttings, announcing federal grants and contracts, sending out district-wide mailings, keeping their large staffs busy chasing passports and wayward Social Security checks, and accumulating enough money from PACs and lobbyists to make the strongest potential challengers seek alternative careers.

This is what Gary Jacobson, a political scientist and a scholar of the electoral system, has called "the fundamental flaw" in our political system: "great individual *responsiveness*, equally great collective *irresponsibility*."

The United States isn't alone; all industrial democracies suffer from the special-interest malady. Britain, the oldest, had such an advanced case that the disorder was first called the "British disease." Political economist Mancur Olson, in his book *The Rise and Decline of Nations* and in other writings, shows that the longer a society enjoys stability, the more special-interest groups it accumulates and, not coincidentally, the slower its economy grows. He calls the illness "institutional sclerosis." His theory helps explain the puzzle of "stagflation," the combination of stagnant economic growth and rapid inflation of prices and wages in the 1970s and early 1980s that seemed to confound classic economic theory. Olson's thesis also provides a reason why the United States is losing its competitive edge to Japan, West Germany, Taiwan, and South Korea. They all began after World War II with clean slates, politically as well as industrially.

Olson's basic principle is that small groups have more incentive to take a larger share of the pie for themselves than they do to work toward enlarging the pie for everyone. Furthermore, narrow organizations such as labor unions, trade associations, or cartels are more likely to form than large, encompassing groups representing the interests of all citizens. In time, self-serving combinations proliferate and society becomes, as Olson puts it, "like a china shop filled with wrestlers battling over the china and breaking far more than they can carry away."

Washington looks very much like Olson's china shop, full of muscular groups clamoring for favors at the expense of the majority of citizens. Dairy farmers have large cooperatives and well-financed PACs to push for expensive federal subsidies and government-sanctioned cartels that push up prices for milk drinkers, cheese eaters, and ice-cream lovers, who themselves have no organized representation. Textile companies and the garment workers' union ask for protection from inexpensive imports, but shoppers have no spokesman in Washington. Construction unions demand government protection from non-union contractors, pushing up the price of apartments, factories, shops, and offices. Gun manufacturers and owners have the National Rifle Association, while people who wish to avoid being machine-gunned are on their own. The *Washington Representatives* directory lists more than 8,500 groups with agents in the capital. Even the lobbyists have lobbies: the American Society of Association Executives represents trade-association officials, the American League of Lobbyists serves the growing number of independent practitioners, and the National Association of Business Political Action Committees consists mainly of corporation-sponsored PACs. . . .

The paralysis is especially severe when one party holds the White House and the other retains control of one or both chambers of Congress, as has been the case for all but four years since Richard Nixon took office in 1969. . . .

The campaign-finance laws make a bad situation worse. The reforms of the 1970s malfunctioned. No longer is political cash being passed around in brown paper bags; the money is mostly out in the open now, flowing through legally sanctioned channels that give it official approval. The reforms turned what had once been a subterranean trickle of special-interest money into a roaring cascade. . . .

There is no denying the good intentions of many who favor spending limits, an understandable but superficial response to the rising cost of elections and the growth of PACs. However, limits won't do anything to provide more abundant funds for challengers or less troublesome sources of financing for incumbents. If lawmakers set limits too low, as it is in their narrow self-interest to do, challengers will be prevented from spending the sums necessary to match the built-in advantages of incumbents. Voters will have even fewer choices, and less influence. . . .

True reform will require a program endorsed by both parties, one potent enough to return power to voters and to cure the paralysis that grips Congress. To arouse the interest of a skeptical public, it needs to be as progressive and exciting as the tax-reform bill of 1986. To work, it will require much stronger enforcement.

★★

The following selection presents a fascinating analysis of the unintended undemocratic consequences of campaign finance reform. The author concludes that reform proposals favor certain political elites, support the status quo, and even discourage citizen participation in the political process.

Bradley A. Smith teaches law at Yale University. In this piece, Smith's major points are:

1. Campaign finance reforms have been based on faulty assumptions and are generally undemocratic.
2. Some of these faulty assumptions are that too much money is spent on campaigns; that campaigns based on small contributions are more democratic; and that money buys elections.
3. Campaign finance reform has had some negative consequences, including entrenching the status quo, encouraging donors to influence legislation, favoring certain elites, and favoring wealthy candidates.
4. The assumptions behind campaign finance laws are directly contrary to the assumptions underlying the First Amendment.

26

Bradley A. Smith

CAMPAIGN FINANCE REFORM: FAULTY ASSUMPTIONS AND UNDEMOCRATIC CONSEQUENCES

★★★

The agenda of the campaign finance reform movement has been to lower the cost of campaigning, reduce the influence of special interests, and open up the political system to change. In 1974, reformers gained their greatest victory, passing major amendments to the Federal Elections Campaign Act. Nevertheless, by 1996, congressional campaign spending, in constant dollars, nearly had tripled.

Congressional election contributions by political action committees (PACs) increased from $20.5 million in 1976 to $189 million in 1994. Since 1974, the number of PACs has risen from 608 to more than 4,500. House incumbents outspent challengers in 1996 by almost four to one. Meanwhile, incumbent reelection rates in the House reached record highs in 1986 and 1988, before declining slightly in the 1990s. What went wrong?

The problem is that reform has been based on faulty assumptions and is, in fact, irretrievably undemocratic. Reform proposals inherently favor certain political elites, support the status quo, and discourage grassroots political activity.

FAULTY ASSUMPTIONS

Too much money is spent on campaigns. The language in which political campaigns are described in the press reinforces the perception that too much money is spent on them. Candidates "amass war chests" with the help of "special interests" which "pour their millions" into campaigns. "Obscene" expenditures "career" out of control or "skyrocket" upwards. Yet, to say that too much money is spent on campaigning is to beg the question, "compared to what?" For instance, Americans expend two to three times as much money each year on potato chips as on political campaigns.

In the two-year period ending in November 1996, approximately $800 million was spent by all congressional general election candidates. Although this set a record for congressional races, it amounts to about $4 per eligible voter, spent over a two-year period. Total direct campaign outlays for all candidates for local, state, and federal elections over the same period can be estimated around $2.5 billion, or about $12 per eligible voter over the two-year cycle. By comparison, Procter & Gamble and Philip Morris, the nation's two largest advertisers, budget roughly the same amount on advertising as is laid out by all political candidates and parties.

Increased campaign spending does translate into a better informed electorate, and voter understanding of issues grows with the quantity of campaign information received. Candidate ads are the major source of voter information. Lower campaign spending will result in less public awareness and understanding of issues. Considering the importance of elections to any democratic society, it is hard to believe that direct expenditures of approximately $10 per voter for all local, state, and national campaigns over a two-year period is a crisis requiring government regulation and limitations on spending.

Campaigns based on small contributions are more democratic. As many as 18 million Americans make some financial contribution to a political party, candidate, or PAC in an election cycle. No other system of campaign funding anywhere in the world enjoys so broad a base of support. Yet, this amounts to just 10% of the voting-age population. Even though this figure represents a far broader base of contributors than historically has existed, it has not made the political system more democratic and responsive.

In many cases, those candidates who best are able to raise campaign dollars in small contributions are those who are most emphatically out of the mainstream. Republican Barry Goldwater's 1964 presidential campaign, for example, garnered $5.8 million from 410,000 small contributors before he suffered a landslide defeat. On his way to an even more crushing defeat in 1972, Democrat George McGovern raised almost $15 million from small donors, at an average of approximately $20 per contributor.

Assuming that reliance on numerous small contributions makes a campaign in some way more democratic, the most "democratic" campaign of recent years was the 1994 Senate race of Republican Oliver North. He amassed approximately $20 million, almost entirely from small contributors, and outspent his nearest rival by nearly four-to-one. Yet, he lost to an unpopular opponent plagued by personal scandal.

With the exception of the occasional candidate such as McGovern or North, Americans are unwilling, individually, to contribute enough money in small amounts to run modern campaigns. The likelihood that what any individual does will matter simply is too small to provide most voters with the incentive to give financially to candidates. If large contributions were banned totally, there would not be enough money available to finance campaigns at a level that informs the electorate.

Money buys elections. A candidate with little or no money to spend is unlikely to win most races. Furthermore, the one expending the most wins more often than not. The correlation between spending and victory, though, may stem simply from the desire of donors to contribute to candidates who are likely to win, in which case the ability to win attracts money, rather than the other way around. Similarly, higher levels of campaign contributions to a candidate may reflect a level of public support that is manifested later at the polls.

A greater outlay does not necessarily translate into electoral triumph. Having money means having the ability to be heard; it does not mean that voters will like what they hear. In 1994 House of Representative races, for example, 34 Republicans defeated Democratic incumbents, spending on average two-thirds as much as their opponents. In 1996, several Senate candidates won despite being outspent. Republican Michael Huffington spent nearly $30 million of his own money in the 1994 California senatorial race, only to come up empty-handed.

Money is a corrupting influence on the legislature. A substantial majority of those who have studied voting patterns on a systemic basis agree that campaign contributions affect very few votes in the legislature. The primary factors in determining a legislator's votes are party affiliation, ideology, and constituent views and needs. Where contributions and voting patterns intersect, this is largely because donors contribute to candidates believed to favor their positions, not the other way around.

These empirical studies often cut against intuition. Experience and human nature suggest that people are influenced by money, even when it does not go directly into their pockets, but into their campaigns. Yet, there are good reasons why the impact of contributions is not so great. First, people who are attracted to public office generally have strong personal views on issues. Second, there are institutional and political incentives to support party positions. Third, large contributors usually are offset in legislative debate by equally well-financed interests that contribute to a different group of candidates. Large PACs and organizations frequently suffer enormous losses in the legislative process.

Moreover, money is not the only political commodity of value. For instance, the National Rifle Association has a large PAC, but also has nearly 3 million members who focus intently, even solely, on NRA issues in their voting. The NRA's power would seem to come less from dollars than from votes. To the extent that it comes from dollars, that, too, is a function of votes—i.e., the group's large membership. Groups advocating gun control frequently complain that the NRA outspends them, but rarely mention that the NRA outvotes them as well.

Campaign finance reformers often pose as disinterested citizens, merely seeking "good government." In fact, there is ample evidence that they have targeted certain types of campaign activities closely tied to political agendas reformers oppose. They therefore favor regulation that would tilt the electoral process in favor of preferred candidates, against popular will.

NEGATIVE CONSEQUENCES

Campaign finance reform has had several negative consequences, which broadly can be labeled "undemocratic." Reform has entrenched the status quo and made the electoral system less responsive to popular opinion, strengthened the power of elites, favored wealthy individuals, and limited opportunities for "grassroots" political activity.

Entrenching the status quo. Contribution limits favor incumbents by making it relatively harder for challengers to raise money to run their campaigns. The need to solicit cash from a large number of small contributors benefits incumbent candidates who have in place a database of past givers, an intact campaign organization, and the ability to raise funds on an ongoing basis from political action committees.

Newcomers with low name recognition have the most difficulty raising substantial sums from small contributors, who are less likely to give to unknowns. Well-known public figures challenging the status quo traditionally have relied on a small number of wealthy patrons to fund their campaigns. Theodore Roosevelt's 1912 Bull Moose campaign was funded almost entirely by a handful of wealthy supporters. Eugene McCarthy's 1968 anti-war campaign relied for seed money on a handful of six-figure donors, including industrialist Stewart Mott, who gave approximately $210,000, and Wall Street banker Jack Dreyfus, Jr., who may have contributed as much as $500,000.

More recently, John Anderson probably would have had more success in his independent campaign for the presidency in 1980 had his wealthy patron, Mott, been able to give unlimited amounts to his campaign. Whereas Ross Perot's 1992 presidential campaign was made possible by the Supreme Court's holding that an individual may spend unlimited sums to advance his own candidacy, contribution limits make it illegal for Perot to bankroll the campaign of another challenger, such as Colin Powell, in the same manner. The Reform Party, started in 1996, was able to get off the ground, in large part, thanks to Perot's money.

Beyond making it harder for challengers to raise cash, contribution limits indirectly reduce spending. This further works against challengers. Incumbents begin each election with significant advantages in name recognition. They are able to attract press coverage because of their office and often receive assistance from their office staffs and government-paid constituent mailings. Through patronage and constituent favors, they can add to their support.

To offset these advantages, challengers must expend money. Studies have found that the effect of each dollar spent is much greater for challengers than for incumbents because most voters already have some knowledge about incumbents and their records. Since spending is so much more important for challengers than incumbents, lower limits tend to hurt the former more.

Set low enough, contribution and spending limits make it almost impossible for challengers to attain the critical threshold of name recognition at which point a race becomes competitive. The bills introduced unsuccessfully in the last two Congresses by Senators John McCain (R.-Ariz.) and Russell Feingold (D.-Wis.) included spending limits. In 1994 and 1996, every challenger who spent less than the limits in the McCain-Feingold bill lost, but each incumbent who expended less than the proposed limits won.

Influence peddling and accountability. Like all political activity, the purpose of campaign contributions is to influence public policy. Contributors may adopt a legislative strategy, attempting to influence votes in the legislature, or an electoral strategy, aimed at influencing who wins elections. Influence peddling only becomes a problem when legislative strategies are pursued; under an electoral strategy, groups are trying to persuade the public to vote for a preferred candidate, and there is nothing wrong with that. Yet, contribution limits—the most popular reform measure—encourage legislative strategies by PACs and other monied interests.

Campaign contributors must weigh the costs and benefits of each strategy. Normally, they prefer an electoral strategy, aimed at convincing voters to elect like-minded candidates to office. Money given to a losing challenger is not merely a waste, it can be counterproductive, since such contributions increase the enmity of the incumbent. Because incumbents win most races, an electoral strategy of supporting challengers is a very high risk.

The alternative is to give to the incumbent in the hope that a legislative strategy might succeed, at least by minimizing otherwise hostile treatment aimed at the contributor's interests. When contributions are limited to an amount unlikely to change the result of an election, rational donors are forced into a legislative strategy. Thus, to the extent that campaign contributions influence legislative policymaking, limits are likely to make the situation worse.

Furthermore, PACs—and the interests they represent—play an important role in monitoring an office-holder's record. In most cases, it will not be rational for individuals to devote considerable time to monitoring the performance of elected officials, but, by banding together with others having similar concerns, they can perform that function at a reasonable cost. PACs are an important part of this process. Thus, contribution limits may reduce legislative monitoring, leading to a legislature ever more isolated from the people.

Favoring select elites. Campaign finance reform usually is sold as a populist means to strengthen the power of "ordinary" citizens against "big money" interests. In fact, campaign finance reform has favored select elites and further isolated individuals from the political process.

There are a great many sources of political influence. Hollywood personalities, by virtue of their celebrity, may receive an audience for their political views they would not have otherwise. They may be invited to testify before Congress, despite their lack of any particular expertise, or use their celebrity to assist campaigns through appearances at rallies. Successful academics may write powerful articles that change the way people think about issues. Labor organizers have at their disposal a vast supply of manpower that can be used to support favored candidates. Successful entrepreneurs may amass large sums of money, which can be applied for political purposes. Media editors, reporters, and anchors can shape not only the manner in which news is reported, but what is reported. Those with marketing skills can raise funds or produce advertising for a candidate or cause.

Newspapers, magazines, and TV and radio stations can spend unlimited sums to promote the election of favored candidates. Thus, Katherine Graham, the publisher of the *Washington Post*, has at her disposal the resources of a media empire to promote her views, free from the campaign finance restrictions others are subjected to. News anchor Peter Jennings is given a nightly forum on national TV on which to express his opinions.

Media elites are not the sole group whose influence is heightened by campaign spending and contribution limits. Restricting the flow of money into campaigns increases the relative importance of in-kind contributions, and so favors those who are able to control large blocks of manpower, rather than dollars. Limiting contributions and expenditures does not particularly democratize the process, but merely shifts power from people who give money to those whose primary contribution is time, media access, or some other attribute—i.e., from small business groups to labor unions and journalists. Other beneficiaries of campaign finance limitations include political middlemen; public relations firms conducting "voter education" programs; lobbyists; PACs, such as Emily's List, which "bundle" large numbers of $1,000 contributions; and political activists. These individuals probably are less representative of public opinion than the wealthy philanthropists and industrialists who financed campaigns in the past.

Campaign finance restrictions do not make the system more responsive to the interests of the middle and working class. Efforts to assure equality of inputs into the campaign process are less likely to guarantee popular control than is the presence of multiple sources of political power. Campaign finance regulation reduces the number of voices and increases the power of those groups whose form of contribution remains unregulated.

Favoring wealthy candidates. Though campaign finance restrictions aim to reduce the role of money in politics, they have helped to renew the phenomenon of the "millionaire candidate," of whom Huffington and Perot arguably are the most celebrated examples. The Supreme Court has held that Congress may not limit constitutionally the amount a candidate can spend on his or her own campaign. Access to unlimited amounts, coupled with restrictions on raising money, favors those candidates who can contribute large sums to their own campaigns from personal assets. A Michael Huffington, Herb Kohl, or Jay Rockefeller becomes a particularly attractive candidate precisely because personal wealth provides a direct campaign advantage that cannot be offset by a large contributor to the opposing candidate.

At the same time that contribution limits help wealthy candidates, they tend to harm working-class political interests. A candidate with many supporters who can afford to give the legal limit may be relatively unscathed by "reform" legislation. However, candidates with large constituencies among the poor and working class traditionally have obtained their campaign funds from a small base of wealthy donors. By limiting the ability of wealthy individuals such as Stewart Mott or Augustus Belmont to finance these efforts, working-class constituencies may suffer.

Favoring special interests. Campaign finance regulation also is undemocratic in that it favors well-organized special interests over grassroots political activity. Limitations on campaign contributions and spending require significant regulation of the campaign process. They favor those already familiar with the regulatory machinery and people with the money and sophistication to hire the lawyers, accountants, and lobbyists needed to comply with complex filing requirements. Such dynamics naturally will run against newcomers to the political arena, especially those who are less educated or less able to pay for professional services.

As opportunities to gain an advantage over an opponent through use of the regulatory process are created, litigation has become a major campaign tactic. One can expect such tactics to be used most often by those already familiar with the rules, and there is some evidence that campaign enforcement actions are directed disproportionately at challengers, who are less likely to have staff familiar with the intricacies of campaign finance regulation.

Perhaps those most likely to run afoul of campaign finance laws—and thus to be vulnerable to legal manipulations aimed at driving them from the political debate—are those engaged in true grassroots activities. For instance, in 1991, the *Los Angeles Times* reviewed Federal Election Commission files and found that one of the largest groups of campaign law violators consisted of "elderly persons . . . with little grasp of the federal campaign laws."

Even sophisticated interest groups have found campaign finance laws a substantial hindrance to grassroots campaign activity and voter education efforts. In 1994, the U.S. Chamber of Commerce and American Medical Association decided not to publish and distribute candidate endorsements to thousands of their dues-paying members, under threats of litigation from the Federal Election Commission. Under FEC regulations, just 63 of the Chamber of Commerce's 220,000 dues-paying members qualified as "members" for the purposes of receiving the organization's political communications. Similarly, the FEC had held that it would be unlawful for the AMA to distribute endorsements to about 44,500 of its members.

The First Amendment was based on the belief that political speech was too important to be regulated by the government. Campaign finance laws operate on the directly contrary assumption that campaigns are so important that speech must be regulated. Campaign finance laws constitute an arcane web of regulation that has led to citizens being fined for distributing homemade leaflets and trade groups being prohibited from communicating with their members.

The solution to the campaign finance dilemma is to recognize the flawed assumptions of the campaign finance reformers, dismantle the Federal Elections Campaign Act and the FEC bureaucracy, and take seriously the system of campaign finance "regulation" that the Founding Fathers wrote into the Bill of Rights: "Congress shall make no law . . . abridging the freedom of speech."

Political consultants are the center of the real world of rough-and-tumble politics. They know that politics is a contact sport, but unlike other sports politics does not have a clearly defined set of rules. Neither umpires nor referees exist to call balls and strikes, fouls, or when players are out of bounds. Politics follows Machiavelli, not Robert's Rules of Order.

In the following selection, a leading political consultant gives a first-hand account of the rough world of modern political campaigns, and shows how far political realities have taken us from the ideal democratic model.

Ed Rollins is a longtime Republican campaign strategist. Rollins' major points are:

1. The pressure of campaigning is intense and exciting—but not glamorous.
2. Campaigns are even tougher on the candidates.
3. The six most significant factors making the current campaign system "dysfunctional" are attack ads; the media; campaign financing; confrontational politics; the power of special interests; and the lack of term limits.

27

Ed Rollins

BARE KNUCKLES AND BACK ROOMS

So now I could quit the political game—and believe me, there were no regrets. I had never intended to run campaigns for a living. As a young man, I considered governing the real work; campaigning was just something you did to get your boss reelected so you could continue to serve. But I'd come to love the rough and tumble of a hard-fought race, and for the most part the political consulting business had been very good to me. Now, at age 51, I couldn't take the physical punishment anymore. But the deeper problem was that I was sick of the life.

Few people have any sense for what it's really like to run a campaign. As George Bush would say, the job is wall-to-wall Tension City. You're constantly hounded by the candidate, his or her spouse, the opposition, your staff, and the media. Before one fire burns out, another is smoldering. Long-range planning is tomorrow's crisis. Between juggling the demands of six races and my business, I spent twenty nights in my own bed in 1994, and there were plenty of times I literally couldn't remember the name of the hotel where I was staying. It got to the point where I lived for airplanes just so I could sleep for two hours without hearing a phone ring. And it's not just telephones—the cellular phone, the fax machine, and the relentlessly buzzing pager are now part of the consultant's standard operating equipment.

If you're physically present in a campaign only a day or two a week, the candidate and his staff want every minute of your time. The pressure is unbelievable, and it only gets worse as election day approaches. You work eighteen or twenty hours a day, and if you can't handle stress and make quick decisions, you're a goner. You can't delay a decision, because another critical one will be facing you shortly. You never forget that one bad call on a commercial can waste a million dollars and cost your candidate the election.

Meanwhile, your other campaigns still want you making the decisions and offering guidance, so even when you're elsewhere, you're talking on the phone constantly to them. After all, if you do your job well, the candidate becomes addicted to you and needs your daily counsel. . . .

Adding insult to injury, our public image isn't exactly terrific. Most people seem to think political consultants are a bunch of unprincipled hired guns engaged in a glamorous profession that makes us rich and famous. They're not just wrong about the money—they're wrong on all counts. The vast majority of consultants start in politics because they believe in somebody or a cause. But after a while, we see our new client or opponent make the same mistakes we watched another guy make two or four or eight years ago. With each election cycle, we lose patience and become more hardened and cynical. Maybe that's why so many of us eat too much, smoke too much, and drink too much. Add these vices to the fact that we spend too many nights alone in motels in far-off cities and you've got a lot of ulcers, coronaries, and divorces waiting to happen. . . .

So is the life of a political consultant exciting? Absolutely. But glamorous? Forget about it!

But consultants (including me) really shouldn't complain—hell, until fairly recently our job didn't even exist. Thirty years ago, when I started out in this business, campaigns were managed by political or personal confidants. Nixon's 1960 campaign was run by Bob Finch, his former administrative assistant. Ted Sorenson was Jack Kennedy's aide and speechwriter. Those days are gone. The modern campaign is the bailiwick of hired guns—political gypsies skilled in the mechanics of polling, fundraising, media buys, and driving a message. The process has become so complex that anyone who tries to do it without people like me is a fool. . . .

Modern campaigns are tough on the people who run them, but they're toughest on the candidates themselves. That's why the once-noble profession of politics has had so much trouble attracting—and keeping—good people.

Look at the distinguished list of Republicans who chose not to run for president this time—several of whom might make a better president than either Bill Clinton or Bob Dole. And look at the roster of prominent senators from both parties who have chosen to retire in 1996. Many of them delivered the same valedictory: They're sick of gridlock, sick of the rat race, and sick of the system.

Let's face it—nobody's happy with what's happening to our political process. Politicians and the people who elect them sense that things have gone haywire. The electorate in particular is disgusted with what passes for politics in this country today.

When running for federal office is such miserable duty that the best and the brightest abandon ship in droves—or aren't even interested in booking passage—we're careening toward disaster. In my opinion, here are the six most significant factors why the system is currently dysfunctional.

Attack ads. Negative commercials are the biggest problem in politics today. Negative-media campaigns are destroying politics. Unlike any other business, in which you try to convince the consumer your product is superior, the essence of campaigning today is winning by destroying the opponent and being the lesser of two evils. Think about it: If every oil company talked about how their business rivals polluted the environment and every carrier in the airline industry ran commercials about how many people were killed in competitors' plane crashes—and the competition responded in kind—nobody would feel safe driving or flying anywhere. That's not much different from what's happening in politics today.

Here's the ugly truth they never teach you in civics class: Negative ads work. It's easier to defeat your opponent than to get elected yourself. Not all that long ago, campaigns were issue-driven. Now they're character-driven. Party labels are essentially meaningless. Issues don't matter as much as the message, and the message doesn't count anywhere near as much the messenger. So the campaign trains its sights on the messenger. You go out and tarnish their personality, you run ads that beat the living daylights out of them.

The name of the game is proving that your opponent is dishonest or has some character flaw. These attack ads go well beyond setting the record straight or laying out policy differences. And unfortunately, American voters have now been conditioned to believe the worst, which is why negative ads are so effective. The 1994 California Senate race was the first I've ever seen where the negative ratings of *both* candidates went over 50 percent.

The worst part of it is watching candidates who deserve better get trashed and even destroyed. George Nethercutt was so clean he squeaked, but Tom Foley's campaign spent six weeks telling voters Nethercutt wanted to cut Medicare, Social Security, and aid to schools, and Nethercutt's negatives exploded. Families get dragged into the muck, too. If a candidate has a daughter who's had an abortion or has a son who's a homosexual, the opposition will know about it, and somebody will probably print it. I've encountered several good potential candidates who decided not to run because their kids had been picked up for smoking marijuana or driving while intoxicated. And there's no statute of limitations. Candidates get nailed for not paying their nanny's Social Security taxes twenty years ago. A spouse's tax shelters and business dealings—not to mention the messy divorce from a previous marriage—are all fair game.

The idea is to put a thought or phrase into the voter's head that reinforces pre-conceived ideas: Bob Dole's been around so long he's obviously part of the problem; Bill Clinton's so smooth and slick he's probably dishonest.

Nasty things have been said about office seekers since the beginning of our democracy. The difference from those early whispering campaigns is TV. Television reaches huge numbers of consumers directly and can pound home a negative message in millions of living rooms night after night. That's the up-front technique—the sneak attacks now come by way of telephone banks. A typical example is calling a senior citizen's home under the guise of doing a poll and slipping in this message: "Are you aware that Candidate X is for abolishing Social Security?" It happens all the time.

I'm not so naive as to think negative ads will go away. The 1994 elections and the early Republican primaries this year were as negative as any in recent history. But there was a time in our history when politics had *some* rules. The only way to stop gutter politics is to make the candidates deliver every negative attack personally. It's easier to get away with disembodied words. If you're slinging the mud yourself, you'll be more careful. But don't count on anything that sensible happening. Willie Horton has become the norm, not the extreme. He'll be back.

The insatiable media. The fundamental difference between the old and new ways of campaigning is the crushing intensity of electronic coverage and the incredible cost of competing on television. When I started out, television was a fairly new phenomenon. Now, even podunk stations have two or three hours of news programming to fill every day. The networks are even hungrier, and CNN never sleeps.

Fifteen years ago, we'd say that overnight is a lifetime in politics—and that was before cable. Nowadays, if CNN has it, you damn well better have your response in an hour, or your candidate has lost the war of the visuals. Television is such a staple of modern society that for most voters, it's not real until it's on the tube. Unfortunately, scandal and sensationalism are the order of the day. And of all the media, television has most avidly bought into the notion that people running for office either aren't honest or have something to hide.

The print media isn't far behind. There's a whole new breed of reporter out there who went to journalism school in the post-Watergate period. These hotshots are activists. They don't want to report the news; they want to be participants in the process. They know it's increasingly harder to get into print without a "holy shit" story, as it's known in the trade. They also know that if you can make a splash with your stories, you'll get invited onto the network talking-head shows. From there, it's a short distance to fat speaking fees. A surprising number of reporters make more on the lecture circuit than they do on their day jobs. Reporting pays the grocery bill, but being a celebrity journalist can pay for your kid's college tuition and a condo in Ocean City.

The bottom line is that these new-age reporters are willing to push the envelope—so they'll bite on a bullshit tip more readily. When I hear reporters talk about stories "too good to check," I know they're not joking.

Political reporters are also far more partisan than they used to be. The vast majority of them think they're objective. But as a breed, most are liberal and Democratic—and absolutely biased against Republicans, culturally and ideologically. Consequently, there's a shared mind-set among most reporters. Their value systems are in lockstep, so even when a reporter is trying to be balanced, the subtle influence of his (or her) peers means that he's probably still going to be slanted. And it's human nature for a reporter to give more weight to the side of a story that's closer to his own beliefs.

In 1992, for example, several prominent reporters made little effort to conceal their affection for Bill Clinton. And even when reporters weren't kissing Clinton's ass or encouraging their editors to bury negative information about him on page nineteen, many of them were quietly leading cheers for him from the sidelines. Why? Because he was one of them. They liked him and didn't like Bush, which was obvious to anyone mixing and mingling with them.

Here's a perfect example from the 1993 New Jersey governor's race. In the final days of the campaign, the race had closed to a dead heat. I did several background interviews with reporters and predicted that Christie Whitman would win. I could tell from their questions they thought I was nuts, despite my reputation for not bullshitting the press. When James Carville backgrounded those same reporters, they all believed him when he said Jim Florio was eight to ten points up. Those reporters may have been "objective," but they gave Carville the benefit of the doubt because they shared his political beliefs and wanted his candidate to win. You'll never convince me the attitude of the media doesn't contribute to skewed coverage.

I'm not one of those media critics who think journalistic ethics is an oxymoron. But I do think some reporters are less principled than they used to be, and it's bound to get worse before it gets better—if it ever gets better.

Dysfunctional campaign financing. When I was recruiting candidates at the White House and the NRCC [National Republican Congressional Committee], the first question most of them asked was how much money they needed to win. I'd always say that while no amount of cash can guarantee a victory, the amount needed to be viable was larger than they thought.

The sticker shock only gets worse. Several credible candidates decided not to run for president this year because they weren't sure they could raise the $20 million to $30 million needed to be a serious contender. The unrelenting and ever-growing need for money has put our politicians in the position of succumbing to the siren song of well-heeled special interests and the cynical process of constant fundraising. In particular, the bottomless need for more money helps keep the power of political action committees intact. Unfortunately, the PAC system is an incumbent's best friend. The ease by which an incumbent can fatten his campaign war chest without going more than a few blocks from the Capitol to a PAC fundraiser is appalling. When the Democrats ran Congress, most of the PAC money went to them. Now the Republicans demand the same largesse—and get it.

The irony is that PACs came about out of a desire to reform the system by limiting the huge sums that individuals or corporations could previously give to candidates. In the end, the voters get screwed. Most incumbents raise at least half their campaign money from PACs. A great deal of that money is controlled by the lobbyists peddling their influence on Capitol Hill. Is there any wonder that the larger PACs have enormous influence over the drafting and passage of legislation?

Genuine campaign finance reform will only occur through a constitutional amendment eliminating PACs and prohibiting wealthy individuals to spend their own fortunes. If it doesn't happen soon, the system will only get more corrupt and fewer challengers will be competitive.

Confrontational politics. Since this Congress convened, confrontational politics has been the order of the day. It's the ugliest climate I've ever seen on Capitol Hill. The truth is, voters are sick of it.

When I came to Washington in 1973, there was still a sense of order and civility to the political process. You fought as partisans during the day, but called a truce at nightfall. Now, with the election of a Republican House and the elevation of Newt Gingrich to Speaker, partisan warfare is the rule and fraternization with the enemy is a near-capital offense.

Serious polarization is the inevitable result. In the House, Democrats are fewer and more liberal; Republicans are greater in number and far more conservative. To the seventy-three freshman GOP members, ending the era of big government is a sacred duty. Yet the solutions to resolving many of our most serious problems lie in the center, and require bipartisan support.

Gingrich is a street fighter of the first order and is loath to compromise. The Democrat leadership is equally partisan and ruthless in trying to save the old order. But Newt and his often intemperate rhetoric set the tone. The last Speaker as mean and partisan was Jim Wright. Gingrich brought him down and sent him back to Texas in disgrace. The Democrats will be satisfied with nothing less for Gingrich. Live by the sword, die by the sword.

When I worked for President Reagan, the Democrats were just as partisan, and divided government didn't work much better then than it does now. But people *thought* it worked. No matter how bitterly they fought one another on issues of substance, Reagan and Speaker Tip O'Neill always seemed to be standing in the Rose Garden to celebrate signing some bill. That was reassuring to the country. The opposite is true today: It's not working, and it doesn't look like it's working, either. The public doesn't trust Clinton and they don't like Gingrich. And as the campaign heats up, it's bound to get worse.

The power of special interests. As the clout of political parties has diminished in the last several decades, special interest groups have risen to fill the void in the political process. Organizations as diverse as labor unions, church groups, and hunting clubs now affect campaigns as much as the old ward bosses of Boston and Chicago. The single issue that such groups support can become the litmus test that mobilizes the membership on election day.

The conservative religious movement is now a critical part of the coalition for any successful Republican candidate. Labor unions fill the same role for Democrats. Candidates endorsed by such organizations are increasingly expected to march in lockstep or pay a heavy price. In the future, the power of these groups will continue to grow. Big labor plans to spend upward of $35 million to defeat Republican House candidates in the fall. Small business groups are planning a similar blitz for Republicans. To try to get elected without the support of single-issue groups like these is becoming damn near impossible.

The lack of term limits. Every place I go, people ask me why better people don't run for office. The truth is good people do run, and some good ones win. But the vast majority lose, because the power of money and incumbency stacks the system against challengers. Once in a generation, as in 1974 and 1994, a frustrated public will decide on radical change and throw a lot of incumbents out. But year in and year out, many good people don't stand a chance of winning.

Turnover in politics is healthy. Making a career of holding office isn't. More than one person in a congressional district of 600,000 people can represent the community's views. If we don't make politics more competitive, more good people will decide not to bother. That's why I support a twelve-year limit for congressional membership, but I wouldn't stop there. We should change the Constitution to create a four-year term for House members and require all members to run in the presidential election year. That would cut down on the cost and duration of campaigning, and eliminate year-round fundraising. Today we get one year of governing and one year of campaigning in a two-year term. This way we'd get three and one. Congress could take more time studying complex issues and could enact multiyear budgets. And if every member had to run with his party's nominee, party platforms would have more relevance, and members would be more accountable to a president's agenda.

The cumulative effect of these six factors is that voters don't like or trust *any* of the people they send to Washington. They believe instead that politicians and parties have developed tin ears—and they're right. Our representatives don't listen to the people as they're charged to do; instead, they heed the loudest and most seductive voices. Even the most highly regarded officeholders are deemed long on rhetoric and short on substance. They don't seem to have the best long-term interests of the country uppermost in their minds.

Whether the public best knows the author of the following selection, Bill Bradley, as a Knicks star or an outstanding Senator from New Jersey is a matter of debate. Bradley's Senate colleagues respected him as much for his political acumen and expert knowledge of public policy issues as his former NBA competitors were impressed with his athletic talents. After a decade in the Senate, Michael Barone wrote, "Bradley has already produced a major reform of our tax system and attracts respectable attention whenever he weighs in on a major issue. He has demonstrated a special strength of character and self-discipline not often seen in politicians and a piercing insight into issues that goes quickly beyond the conventional wisdom and to the heart of the matter."[1]

Bill Bradley was the kind of deliberative Senator the framers of the Constitution wanted and expected. Senator Bradley found, however, that political campaigning is anything but a deliberative process in which candidates debate important issues of public policy. Bradley describes in the following selection how fundraising became the overriding issue of his political campaigns.

Bill Bradley served as a United States Senator from New Jersey from 1979 to 1996; formerly, he was a Rhodes Scholar and played for the New York Knicks from 1967 to 1977. Bradley was elected to the basketball Hall of Fame in 1983, and is positioning himself for a presidential run in 2000. Bradley's main points in this selection are:

1. The *Buckley* ruling, allowing Bradley to use as much of his personal funds as he wanted to finance his first campaign, gave him a chance in his first campaign. Other funds were raised by personalizing the campaign "to rich people."
2. Raising funds between elections is important in dissuading potential candidates from running in opposition, and also for building mailing lists and other campaign infrastructures. Fundraising therefore consumes a great deal of time even when there is no election pending. Fundraising can also become a personal challenge.
3. Raising so much money, however, had an unexpected result. Maintaining the infrastructure took a lot of the funds, and the campaign became susceptible to charges that they had raised too much money. The idea that he had raised too much money also made Bradley susceptible to concerns about donors' influence and access to the Senator, and lessened the seriousness with which his calls for campaign finance reform were received.
4. The only solution is a constitutional amendment for total voluntary public funding of campaigns.

28

Bill Bradley

TIME PRESENT, TIME PAST

In my first campaign, I spent about 40 percent of my time raising money. I made a list of all the people I had known in my life who I thought could afford to contribute money on any scale to my campaign. I then either visited or called them to ask for a contribution. Finding the person who would raise money as well as give it was impor-

---

[1]Michael Barone and Grant Ujifusa, *The Almanac of American Politics, 1990* (Washington, D.C.: National Journal, 1990), pp. 744–745.

tant, and not easy. After about four months of these attempts, a few things were clear. People whom I had pegged as sure contributors because of an association with me over many years became elusive. One man with whom I had had business dealings as a Knick for ten years said he would like to help, but his help would be more generous if I shared his interests, such as the new Broadway play he was financing. I invested seventeen thousand dollars of my own money in the play, which failed shortly after its opening, and the man responded by throwing a cocktail party in New York that raised eight thousand dollars. With this kind of balance sheet, I'd go broke before the campaign was financed.

In 1978, I was known as a basketball player, not as a politician. Though my celebrity might attract two hundred people instead of fifty to hear me speak, the result would be that I had two hundred people before whom I could fail if I had nothing to say. Giving money to a basketball player who was running for the U.S. Senate was not something most people were eager to do. As I often noted in my speeches in that first campaign, "I took a different road to the U.S. Senate." To most potential contributors, the road was often so far off the beaten track that they couldn't find it.

I would stand before twenty or thirty or eighty people in a living room and pour my heart out. If they liked what they heard, or they felt that I answered questions competently enough, they would make a contribution. For a while, I felt that contributors were as cold as the ice that encased New Jersey month after month in that winter of 1978.

Slowly, the lifetime-association list began to yield results. A call, a second call, a third call determined whether a friend would put his money where his mouth was. The results were sometimes surprising. I raised more money from NBA players than from Princeton alumni. I was told so often that "the check is in the mail" that I could only conclude that an amazing number were being lost by the post office. The leaders of the organized Jewish community, with several notable exceptions, told me candidly before the primary that they were supporting the Republican incumbent, Clifford Case, who had been a friend of Israel for twenty-four years. Acquaintances who had long professed undying admiration for me begged off by saying, "But you're a Democrat!" Surprisingly, I found that California, fertile from the Laker-Knick rivalry of my basketball days, yielded an impressive amount.

There were also journeys that ended in failure. On one particularly disastrous trip, a luncheon organized by a self-described old friend did not yield enough to pay for the food. Thereafter, the worst fund-raising event of any trip received an award called "The Ernie," named after the host of that first negative-cash-flow luncheon.

On another occasion, an oilman basketball fan offered to host a fund-raiser at his Fifth Avenue apartment. On the day of the event, there was a blizzard. He insisted that the event go on anyway. I will never forget how the vast oak floor of his apartment gleamed, as only a few people were scattered around it during my pitch. My original finance committee of twenty-one, who were primarily personal friends of my finance chairman, had raised all they could raise in the first three months of the campaign. After that, it was one phone call and one coffee visit and one luncheon visit at a time.

Two factors helped me with money in 1978. Politics is full of talkers, not doers. My major primary opponent, Dick Leone, couldn't parlay Governor Brendan Byrne's support into contributions. Byrne backed him, but he didn't dislike me. Besides, rarely did Byrne make fund-raising calls. Without more pressure, the fund-raisers and contributors associated with state politics, whom my opponent had counted on to raise his money, took a pass. Leone was competent, honest, predictable, and not at all well known to the public. I was a newcomer to politics, and much more widely known. On top of that advantage was the loophole created by the Supreme Court's decision in *Buckley* v. *Valeo*. I could contribute and/or loan my own campaign an unlimited amount of money. I determined, given what I had made playing basketball, that I could provide up to two hundred and fifty thousand dollars—part loan, part contribution. That was about 19 percent of my whole budget, and, more important, it assured me that I could compete even if I didn't raise as much as I had hoped. With the existence of that self-generated cushion, I was able to raise more. When potential contributors see a campaign with money, they assume it's well run, and they are more likely to make a contribution. Everyone likes to be with a winner, whether in basketball or politics.

The *Buckley* v. *Valeo* loophole had given me a shot at victory even before I declared. In the years ahead, the loophole would become as wide as a barn door for others. Four years later in New Jersey, Frank Lautenberg, a wealthy computer executive with no elective experience, would spend over three and a half million dollars of his own money to win a U.S. Senate seat. In Pennsylvania, the son of the Heinz Ketchup fortune spent more than three million dollars of his own money to get elected to the Senate. In West Virginia, the great-grandson of John D. Rockefeller spent ten million two hundred and fifty thousand dollars of his own money to get three hundred and seventy thousand votes. In Wisconsin in 1988, Herb Kohl promised to spend primarily his own money in his Senate campaign; seven and a half million dollars later, he won. Michael Huffington was one candidate of immense wealth who fell short of joining the "rich caucus," composed, not so facetiously, of senators who "bought" their seats themselves. In 1994, Huffington spent an unprecedented twenty-eight million dollars of his own money trying to win a U.S. Senate seat from California, unsuccessfully.

Whereas a candidate could contribute as much of his own money as he chose, he could accept individual contributions of only two thousand dollars from others—one thousand of it for the primary and one thousand for the general election. Pat Moynihan used to joke that under the old fund-raising system a politician risked being obligated to twenty rich people who gave him one hundred thousand dollars each, but under the new system a politician risked obligating himself to a whole class of people who could afford to give two thousand dollars each.

Money was raised in the new system by personalizing your candidacy to rich people. The sequence of the hoped-for events always began in the same places—a living room in Summit, Cherry Hill, Chevy Chase, Evanston, Scarsdale, Short Hills, Scottsdale, Beverly Hills, Portola Valley, Ladue, River Oaks, Bloomfield Hills, Shaker Heights, Bryn Mawr, Palm Beach, Nantucket, Easthampton, Palm Springs. The activity was usually the same. A group of well-dressed guests awaited your arrival. After saying hello to the hostess, you ducked into the bathroom to straighten your tie, and then gradually moved around the room exchanging pleasantries with individual guests and snatching vegetables or shrimp from the buffet. The host would call the people into the living room or onto the patio, and you would stand in front of the fireplace or next to the pool as the host introduced you, to make a few comments and answer questions. Once you had impressed a house party, you hoped to use that base to build support for future small breakfasts or larger luncheons, and finally to attract an expanded group of supporters who would run a big dinner with a thousand tickets at a thousand dollars per person. Often in the chase for campaign money you met bright, talented people; occasionally, a friendship developed. But just as often the people who attended fund-raisers blurred in your memory and events and locations began to look very much the same.

For their part, many of the people in these living rooms met fifteen, or even twenty, candidates in one political season. As they observed more politicians, their standards rose, their questions became more pointed, and their demands intensified. Many of them wanted more than competence in the candidate. Increasingly, they looked for commitments. An hour in front of a group of insistent fund-raisers became as challenging as addressing a group of newspaper editors. Politicians who go through this process have to get used to people looking them over as if they were a piece of meat in the supermarket.

Many hosts had a den in which one wall was covered by pictures of the host with an array of Democratic presidential aspirants and well-known senators or congresspeople. I always enjoyed seeing who had preceded me on the hotspot in front of the fireplace. Some hosts were cause oriented. They raised money from fellow believers. Whether the bond was the whales, the environment as a whole, capital gains, gun control, fiscal prudence, oil, Israel, India, Greece—unless you shared the group's views on a particular issue, it was unlikely that you would raise much money. Other hosts, whose walls were covered with paintings, opened their homes out of friendship. They were kindred spirits in a nonpolitical sense—old friends and business associates, basketball fans, lovers of art, those in search of a new experience; they all raised money without implied conditions, and they were my preferred fund-raisers. My goal was to find what I came to regard as "monogamous" fund-raisers—people who asked others for money only on my behalf and who had friends untapped by other politicians.

In the nineteenth century, senators were on the payroll of the railroads and the power companies. The historian Henry Adams referred to American democracy as "government of the people, by the people, and for the benefit of senators." There were scandals such as Crédit Mobilier, in which congressmen (including future president James Garfield) made money out of investments in railroad construction that their votes had helped to finance. The Crédit Mobilier revelations brought only censure from the Republican Congress. Then there were the distillers who bribed Treasury officials in order to evade taxes on whiskey. William Belknap, Grant's secretary of war, was impeached on charges of accepting bribes from traders at Indian reservations and resigned. In these cases there was little pretense of serving the public interest. President Grant could lead an army, but he couldn't tell a rogue from a saint in his own presidential administration.

Today, the flow of money into politics is more complicated but equally destructive. Its biggest channels are the contributions of political-action committees, or PACs. There are corporate PACs, funded by the voluntary contributions of a company's employees; union or trade-association PACs funded by the contributions of members; and free-standing or cause PACs, funded by those who believe in the cause.

PACs are a loophole in the 1974. law. Each can give a candidate five thousand dollars in the primary election and five thousand dollars in the general election.

Corporate PACs have replaced the corporate sinecures for senators and congresspeople. In some campaigns, they represent 50 percent of total contributions. The five-thousand-dollar limit for PACs allows corporate interests to have a bigger impact on campaigns than individuals, with their thousand-dollar limitation. Many PACs buy access as insurance against changes in law adverse to their corporate interest. The contributor assumes that the corporation's Washington representative, who oversees the PAC allocations, can get an audience with the elected official, or at least with the official's staff, to make the special-interest case. Occasionally, that meeting results in report language that accompanies passage of a bill, or a colloquy on the floor between two senators, with the intent of directing the regulators to interpret a section of the law in a way that favors the special interest. In rare instances, the meeting produces an amendment that alters an effective date for a tax provision or a regulation in favor of the corporation. To assure a willing ear whatever the elective outcome, corporate PACs frequently give to both parties, like prudent businessmen hedging their risks. Those who control PACs are often blunt in their quest for any information that might affect their interests. Once, at a big PAC fund-raiser for the Democratic Party, a Washington PAC representative came up to me and said, "Senator, you've lost a lot of weight. What's the matter? Have you got AIDS?"

Occasionally, a politician will raise money through direct-mail solicitation aimed at targeted mailing lists. This approach yields many small contributions, but it takes time and a big investment up front. If 3 percent of those mailed to actually respond, the mailing is considered a success. Once someone contributes, you can probably get that person to contribute a second or third time during the campaign, but, as with compound interest, it takes time before big money builds up. The greatest returns come from strident appeals to large but narrow constituencies. Jesse Helms and Oliver North have raised gigantic amounts of money by appealing to a dedicated base of right-wing Americans who give when buttons marked "communism," "big government," "abortion," "homosexuals," "birth control," and "secular humanism" are pushed.

Jesse Helms's National Congressional Club hovers over North Carolina politics like a specter. It has sizable direct-mail fund-raising capabilities established over twenty-three years. The tactics are transparent: Helms offers an outrageous amendment in the Senate and insists on a vote. The Congressional Club puts that vote in a direct-mail piece targeted at ultraconservatives, and the money rolls in. Liberals, such as Ted Kennedy and Barbara Boxer, touch different buttons: "abortion rights," "right-wing fanaticism," "civil liberties," "gun control." Helms uses Kennedy and Kennedy uses Helms to energize the direct-mail contributions of the right and the left. They are like partners in a dance for dollars.

A more recent innovation is telemarketing, but the targeted blind solicitation by a telemarketing firm is not as successful as an appeal by the candidate. A Democratic Senate challenger in 1994 proclaimed to me in October that he had a shot at winning because of his fund-raising prowess on the telephone. He claimed that for six to eight hours every day for nine months, with two fund-raising assistants handing him names, he had sat in a room calling people he didn't know and asking for money. He told me that he had made more than four thousand calls since the first of the year. (He lost.) Usually, however, the financial base of federal legislators comes from PACs and the rich. To have enough money for a statewide campaign in New Jersey, I had to raise an average of twenty thousand dollars per week for six years. I raised more than double that amount for my 1990 reelection. . . .

In my 1990 campaign, money proved to be my Achilles' heel. When I first thought about running for elective office in New Jersey in a 1974 congressional race, the question of money loomed very large. Consultants and advisers reiterated the point that, without enough money, good people had lost. I didn't run that year, but I remembered the advice. In my first Senate race, I didn't need sizable amounts, because mainstream Republicans felt no strong affinity for my opponent, who was a newcomer and had upset the incumbent. I had sufficient funds, with my own seed money and the help of friends. The total I spent in 1978 was close to one and a half million dollars. In 1984, I raised four and a half million dollars, in a contest against an unknown opponent, and I used the money chiefly to pay for television ads. As I went into the six-year 1990 cycle, I started raising money in 1985 with the goal of building up a huge campaign war chest.

First of all, I believed that if I had millions in the bank I would draw a weak opponent—a pre-emptive strategy that had worked in 1984. With approval ratings of nearly 80 percent or more and an apparently unlimited fund-raising capacity, I felt that most potentially difficult opponents would pass, thereby allowing me to save resources in the long run. A large war chest is part of an incumbent's armor.

Second, raising a large war chest would give me the flexibility to run for national office. If I had several million dollars in the bank and drew a weak opponent in 1990, I could bank the surplus for a potential 1992 presidential run. Walter Mondale won the Democratic nomination in 1984 because the more than eighteen million dollars he raised allowed him to offset the bump that Gary Hart got from his early victory in New Hampshire. Dick Gephardt told me after his 1988 presidential run that he had concluded that money was without question the most important component of a presidential campaign. I was far from decided on a run, but as someone who wanted to keep options open, I considered this a cost-free strategy.

Third, I went along with grandiose recommendations by my staff that I build a polling-and-computer infrastructure that could be transferred to a national effort. In 1987, we started polling in markets other than New Jersey. The purpose was to help me understand what constituencies certain colleagues had to deal with, so that I could garner wider support for my legislative initiatives in behalf of New Jersey. In addition to that legitimate rationale was the ambitious goal of charting the country with our own "typologies." We had developed a set of voter types into which we classified people. These categories were value-based—that is, we asked questions that defined the respondent's values—and after polling in this way we could target our communications to a particular group based not on issues but on shared values. If we honed this communication-and-polling technique, it would become an advantage few other politicians could boast. In addition to the polling, we made an investment in a large, secure computer system that could quickly be expanded in a national effort. These two investments together cost nearly two million dollars.

Fourth, I wanted to be prepared for the unforeseen. If my preemptive strategy failed and I found myself running against a wealthy opponent who would spend personal money, I couldn't match this overnight. A rich candidate could write a check for a three-million-dollar TV-ad buy in October and run a strong race. I had to raise that amount over nearly two years. Never wanting to be unprepared, I raised the money.

Fifth, in the years leading up to 1990, I began to realize I could no longer be personally indifferent to money. My family's relatively comfortable circumstances when I was young, and my generous salary with the Knicks, had created a life in which I rarely thought about money. Combined with my natural frugality—my teammates joked that I had kept the first dollar I'd ever earned, which is one of the reasons they called me Dollar Bill—my income had always been enough for me to do what I wanted. After I became a senator, however, the bulk of my annual income consisted of my Senate salary. Nearly all assets that I owned I had owned when I became a senator. Since I felt there were no acceptable ways to make investments without conflict of interest, I didn't invest in stocks and I refused to buy real estate other than a Washington home. The only financial assets I owned or acquired were some government bonds and notes. Far from amassing wealth, I was liquidating assets just to pay ongoing bills. I once calculated that being in the Senate, as opposed to holding another job in New Jersey, cost me more than half my Senate salary. After subtracting the expense of living in Washington and New Jersey, with the accompanying two sets of cars, homes, and electricians, I had little left. I suppose I could have shared a one-room bachelor apartment in Washington and commuted from New Jersey to the Senate, but I wasn't prepared to do that to my family. Because I wasn't, the expenses mounted quickly. The normal impulse to count up your assets was for me a painful one. I was watching them decline. It was as if my assets were grains of sand streaming from the top half of an hourglass. This personal financial pressure had implications for the campaign. Unable to dip into personal funds to support my campaign in a crunch, as I had in 1978, I needed a large campaign fund in the bank to cushion against the unknown.

Sixth, fund-raising became a challenge, a game played in competition with myself. By the end of 1988, I had raised as much money as I had spent in the 1984 campaign. I still had no opponent on the horizon. The New Jersey Republicans regarded as tough opponents by conventional political thinkers chose not to run. Still I kept raising money. If we pulled in fifty thousand dollars, I wanted seventy-five thousand dollars at the next event. If we succeeded with a two-hundred-and-fifty-thousand-dollar dinner, why not a five-hundred-thousand-dollar dinner? Everyone felt triumphant when we surpassed our goals. Other senators regarded me with envy. The fund-raising ability became a part of a generally perceived political strength. How could you have too much money?

Fund-raising in 1989 and 1990 took less of my time than it had in 1984 and much less than it had in 1978. The campaign fund-raising operation was led by Betty Sapoch, a friend of twenty-five years. If the effort was not the best in the country, it was close to it. Betty made thousands of people feel good about giving more to a politician than they had ever anticipated they would. In that sense, she had a little Mark Hanna in her. She paid attention to details, insisting on stylish table decorations at dinners and quick thank-you notes afterward. She was an extraordinary networker, always available to listen, and over time she developed a unique capacity to field complaints in a way that made a caller feel better about me after the call. One night in 1989, with a dinner at the Waldorf-Astoria in New York, she directed an effort that raised a million dollars. She collected six hundred thousand dollars at a dinner in Los Angeles a few months later. In both places, I had good and influential friends who were willing to ask their friends and associates to contribute, but Betty put it all together. I traveled to Austin, Dallas, Houston, and El Paso to raise money. I visited Chicago several times, for fifty-thousand-dollar events in people's homes and a two-hundred-and-fifty-thousand-dollar event in a hotel. Friends and interested supporters hosted luncheons or cocktail parties in Palm Beach, Miami, Jacksonville, and Fort Lauderdale. Other friends offered to organize smaller fund-raisers in Baltimore, Atlanta, St. Louis, Kansas City, Denver, and Seattle. The country became dotted with Bradley fund-raisers, and money kept pouring in.

Only 10 percent of it came from PACs. The largest amount came in contributions of two hundred and fifty dollars to two thousand dollars from individuals all over the country. Contributors from New Jersey, New York, and Pennsylvania formed the core of my support, with California close behind. Ultimately, we raised a total of $12.9 million. But it did not make me invincible. Instead, it became a string that almost undid my political career when it was yanked.

Setting up the administrative pieces that could be transferred to a national campaign and maintaining an active fund-raising operation for five years yielded a very high "burn rate," meaning that although we were raising a lot of money, we were spending a lot on polls, offices, fund-raising staff, and computer programs and hardware. The fund-raising and political infrastructure became so expensive that much of what we raised was sopped up by it. Once we had raised the money, few people focused on the net—the amount we needed to spend after Labor Day in 1990. This insouciance led to some wasteful expenditures. For example, in the early summer of 1990, to counter the charges of my opponent, Christine Todd Whitman, that we had too much money, we ran public-service television commercials warning about lead poisoning in the environment. Some in the campaign felt that the commercials might save people's lives, and perhaps they did, but they produced little goodwill and resulted in less money in the bank.

People gave money to my campaign for different reasons. Many contributed because they were personal friends who wished me well. Many contributed because they had known me from my days on the road playing basketball, or from a particular legislative effort such as tax reform or Third World debt. Some admired speeches I had made on Russia, Japan, or trade policy. Some gave because they had followed my Senate service and supported my overall voting record. Others contributed because my personal friends asked them to and they wanted to please those friends. Finally, there were some contributors who wanted to get in on the ground floor of a presidential campaign. I mistook their support of me as being a more personal commitment than it was. During 1992, I discovered that virtually every person of significant means who was a Democrat and had supported me in 1989–90 had given to Bill Clinton or Bob Kerrey or Tom Harkin or Paul Tsongas in their presidential campaigns. So much for monogamous fund-raisers.

When it comes to what people get for their political contributions, I'm more Harry Truman than LBJ. Those who have given out of friendship, a sense of values, or admiration of my record have never asked for anything. I tried to make sure that no one gave money with expectations of receiving a favor. When it comes to fund-raising ethics, I'm similar to a friend who, in a response to a CIA lie-detector test, answered the question "Do you advocate overthrowing the government of the United States?" in the negative. The alarms went off, indicating that he had lied. The question was asked again. Same response. The question was changed to "Do you advocate overthrowing the government of the United States by *unlawful means?*" This time when my friend said no, he passed the test. I, too, had become hyperconscious of fine distinctions. I often saw potential conflicts of interest in harmless circumstances.

Like many of my colleagues in the Senate, I go to great extremes to ensure that no one can ever sustain a question of ethics about my service. In the 1990 campaign, this obsession with rectitude translated into having a full-time campaign accountant and bookkeeper, two law firms on call for specific legal questions, and a campaign manager whose greatest strength was his honesty and financial-accounting skills. All of this cost money.

Contributions were meticulously logged in the new computer system. Biographical data, such as hobbies, education, and children's names, were quickly entered—or, for those with biographical gaps, obtained in follow-up calls. With more than seventy-five thousand contributors, such information would assure more personal communication in mailings to a larger number of my supporters. The nightmare of my public service is that someone on my staff to whom I have delegated authority will make an ethical error out of ignorance or fatigue, such as failing to record the name of a contributor or the correct amount of the contribution. Most campaigns are run out of a shoebox—that is, contribution cards and financial records are not well ordered or computerized. Though I took every extra precaution, politics is full of trapdoors.

My desire to be super-clean made me vulnerable to any hint of criticism about fund-raising. Like Woodrow Wilson, who worried about criticism of his perfectly legal professor's pension, I had tried to set a high moral tone in my campaign. I had seen no theoretical conflict between idealism and raising money. Now, in a kind of political judo, the money was what my opponent was using against me.

By the summer of 1990, the press had begun to depict the race as David against Goliath. When I started in politics, every time my name was mentioned it was "Bill Bradley, former New York Knick." Now it was "Bill Bradley, the candidate who raised twelve million dollars." The press did not focus on what I stood for or what I had accomplished; the money overshadowed everything else. In isolation and without explanation, the amount looked embarrassing. When I supported campaign-finance reform, my opponent's campaign said that it was "similar to someone eating giant éclairs and saying they're observing Lent." But it was too late to do anything about it. I had raised too much money for a New Jersey Senate campaign, and in that campaign I could hardly allude to the money's potential national purposes, or to the five-year burn-rate problem. As with the state-tax revolt I was saddled with, I just had to get through it.

When the fall campaign began, of the nearly twelve million dollars we had raised up to that point, only five million remained in the bank. Over the next eight weeks, we spent three million dollars on television advertising alone. The money that had been laboriously raised over five years poured out in days. After the narrow election victory, a college friend of mine who had raised more than a hundred thousand dollars for the campaign complained loudly that we had ended up with less than a million dollars in the bank. He and his friends had thought that the goal of all the fundraising was a presidential war chest.

The 12.9-million-dollar lesson was indeed expensive. I had started out with the highest of motives and had followed every rule in the book. I had lived my life so as never to have a blemish, and yet somehow I felt tarnished by the fund-raising success of 1985–90. It was as if I were walking around with a scarlet dollar sign on my chest. At a minimum, it made me see the folly of the fund-raising strategy. The antidote, I realized, was twofold: a holiday from fund-raising, and fighting for campaign-finance reform with a new sense of urgency.

With the decline of the parties as sources of funds, individual congresspeople must raise their own money. There is no Lyndon Johnson delivering rescue money for Democrats in the final weeks of the election. The quest for money for the next election begins only months after the last one. It is constant. It drains time and energy from the lives of many elected officials and opens doors to unending speculation about corruption, influence peddling, or, in my case, misguided conceptions of what constitutes preparedness. One senator complaining to me about the current system recalled how he ran into a colleague at 4 A.M. in the Dallas airport. Both were changing planes, having come from fund-raisers in different cities, and both were waiting to get an early-morning flight back to Washington for a day of Senate votes.

Certain interests do attempt to buy off congresspeople with contributions—not overtly but by ingratiating themselves. I've actually been visited by cause PACs urging that I not support campaign-finance reform if it impedes their use of money in the political process. It's a mark of how bad things have gotten that they make these requests without blushing. When corporate PACs displace parties as funding sources, politicians answer to such interest groups more than to their party leaders. After all, the political leaders don't help them when they're in the greatest need. What is threatened is not only any sense of loyally serving a party's interests but also the sense of serving even the "public interest."

Finally, there are the independent PACs, which don't give money to a candidate but spend their own money to champion a specific issue. For example, the National Rifle Association has a PAC that runs negative TV commercials against candidates who disagree with them on gun control. If one candidate opposes gun control and the other one supports it, an anti-gun-control commercial can make a difference, even though the campaign and the independent PAC are technically separate. Policing the contacts an independent PAC may or may not make with a friendly candidate is virtually impossible.

Beyond PACs, big money enters politics through something called the "coordinated campaign," which is supposedly a party effort to register voters and to get them out to vote for all the candidates on the party ticket that year in a particular state. The candidate at the top of the ticket usually controls the expenditures, which means that the candidate's campaign manager usually places as many campaign workers as possible on the payroll of the coordinated campaign. That way the candidate's campaign war chest can be saved to buy TV ads. There are no limits on the amount of money that someone can give to a coordinated campaign, and in a national election there is one in each state. Wealthy individuals who want to help a presidential nominee have given more than five hundred thousand dollars in one year to separate state-coordinated campaigns. And that is after the campaign reform of 1974.

Senator Fritz Hollings says that his Senate colleagues aren't corrupt, the system is corrupt. Fundamental campaign-finance reform must be comprehensive and embodied in an amendment to the U.S. Constitution. TV and mail costs should be dramatically discounted to reflect the public ownership of the airwaves and the public interest in an informed electorate. There should be voluntary taxpayer funding, but no PACs, no big contributions to special committees, no unaccounted-for money for state parties to use in behalf of candidates, and no rich candidates able to buy an election with their wealth. The amount of money candidates get should depend on how much the citizens of their state give them through a nondeductible check-off of up to five thousand dollars above their tax liability on their federal tax returns. The money from the tax check-off would go into a fund that, eight weeks before the general election, would be distributed equally to Republican, Democratic, or qualified independent candidates. Candidates would have to live with what the people of their state gave them. If that means that there will not be enough money to inform voters about the views of the candidates (money for the presidential check-off is dropping), it will be the voters themselves who will suffer. But at least it will be their choice; the point is that the citizens will be in charge. If candidates in different years are given different amounts for a campaign, their circumstances will be no less uncertain than those most Americans face every day. Some senators have suggested a combination of spending limits based on population and media costs in a state and a national lottery dedicated to public financing of federal campaigns. At least as another form of voluntary citizen financing, a lottery would also effect change. Money in politics is similar to the ants in your kitchen. Just when you think you've got them blocked, they find another way to get in. Only hermetically sealing the kitchen off will work—which means total voluntary public funding of campaigns encompassed by a constitutional amendment. Anything less means that democracy can still be corrupted.

The fund-raiser in Seattle in 1992 was similar to hundreds of others I had attended over my fourteen years in the Senate. The candidate this time was Patty Murray, running for the Senate to succeed Brock Adams. . . .

Most fund-raisers involve a mixed Republican and Democratic audience, so frequently the pitch is not even supposed to be partisan. The less ideological and more personal the approach, the better. That individualized, non-threatening manner had become my style. I was trying to make them like me.

It was a successful style for fund-raisers. But what was my purpose? I had reasoned that if I didn't polarize people, I could more easily build a legislative coalition. But passing laws and mobilizing a country require different styles. Until 1991, when I began to speak from my gut as well as my head, I had been content to follow a nonconfrontational strategy that had always allowed me to achieve my goals. I was smooth, not sharp-edged; bland, not "exciting." Understatement was my trademark. Intellectual analysis was my approach. The modest format of a town meeting or a small fund-raiser suited me better than delivering the partisan stem-winder or the prophetic jeremiad. I wore discretion as a badge. I almost never assigned blame for our predicament, or knowingly offended an audience, even if I thought they were dead wrong. As a result, my words rarely had the ring of truth to the nonpolitical observer.

The event in the Seattle living room was a perfect occasion for the same old stuff. Lynn Cutler finished her introduction. I took a few steps out of the corner toward the center of the room and started to talk. Picking individuals in the room, I elaborated on anecdotes each of them had told me about Patty. I spoke about her record in the state legislature and the status of her campaign. I said that Patty's opponent had raised $3.4 million to her $1.3 million. I said how difficult it was for a woman to raise money—there were organizations, such as Emily's List or the Women's National Political Caucus, that gave money only to women, but rarely did a woman's hardest efforts result in a war chest equal to that of her male opponent. I pointed out that most of Patty's money had come from women in small contributions of, on average, forty-seven dollars. I thanked them for coming to this five-hundred-dollar-per-person fund-raiser. They laughed, since the tickets were a hundred dollars. I told them to make their individual contributions as close as possible to five hundred dollars by the end of the campaign, and to do it just for me. They laughed again. I urged them to think of the historic nature of this race, telling them that good candidates sometimes lose when they haven't been able to raise enough money to get their message out. I said that over time I'd learned never to take anything for granted. I pointed out that Patty's opponent had made a grievous gaffe in the last debate, so we had a chance against his superior financial resources, if Patty could just raise enough to remind people about it. I suggested that Patty's race was an advertisement for the need for campaign-finance reform. I said that we needed her vote for reform and her voice for women. I said to give more now so that Patty would be in the Senate for them and for the state of Washington. I said that of all the things someone could give, time and money were the two most important. And at this stage in the campaign, what Patty needed was money, money, money. So give, give, give.

As I spoke, I couldn't imagine Woodrow Wilson saying what I was saying. For LBJ, the gathering would have been too insignificant. Harry Truman would have frowned at the direct solicitation, and Mark Hanna, the man who started us down this crazy fund-raising path—well, Mark Hanna was popping a chocolate into his mouth and smiling.

CHAPTER 7

FOREIGN POLICY

What's the "Right" Thing To Do, and How Do We Do It?

America's relations with the world, like its domestic politics, involve paradoxes, complexities, and compromises. Some of these are the result of conflicts between the nation's idealism and its strongly pragmatic and realistic approach to international affairs. Other difficulties stem from the role of domestic political forces in the decisionmaking processes that drive foreign policy. Given these factors, it is not surprising that the nation's foreign policy is a constant source of contention and public debate.

In this selection, former Secretary of State Henry Kissinger outlines the paradoxes that lie at the core of many of America's foreign policy dilemmas. Kissinger argues that American idealism must be balanced with realistic assessments of America's national interests.

Born in Germany in 1923, Henry Kissinger is one of the twentieth century's leading experts on foreign policy. A Professor of Government at Harvard University from 1962 to 1971, Kissinger was an adviser to Presidents Eisenhower, Kennedy, and Johnson. Kissinger served as the National Security Council's executive secretary from 1969 to 1971, and from 1971 to 1976 he served as Secretary of State. Kissinger shared the 1973 Nobel Peace Prize with Vietnamese statesman Le Duc Tho.

Kissinger's main points in this selection are:

1. The United States encompasses conflicting themes in its foreign policy. No country in the twentieth century has been so reluctant to become involved in world affairs yet been so willing to make far-reaching commitments and alliances. The key to this paradox is that America sees itself as both a beacon to the world, leading by example, and also as a crusader, destined to intervene on behalf of democracy around the world.

2. The United States can neither withdraw from nor dominate "the new world order."

3. American idealism, symbolized by Woodrow Wilson, and realism, symbolized by Theodore Roosevelt, need to be considered and included in decisions about the direction of American foreign policy. "American idealism needs the leaven of geo-political analysis to find its way through the maze of new complexities."

4. America's successes will be partial in coming years, and proponents of America's goals abroad must be patient.

29

Henry Kissinger

DIPLOMACY

★★★

THE NEW WORLD ORDER

Almost as if according to some natural law, in every century there seems to emerge a country with the power, the will, and the intellectual and moral impetus to shape the entire international system in accordance with its own values. In the seventeenth century, France under Cardinal Richelieu introduced the modern approach to international relations, based on the nation-state and motivated by national interest as its ultimate purpose. In the eighteenth century, Great Britain elaborated the concept of the balance of power, which dominated European diplomacy for the next 200 years. In the nineteenth century, Metternich's Austria reconstructed the Concert of Europe and Bismarck's Germany dismantled it, reshaping European diplomacy into a cold-blooded game of power politics.

In the twentieth century, no country has influenced international relations as decisively and at the same time as ambivalently as the United States. No society has more firmly insisted on the inadmissibility of intervention in the domestic affairs of other states, or more passionately asserted that its own values were universally applicable. No nation has been more pragmatic in the day-to-day conduct of its diplomacy, or more ideological in the pursuit of its historic moral convictions. No country has been more reluctant to engage itself abroad even while undertaking alliances and commitments of unprecedented reach and scope.

The singularities that America has ascribed to itself throughout its history have produced two contradictory attitudes toward foreign policy. The first is that America serves its values best by perfecting democracy at home, thereby acting as a beacon for the rest of mankind; the second, that America's values impose on it an obligation to crusade for them around the world. Torn between nostalgia for a pristine past and yearning for a perfect future, American thought has oscillated between isolationism and commitment, though, since the end of the Second World War, the realities of interdependence have predominated.

Both schools of thought—of America as beacon and of America as crusader—envision as normal a global international order based on democracy, free commerce, and international law. Since no such system has ever existed, its evocation often appears to other societies as utopian, if not naïve. Still, foreign skepticism never dimmed the idealism of Woodrow Wilson, Franklin Roosevelt, or Ronald Reagan, or indeed of all other twentieth-century American presidents. If anything, it has spurred America's faith that history can be overcome and that if the world truly wants peace, it needs to apply America's moral prescriptions.

Both schools of thought were products of the American experience. Though other republics have existed, none had been consciously created to vindicate the idea of liberty. No other country's population had chosen to head for a new continent and tame its wilderness in the name of freedom and prosperity for all. Thus the two approaches, the isolationist and the missionary, so contradictory on the surface, reflected a common underlying faith: that the United States possessed the world's best system of government, and that the rest of mankind could attain peace and prosperity by abandoning traditional diplomacy and adopting America's reverence for international law and democracy.

America's journey through international politics has been a triumph of faith over experience. Since the time America entered the arena of world politics in 1917, it has been so preponderant in strength and so convinced of the rightness of its ideals that this century's major international agreements have been embodiments of American values—from the League of Nations and the Kellogg-Briand Pact to the United Nations Charter and the Helsinki Final Act. The collapse of Soviet communism marked the intellectual vindication of American ideals and, ironically, brought America face to face with the kind of world it had been seeking to escape throughout its history. In the emerging international order, nationalism has gained a new lease on life. Nations have pursued self-interest more frequently than high-minded principle, and have competed more than they have cooperated. There is little evidence to suggest that this age-old mode of behavior has changed, or that it is likely to change in the decades ahead.

What *is* new about the emerging world order is that, for the first time, the United States can neither withdraw from the world nor dominate it. America cannot change the way it has perceived its role throughout its history, nor should it want to. When America entered the international arena, it was young and robust and had the power to make the world conform to its vision of international relations. By the end of the Second World War in 1945, the United States was so powerful (at one point about 35 percent of the world's entire economic production was American) that it seemed as if it was destined to shape the world according to its preferences.

John F. Kennedy declared confidently in 1961 that America was strong enough to "pay any price, bear any burden" to ensure the success of liberty. Three decades later, the United States is in less of a position to insist on the immediate realization of all its desires. Other countries have grown into Great Power status. The United States now faces the challenge of reaching its goals in stages, each of which is an amalgam of American values and geopolitical necessities. One of the new necessi-

ties is that a world comprising several states of comparable strength must base its order on some concept of equilibrium—an idea with which the United States has
never felt comfortable.   .

* * *

For [Theodore] Roosevelt, muscular diplomacy in the Western Hemisphere was
part of America's new global role. The two oceans were no longer wide enough to insulate America from the rest of the world. The United States had to become an actor
on the international stage. Roosevelt said as much in a 1902 message to the Congress:
"More and more, the increasing interdependence and complexity of international political and economic relations render it incumbent on all civilized and orderly powers
to insist on the proper policing of the world."

Roosevelt commands a unique historical position in America's approach to international relations. No other president defined America's world role so completely in terms
of national interest, or identified the national interest so comprehensively with the balance of power. Roosevelt shared the view of his countrymen, that America was the best
hope for the world. But unlike most of them, he did not believe that it could preserve the
peace or fulfill its destiny simply by practicing civic virtues. In his perception of the nature
of world order, he was much closer to Palmerston or Disraeli than to Thomas Jefferson.

A great president must be an educator, bridging the gap between his people's future and its experience. Roosevelt taught an especially stern doctrine for a people
brought up in the belief that peace is the normal condition among nations, that there
is no difference between personal and public morality, and that America was safely insulated from the upheavals affecting the rest of the world. For Roosevelt rebutted each
of these propositions. To him, international life meant struggle, and Darwin's theory
of the survival of the fittest was a better guide to history than personal morality. In
Roosevelt's view, the meek inherited the earth only if they were strong. To Roosevelt,
America was not a cause but a great power—potentially the greatest. He hoped to be
the president destined to usher his nation onto the world scene so that it might shape
the twentieth century in the way Great Britain had dominated the nineteenth—as a
country of vast strengths which had enlisted itself, with moderation and wisdom, to
work on behalf of stability, peace, and progress. . . .

Had American thinking on foreign policy culminated in Theodore Roosevelt,
it would have been described as an evolution adapting traditional principles of European statecraft to the American condition. Roosevelt would have been seen as the
president who was in office when the United States, having established a dominant
position in the Americas, began to make its weight felt as a world power. But American foreign-policy thinking did not end with Roosevelt, nor could it have done so.
A leader who confines his role to his people's experience dooms himself to stagna-
tion; a leader who outstrips his people's experience runs the risk of not being understood. Neither its experience nor its values prepared America for the role assigned to it by Roosevelt.

In one of history's ironies, America did in the end fulfill the leading role Roosevelt had envisioned for it, and within Roosevelt's lifetime, but it did so on behalf of
principles Roosevelt derided, and under the guidance of a president whom Roosevelt
despised. Woodrow Wilson was the embodiment of the tradition of American excep-

tionalism, and originated what would become the dominant intellectual school of American foreign policy—a school whose precepts Roosevelt considered at best irrelevant and at worst inimical to America's long-range interests.

In terms of all established principles of statecraft, Roosevelt had by far the better of the argument between these two of America's greatest presidents. Nevertheless, it was Wilson who prevailed: a century later, Roosevelt is remembered for his achievements, but it was Wilson who shaped American thought. Roosevelt understood how international politics worked among the nations then conducting world affairs—no American president has had a more acute insight into the operation of international systems. Yet Wilson grasped the mainsprings of American motivation, perhaps the principal one being that America simply did not see itself as a nation like any other. It lacked both the theoretical and the practical basis for the European-style diplomacy of constant adjustment of the nuances of power from a posture of moral neutrality for the sole purpose of preserving an ever-shifting balance. Whatever the realities and the lessons of power, the American people's abiding conviction has been that its exceptional character resides in the practice and propagation of freedom.

Americans could be moved to great deeds only through a vision that coincided with their perception of their country as exceptional. However intellectually attuned to the way the diplomacy of the Great Powers actually operated, Roosevelt's approach failed to persuade his countrymen that they needed to enter the First World War. Wilson, on the other hand, tapped his people's emotions with arguments that were as morally elevated as they were largely incomprehensible to foreign leaders. . . .

In Wilsonianism was incarnate the central drama of America on the world stage: America's ideology has, in a sense, been revolutionary while, domestically, Americans have considered themselves satisfied with the *status quo*. Tending to turn foreign-policy issues into a struggle between good and evil, Americans have generally felt ill at ease with compromise, as they have with partial or inconclusive outcomes. The fact that America has shied away from seeking vast geopolitical transformations has often associated it with defense of the territorial, and sometimes the political, *status quo*. Trusting in the rule of law, it has found it difficult to reconcile its faith in peaceful change with the historical fact that almost all significant changes in history have involved violence and upheaval.

America found that it would have to implement its ideals in a world less blessed than its own and in concert with states possessed of narrower margins of survival, more limited objectives, and far less self-confidence. And yet America has persevered. The postwar world became largely America's creation, so that, in the end, it did come to play the role Wilson had envisioned for it—as a beacon to follow, and a hope to attain.

* * *

Western-style democracy presupposes a consensus on values that sets limits to partisanship. America would not be true to itself if it did not insist on the universal applicability of the idea of liberty. That America should give preference to democratic governments over repressive ones and be prepared to pay some price for its moral convictions is beyond dispute. That there is an area of discretion which should be exercised in favor of governments and institutions promoting democratic values and human rights is also clear. The difficulty arises in determining the precise price to be paid and its relationship to other essential American priorities, including national security and the overall geopolitical balance. If American exhortations are to go beyond patriotic rhetoric, they must reflect a realistic understanding of America's reach. America must be careful not to multiply moral commitments while the financial and military resources for the conduct of a global foreign policy are being curtailed. Sweeping pronouncements not matched by either the ability or the willingness to back them up diminish America's influence on all other matters as well.

The precise balance between the moral and the strategic elements of American foreign policy cannot be prescribed in the abstract. But the beginning of wisdom consists of recognizing that a balance needs to be struck. However powerful America is, no country has the capacity to impose all its preferences on the rest of mankind; priorities must be established. Even if the resources for it existed, undifferentiated Wilsonianism would not be supported once the American public clearly understood its corollary commitments and involvements. It runs the risk of being turned into a slogan to escape difficult geopolitical choices by means of pronouncements involving little apparent risk. A gap is threatening to open up in America's policy between its pretensions and its willingness to support them; the nearly inevitable disillusionment too easily turns into an excuse for withdrawing from world affairs altogether.

In the post–Cold War world, American idealism needs the leaven of geopolitical analysis to find its way through the maze of new complexities. That will not be easy. America refused to dominate even when it had the nuclear monopoly, and it disdained the balance of power even when conducting, as during the Cold War, what was in effect a spheres of interest diplomacy. In the twenty-first century, America, like other nations, must learn to navigate between necessity and choice, between the immutable constants of international relations and the elements subject to the discretion of statesmen.

Wherever the balance is established between values and necessity, foreign policy must begin with some definition of what constitutes a vital interest—a change in the international environment so likely to undermine the national security that it must be resisted no matter what form the threat takes or how ostensibly legitimate it appears. During its heyday, Great Britain would have gone to war to prevent the occupation of the Channel ports in the Low Countries even if they had been taken over by a major power governed by saints. For the greater part of American history, the Monroe Doctrine served as an operating definition of the American national interest. Since Woodrow Wilson's entry into World War I, America has avoided defining a national interest with the argument that it was not opposed to change as such, but to the use of force to bring it about. Neither definition is adequate any longer; the Monroe Doctrine is too restrictive, Wilsonianism is both too vague and too legalistic. The controversy surrounding almost all American military actions in the post–Cold War period shows that a wider consensus on where America should draw the line does not yet exist. To bring it about is a major challenge to national leadership.

* * *

In launching itself for the third time in this century on creating a new world order, America's dominant task is to strike a balance between the twin temptations inherent in its exceptionalism: the notion that America must remedy every wrong and stabilize every dislocation, and the latent instinct to withdraw into itself. Indiscriminate involvement in all the ethnic turmoil and civil wars of the post-Cold War world would drain a crusading America. Yet an America that confines itself to the refinement of its domestic virtues would, in the end, abdicate America's security and prosperity to decisions made by other societies in faraway places and over which America would progressively lose control.

When, in 1821, John Quincy Adams warned Americans against the penchant to slay "distant monsters," he could not have imagined the sheer number and magnitude of monsters that would exist in the post-Cold War world. Not every evil can be combated by America, even less by America alone. But some monsters need to be, if not slain, at least resisted. What is most needed are criteria for selectivity.

America's leaders have generally stressed motivation over structure. They have placed more emphasis on affecting the attitudes than the calculations of their counterparts. As a result, American society is peculiarly ambivalent about the lessons of history. American films often depict how some dramatic event transforms a villain into a paragon of virtue (sometimes cloyingly so)—a reflection of the pervasive national belief that the past has no final claim and that new departures are always possible. In the real world, such transformations are rarely observed in individuals, even less so among nations which are composites of many individual choices.

The rejection of history extols the image of a universal man living by universal maxims, regardless of the past, of geography, or of other immutable circumstance. Since the American tradition emphasizes universal truths rather than national characteristics, American policymakers have generally preferred multilateral approaches to national ones: the agendas of disarmament, nonproliferation, and human rights rather than essentially national, geopolitical, or strategic issues.

The American refusal to be bound by history and the insistence on the perpetual possibility for renewal confer a great dignity, even beauty, on the American way of life. The national fear that those who are obsessed with history produce self-fulfilling prophecies does embody a great folk wisdom. Still, Santayana's dictum that those who ignore history are condemned to repeat it can be supported by even more examples.

A country with America's idealistic tradition cannot base its policy on the balance of power as the sole criterion for a new world order. But it must learn that equilibrium is a fundamental precondition for the pursuit of its historic goals. And these higher goals cannot be achieved by rhetoric or posturing. The emerging international system is far more complex than any previously encountered by American diplomacy. Foreign policy has to be conducted by a political system that emphasizes the immediate and provides few incentives for the long range. Its leaders are obliged to deal with constituencies that tend to receive their information via visual images. All this puts a premium on emotion and on the mood of the moment at a time that demands rethinking of priorities and an analysis of capabilities.

History, however, will not excuse failure by the magnitude of the task. What America must master is the transition from an age when all choices seemed open to a period when it can still accomplish more than any other society if it can only learn its limits. Through most of its history, America knew no foreign threat to its survival. When such a threat finally emerged during the Cold War, it was utterly defeated. The

American experience has thus encouraged the belief that America, alone among the nations of the world, is impervious and that it can prevail by the example of its virtues and good works.

In the post–Cold War world, such an attitude would turn innocence into self-indulgence. At a time when America is able neither to dominate the world nor to withdraw from it, when it finds itself both all-powerful and totally vulnerable, it must not abandon the ideals which have accounted for its greatness. But neither must it jeopardize that greatness by fostering illusions about the extent of its reach. World leadership is inherent in America's power and values, but it does not include the privilege of pretending that America is doing other nations a kindness by associating with them, or that it has a limitless capacity to impose its will by withholding its favors. For America, any association with *Realpolitik* must take into account the core values of the first society in history to have been explicitly created in the name of liberty. Yet America's survival and progress will depend as well on its ability to make choices which reflect contemporary reality. Otherwise, foreign policy will turn into self-righteous posturing. The relative weight to be given to each of these components and the price associated with every priority define both the challenge and the stature of political leaders. What no leader must ever do is to suggest that choice has no price, or that no balance needs to be struck.

In traveling along the road to world order for the third time in the modern era, American idealism remains as essential as ever, perhaps even more so. But in the new world order, its role will be to provide the faith to sustain America through all the ambiguities of choice in an imperfect world. Traditional American idealism must combine with a thoughtful assessment of contemporary realities to bring about a usable definition of American interests. In the past, American foreign policy efforts were inspired by utopian visions of some terminal point after which the underlying harmony of the world would simply reassert itself.

Henceforth, few such final outcomes are in prospect; the fulfillment of America's ideals will have to be sought in the patient accumulation of partial successes. The certitudes of physical threat and hostile ideology characteristic of the Cold War are gone. The convictions needed to master the emerging world order are more abstract: a vision of a future that cannot be demonstrated when it is put forward and judgments about the relationship between hope and possibility that are, in their essence, conjectural. The Wilsonian goals of America's past—peace, stability, progress, and freedom for mankind—will have to be sought in a journey that has no end. "Traveler," says a Spanish proverb, "there are no roads. Roads are made by walking."

David Gergen served in the White House under Presidents Nixon, Ford, Reagan, and Clinton, and he has offered political analysis for *U.S. News & World Report* as well as *The MacNeil/Lehrer Newshour* on public television. In this selection, David Gergen discusses the numerous forces that influence the direction of American foreign policy. The fragmented American system provides a role for these diverse groups, encouraging free debate but simultaneously complicating the task of designing and implementing coherent international policies.

The main points of this selection are:

1. Foreign policy decisionmakers no longer confront a simple, East-West dichotomy. "[T]he world has turned out to be much messier in the post–cold war era than most had expected."
2. A variety of factors must be considered and included when devising foreign policy: competing advisers with differing opinions, a fragmented Congress, an uncertain public, fickle media coverage, and weak allies.
3. Foreign policy is thus no longer a matter of achieving or defending certain ideals in a bipolar world. It is a matter of lining up support, explaining concepts, and holding coalitions together. This reality makes the creation and implementation of American foreign policy much more complex than many realize.

30

David Gergen

FOREIGN POLICY AND DOMESTIC CIRCUMSTANCES

ADAPTING U.S. FOREIGN POLICY MAKING
TO CHANGING DOMESTIC CIRCUMSTANCES

Toward the end of the Gorbachev era, Georgy Arbatov wryly warned his friends in the West that the Soviet Union was going to do something very dangerous to us: "We're going to deny you an enemy." While Arbatov was of course wrong in a fundamental sense—the collapse of the Soviet empire has left the world a good deal safer from fear of a nuclear holocaust—he was prescient in another: the demise of its archrival has also made the conduct of U.S. foreign policy a great deal more complicated than in the past.

During most of the cold war, the marshaling of support for foreign policy initiatives was relatively straightforward for a president. Most Americans agreed that the Soviets posed a deadly threat and that the United States must "pay any price, bear any burden" in the defense of freedom around the world. In Congress, Democrats and Republicans alike willingly voted during the Kennedy years for defense budgets that were more than twice the size of today's, measured as a share of the gross domestic product (GDP). The public, if anything, tended to be more hawkish. The press was generally supportive. And allies overseas quickly fell into line behind U.S. policies. To the extent that economic conflicts arose among the industrialized nations, they were downplayed in the interest of political harmony.

The Vietnam War obviously splintered some of that bipartisan, domestic consensus on foreign policy, at least on the matter of using force to settle disputes on the periphery of the Soviet empire. But on the central issue of matching the direct threat of the Soviet military, the United States remained firmly united. Indeed, by the end of the 1970s, the perception that the country might be slipping led to a strong public desire for beefing up the armed forces and gave Ronald Reagan the impetus to undertake the biggest defense build-up in peacetime history. How long ago that all seems now.

Today the United States has neither a recognized enemy nor a strategy for shaping the world's future. During the early months of confrontation with Iraq, George Bush often spoke about creating a "new world order" and even planned to give a series of four commencement addresses after the war, outlining his vision; in the event, he gave only one of the speeches and the phrase dropped from his lexicon. Bill Clinton spoke broadly about foreign policy during his campaign, but in his opening months his primary preoccupations have been domestic.

Just as importantly, the world has turned out to be much messier in the post–Cold War era than most had expected. Indeed, the euphoria that greeted the liberation of Eastern Europe and the fall of the Soviet Union has given way to a sober, rather pessimistic view that the world is sliding toward disequilibrium as smaller conflicts break out, tensions rise, and the industrialized nations dither on the sidelines. History has not ended, it is said; it had merely been frozen, and the old ethnic and nationalistic hatreds are now thawing. Despite its preeminence as the world's single superpower—first in military, political, economic, and cultural influence—the United States seems unable to imprint its own sense of order. Observers such as James Schlesinger, Zbigniew Brzezinski, and Daniel Patrick Moynihan all write rather darkly about prospects ahead. No wonder some foreign policy buffs grow nostalgic for the simplicities of the cold war.

Lining Up Support for Military Engagements

Just how complicated and difficult the conduct of foreign policy has become in the new era is best illustrated by the imposing array of forces a president must now align in his favor in order to undertake a military engagement by U.S. troops. Sending in forces for a brief, police-type action, as in Panama, does not require much advance effort, but something more dangerous, as in Kuwait and the former Yugoslavia, is incredibly demanding. Consider the players the president must corral in his corner:

Competing advisers: The question of when and how to commit the United States to an overseas venture seems to arouse conflicts among presidential advisers far more than in the cold war period. . . .

A balky Congress: Since Vietnam and passage of the War Powers Act in 1973, Congress has insisted that it have a large voice in any decision to send troops into combat. The executive branch has long disagreed with leaders on the Hill about the extent of congressional approval required by the Constitution, but as a political matter, the fact that Bush sought authorization from both chambers prior to launching an attack against Saddam Hussein's forces will probably make it imperative that future presidents obtain similar support before starting major missions.

The problem for the executive is that Congress wants to share authority but won't share equal responsibility. In early debates on Bosnia, for example, members took to the floor demanding a chance to vote and, in the same breath, demanded that before they voted yea, the president—not they—must muster support among voters back home. In the case of Kuwait, members wanted advance support of both the voters and the United Nations Security Council. Few are the members who are willing to step forward in a dicey situation and help the president take his case to the country (Senators Richard Lugar, Joseph Lieberman, and Robert Dole are among the exceptions). It's mostly, "After you, Alphonse."

Moreover, the disappearance of the Soviet threat has also scrambled the old coalitions that were for and against military action. Now a president must start afresh in every conflict, seeing whom he can line up. One irony of the new era, it has been said, is that some liberals have become extremely enthusiastic about using force everywhere, even as they work to dismantle the defense establishment, while some conservatives never want to use force any more, even as they work to preserve the biggest military in the world. With so little help from Congress, a president is almost on his own in convincing the country that the United States must take action.

An uncertain public: With no obvious enemy lurking over the horizon, the public is paying even less attention to international affairs than in the past. That's hardly encouraging for a president who must look to the public for guidance: after all, a poll by ABC and the *Washington Post* in the early 1980s found that when people were asked which of two countries, the United States or the Soviet Union, was a member of NATO, only 47 percent could identify the United States (a flip of the coin, it was noted, would have produced more right answers).

In today's context, the lack of public attention often means that polls probing opinion on overseas conflicts are often haunted by "mushiness," a phrase Daniel Yankelovich introduced a few years ago to describe the vast uncertainties and volatility of opinion when people have only the vaguest idea of what's at stake. One week in spring 1993, polls said, for example, that Americans were prepared to use force to stop the Serbs in Bosnia; the next week, polls showed just the reverse. For a president, such uncertainty makes all the more challenging the task of building stable public support for a military engagement. He knows that as soon as he sends troops, Americans will automatically "rally 'round," but if something goes wrong or conflict turns into "quagmire," support will melt away. And a president knows that the public won't take its cues just from him; people will also pay a great deal of attention to what they see on their television screens. Yet another player enters the game.

A wandering television eye: . . . For a president, the degree to which the modern media—print as well as television—can shape the public's foreign policy agenda is a mixed blessing, indeed. In some cases, the fact that the media ignore a problem of serious interest to the government makes it more difficult to generate support for action there; more often, the media may goad a president to action, even when no large U.S. interest is at stake. And as many presidents have found, the press can be notoriously fickle, helping to build public attention in a potential conflict and then on the eve of potential military action, as in Kuwait and Bosnia, nearly frightening the public out of a military response because of all the horrible consequences that may flow. Every contemporary White House thus finds the modern media both unpredictable and difficult to master as it tries to marshal public support for its international initiatives.

Weak allies: In an . . . American Assembly session [at Columbia University], participants agreed upon a central recommendation: in the post–cold war era, the United States must learn to share responsibility with its allies far more than it has in the past. Unilateralism is out; multinationalism is in. Right? But what if the allies aren't willing to play? What if their governments are in so much trouble at home that their leaders aren't willing to take risks, or they roll out arguments that because of history and legal constraints at home, they can't help? Is the West to be paralyzed? How far should the United States go in bullying others to follow its lead? Should it resort to unilateral action? Or should it shrug and walk away, taking the view that it cannot and should not be the world's keeper? Those questions are certainly on the table after the long, agonizing failure of the industrialized nations in addressing the slaughter in Yugoslavia. They also underline just how tricky it can be for an American president to serve as leader of a coalition, especially as leaders such as Margaret Thatcher and Brian Mulroney pass from the scene.

A wavering Security Council: The issue of allied support is important not only in and of itself—NATO is vitally affected, of course—but is also tied to prospects for support in the United Nations Security Council. The Security Council is in turn linked to support in Congress: in the cases of both Kuwait and Bosnia, Congress wanted the Security Council to give its blessing before it would vote in favor of committing U.S. troops. These linkages are all rather novel but seem destined to become a fixture of the new era.

Again, however, the challenges grow ever bigger for a president. Assuming the White House can line up the British and French through alliance talks, it faces separate and thorny considerations at the United Nations in lining up the Russians and Chinese. Boris Yeltsin showed that the Russians still have their own interests to pursue, independent of his patrons in the West, in his approach to the Serbs. China could become even more problematic in years ahead. Their economy is bounding ahead so rapidly that Chinese leaders may wish to exercise more muscle at the UN than in the past; and the pressures arising from within the Democratic party for Clinton to toughen U.S. policies toward Beijing could easily complicate efforts to win Chinese cooperation at the United Nations.

In short, it won't be easy for Clinton—and probably for his successors—to ride high in the saddle, solving the world's problems. A president's horse has so many hurdles to clear—his own advisers, Congress, public opinion, the press, allies, the Security Council—and any one of them could trip him up. . . .

In the introduction to its report, *Changing Our Ways*, the national commission set up by the Carnegie Endowment pointed out that we have now reached the third great watershed of the twentieth century. The first came after World War I, and the United States blew it. "Despite Woodrow Wilson's good intentions, our response was too idealistically conceived, too rigidly presented." The second came after World War II, and America succeeded beyond its best dreams. "There were moments (during the cold war) when we were not true to our ideals at home or abroad. But the policies put into play starting in 1947 ultimately succeeded in their fundamental objective four decades later—the containment and defeat of Soviet Communism." The end of the cold war brings us to a third watershed. The Carnegie group summed it up:

> Now America once again faces a rare opportunity, an open but fleeting moment in world history. We must seize it now. This is our chance to ensure that recent enemies become future friends and that present allies do not become new antagonists. This is our chance to shape new forms of leadership before the fluid trends of the moment harden into something not to our liking.

Well said.

American foreign policy often looks inconsistent and uncoordinated, leading to criticism that America's world leadership is drifting and confused. Observers often yearn for the simpler days of the Cold War, when "containing communism" summed up foreign policy in a neat package. The previous selections looked at some of the ideological and institutional factors that fragment today's foreign policy. The following essay, by Edward N. Luttwak, examines some of the international dynamics that complicate the making of foreign policy in the post-Cold War world. Luttwak, director of geo-economics at the Center for Strategic and International Studies, argues that a seemingly confused yet flexible foreign policy can be well-suited to meet America's diverse goals. The ideal of a simple and straightforward foreign policy must sometimes give way to the complex reality of world affairs.

Luttwak makes the following major arguments:

1. Since the end of the Cold War, and especially since the beginning of Bill Clinton's presidency, critics have charged that American foreign policy lacks a coherent and consistent vision or direction.

2. American policy toward China exemplifies this supposedly rudder-less foreign policy. Critics argue that a clear "line" to guide relations with China would minimize confusion and strengthen our foreign policy.
3. A foreign policy that looks incoherent may actually maximize the United States' leverage in world affairs, despite the complexity and the frustration associated with such a policy.

31

Edward N. Luttwak

WHY WE NEED AN INCOHERENT FOREIGN POLICY

★★★

A solidly practical, one-thing-at-a-time pragmatism is the Anglo-Saxon virtue in the realm of foreign affairs, as in most things. Conversely, the attempt to interpret systematically and individually all sorts of diverse phenomena is a Teutonic vice of the likes of von Clausewitz. But sometimes vice must prevail.

Consider for example the standard criticism of U.S. foreign policy since the end of the Cold War, and more especially since the beginning of Bill Clinton's presidency. With rare unanimity, the most varied voices, from the ambassadors of traditional allies at Washington dinner parties to truculent government spokesmen in Beijing, not to mention a multitude of academic and journalistic commentators, insistently criticize the lack of any coherent scheme in the overall conduct of U.S. foreign policy. Worse still, they denounce the mixed signals and contradictory actions that abound even in U.S. dealings with single countries.

U.S. DOUBLE-DEALINGS IN CHINA

Such incoherence has many examples, but perhaps the most extreme, and the country in question is certainly very important, arguably the most important in the long run at least. Chinese officials, and the Hong Kong tycoons who now habitually relay their views, bitterly complain that U.S.-Chinese relations have become fragile because of the bewildering variety of contradictory pressures emanating from the United States.

On the one hand, they point out, China is regularly called upon to act as a responsible Great Power at the United Nations (UN) Security Council, over the disposition of Iraq for example, and confidently expected to cooperate with the United States in stabilizing the Korean peninsula, almost as if it were a strategic ally.

Yet, these Chinese officials complain, the United States now refuses to sell any military equipment whatsoever to China, hampering its very restrained efforts to acquire some of the capabilities that befit a Great Power, which China has only in token numbers: a few squadrons of modern fighters, a few competent warships, last-generation battle tanks, and so on. Adding insult to injury, when China exercises a prosaic right of any independent power, Great or otherwise, by selling its own weapons to friendly countries and other paying customers, the United States feels free to investigate, embarrassingly publicize, and stridently denounce such transactions, while striving to stop the transactions by intimidating the prospective recipients.

Likewise, the United States explicitly endorses the Chinese claim of sovereignty over Taiwan, and consistently rejects the attempts of the Republic of China to regain diplomatic recognition. Yet, when Chinese armed forces conducted military exercises in the Straits of Taiwan, strictly within the norms of international law, and for the declared purpose of dissuading Taiwanese demands for independence (which Washington also opposes), the United States reacted with an anachronistic exercise in gunboat diplomacy, except that the interposition was carried out by aircraft carrier.

Moreover, while thus negating their verbal acceptance of China's sovereignty over one province—Taiwan—Americans outrightly challenge that sovereignty in the case of another—Tibet—through congressional statements and actions in support of Tibetan claims, which sometimes include demands for outright independence. Much worse, the executive branch has now joined in these challenges to Chinese sovereignty by creating the new position of "Tibet coordinator" within the State Department, implying that Tibetan matters no longer belong to the sphere of Washington-Beijing relations on the same footing as concerns for the rest of Chinese territory. One can well imagine how Americans would react if a foreign government were to appoint a "Texas coordinator"—in effect an explicit declaration of the intent to interfere in the domestic affairs of the United States.

Even more contradictory are the commercial pressures. On the one hand, the U.S. secretary of commerce visits China with a large number of accompanying corporate salespeople, explicitly to gain privileged access to China's rapidly growing market—ordinary access is already available to all. At the same time, however, the Office of the U.S. Trade Representative seems bent on dissolving whatever goodwill is thus achieved, by bluntly threatening sanctions from the very outset of negotiations over any dispute at hand—despite the long list of disputes already successfully resolved by Chinese concessions. Again, in this respect too there is an aggravating factor: While acting so harshly with China, the United States seems much more respectful in its economic diplomacy with its subordinate ally Japan, and even with its dependent client South Korea, tolerating any number of transparent evasions of negotiated agreements with only the most feeble protests.

And then there is the vexed question of the dissidents. In many different ways, from formal human rights interventions by the State Department and government-sponsored radio broadcasts, to the varied forms of support offered by academic and eleemosynary institutions, U.S. citizens systematically encourage Chinese citizens to subvert the very same Chinese government with which the United States is so eager to cooperate on a wide range of issues.

The contradictions are certainly sharp, when executive, legislative, and purely private doings are thus conflated. If one accepts Beijing's perspective—overlooking such things as the unbending rigidity of its political repression not least in Tibet, the well-documented sale of nuclear materials and ballistic-missile technology to Pakistan, and the use of prison labor on a huge scale in manufacturing for export as well as domestic consumption—the overall argument may even seem persuasive.

What is certainly true is that the effective leverage of the United States over China at any one moment in time would be far greater if all relevant parties pursued a single, unified policy. That would of course require a prior set of fundamental choices: Is China to be treated as an adversary or as a global-security partner? Is China to be courted as a market for U.S. exports, or is it more important to protect the U.S. market from the flood of Chinese imports?

Adopting a Fixed Line

Once such choices were made, the United States would be ready to adopt an unambiguous "line" toward China, as not only the Soviet Union once did for each country and each issue, but France for example does still, toward countries as varied as Rwanda under its former regime, or China itself.

The diplomats of the Quai d'Orsay are rarely troubled by the doubts and tensions that afflict their U.S. counterparts, as French diplomats implement the logically consistent policies invariably favored by their governments. Nor is there any ambiguity about the scope of the diplomats' responsibilities: The execution of foreign policy is the realm of professional diplomacy, with no parliamentary intrusions tolerated, and still less those of mere private groupings pursuing idealistic agendas. Naturally, so much consistency and clarity evokes the deference of all respectable mass media, as of most other French institutions—academic, commercial, industrial, or financial—all of which very helpfully have strong government ties.

U.S. society is much different; the U.S. Congress lacks the inhibitions of the French National Assembly, U.S. mass media are little given to deference, and few private institutions strive to adhere as closely as possible to government policies, unless these policies happen to coincide with their own goals. Nevertheless, if the executive branch at least made its own clear-cut choices to set a "line" for each country and issue, it would finally have a consistent set of priorities for each.

Not every new dilemma that came along would thereby be automatically resolved. But the chronic problems, at least, would each have their preordained solutions, to determine for example if human rights complaints are to be vigorously pressed, or merely recorded in obscure documents to comply ritualistically with legislated requirements.

As to commerce, the administration would either seek privileged access to the Chinese market for U.S. exporters at the expense of other potential exporters, then tolerate with equanimity the liberties attending commensurate Chinese penetrations of the U.S. market, or else insist on the strict application of each and every multilateral or bilateral rule, freely using the threat of sanctions to enforce compliance.

DEALING WITH CHINA AS PARTNER

With far broader consequences, if the choice were made to turn China into a global strategic partner, outstanding issues would be resolved by systematic negotiations within the framework of standing bilateral arrangements, instead of through the present admixture of quiet deals, failed understandings, and angry polemics.

Most notably, the administration might agree to resume the sale of selected weapons and military technologies to China, in exchange for satisfactory restraints on Chinese military exports to third countries and the outright termination of all nuclear and long-range missile exports.

In addition to the important case of Korea, there would likewise be consultations on any other regional issues in which China had a significant stake, from Burma (Myanmar) to the different West Asia conflicts. As in the case of U.S. dealings with other friendly powers, the aim would be to minimize the effects of divergent interests and to eliminate unnecessary frictions, even if no close cooperation could ensue.

A strategic partnership, even if rather loose, does require each side to defer to the recognized core interests of the other. Accordingly, Beijing would presumably have to stop providing any form of verbal or substantive support to countries actively hostile to the United States—most important, Iran. The United States for its part would have to refrain from interfering in the Chinese disposition of Hong Kong, specifically by denying even purely verbal support for local dissidence. More broadly, the executive branch would have to stop all forms of interference in the domestic affairs of China under the human rights rubric, except insofar as inflexibly mandated by laws, for example the annual State Department assessment of human rights shortcomings. Similarly, Taipei and Beijing would have to be left to resolve their differences as best they could, within the context of their own bilateral balance of power, with no further U.S. intrusions.

Consistent with that choice, the administration in office would adopt the most minimalist interpretation possible of the security and military-supply commitments legally prescribed by the Taiwan Relations Act. China for its part would tacitly be expected to refrain from any use of force against Taiwan—which would not be necessary anyway once Taiwan were left isolated and unprotected.

DEALING WITH CHINA AS ADVERSARY

Conversely, if the administration decided that China is inevitably destined to be the Soviet Union's successor as the principal adversary of the United States, most of the foregoing policy prescriptions would have to be reversed.

The denial to China of any form of military supply would have to be made permanent, and much stronger efforts than hitherto would have to be made to persuade other countries to stop supplying weapons or relevant technology to China. As for Chinese weapon and nuclear exports, they would have to be countered yet more vigorously, with Washington dissuading potential recipients by threats or inducements.

It would also become a fixed U.S. practice to press human rights complaints as insistently as possible and enhance mass media and other informational activities aimed at China and Hong Kong. Chinese conduct in the latter would be attentively monitored and promptly denounced, as appropriate.

More substantively, to force China onto the defensive, it would be advantageous to affirm the broadest possible interpretation of the Taiwan Relations Act, and to support Tibetan demands for cultural autonomy, generously defined.

The choice to oppose China systematically would imply much more than all that for U.S. foreign policy worldwide. In the first place, most obviously, it would dictate a reordering of priorities in U.S. dealings with a good number of other Asian countries, to seek their active participation in the containment of China. That would in turn require the offer of enhanced security guarantees by the United States, as well as a much more forthcoming attitude in supplying weapons, and possibly also an increased presence of U.S. military forces, which might well have implications for the overall defense budget. It is evident that any unrelated disputes with Asian countries would have to be resolved under the new order of priorities, if they are otherwise willing to cooperate in the containment of China.

The redirection of U.S. foreign policy would have to extend far beyond East Asia, beginning with Russia. In what would inevitably amount to a major and prolonged diplomatic campaign, the maximum aim would be to secure an active Russian participation in the containment of China; the minimum aim would be to reduce as much as possible any form of Russian security cooperation with Beijing, notably including arms sales. Just as inevitably, nothing is likely to be achieved without the offer of suitable inducements to Moscow, including the reversal of policies that Russia opposes, beginning of course with the enlargement of the North Atlantic Treaty Organization (NATO) to the East. Indeed, NATO would have to be effectively abolished, or drastically redefined, to meet Russian objections. As it is, some supporters of expansion envisage Russian membership in a new NATO that would function as an alliance of democratic states. In a new foreign policy recast to serve the central aim of containing China, Russia would be elevated as the leading partner of the United States in that sort of NATO. Many other changes would logically have to follow in U.S. policy toward its present European allies, and indeed toward Europe and its institutions as a whole, to achieve consistency with the new priority of containing China with Russian cooperation.

Once China is declared the main adversary, it is bound to react. To be sure, it has only a modest capacity to hurt U.S. interests economically or in any other way, while its military weakness would no doubt rule out any dangerous direct confrontations. But Beijing could do much to harm the United States indirectly, by supporting whatever countries and nonstate groups are still willing actively to oppose it, by violent means too. Chinese military supplies, technology transfers, and diplomatic backing—including the use of Beijing's UN Security Council veto on these groups' behalf, would greatly strengthen surviving anti-American elements worldwide, which are now bereft of any Great Power support. Naturally, the United States would have to anticipate such Chinese reactions, not only by defensive preparations and precautions, but also by urgent efforts to repair U.S. relations with the prospective beneficiaries of Beijing's support, including Iran and North Korea. In other words, to better confront the main adversary, lesser adversaries would have to be conciliated. Again, that could not be accomplished without concessions, this time to so-called "rogue" states.

WEIGHING THE OPTIONS

Upon examining both alternatives for a truly coherent and consistent policy towards China, one can only conclude that there is much to be said for incoherence and inconsistency. Different as they are, each alternative has disturbing, indeed alarming, implications. As compared to their costs and risks, starting with the divisive domestic debate that would precede their adoption, whatever dissatisfactions arise from the current mixture of incoherent policies seem almost inconsequential. Actually, despite their disorder, the diverse policies now pursued jointly provide what both of the coherent alternatives do not: a muddled but prudent moderation. . . .

ONE VOTE FOR INCOHERENCE

All this does not mean that the present, incoherent foreign policies of the United States are the best possible foreign policies, implemented in the best possible manner. It does mean, however, that in the wake of the Soviet collapse, there is such a thing as a *culminating point of success* in maximizing the leverage of the United States on the world scene. To overshoot that point, to exceed the limit of what others can accept with sufficient equanimity—in other words, to demand some form of coherent foreign policy—could in fact result not in further increases in power or influence, but in their diminution.

The Bosnian situation continues to be an example of an extremely complex and difficult foreign policy issue facing American government. Debate abounds over the proper response to human rights abuses in the region, and over the degree to which the conflict involves American national interests.

Richard C. Holbrooke is a career diplomat who, in 1998, served as the United States' chief representative at the United Nations. Holbrooke has previously served as Assistant Secretary of State for East Asian and Pacific Affairs (1977–1981), Ambassador to Germany (1993–1994), and Assistant Secretary of State for European and Canadian Affairs (1994–1996). Holbrooke was the United States' principal negotiator at the Dayton Conference in 1995, leading the U.S. effort to broker a solution to the highly complex problems brought on by the collapse of the former Yugoslavia. While the Dayton accords have not yet completely fulfilled their goal of creating a stable and unified Bosnian state, they have provided the framework for a fragile peace and the foundation for future advances.

The following selection is from Holbrooke's account of the negotiations at Dayton. The author recounts the Clinton Administration's response to the Dayton accords, demonstrating that diverse elements involved in American foreign policy can still come together behind a particular initiative, and that implementation of that initiative still faces challenges. Holbrooke argues that the dichotomy of American pragmatism and American idealism is a false one: when it came to implementing foreign policy in Bosnia, "our strategic interests and human rights supported and reinforced each other."

Holbrooke's major points are:

1. Bosnia has been a tricky situation for American foreign policy.
2. Once the Clinton Administration settled on the Dayton accords as the guide to future policy, the leadership of the White House was able to influence the other dynamics in American foreign policy. Still, they had to convince many interests—Congress, the public, leaders in Europe—to get behind the Dayton agreement.
3. The idealism-realism dichotomy is a false one: America's national interest as well as the defense of human rights inform and support U.S. policy on Bosnia.

32

Richard C. Holbrooke

TO END A WAR

Between 1991 and 1995, close to three hundred thousand people were killed in the former Yugoslavia. The international response to this catastrophe was at best uncertain and at worst appalling. While both the United States and the European Union initially viewed the Balkan wars as a European problem, the Europeans chose not to take a strong stand, restricting themselves to dispatching U.N. "peacekeepers" to a country where there was no peace to keep, and withholding from them the means and the authority to stop the fighting. Finally, in late 1995, in the face of growing atrocities and new Bosnian Serb threats, the United States decided to launch a last, all-out negotiating effort. This is the story of how, belatedly and reluctantly, the United States came to intervene and how that intervention brought the war in Bosnia to an end.

In the last two years, many people have asked me what the negotiations were really like. This cannot be answered with a dry account of positions taken and agreements reached. The fourteen weeks that form the core of this story were filled with conflict, confusion, and tragedy before their ultimate success. The negotiations were simultaneously cerebral and physical, abstract and personal, something like a combination of chess and mountain climbing. This was not a theoretical game between nation-states, but a dangerous and unpredictable process. . . .

Today, public service has lost much of the aura that it had when John F. Kennedy asked us what we could do for our country. To hear that phrase before it became a cliché was electrifying, and it led many in my generation to enter public service. For me, it was the Foreign Service, which I joined right after graduating from college. Less than a year later I found myself in Saigon. It seems like yesterday, but this was almost thirty-six years ago. I do not wish to suggest that in some distant "golden age" all was altruism and that today idealism is dead. Such easy myths may satisfy, but they are not true; every era has both heroes and scandals. But in an age when the media pays more attention to personalities than to issues, Americans may conclude that public service is either just another job, or a game played for personal advancement.

Such views are sadly deficient. The public sector contains countless men and women who, whether liberal or conservative, still believe in hard work, high ethical standards, and patriotism. . . .

My own government experiences over the last thirty-five years have led me to conclude that most accounts of major historical events, including memoirs, do not convey how the process appeared at the time to those participating in it. This derives, in part, from the historian's need to compress immensely complicated and often contradictory events into a coherent narrative whose outcome the reader (unlike the participants at the time) already knows. Other, more subtle factors are also at work: the natural tendency of memoirists to present themselves in a favorable light; a faulty memory or incomplete knowledge; and the distorting effect of perfect hindsight. A memoir sits at the dangerous intersection of policy, ambition, and history, where it is tempting to focus on instances of good judgment, and to blur or forget times when one made a mistake.

Hindsight tends to give historical narrative a sense of inevitability. But there was nothing predetermined about the outcome of the Bosnia negotiations. In August 1995, when they began, it was almost universally believed that they would fail, as all previous efforts had. And we knew that if we failed, the war would continue. . . .

An hour after the Dayton initialing ceremony, Kati and I flew with General Shalikashvili to New York. Leaving Wright-Patterson Air Force Base was like release from a comfortable prison; we slowly rediscovered the outside world. Still, after twenty-one days of isolation, normal life seemed far away. The extraordinary public reaction to the Dayton agreement was immensely gratifying, but in the rush of tasks that needed to be done, there was no time to savor it.

Meeting with the President

The next day, November 22, we met at the White House in an atmosphere that combined relief, pride, and apprehension. [National Security Advisor Anthony] Lake's opening quip reflected the tone: "We're in a heap of trouble now—but it's the right kind of trouble." The President, arriving with [Vice President] Gore a few moments later, thanked everyone, and joked, "I was all set for a disappointment."

Asked to begin, I said that the arrest of Karadzic and Mladic was the most critical issue that was not resolved at Dayton. I repeated my view that if the two men, particularly Karadzic, the founder and leader of a still-unrepentant separatist movement, remained at large, full implementation of the agreement would be impossible. The President concurred, saying, "It is best to remove both men." Without giving a direct instruction, he asked the military to reconsider the issue.

He then shifted to a more immediate issue: gaining public and congressional support for the policy. "I must be brutally honest with the American people," he said. "When I address the people I must be sure our military and intelligence people have signed off. I must be honest about what we are getting into."

Vice President Gore said Dayton was a gamble worth taking. He paused for a moment, and his face took on a sharp focus. "I want to make an important practical point regarding the [Joint Chiefs of Staff] and the Pentagon," he said, looking directly at the Defense representatives in the room. "I've had lots of conversations with the Congress. They have told me that our military representatives on the Hill usually leave their audience more uncomfortable than when they arrived. I'm not saying they are trying to undercut our policy, but they are losing us votes up there."

After a brief, stunned silence, Deputy Defense Secretary John White took up the challenge: "We need answers that Shali and his colleagues can all feel comfortable with."

The President stepped in to support Gore. "My sense," he said, "is that the diplomatic breakthrough in Dayton has given us a chance to prevail in Congress and in the nation. People see the stakes and the big picture. But we can't get congressional support without Defense and the military fully behind this. We must show Congress the stakes and the consequences. We can't promise them zero casualties, but we have to convey a high level of confidence in our capacity to carry out the mission and to manage the gaps in the agreement. Your people have body language. It's not a question of being dishonest, but we can't close the deal without the Pentagon's support." He looked directly at Shalikashvili. "I know there has been ambivalence among some of your people—not you, Shali, but some of your people—about Bosnia," he said, "but that is all in the past. I want everyone here to get behind the agreement."

The two men rose to leave, and we all rose with them. Their message would have a substantial effect. When the President and Vice President tell their senior aides to get with the program, and when they say it with vigor and even an unmistakable sternness, it does wonders for a divided or reluctant bureaucracy. I wondered if the two men had coordinated their comments; a year later the President told me that they had.

Congress and the Public

While the public applauded our diplomatic efforts, opinion polls put public opposition to the deployment of American forces to Bosnia at around 70 percent. This was understandable. For almost four years, Americans had watched television pictures of United Nations troops being killed and wounded while unable to defend themselves adequately. Most Americans assumed we were sending our own troops into a similar situation, where they would suffer heavy casualties.

Sending American troops to Bosnia would be the single most unpopular action of President Clinton's entire first term. Although the public was proud of the American diplomatic role in ending the war, we had to convince them that the American deployments would be different from those of the U.N., that NATO would shoot first and ask questions later—and that the deployment was in our national interest. *Newsweek* wryly captured the paradoxical situation in its first post-Dayton issue in an article by Evan Thomas and John Barry:

> Hail Pax Americana! Salute the return of the superpower! Or, then again, maybe not. The foreign-policy establishment may cheer, and Balkan brigands may head for the hills, but ordinary Americans are decidedly wary of sacrifices ahead. . . . Most voters regard Bosnia as someone else's civil war. It will be up to President Clinton to convince them otherwise. . . . Baffled by Bosnia or distracted by domestic concerns, most Americans have not begun to realize the reach and depth of the U.S. commitment made last week in Dayton.

Some important members of Congress immediately came to our support: Senators Lieberman, Biden, and Lugar once again were in the forefront. Some qualified their support by tying it to a tight "exit strategy." Since the Administration had written a one-year timetable into the Dayton agreement, we could not object. Many others opposed the policy outright. Such a position was essentially cost-free, since the Congress knew that the President would send troops regardless of what it did (barring an absolute cutoff of funds, which was very unlikely). Thus members of Congress could take a politically popular position without having to worry about its consequences. Speaker Gingrich predicted that the Administration would win "guarded approval, even acquiescence through inaction" and produced an artfully evasive resolution that allowed his colleagues in the House to vote both sides of the issue; they could give, as he put it, "very strong support for the troops [while objecting to] the president's policy."

In this atmosphere Donilon, Burns, and McCurry coordinated an intense public relations campaign. The President invited many members of Congress to the White House for briefings, and sent Christopher, Perry, Shalikashvili, and me to the Hill. In December we organized two large congressional delegations to the Balkans. Almost seventy members, an astonishing 15 percent of the entire House, went on these trips. Without exception, the members who went came back swayed in favor of the policy, although participation did not automatically mean full support. Cynthia McKinney, a first-term Democrat from an overwhelmingly black district in Georgia, who had previously focused on domestic issues and expressed great skepticism about foreign "giveaways," was typical. She told me later, "The trip changed my life. It made me realize that we have to undertake some of the same responsibilities overseas that we need to do at home, and that we must find a way to do both."

Europe: Applause and Shock

Dayton shook the leadership elite of post–Cold War Europe. The Europeans were grateful to the United States for leading the effort that finally ended the war in Bosnia, but some European officials were embarrassed that American involvement had been necessary. Jacques Poos's 1991 assertion that Europe's "hour had dawned" lay in history's dustbin, alongside James Baker's view that we had no dog in that fight.

"One cannot call it an American peace," French Foreign Minister de Charette told the press, "even if President Clinton and the Americans have tried to pull the blanket over to their side. The fact is that the Americans looked at this affair in ex-Yugoslavia from a great distance for nearly four years and basically blocked the progression of things." But de Charette also acknowledged that "Europe as such was not present, and this, it is true, was a failure of the European Union." Prime Minister Alain Juppé, after praising the Dayton agreement, could not resist adding, "Of course, it resembles like a twin the European plan we presented eighteen months ago"—when he was Foreign Minister. Agence France-Presse reported that many European diplomats were "left smarting" at Dayton. In an article clearly inspired by someone at the French Foreign Ministry, *Le Figaro* said that "Richard Holbrooke, the American mediator, did not leave his European colleagues with good memories from the air base at Dayton." They quoted an unnamed French diplomat as saying, "He flatters, he lies, he humiliates: he is a sort of brutal and schizophrenic Mazarin."* President Chirac's national security assistant, Jean-David Levitte, called to apologize for this comment, saying it did not represent the views of his boss. I replied that such minidramas were inevitable given the pressures and frustrations we faced at Dayton and were inconsequential considering that the war was over.

With two weeks remaining before the formal signing of the agreement in Paris, Karadzic raised temperatures again in the region. Although he had signed the agreement under Milosevic's pressure, he announced that Sarajevo would "bleed for decades" unless we changed the Dayton terms. In response, we said that we would not change the agreement. Defending the most problematic part of American policy, Perry predicted that "one year will be sufficient to break the cycle of violence in Bosnia." Perry broke the year down into two phases, four to six months to enforce a truce and disarmament, and another six months to create a secure environment. As it turned out, he was overly pessimistic on the first task, and overly optimistic on the second.

There was much work left before the signing ceremony. NATO had to send sixty thousand troops to Bosnia—the largest troop movement in Western Europe since World War II—and deploy thousands more off the Adriatic coast and at a forward logistics base in Hungary. On the civilian side, a series of high-level conferences were jammed into the two weeks immediately preceding the Paris ceremony. First came the annual NATO Foreign Ministers meeting in Brussels on December 5 and 6, which focused heavily on Bosnia. One day later, the scene shifted to Budapest for the annual meeting of the Foreign Ministers of the OSCE, who had to set up the machinery to oversee the elections in Bosnia as called for in the Dayton Peace Agreement. On December 8, the British convened a high-level "Implementation Conference" in London to discuss how to handle the nonmilitary parts of Dayton. Warren Christopher and John Kornblum attended the first two conferences, while Strobe Talbott and Bob Gallucci led the American team to London and Budapest. Meanwhile, I reassembled the

---

*Cardinal Jules Mazarin, a famously cunning and powerful seventeenth-century prelate, succeeded Cardinal Richelieu as chief minister to Louis XIII.

negotiating team and returned to the Balkans to pin down the final details for the Paris ceremonies.

This blizzard of diffused activity demonstrated the key difference between the negotiations and the phase that was beginning. The previous fourteen weeks had been highly focused. Now a wide-ranging effort, involving thousands of civilian and military personnel from the United States and other countries, was about to begin. Unfortunately, we had created a structure for implementing Dayton in which responsibility and authority would rest with no single individual or institution. . . .

AMERICA, EUROPE, AND BOSNIA

From the beginning of Yugoslavia's collapse, Americans divided into two groups, broadly defined: those who thought we should intervene for either moral or strategic reasons, and those who feared that if we did, we would become entangled in a Vietnam-like quagmire. As awareness of ethnic cleansing spread, the proportion of those who wanted the United States to "do something" increased, but they probably never constituted a majority.

Nonetheless, in only eighteen weeks in 1995—when the situation seemed most hopeless—the United States put its prestige on the line with a series of high-risk actions: an all-out diplomatic effort in August, heavy NATO bombing in September, a cease-fire in October, Dayton in November, and, in December, the deployment of twenty thousand American troops to Bosnia. Suddenly, the war was over—and America's role in post–Cold War Europe redefined.

Had the United States not intervened, the war would have continued for years and ended disastrously. The Bosnian Muslims would have been either destroyed, or reduced to a weak landlocked ministate surrounded by a Greater Croatia and a Greater Serbia. Fighting would eventually have resumed in eastern Slavonia. Europe would have faced a continued influx of Balkan refugees. And tens of thousands more would have been killed, maimed, or displaced from their homes.

But questions remain: Was American involvement in the national interest? How did it affect America's role in the world? Did Dayton bring peace to Bosnia, or only the absence of war? What might we have done better, or at least differently? Can Bosnia survive as a single multiethnic country, as called for in Dayton, or will it eventually divide into two or three ethnically based states? These issues, and others, deserve further attention.

American Leadership

By the spring of 1995 it had become commonplace to say that Washington's relations with our European allies were worse than at any time since the 1956 Suez crisis. But this comparison was misleading; because Suez came at the height of the Cold War, the strain then was containable. Bosnia, however, had defined the first phase of the post–Cold War relationship between Europe and the United States, and seriously damaged the Atlantic relationship. In particular, the strains endangered NATO itself just as Washington sought to enlarge it.

The Clinton Administration was severely criticized for reneging on our commitments to European security and for lowering the general priority accorded to foreign affairs—in short, for weak leadership in foreign policy. These charges deeply troubled the Administration's senior foreign-policy officials, especially when, ironically, they often came from those who opposed American involvement in Bosnia. In its own eyes, the Clinton Administration had laid down a strong track record in post–Cold War Europe: it had built a new relationship with Russia and the other former Soviet republics; started to enlarge NATO; tackled the Irish problem; strengthened American ties with the Baltic nations and Central Europe; and gained congressional approval for the NAFTA and GATT trade agreements. Nonetheless, the perception that Washington had turned away from Europe at the end of the Cold War was hard to shake as long as we did nothing about Bosnia.

Dayton changed this almost overnight. Criticism of President Clinton as a weak leader ended abruptly, especially in Europe and among Muslim nations. Washington was now praised for its firm leadership—or even chided by some Europeans for *too much* leadership. But even those who chafed at the reassertion of American power conceded, at least implicitly, its necessity. As I suggested at the time, this was not a serious problem; it was better to be criticized for too much leadership than for too little.

After Dayton, American foreign policy seemed more assertive, more muscular. This may have been as much perception as reality, but the perception mattered. The three main pillars of American foreign policy in Europe—U.S.-Russian relations, NATO enlargement into Central Europe, and Bosnia—had often worked against each other. Now they reinforced each other: NATO sent its forces out of area for the first time in its history, and Russian troops, under an American commander, were deployed alongside them. "Clinton managed to pull off the seemingly impossible," wrote Russia's former Prime Minister, Yegor Gaidar, "to implement NATO enlargement without causing irreparable damage either to democratic elements in Russia's political establishment or to U.S.-Russian relations." De Charette had it right: "America *was* back."

Strategic considerations were vital to our involvement, but the motives that finally pushed the United States into action were also moral and humanitarian. After Srebrenica and Mount Igman the United States could no longer escape the terrible truth of what was happening in Bosnia. A surge of sentiment arose from ordinary Americans who were outraged at what they saw on television and from senior government officials who could no longer look the other way. Within the Administration, the loss of three friends on Mount Igman carried a special weight; the war had, in effect, come home.

Despite American pride over Dayton, our own record in the former Yugoslavia was flawed. The tortured half-measures of the United Nations and the European Union had been inadequate, to be sure, but they had kept the Bosnian Muslims from complete destruction for several years. And the Europeans continued to pay the bulk of the bills, without getting sufficient credit from the American public or the Congress, which, immediately after Dayton, told the Europeans that they would have to carry the burden for civilian reconstruction. Thus, the richest nation in the world, in the midst of its strongest economic performance in thirty years, offered the former Yugoslavia a relatively insignificant amount of aid. Furthermore, despite valiant efforts by John Kornblum, implementation of the Dayton agreement was initially half-hearted. Only in mid-1997, with the arrival of Bob Gelbard and General Clark, did the implementation effort begin to show the energy required.

AMERICA, STILL A EUROPEAN POWER

Even with the Cold War over, what happens in Europe still matters to the United States. This is not self-evident to most Americans, who thought the need for direct American involvement in Europe—and for that matter, most of the rest of the world—would end or decline sharply with the fall of communism.

But American involvement in Europe is not limited to crusades against fascism or communism. Deeper, less tangible factors tie the two continents together. Three times earlier in this century, the United States engaged deeply on the European continent: in World War I, in World War II, and in the Cold War. After each of the first two involvements, the United States withdrew, or began to withdraw, from the continent: in 1919-20, when it decided not to join the international institution President Wilson had helped create, and in 1945-47. After World War II, America's leaders recognized that the country's national interests required a continued involvement in Europe, as well as in Asia.* But when their initial policy, based on the effectiveness of the United Nations, failed because it required the positive participation of the Soviet Union, the Truman Administration quickly recognized its initial misjudgment of Moscow and entered into the century's third American engagement in Europe, one that led to the collapse of the Soviet Union at the end of 1991.

Then, after fifty years of costly involvement in Europe, Americans hoped to focus on domestic priorities and disengage as much as possible from international commitments. Although understandable, this hope was unrealistic. Well before the Bosnia negotiations began, I argued that "an unstable Europe would still threaten essential security interests of the United States." But, with the disappearance of the Soviet Union, most Americans no longer believed this. There was no clear and present threat to the Western democracies, no Hitler or Stalin. Moreover, for the first time since 1917, Russia and its former republics had to be incorporated into Europe's security structure rather than excluded from it. This new European security structure could not be built while part of it, the former Yugoslavia, was in flames. Settling Bosnia was necessary, although not sufficient, for true stability and long-term economic growth in Europe.

The policies of the last half century produced unparalleled peace and prosperity for half a century—but for only half a continent. With the war over in Bosnia, building a new European security architecture that included both the United States and Russia could finally proceed. NATO, long the private preserve of the nations on one side of the Iron Curtain, could gradually open its doors to qualified Central European nations—in a manner that neither threatened Russia nor weakened the alliance.

---

*It is noteworthy that, in contrast to Europe, the United States has maintained military forces in East Asia and the Pacific continuously for one hundred years, since 1898, except when the Japanese drove us from the area in 1942-43.

Meanwhile, a new role for Russia, Ukraine, and the other parts of the former Soviet Union was being defined through new agreements like the Founding Act, which created a formal relationship between Russia and NATO yet did not give Russia a veto power over NATO activities. Other existing institutions, like the Organization for Security and Cooperation in Europe (OSCE), were strengthened and expanded.

Leadership Without Unilateralism

The great architect of European unity, Jean Monnet, once observed, "Nothing is possible without men, but nothing is lasting without institutions." It has become commonplace to observe that achieving Monnet's vision is far more difficult in the absence of the unifying effect of a common adversary. But we should not wax nostalgic for the Cold War. It is now institutional and structural problems that inhibit progress on both sides of the Atlantic.

The United States has survived divided government between the Executive Branch and the Congress for much of the last two decades. But a bloated bureaucratic system and a protracted struggle between the two branches have eroded much of Washington's capacity for decisive action in foreign affairs and reduced our presence just as our range of interests has increased. The United States continues to reduce the resources committed to international affairs even as vast parts of the globe—the former Soviet bloc, China—and new issues that once lay outside its area of direct involvement now take on new importance and require American attention. One cannot have a global economic policy without a political and strategic vision to accompany it, as the 1997–98 economic crisis in East Asia has shown.

If the search for a process that can produce coherent policies is difficult in Washington, it seems to be virtually impossible in the new Europe. Carl Bildt has made a useful observation: the United States, he points out, has to harmonize "institutional views" while Europe has to coordinate "national views." Bildt, who saw the two systems from a unique vantage point, observed:

> In Washington everything has to be formulated and shaped in a continuous compromise between the State Department, the Defense Department, the Treasury, intelligence agencies, and purely domestic factors. The rivalry between these various interests sometimes runs very deep. A great deal of blood can be spilt in the course of inter-agency debates in Washington. *But when this apparatus finally decides on a policy, the United States then has the resources to implement its policy which is almost completely lacking in Europe* [emphasis added].

A Question of Evil: A Personal Note

Advocates of realpolitik, like three of its most famous American practitioners, Richard Nixon, Henry Kissinger, and George Kennan, have long argued that American advocacy of human rights conflicted with America's true national security interests, amounted to interference in the internal affairs of other nations, and weakened the nation's strategic and commercial interests. In his most recent book, *Diplomacy*, Kissinger portrayed American foreign policy as a constant struggle between realism, symbolized by Theodore Roosevelt, and idealism, as epitomized by Woodrow Wilson. Kissinger, who strongly favored TR, wrote, "The American experience has encouraged the belief that America, alone among the nations of the world, is impervious and that it can prevail by the example of its virtues and good works. In the post–Cold War world, such an attitude would turn innocence into self-indulgence."

Under Presidents Nixon, Ford, and Bush, such "realist" theories were in the ascendancy. (The Carter Administration and the Reagan Administration, after the forced departure of Secretary of State Al Haig, took much more assertive positions on human rights.) But based on personal experiences in the late 1970s with authoritarian leaders like Ferdinand Marcos of the Philippines and Park Chung Hee of South Korea—both of whose corrupt strongman regimes were peacefully replaced by democracies—I came to the conclusion that the choice between "realists" and "idealists" was a false one: in the long run, our strategic interests and human rights supported and reinforced each other, and could be advanced at the same time. In short, American foreign policy needed to embrace both Theodore Roosevelt and Woodrow Wilson. These thoughts were never far from my mind as we searched for a way to end the war.

CHAPTER 8

CIVIL SOCIETY AND COMMUNITY

Who Are We and What Do We Want From Each Other?

The relationship of the individual to the larger society has interested philosophers and political pundits for thousands of years. Currently, many Americans decry a breakdown in "civil society." The fear is that as individuals retreat from civic obligations, the social ties that bind us together as a nation become frayed and the very notion of a "community"—of people working together for the benefit of all—can become forgotten. This happens when people stop taking a formal part in the lives of their communities and its organizations.

At the same time, though, America has always had a vibrant sense of individualism, a feeling of freedom—nobody forces individuals to go to PTA meetings or even to vote, for that matter. We block attempts by organizations and by government itself to intrude too far into our personal lives, and we are ever vigilant against Big Brother–style efforts to compel individual behavior.

These ideals—individualism and the common good—are not as isolated from each other as they might appear. America has a unique awareness of how seemingly individualistic, self-interested behavior can work for the benefit of both the individual and the community. Tocqueville called this "self-interest rightly understood." Thus, individualized behavior does not necessarily threaten the stability of the republic or the ability of our nation to work together for mutual benefits. Nevertheless, there are important reasons why we need to be concerned with the balance between our private behavior as individuals and our interest, as citizens, in the common good. America is not likely to destroy itself if membership in traditional organizations declines, but we need to understand how new developments and new technologies can help, or hinder, our search for a community based on individual freedom.

Alexis de Tocqueville came to America in the early nineteenth century to observe and write about what the world viewed as a tenuous new experiment in democracy. Tocqueville saw democracy as the wave of the future, and the drive toward equality as a dominant political force. His famous treatise, *Democracy in America*, was published in 1833 and became an immediate best seller in America and Europe. Tocqueville, an aristocrat himself, lauded the American experiment, extolled American virtues, and viewed American democracy as the future paradigm for all governments.

The French Revolution, unlike the American Revolution, had failed to create a stable and lasting democratic government. At the time of a second democratic revolution in 1848, Tocqueville in the same year wrote in the preface to his book: "Let us look to America, not in order to make a servile copy of the institutions that she has established, but to gain a clearer view of the polity that will be the best for us; let us look there less to find examples than instructions; let us borrow from her the principles, rather than the details, of her laws."

Tocqueville admired many aspects of American society, particularly the large number of voluntary civic associations. In the following selection from *Democracy in America*, Tocqueville compares aristocratic and democratic virtues. He grapples with the question of how liberty, equality, and the pursuit of self-interest are linked in American culture to support a democratic civic society.

Tocqueville's major points are:

1. Americans do not sacrifice for others because it is noble to do so, but because sacrifice serves the individual's self-interest. Tocqueville calls this "self-interest rightly understood."
2. Self-interest rightly understood produces a continual progression of small sacrifices, rather than great acts of self-sacrifice. This draws Americans to sacrifice for the good of all as a force of habit.
3. There is "a close bond" between freedom and productive industry, but the freedom to pursue material benefits in a democracy can lead people to overlook the connection between individual prosperity and the prosperity of the community.
4. In turn, inattention to public concerns opens avenues for despots to seize power. As people come to oppose the disruptions caused by the "turmoil of freedom," they may seek leaders who will maintain order and tranquility. Small factions can thus enslave nations.
5. Americans, especially, are threatened by a peculiar dynamic of equality. Equality can compress will and action, circumscribing behavior into ever narrower channels.
6. The desire to be led and yet remain free encourages intermittent participation at special times like elections, and an attention to private things at other times. Surrendering power to the nation at large, though, risks succumbing to a "soft despotism" that rules by controlling the habits of behavior. As people give ever more control of administrative details to the government, they may lose the freedom of choice and will in everyday things.

33

Alexis de Tocqueville

Individualism, Self-Interest, and Community

★★★

How the Americans Combat Individualism by the Principle of Self-Interest Rightly Understood

When the world was managed by a few rich and powerful individuals, these persons loved to entertain a lofty idea of the duties of man. They were fond of professing that it is praiseworthy to forget oneself and that good should be done without hope of reward, as it is by the Deity himself. Such were the standard opinions of that time in morals.

I doubt whether men were more virtuous in aristocratic ages than in others, but they were incessantly talking of the beauties of virtue, and its utility was only studied in secret. But since the imagination takes less lofty flights, and every man's thoughts are centered in himself, moralists are alarmed by this idea of self-sacrifice and they no longer venture to present it to the human mind. They therefore content themselves with inquiring whether the personal advantage of each member of the community does not consist in working for the good of all; and when they have hit upon some point on which private interest and public interest meet and amalgamate, they are eager to bring it into notice. Observations of this kind are gradually multiplied; what was only a single remark becomes a general principle, and it is held as a truth that man serves himself in serving his fellow creatures and that his private interest is to do good.

I have already shown . . . by what means the inhabitants of the United States almost always manage to combine their own advantage with that of their fellow citizens; my present purpose is to point out the general rule that enables them to do so. In the United States hardly anybody talks of the beauty of virtue, but they maintain that virtue is useful and prove it every day. The American moralists do not profess that men ought to sacrifice themselves for their fellow creatures *because* it is noble to make such sacrifices, but they boldly aver that such sacrifices are as necessary to him who imposes them upon himself as to him for whose sake they are made.

They have found out that, in their country and their age, man is brought home to himself by an irresistible force; and, losing all hope of stopping that force, they turn all their thoughts to the direction of it. They therefore do not deny that every man may follow his own interest, but they endeavor to prove that it is the interest of every man to be virtuous. I shall not here enter into the reasons they allege, which would divert me from my subject; suffice it to say that they have convinced their fellow countrymen.

Montaigne said long ago: "Were I not to follow the straight road for its straightness, I should follow it for having found by experience that in the end it is commonly the happiest and most useful track." The doctrine of interest rightly understood is not then new, but among the Americans of our time it finds universal acceptance; it has become popular there; you may trace it at the bottom of all their actions, you will remark it in all they say. It is as often asserted by the poor man as by the rich. In Europe the principle of interest is much grosser than it is in America, but it is also less common and especially it is less avowed; among us, men still constantly feign great abnegations which they no longer feel.

The Americans, on the other hand, are fond of explaining almost all the actions of their lives by the principle of self-interest rightly understood; they show with complacency how an enlightened regard for themselves constantly prompts them to assist one another and inclines them willingly to sacrifice a portion of their time and property to the welfare of the state. In this respect I think they frequently fail to do themselves justice; for in the United States as well as elsewhere people are sometimes seen to give way to those disinterested and spontaneous impulses that are natural to man; but the Americans seldom admit that they yield to emotions of this kind; they are more anxious to do honor to their philosophy than to themselves.

I might here pause without attempting to pass a judgment on what I have described. The extreme difficulty of the subject would be my excuse, but I shall not avail myself of it; and I had rather that my readers, clearly perceiving my object, would refuse to follow me than that I should leave them in suspense.

The principle of self-interest rightly understood is not a lofty one, but it is clear and sure. It does not aim at mighty objects, but attains without exertion all those at which it aims. As it lies within the reach of all capacities, everyone can without difficulty learn and retain it. By its admirable conformity to human weaknesses it easily obtains great dominion; nor is that dominion precarious, since the principle checks one personal interest by another, and uses, to direct the passions, the very same instrument that excites them.

The principle of self-interest rightly understood produces no great acts of self-sacrifice, but it suggests daily small acts of self-denial. By itself it cannot suffice to make a man virtuous; but it disciplines a number of persons in habits of regularity, temperance, moderation, foresight, self-command; and if it does not lead men straight to virtue by the will, it gradually draws them in that direction by their habits. If the principle of interest rightly understood were to sway the whole moral world, extraordinary virtues would doubtless be more rare; but I think that gross depravity would then also be less common. The principle of interest rightly understood perhaps prevents men from rising far above the level of mankind, but a great number of other men, who were falling far below it, are caught and restrained by it. Observe some few individuals, they are lowered by it; survey man kind, they are raised.

I am not afraid to say that the principle of self-interest rightly understood appears to me the best suited of all philosophical theories to the wants of the men of our time, and that I regard it as their chief remaining security against themselves. Towards it, therefore, the minds of the moralists of our age should turn; even should they judge it to be incomplete, it must nevertheless be adopted as necessary.

I do not think, on the whole, that there is more selfishness among us than in America; the only difference is that there it is enlightened, here it is not. Each American knows when to sacrifice some of his private interests to save the rest; we want to save everything, and often we lose it all. Everybody I see about me seems bent on teaching his contemporaries, by precept and example, that what is useful is never wrong. Will nobody undertake to make them understand how what is right may be useful?

No power on earth can prevent the increasing equality of conditions from inclining the human mind to seek out what is useful or from leading every member of the community to be wrapped up in himself. It must therefore be expected that personal interest will become more than ever the principal if not the sole spring of men's actions; but it remains to be seen how each man will understand his personal interest. If the members of a community, as they become more equal, become more ignorant and coarse, it is difficult to forsee to what pitch of stupid excesses their selfishness may lead them; and no one can foretell into what disgrace and wretchedness they would plunge themselves lest they should have to sacrifice something of their own well-being to the prosperity of their fellow creatures.

I do not think that the system of self-interest as it is professed in America is in all its parts self-evident, but it contains a great number of truths so evident that men, if they are only educated, cannot fail to see them. Educate, then, at any rate, for the age of implicit self-sacrifice and instinctive virtues is already flitting far away from us, and the time is fast approaching when freedom, public peace, and social order itself will not be able to exist without education.

How the Taste for Physical Gratifications is United in America to Love of Freedom and Attention to Public Affairs

. . . There is a close bond and necessary relation between these two elements, freedom and productive industry.

This proposition is generally true of all nations, but especially of democratic nations. I have already shown that men who live in ages of equality have a continual need of forming associations in order to procure the things they desire; and, on the other hand, I have shown how great political freedom improves and diffuses the art of association. Freedom in these ages is therefore especially favorable to the production of wealth; nor is it difficult to perceive that despotism is especially adverse to the same result.

The nature of despotic power in democratic ages is not to be fierce or cruel, but minute and meddling. Despotism of this kind, though it does not trample on humanity, is directly opposed to the genius of commerce and the pursuits of industry.

Thus the men of democratic times require to be free in order to procure more readily those physical enjoyments for which they are always longing. It sometimes happens, however, that the excessive taste they conceive for these same enjoyments makes them surrender to the first master who appears. The passion for worldly welfare then defeats itself and, without their perceiving it, throws the object of their desires to a greater distance.

There is, indeed, a most dangerous passage in the history of a democratic people. When the taste for physical gratifications among them has grown more rapidly than their education and their experience of free institutions, the time will come when men are carried away and lose all self-restraint at the sight of the new possessions they are about to obtain. In their intense and exclusive anxiety to make a fortune they lose sight of the close connection that exists between the private fortune of each and the prosperity of all. It is not necessary to do violence to such a people in order to strip them of the rights they enjoy; they themselves willingly loosen their hold. The discharge of political duties appears to them to be a troublesome impediment which diverts them from their occupations and business. If they are required to elect representatives, to support the government by personal service, to meet on public business, they think they have no time, they cannot waste their precious hours in useless engagements; such idle amusements are unsuited to serious men who are engaged with the more important interests of life. These people think they are following the principle of self-interest, but the idea they entertain of that principle is a very crude one; and the better to look after what they call their own business, they neglect their chief business, which is to remain their own masters.

As the citizens who labor do not care to attend to public affairs, and as the class which might devote its leisure to these duties has ceased to exist, the place of the government is, as it were, unfilled. If at that critical moment some able and ambitious man grasps the supreme power, he will find the road to every kind of usurpation open before him. If he attends for some time only to the material prosperity of the country, no more will be demanded of him. Above all, he must ensure public tranquillity: men who are possessed by the passion for physical gratification generally find out that the turmoil of freedom disturbs their welfare before they discover how freedom itself serves to promote it. If the slightest rumor of public commotion intrudes into the petty pleasures of private life, they are aroused and alarmed by it. The fear of anarchy perpetually haunts them, and they are always ready to fling away their freedom at the first disturbance.

I readily admit that public tranquillity is a great good, but at the same time I cannot forget that all nations have been enslaved by being kept in good order. Certainly it is not to be inferred that nations ought to despise public tranquillity, but that state ought not to content them. A nation that asks nothing of its government but the maintenance of order is already a slave at heart, the slave of its own well-being, awaiting only the hand that will bind it.

By such a nation the despotism of faction is not less to be dreaded than the despotism of an individual. When the bulk of the community are engrossed by private concerns, the smallest parties need not despair of getting the upper hand in public affairs. At such times it is not rare to see on the great stage of the world, as we see in our theaters, a multitude represented by a few players, who alone speak in the name of an absent or inattentive crowd: they alone are in action, while all others are stationary; they regulate everything by their own caprice; they change the laws and tyrannize at will over the manners of the country; and then men wonder to see into how small a number of weak and worthless hands a great people may fall.

Hitherto the Americans have fortunately escaped all the perils that I have just pointed out, and in this respect they are really deserving of admiration. Perhaps there is no country in the world where fewer idle men are to be *met* with than in America, or where all who work are more eager to promote their own welfare. But if the passion of the Americans for physical gratifications is vehement, at least it is not indiscriminate; and reason, though unable to restrain it, still directs its course.

An American attends to his private concerns as if he were alone in the world, and the next minute he gives himself up to the common welfare as if he had forgotten them. At one time he seems animated by the most selfish cupidity; at another, by the most lively patriotism. The human heart cannot be thus divided. The inhabitants of the United States alternately display so strong and so similar a passion for their own welfare and for their freedom that it may be supposed that these passions are united and mingled in some part of their character. And indeed the Americans believe their freedom to be the best instrument and surest safeguard of their welfare; they are attached to the one by the other. They by no means think that they are not called upon to take a part in public affairs; they believe, on the contrary, that their chief business is to secure for themselves a government which will allow them to acquire the things they covet and which will not debar them from the peaceful enjoyment of those possessions which they have already acquired.

Democratic governments may become violent and even cruel at certain periods of extreme effervescence or of great danger, but these crises will be rare and brief. When I consider the petty passions of our contemporaries, the mildness of their manners, the extent of their education, the purity of their religion, the gentleness of their morality, their regular and industrious habits, and the restraint which they almost all observe in their vices no less than in their virtues, I have no fear that they will meet with tyranny in their rules, but rather with guardians.

I think, then, that the species of oppression by which democratic nations are menaced is unlike anything that ever before existed in the world; our contemporaries will find no prototype of it in their memories. I seek in vain for an expression that will accurately convey the whole of the idea I have formed of it; the old words *despotism* and *tyranny* are inappropriate: the thing itself is new, and since I cannot name, I must attempt to define it.

I seek to trace the novel features under which despotism may appear in the world. The first thing that strikes the observation is an innumerable multitude of men, all equal and alike, incessantly endeavoring to procure the petty and paltry pleasures with which they glut their lives. Each of them, living apart, is as a stranger to the fate of all the rest; his children and his private friends constitute to him the whole of mankind. As for the rest of his fellow citizens, he is close to them, but does not see them; he touches them, but he does not feel them; he exists only in himself and for himself alone; and if his kindred still remain to him, he may be said at any rate to have lost his country.

Above this race of men stands an immense and tutelary power, which takes upon itself alone to secure their gratifications and to watch over their fate. That power is absolute, minute, regular, provident, and mild. It would be like the authority of a parent if, like that authority, its object was to prepare men for manhood; but it seeks, on the contrary, to keep them in perpetual childhood: it is well content that the people should rejoice, provided they think of nothing but rejoicing. For their happiness such a government willingly labors, but it chooses to be the sole agent and the only arbiter of that happiness; it provides for their security, foresees and supplies their necessities, facilitates their pleasures, manages their principal concerns, directs their industry, regulates the descent of property, and subdivides their inheritances: what remains, but to spare them all the care of thinking and all the trouble of living?

Thus it every day renders the exercise of the free agency of man less useful and less frequent; it circumscribes the will within a narrower range and gradually robs a man of all the uses of himself. The principle of equality has prepared men for these things; it has predisposed men to endure them and often to look on them as benefits.

After having thus successively taken each member of the community in its powerful grasp and fashioned him at will, the supreme power then extends its arm over the whole community. It covers the surface of society with a network of small complicated rules, minute and uniform, through which the most original minds and the most energetic characters cannot penetrate, to rise above the crowd. The will of man is not shattered, but softened, bent, and guided; men are seldom forced by it to act, but they are constantly restrained from acting. Such a power does not destroy, but it prevents existence; it does not tyrannize, but it compresses, enervates, extinguishes, and stupefies a people, till each nation is reduced to nothing better than a flock of timid and industrious animals, of which the government is the shepherd.

I have always thought that servitude of the regular, quiet, and gentle kind which I have just described might be combined more easily than is commonly believed with some of the outward forms of freedom, and that it might even establish itself under the wing of the sovereignty of the people.

Our contemporaries are constantly excited by two conflicting passions: they want to be led, and they wish to remain free. As they cannot destroy either the one or the other of these contrary propensities, they strive to satisfy them both at once. They devise a sole, tutelary, and all-powerful form of government, but elected by the people. They combine the principle of centralization and that of popular sovereignty; this gives them a respite: they console themselves for being in tutelage by the reflection that they have chosen their own guardians. Every man allows himself to be put in leading-strings, because he sees that it is not a person or a class of persons, but the people at large who hold the end of his chain.

By this system the people shake off their state of dependence just long enough to select their master and then relapse into it again. A great many persons at the present day are quite contented with this sort of compromise between administrative despotism and the sovereignty of the people; and they think they have done enough for the protection of individual freedom when they have surrendered it to the power of the nation at large. This does not satisfy me: the nature of him I am to obey signifies less to me than the fact of extorted obedience.

I do not deny, however, that a constitution of this kind appears to me to be infinitely preferable to one which, after having concentrated all the powers of government, should vest them in the hands of an irresponsible person or body of persons. Of all the forms that democratic despotism could assume, the latter would assuredly be the worst.

When the sovereign is elective, or narrowly watched by a legislature which is really elective and independent, the oppression that he exercises over individuals is sometimes greater, but it is always less degrading; because every man, when he is oppressed and disarmed, may still imagine that, while he yields obedience, it is to himself he yields it, and that it is to one of his own inclinations that all the rest give way. In like manner, I can understand that when the sovereign represents the nation and is dependent upon the people, the rights and the power of which every citizen is deprived serve not only the head of the state, but the state itself; and that private persons derive some return from the sacrifice of their independence which they have made to the public. To create a representation of the people in every centralized country is, therefore, to diminish the evil that extreme centralization may produce, but not to get rid of it.

I admit that, by this means, room is left for the intervention of individuals in the more important affairs; but it is not the less suppressed in the smaller and more privates ones. It must not be forgotten that it is especially dangerous to enslave men in the minor details of life. For my own part, I should be inclined to think freedom less necessary in great things than in little ones, if it were possible to be secure of the one without possessing the other.

Subjection in minor affairs breaks out every day and is felt by the whole community indiscriminately. It does not drive men to resistance, but it crosses them at every turn, till they are led to surrender the exercise of their own will. Thus their spirit is gradually broken and their character enervated; whereas that obedience which is exacted on a few important but rare occasions only exhibits servitude at certain intervals and throws the burden of it upon a small number of men. It is in vain to summon a people who have been rendered so dependent on the central power to choose from time to time the representatives of that power; this rare and brief exercise of their free choice, however important it may be, will not prevent them from gradually losing the faculties of thinking, feeling, and acting for themselves, and thus gradually falling below the level of humanity.

I add that they will soon become incapable of exercising the great and only privilege which remains to them. The democratic nations that have introduced freedom into their political constitution at the very time when they were augmenting the despotism of their administrative constitution have been led into strange paradoxes. To manage those minor affairs in which good sense is all that is wanted, the people are held to be unequal to the task; but when the government of the country is at stake, the people are invested with immense powers; they are alternately made the playthings of their ruler, and his masters, more than kings and less than men. After having exhausted all the different modes of election without finding one to suit their purpose, they are still amazed and still bent on seeking further; as if the evil they notice did not originate in the constitution of the country far more than in that of the electoral body.

It is indeed difficult to conceive how men who have entirely given up the habit of self-government should succeed in making a proper choice of those by whom they are

to be governed; and no one will ever believe that a liberal, wise, and energetic government can spring from the suffrages of a subservient people.

The conservative author of the following selection argues that liberty and good government depend upon private and public virtue. Government always reflects a set of values,
and the question is, whose values will prevail? The answer, according to the author, is
that a majority of Americans accept a set of core values that define virtue. These values
must be recognized, resurrected, and implemented in all walks of public and private life.
    William J. Bennett served as chairman of the National Endowment for the Humani-
ties from 1981 to 1985, and as Secretary of Education under President Ronald Reagan
from 1985 to 1988. From 1989 to 1991, Bennett served as President George Bush's "drug
czar." Since then, Bennett has written widely on American morals and values, including
the best-selling *Book of Virtues*.
    In this selection, Bennett writes:

1. Right and wrong, and personal responsibility, are fundamental subjects of public policy.
2. Public and private spheres overlap, and the argument that they are isolated and discrete is an oversimplification.
3. "Cultural" issues are every bit as important as "real" issues like the budget deficit. Ignoring the importance of culture and values is unrealistic. Citizens need to join the
   debate over what values will guide the nation.

34

William J. Bennett

THE DE-VALUING OF AMERICA

. . . [There is a] need in public policy to address fundamental matters of right and
wrong, and personal responsibility.
    . . . The modern liberal sensibility is quite often allergic to the most serious ques-
tions of culture, spirit, and values. Money, technology, and bureaucracy: the liberal-
left will talk about and work on them incessantly, vigorously, and enthusiastically. But
when the subject is character, personal responsibility, and right and wrong, they tend
to grow uncomfortable and diffident.

I understand the discomfort and the diffidence. Ours is a society deliberately and wisely divided into separate spheres of private and public action. Liberty requires it. But as our Founders understood, liberty also requires a strong measure of virtue in each sphere. The public good rests its foundation on the qualities of private men and women. Madison wrote in *Federalist* #55 that a government devoted to liberty "presupposes the existence of these qualities in a higher degree than any other form." In America, general liberty cannot survive a dearth of virtue and public policy cannot succeed without addressing the issue of values directly.

Public action should not and need not extend its full reach into strictly private terrain. But the public and private spheres approach each other at many points. And when the private sphere comes forward in partial ill-health, then public *conversation*, at least, should not ignore it by an embarrassed silence. What this means concretely is that we must confront our discomfort and talk openly and candidly about the moral good as an essential part of our lives together.

I know the automatic response from some quarters, since I have heard it more than a few times during my government career: "The Puritans are coming, the Puritans are coming!" But Cotton Mather has been dead for more than 250 years, and this country is hardly at risk of a renewed interest in his thinking. We need to have a calm, complete, and honest talk about some of the most troubling aspects of contemporary American culture. The longer we wait, the more trouble we'll see. The longer we avoid these questions, the worse things will get.

C. S. Lewis wrote in *The Abolition of Man:* "We make men without chests and expect of them virtue and enterprise. We laugh at honor and are shocked to find traitors in our midst. We castrate and then bid the geldings be fruitful." If we ridicule and caricature traditional religious beliefs, standards of decency, and virtue as the hang-up of uptight, obsessive prudes, there will be a cost. It will be primarily to our children.

It needn't be this way. The subject of my most recent government post is a good example. Drug use is a problem with obvious and devastating public consequences, but a problem first and foremost of private behavior, of morality. . . . [O]ur public conversation about drugs was until recently devoted largely to aimless handwringing and expressions of despair. Today, things look very different. Every available piece of evidence suggests that overall the drug problem is getting better, not worse. No doubt that official action has helped. The federal government and many states are now effectively spending record amounts of money on drug interdiction, law enforcement, education, and treatment. We are deploying that money more intelligently and less haphazardly than in the past. All these steps are useful. But something even more important has happened: we have recovered our public mind, our moral clarity, about a dangerous private behavior.

Embarrassment in this area has faded; in fact, it now seems almost antiquated. Taking drugs is wrong. Almost everyone says so, and they say it out loud, and often. Americans want this problem over. And the private voices give strength to the official actions; indeed, they are a necessary condition of the effectiveness of those actions. The result is that fewer and fewer people are taking drugs. It is not a simple process, this "American capacity for self-renewal," as one historian described it. But it is definite, discernible, and replicable. And the first step here, as in so many other areas, involves an open attempt to grapple with moral principles, with principles of behavior and conduct.

The popular press and political commentators often portray cultural issues as a sideshow, a distraction from the more "real" and "pressing" issues we face like, say, the federal budget deficit. A university professor was quoted in *The New York Times* as saying that President Bush had lost his ability to announce any new initiatives that cost money, and "that's why you see these symbolic causes—the flag, abortion, family values." That is a cynical attitude and it is flat-out wrong. Cultural issues are every bit as "real"—indeed, they are more real, more important, and have more impact on the lives of our children.

Nothing more powerfully determines a child's behavior than his internal compass, his beliefs, his sense of right and wrong. If a child firmly believes, if he has been taught and guided to believe, that drugs, promiscuity, and assaulting other people are wrong things to do, this will contribute to his own well-being and to the well-being of others. And if this lesson is multiplied a million times—that is, taught a million times—we will have greater and broader well-being, fewer personal catastrophes, less social violence, and fewer wasted and lost lives. The character of a society is determined by how well it transmits true and time-honored values from generation to generation. Cultural matters, then, are not simply an add-on or an afterthought to the quality of life of a country; they determine the character and essence of the country itself. Private belief is a condition of public spirit, personal responsibility a condition of public well-being. The investment in private belief must be constantly renewed.

During the last twenty-five years, we didn't make much of an investment and we received little return. Many of America's intellectual elite perpetrated a doctrine of *de facto* nihilism that cut to the core of American traditions. While the doctrine never fully took hold among most Americans, it did make significant inroads. A lot of people forgot, and many others willfully rejected, the most basic and sensible answers to first questions, to questions about what contributes to our social well-being and prosperity, what makes for individual character and responsibility, and what constitutes a "good society."

The public has been too quiescent and too accepting about what has been inflicted on them from the upper strata of society and the permanent political establishment in Washington. Too often they elected to sit on the sidelines, in part because legions of officials, special interest groups, professors, and commentators belittle mainstream American values and participation; often they belittle and patronize mainstream Americans themselves. "We know better," the elite establishment said. "Leave it to us, the enlightened experts, and everything will turn out just fine." Too often many people did what was asked of them. The results are now in.

Significant portions of American society have been culturally deconstructed. This has had particularly devastating effects on our institutions: schools, colleges and universities, mainline churches, the legal profession, the Congress, and others. The assault was made primarily by people who held left-liberal political views, who believed that these institutions were corrupt, unsuitable, unworthy and unfit, and so they decided to remake them in their image, for their own purposes.

The good news is that this cultural virus has created its own antibodies. Americans are regaining the confidence to express publicly the common sense sentiments they hold privately. They are learning again that the things a society collectively chooses to affirm and condemn, encourage and discourage, make all the difference. This is true whether we are talking about curricular basics or curricular fluff; welfare or workfare; marriage or out-of-wedlock births; regard or disdain for religion in the public square; color blindness or color consciousness; or drug use as acceptable or unacceptable. This renewed understanding on a whole range of social issues is the critical first step in the "revaluing" of America. Values that were once in exile are being welcomed home. The American people are renewing their commitment to our common principles. And so the task of cultural reconstruction has begun. But it is nowhere near complete, and it is least complete in the institutions that have borne the brunt of two decades of wrong-headed cultural and public policy.

Michael Barone and Grant Ujifusa, editors of the *Almanac of American Politics*, put it this way:

> The [domestic] public sector institutions of which liberals have had custody for the last twenty years—the public schools, central city bureaucracies, university governance—have performed poorly. The people in charge of them have a million excuses: they have a poor quality of students or constituents, they don't have enough money, they must do things according to certain rules and regulations because of internal institutional imperatives. These are the same excuses the military made fifteen or twenty years ago. Fortunately, the leaders of the military stopped making excuses and started reforming. Unfortunately, with very few exceptions, the leaders of liberal public sector institutions are continuing to make excuses and their institutions are continuing to perform poorly. . . . Much of the politics of the 1990s will turn out to be a struggle to reform those parts of the public sector that patently aren't functioning.

The time for excuses is over. The returns are in on the Brave New World of liberal social policy, and they are not good. We now know that the left was peddling from an empty wagon. Today fewer and fewer people are swayed by cultural nihilism and leftist social policy. But though the emperor has no clothes, he still has an empire. A number of critical American institutions are still under liberal tutelage.

What, then, to do? The American people face a great and important political task. They need to reassert their influence on their social institutions: elementary and secondary schools, universities, churches and synagogues, the media, the legal profession, federal, state, and local governments, and the arts. Reclaiming our institutions does not mean subjecting them to a narrow or rigid ideology; it means letting these institutions be governed by what works, by what makes sense, and by insisting that they remain true to their original purposes. In short, we need institutions that more accurately reflect the sentiments and beliefs of the great body of the American people rather than those of the cultural deconstructionists. For the citizenry, this requires greater public scrutiny, attention, and action; institutional accountability and reform; more citizen participation (on school boards, church offices, boards of trustees, and the like); political action; and the recruitment of sympathetic talent to take jobs in, and affect the course of, these institutions. In short, we need to pay attention and act.

Those whose beliefs govern our institutions will in large measure win the battle for the culture. And whoever wins the battle for the culture gets to teach the children. This cultural and institutional reclamation project will not be easy. Midge Decter has written that the Reagan election victories set off a response in the liberal community ranging from deep confusion to panic. The reason this occurred, according to Decter, is that his victories

> bore testimony not so much to a wish for radical new policies as to an open declaration of war over the culture. And a culture war, as the liberals understood far better than did their conservative opponents, is a war to the death. For a culture war is not battle over policy, though policy in many cases gives it expression; it is rather a battle about matters of the spirit.

So be it. Reclaiming our institutions is less a political opportunity than a civic obligation. It involves hard work. But it is work of immense importance. At the end of the day, *somebody's* values will prevail. In America, "we the people" have a duty to insist that our institutions and our government be true to their time-honored tasks. In some instances that means that the American people must roll up their sleeves and work to ensure that their institutions and government reflect their sentiments, their good sense, their sense of right and wrong. This is what a democracy—a government of, by, and for the people—is all about. The debate has been joined. But the fight for our values has just begun.

Civic engagement is the topic of the next reading. Democracy requires a "civic culture" to support it. That culture is one in which enlightened self-interest mutes individualism. Tocqueville pointed out, as does the author of the following reading, that in the American civic culture enlightened individuals strengthen democracy and civic values by joining voluntary associations and engaging in a variety of civic activities that are not dependent directly upon government. Unlike the preceding selection, which deplores the decline of values in our society, the author of this selection concludes that despite a decline of civic engagement in some areas, pervasive democratic values make American democracy the strongest in the world.

Seymour Martin Lipset is a social scientist who has taught at Berkeley, Harvard, Stanford's Hoover Institution, and George Mason University in Virginia. Lipset is one of the most thoughtful students of American character and politics, and his 1960 book, *Political Man,* remains a classic.

In this selection, Lipset's major points are:

1. Individualism is an important part of the American community.
2. Participating in civil society—the social context in which individuals interact—is a "dynamic and sometimes problematic" activity that involves individuals and groups and associations. Individualism in America strengthens the bonds of civil society.
3. Evidence suggests that civic engagement in America may be declining, and that cynicism and mistrust of government may be on the rise.

4. Despite these warning signs, "The American Dream is still alive." The United States has survived major changes in its notions about the state and individualism, and we should bear in mind that many of America's strongest ideals and most cherished values—suspicion of authority, populism, meritocracy, religiosity, and individualism—are intimately related to the realities of crime, low electoral turnouts, deviant behavior, and fluctuating group membership.

35

Seymour Martin Lipset

AMERICAN EXCEPTIONALISM

INDIVIDUALISM, AWARENESS, AND MORALITY

The standard evidence marshaled to argue that America is experiencing a value crisis is unconvincing. However, it is difficult to make the opposite case that morality in America is waxing. There is indeed a widespread perception that traditional values are threatened by recent social, political, and economic developments. In some respects this view is heightened precisely because of moral advances of recent decades, such as the recognition that throughout American history women, homosexuals, and minorities have faced political, economic, and social inequalities. Americanism has clearly not weakened, but the issues that it must address in a modern pluralist society are recognizably more difficult. It is no solution to explain away the real concerns of citizens as mere "hyper-sensitization." The fact that we have strong moral frameworks, rooted in ideals of equality and liberty, around which certain new issues of race, gender, sexual orientation, and the older and continuing concern for the impoverished have coalesced, presents a challenge to American society. Some observers have suggested that an emphasis on communitarian norms is the best way to meet this challenge. This may be true for Canada, Japan, or Europe. The American tradition, however, calls for a different alternative, which may be described as "moral individualism." An emphasis on individual morality is an elemental component of the American polity. As political theorist James Rutherford notes: "The free and equal individual with moral responsibility is the basis of communal solidarity." This is an important assertion—that community in democratic pluralistic America is grounded in the individual as a thinking, moral actor, not in group solidarity.

Oftentimes, the idea of a normative community is contrasted with self-interested atomism (read individualism). But to reiterate individualism is not necessarily a force grinding against the bonds of morality; it is, rather, an integral part of American values. Our national ideology—Americanism—is not merely a context, an environment that bounds or guides individual action; it is a set of values that requires reasoning and reflection in order to produce responsible consequences. The idea that we can be better moral agents by passively soaking up the values of the social context in which we find ourselves is antithetical to the principles of our democratic culture. In the modern environment of individual mobility and societal pluralism, the stability that marked traditional communal contexts is rare. Individuals need to be capable of retaining their ideological engagements even as the world around them changes. A morality grounded in a recognition of individual autonomy is therefore vitally flexible.

INDIVIDUALS IN CIVIL SOCIETY

The moral content of Americanism is only meaningful insofar as it is expressed within a social context, and that context is civil society. Commentaries, derived from Tocqueville, on the importance of civil associations permeate classically liberal (i.e., libertarian) treatments of democratic life, which argue that an idealized individualism is more attractive and more readily attainable than any idealized collectivism.

Central to this American conception of individualism is the importance of civil society and voluntary associations. Zbigniew Rau comments: "Civil society is an association of rational agents who decide for themselves whether to join it and how to act in it. . . . Therefore, the creation of and participation in civil society is caused by and further promotes the reassertion of its members as fully rational and moral agents." These associations—including churches, civic organizations, school boards, and philanthropic volunteer groups—are lifelong training grounds of citizenship and leadership, and create communication networks, conclusions Tocqueville drew from American practice. They strengthen moral bonds and facilitate the understanding of democracy.

But taking part in civil society does not simply mean belonging to collective entities and thereby embedding oneself within a social identity. Rather, it is a dynamic and sometimes problematic process of engagement between the individual and associations linked to interests and ideas. Nor is civil society a gentle, comfortable sphere of activity. It can be rough and challenging. From a critical perspective, David Popenoe correctly analyzes this dimension of civil society: "Outside the moral realm of the family is the world of voluntary friendships, a sphere governed by a marketplace for acceptance. In this outside world, acceptance is a scarce commodity that is allocated through competition; it must be strived for, earned, and maintained, and, hence, is highly conditional." Yet, Popenoe's analogy of civil society to a market is not entirely appropriate. There is nothing inherently common in these two spheres of liberal society, and it is a mistake to ascribe market forces to anything that requires effort and sacrifice, such as voluntarism or church membership.

Alasdair MacIntyre's notion of civil society as "simply an arena in which individuals each pursue their own self-chosen conception of the good life" hardly seems capable of providing a moral context for democracy. Surprisingly, however, the evidence regarding contemporary America suggests that it is. Individuals continue to take an active role in their local religious communities and to do volunteer work, while seven out of ten give money to charity. Though the impression of a narcissistic and materialistic society has been promoted by many commentators, Aileen Ross's assessment . . . that philanthropy is more extensive in America "than in any other part of the world" helps discount such a view.

It is important to recognize that in America, individualism *strengthens* the bonds of civil society rather than weakens them. In his book *Acts of Compassion*, Robert Wuthnow examines national survey data and reports that they reveal a "*positive* relationship between self-oriented value, and placing importance on charitable activities. In other words, people who were the most individualistic were also the most likely to value doing things to help others." This conclusion is significant in light of Gallup surveys taken between 1977 and 1994 which show an increase from 27 to 48 percent in the proportion of respondents reporting having been "involved in any charity or social service activities, such as helping the poor, the sick or the elderly."

Other students of American society have argued, as Tocqueville did, that individualism is related to the continuing vitality of religion and religious organizations. Since most of the country's sects are congregational, not hierarchical, they have fostered individualistic, egalitarian, and populist values, the moral order. And voluntary religion fostered the myriad of voluntary associations in America that so impressed Tocqueville, Bryce, Weber, and other foreign observers. These associations of what has come to be known as civil society create networks of communication among people with common positions and interests helping to sustain the moral order, political parties, and participation. Americans not only remain the most religious and most devout people in Christendom; they also are still the most participatory, the most disposed to belong to and be active in voluntary associations. . . .

The strength of American religion shows no sign of diminishing. Polls by Gallup and others, as we saw earlier, indicate that Americans are the most churchgoing in Protestantism and the most fundamentalist in Christendom. Commenting on the continuity of religious practice in America as revealed in opinion surveys, the political scientist William Mayer concludes that "[w]hen the late 1980s are compared with the late 1930s, church membership may have declined by about five percent, while church attendance may actually be *higher* today than it was fifty years ago." In 1991, 68 percent of the adult population belonged to a church and 42 percent attended services weekly, much higher ratios than in any other industrialized nation. Americans still bear out Tocqueville's observation that they are among the most devout people in Christendom.

THE DECLINE OF CIVIC ENGAGEMENT

Although civil society, association life, is, as Tocqueville also noted, stronger here than elsewhere, the American data, much of which has been assembled by Robert Putnam, indicate that "civic engagement," to use his term, and political commitment have declined in the past three decades. He notes that "participation in many types of civic associations from religious groups to labor unions, from women's clubs to fraternal clubs and from neighborhood gatherings to bowling leagues has fallen off."

Most, but not all, of the available evidence bears out these generalizations. . . .

THE GROWTH OF CYNICISM

Popular involvement in civil society apart, the evidence has been growing that all is not well with the American polity. Over the past three decades, opinion polls show that the citizenry is increasingly distrustful of its political leaders and institutions. When asked about their "confidence" in government, large majorities, here as in almost every country, report that they have "none," "little," or "a fair amount" of trust in the president and the legislative bodies. Those who are strongly positive are minorities, usually small ones.

The United States provides a striking example of this breakdown of respect for authority. Confidence in all United States institutions inquired about in the opinion surveys declined precipitously and steadily from the mid-1960s, though the greatest part of the fall occurred early in that decade. The Louis Harris Poll, which has investigated the subject since 1966, reported in 1994 the lowest level of confidence in government institutions ever. Those expressing a "great deal" of confidence in the executive branch of government constituted only 12 percent of a national sample in 1994, as compared to 24 percent in 1981, and 41 percent in 1966. Trust in Congress was even lower—8 percent in 1994, contrasted with 16 percent in 1981, and 42 percent in 1966. Daniel Yankelovich reports a drastic shift for the worse in response to the question, "How much of the time can you trust the government to do what's right?" In 1964, 76 percent said "always" or "most of the time." The proportion so answering fell to 44 percent in 1984, and then to an all-time low of 19 percent in 1994, a finding reported in the latest Luntz Poll for the Hudson Institute as well.

The University of Michigan Survey Research Center's national election study has been asking: "Would you say the government is pretty much run by a few big interests looking out for themselves or that it is run for the benefit of all the people?" In 1964, 29 percent said it was run for a few big interests. By 1980, the proportion so replying had moved up to 70 percent; in 1992, fully four fifths, 80 percent, expressed this cynical view. A Gallup Poll conducted for the *Times-Mirror* organization in 1994 found that 66 percent of a national sample agreed that the "Government is almost always wasteful and inefficient." A similar percentage said that "most elected officials don't care what people like me think." Again, the data show steady increases in disdain for officeholders. In response to this question, just under half, 47 percent, agreed in 1987, compared to 33 percent in the 1960s.

These doubts manifest themselves in numerous ways, including a decline in voter participation and erosion of the two-party system. The United States, which could once boast that the overwhelming majority of eligible voters cast their ballots, lost that record after 1914 and is experiencing a new pattern of decline. In fact, a much smaller proportion take part in American national elections than in any of the other older democracies, except Switzerland. The percentage voting has fallen from a postwar high point of around two thirds at the beginning of the 1960s to little more than one half in presidential elections today. Considerably fewer take part in lower-level contests, state and city elections, and even the presidential primaries. In reporting on the mid-term primaries in 1994, the Committee for the Study of the American Electorate noted that only 18 percent of the voting age population cast ballots, compared to 24 percent in 1974 and 33 percent in 1966. The November election produced a turnout of 39 percent, up 2 percent from 1990, but still among the lowest reported.

The lack of faith in the traditional American political system also is strikingly revealed by declining regard for the two-party system. In 1994, for the first time in polling history, a majority of those interviewed, 53 percent, told Gallup that they would like to see a third major party, up to 60 percent in 1995. Evidence that this sentiment is not simply symbolic is provided by the support which Ross Perot obtained in the 1992 election and continues to receive in opinion polls in 1994–95. Perot secured the highest percentage of the vote ever attained by a third-party candidate, with the limited exception of Theodore Roosevelt in 1912. Roosevelt, however, was a dissident Republican preferred in the twelve primaries of that year by most of his party's supporters. The 1995 opinion polls show that Perot continues to be endorsed by a fifth of the electorate. And the 1994 election results, like the 1992 ones, are seemingly the consequence of this distrust. The Perot voters, who disliked Bush the incumbent more than Clinton the outsider, turned in overwhelming numbers to support Republican congressional and state candidates in 1994. But the *Times-Mirror* Poll reports continued distrust of Congress and both parties, as of the fall of 1995.

THE LEGACY OF THE 1960s

This erosion of trust in American government is troubling. President Jimmy Carter characterized it in a July 1979 television address to the American people as a "fundamental threat to American democracy." That threat, he said, was a "crisis of confidence . . . that strikes at the very heart and soul and spirit of our national will." He pointed to "a growing disrespect for government and for churches and for schools, the news media and other institutions," and emphasized that "the gap between our citizens and our government has never been so wide." If anything, that gap has now widened. In a report on a 1994 poll evaluating "The New Political Landscape," the *Times-Mirror* Center finds that "Voters' frustration with the political system continues to grow, as does animosity toward the media. . . . The Clinton Administration and the economic recovery have failed to stern the tide of political cynicism. The discontent with Washington that gained momentum in the late 1980s is even greater now than it was in 1992."

TELEVISION'S DISTORTING PICTURE

Why is there so much malaise, so much unrest about the workings of American democracy? The discontent generated in the 1960s does not explain why these feelings have continued or what has sustained them. Politicians tend to blame the media for the lack of trust. I suspect that to some degree they are right. American presidents since George Washington have complained about the way the press covered them. Thomas Jefferson, Andrew Jackson, Abraham Lincoln, and Franklin Roosevelt all felt, correctly, that much of the press was antagonistic. Those on the left, from Jefferson to Roosevelt and Truman, felt that the owners of the press were conservatives and controlled the way their papers wrote about them. Since Lyndon Johnson, presidents have identified media bias as reflecting the views of journalists, not owners, and as leftist or liberal. There can be little doubt that the predominantly left views of reporters affect the way the news is presented. But the political views or interests of those who dominate the media are not the main sources of their emphasis on the failings of elites and institutions. The fact is that good news is not news; bad news is. Planes that land do not constitute a story; planes that crash do. Politicians characterized by honesty, personal integrity, and a good family life are dull; sexually promiscuous, corrupt political figures are interesting. The press looks for failings. The desire to locate and exaggerate scandals among the political, social, and economic elites has always characterized open democratic societies.

The effect of the media is illustrated by the public's concern over the increased risk of criminal victim rates when, "according to the most reliable measure available, total levels of crime in America have fallen, not risen, over the past two decades." A comprehensive review by *The Economist* of the problems involved in evaluating crime statistics dealing with many countries indicates that police reports "often quoted by politicians and given prominence in the media" considerably exaggerate the extent of crime reported in crime-victimization surveys. In polls conducted regularly by Gallup since 1971, "some 50% of Americans have usually thought crime to have risen in the preceding year in their area. Only around 15% believed—often correctly, in all probability—that crime had fallen locally."

There has been a change in the nature of the media, which I think is responsible for perpetuating and extending the loss in trust: the shift from print to television as the major source of news. Television presents the news, conveys the message, in much stronger terms, in much more convincing fashion than newspapers or magazines. The massive transition from print to televised media occurred during the 1960s. The Vietnam War was the first televised war; for the first time, the public could watch the spilling of blood from their living rooms. The impact of the prolonged war on American opinion was to a considerable extent a function of pictorial reportage. And the domination of the camera has continued to grow. All problems of society now reach people almost immediately and in what appears to be an unbiased manner, because the viewer thinks he sees what is happening for himself. And in 1994, the United States led the ownership of television sets, with 81 for every 100 people. The corresponding figure for the European Union was 44, while for Japan it was 62.

There have been other notable changes as well. Norman Ornstein has noted that the increase in reportage on scandals and corruption in government and other institutions is linked to greater disclosure. Sweeping reform of the political process has resulted in a drastic increase in information made possible by the computer, which has been grist for investigative journalism. As important in undermining trust in leaders has been the enormous growth in "prosecutorial zeal," flowing in part from "the reform-era creation of a Public Integrity Section in the Justice Department, which defines its success by the volume of prosecution of public officials." As a result, Ornstein reports, between 1975 and 1989 "the number of federal officials indicted on charges of public corruption increased by a staggering 1,211 percent, whereas the number of non-federal public officials indicted doubled during the same period." There has clearly been more bad news to report about politics, as well as a more effective medium to transmit it.

Paradoxically, the increase in the malaise about politics and the disdain for government may also reflect the growth of dependence on government since the 1930s. Most people in the West, even those in the less statist United States, have come to rely on the state to solve most problems and to provide jobs, security for the aged, and medical care, as well as good schools. Socialism and communism may have collapsed, but heavy reliance on what Robert Dahl describes as an increasingly complex and incomprehensible government has not. We expect much from the state, and we turn against elected officials because of their failure to accomplish what we want them to do. Ironically, the decline in confidence in government in a nation which suspects government, which does not want to rely on it, makes it more difficult for the political leaders to enact new programs and deal with problems that the public would like to see resolved, such as health care.

THE SURVIVAL OF THE AMERICAN DREAM

Given the anger about politics in the United States, what accounts for the continued stability of the American system? Why do we not witness grievous forms of mass unrest? Why is the major protest movement, led by Ross Perot, basically centrist, even conservative with respect to economic and social policy? Part of the answer to the conundrum is that most Americans are not unhappy about their personal lives or prospects; if anything, the opposite is true. They still view the United States as a country that rewards personal integrity and hard work, as one that, government and politics apart, still works. The American Dream is still alive, even if the government and other institutions are seen as corrupt and inefficient. . . .

The American political system, though distrusted and ineffective in dealing with major social issues, is clearly not in danger. Most Americans remain highly patriotic and religious, believe they are living in the best society in the world, and think that their country and economy, in spite of problems, still offer them opportunity and economic security. Although the depression of the 1930s was worse here than in most of Europe, America came out of it with its party system, state institutions, and material values intact. The country will probably do the same today, although it must be acknowledged that the major parties appear somewhat more vulnerable than at any time since the Civil War.

CONCLUSION

To what extent is it still possible to speak of American exceptionalism? It is obvious that America and the rest of the Western world have changed greatly over the past two centuries. From a nation of thirteen states hugging the Atlantic seaboard with a population of 4 million, America has grown to a continent-spanning federation of fifty states and, as of the 1990 Census, 250 million people. Close to 30 million live in California, a state nonexistent in 1789. The country began as an overwhelmingly agrarian society, with more than 90 percent of its work force on the land, many as subsistence farmers. As the country approaches the twenty-first century, only 2 percent are farmers, and the great majority of the population live in sprawling metropolitan regions. From an underdeveloped rural economy which largely relied on Britain for its manufactured goods, it became in the latter decades of the nineteenth century the most prosperous power on earth. In real consumer income terms, it still holds this position, although the emergence of other industrial countries and the reexpansion of Europe has reduced its proportion of the world's production from two fifths after World War II to a quarter in the nineties. The character of its labor force has changed, first with the decline of agriculture and the expansion of industry, and more recently with the decrease in manual jobs and the growth of high-tech and scientific activities accompanied by an increase in white-collar and service jobs and in positions requiring college education. The resultant gap in demand for the growing population of well-educated people and the declining need for unskilled people is producing a sizable income difference, with the share going to the lowest strata falling. Other Western nations have also changed, becoming industrialized, urbanized, better educated. The postfeudal elements that characterized many European countries have declined enormously, although Britain, while also changing, still contains more of these elements than others. In social-structural terms, these countries are becoming Americanized.

The changes that have occurred around the developed world, however, still leave many differences. In comparative terms, the United States remains more religious, more patriotic, more populist and antielitist (the number of elective positions increased between 1987 and 1992 by over ten thousand, while direct involvement of the electorate in the candidate nomination process continues to grow), more committed to higher education for the majority, hence to meritocracy, more socially egalitarian, more prone to divorce, less law-abiding, wealthier in real income (purchasing power) terms, markedly more job-creating, and significantly less disposed to save, than other developed countries. To reiterate, the United States is a "welfare laggard." It remains the least statist Western nation in terms of public effort, benefits, and employment. It is "[t]he reluctant bride of the welfare state, instituting national programs later than most countries . . . and spending a lower share of its national income on social welfare than most. . . ." According to the OECD, the United States provides single-parent families with a much lower level of income support, 37 percent of the average production worker's wage, than any of seven other countries listed in a recent report—Sweden (82%), Canada (69%), Finland (67%), Holland (68%), Austria (53%), Britain (53%), and Australia (52%). Conversely, Americans show a marked preference for private efforts in welfare as in business; they lead the world in philanthropic giving. As Nathan Glazer reports, "non-public resources in American welfare are greater than is found in any other major nation."

However, major changes have occurred which have modified the original American Creed, with its suspicion of the state and its emphasis on individual rights. These include the introduction of a planning–welfare state emphasis in the 1930s, accompanied initially by greater class-consciousness and trade union growth, and the focus on ethnic, racial, and gender group rights which emerged in the 1960s. The first has had a continuing impact in the form of a much expanded government that remains committed to many welfare and regulatory objectives. But, as I noted earlier, the increase has been slowed, in some aspects reversed. Popular sentiment in the mid-1990s seeks to limit welfare and opposes some types of state involvement in the economy that once had considerable support. Election results from 1968 to 1994 indicate Americans want to reduce the role of the state. The Republicans are the most anti-statist major party in the West, but the Clinton New Democrats are not far behind. Trade union membership, as we have seen, has fallen greatly as a share of the labor force, and the significance of class as a variable related to partisan support is much reduced. The economic role of government remains weaker in the United States than in any other industrialized economy. On the other hand, the focus on non-class forms of group rights which came to a head in the 1960s, though still a dynamic force, is under sharper criticism than any time since the Johnson era. These developments appear to be reaffirming the basic emphases on individual success, on equality of opportunity rather than of results.

Finally, it is worth reiterating that various seemingly contradictory aspects of American society are intimately related. The lack of respect for authority, anti-elitism, and populism contribute to higher crime rates, school indiscipline, and low electoral turnouts. The emphasis on achievement, on meritocracy, is also tied to higher levels of deviant behavior and less support for the underprivileged. Intense religiosity is linked to less reliance on contraception in premarital sexual relationships by young people. The same moralistic factors which make for patriotism help to produce opposition to war. Concern for the legal rights of accused persons and civil liberties in general is tied to opposition to gun control and difficulty in applying crime-control measures. The stress on individualism both weakens social control mechanisms, which rely on strong ties to groups, and facilitates diverse forms of deviant behavior.

I would like to conclude with some thoughts derived from an American political scientist, Samuel Huntington; a Canadian scholar who was named after two executed Italian American anarchists, Sacvan Bercovitch; and a communist theorist, Antonio Gramsci. Huntington and Bercovitch both note that an emphasis on a national consensus, a national myth, which some mistakenly see as the meaning of exceptionalism, is not an alternative to a stress on conflict. The consensual myth fosters bitter controversy. Huntington notes periods of creedal passion in American history, intense conflicts seeking to bring "institutions and practices in accord with these values and beliefs. . . . In a political system produced by a major revolution . . . efforts may be made from time to time to renew or reaffirm revolutionary values." Such conflicts and patterns of change can only occur "in a society with an overwhelming *consensus*" on "values." They could not occur "in societies with traditional ideological pluralism, such as most of those of western Europe" and Canada.

Americans fight each other in their efforts to defend or expand the American Creed. Pre–Civil War leaders of the anti-slavery struggle, such as Frederick Douglass and William Lloyd Garrison, or the founder of American feminism, Elizabeth Cady Stanton, like mid-twentieth-century American radicals, demanded changes in order, in Douglass's words, to live up to "the genius of American institutions, to help fulfill its [the nation's] sacred mission." Bercovitch, who cites these radical exponents of the

Creed, first entered the United States during the conflict-ridden 1960s. Expressing his reaction to the creedal passions of the era, he wrote:

> My first encounter with American consensus was in the late sixties, when I crossed the border into the United States and found myself inside the myth of America. Not of North America, for the myth stopped short of the Canadian and Mexican borders, but of a Country that despite its arbitrary frontiers, despite its bewildering mix of race and creed, could believe in something called the True America, and could invest that patent fiction with all the moral and emotional appeal of a religious symbol. . . .
> Here was the Jewish anarchist Paul Goodman berating the Midwest for abandoning the promise; here, the descendant of American slaves, Martin Luther King, denouncing injustice as a violation of the American way; here, an endless debate about national destiny . . . conservatives scavenging for un-Americans, New Left historians recalling the country to its sacred mission.
> Nothing in my Canadian background had prepared me for that spectacle. . . . It gave me something of an anthropologist's sense of wonder at the symbol of the tribe. . . . To a Canadian skeptic, a gentile in God's country . . . [here was] a pluralistic, pragmatic people . . . bound together by an ideological consensus.
> Let me repeat that mundane phrase: *ideological consensus.* For it wasn't the idea of exceptionalism that I discovered in '68. . . . It was a hundred sects and factions, each apparently different from the others, yet all celebrating the same mission. . . .

Gramsci, who also believed that America has a national ideology, wrote in the 1920s that before Italy could become socialist, it had to Americanize socially as well as economically, a development he viewed positively. Like earlier Marxists, he saw the United States as the epitome of a bourgeois democratic society, one that lacked the traditional precapitalist elements which were still to be found in Italy and other European cultures. Of course, the industrialized European countries have begun to resemble the United States economically, as more affluent, and socially, as less status-conscious. In the process, their socialist movements (and the Italian Communist Party, now renamed the Party of the Democratic Left) have redefined their objectives. Not only do their conservatives, like Margaret Thatcher, increasingly advocate classical (Jeffersonian/Jacksonian) liberal doctrines, but as I have documented elsewhere, this ideology is also strongly affecting their left. In line with Marx's anticipation in *Das Kapital* that "the more developed country shows the less developed the image of their future," the United States is less exceptional as other nations develop and "Americanize." But, given the structural convergences in economy and ecology, the extent to which it is still unique is astonishing.

The following reading analyzes for good and ill the way in which new telecommunications technologies impact democracy. New and ever-changing technologies that facilitate the flow of information can vastly increase democratic participation. Technology also makes centralized control over information possible. How telecommunications technologies are used will determine the future of democracy.

Benjamin R. Barber is Walt Whitman Professor of Political Science at Rutgers University. His major points in this essay are:

1. The relationship of new telecommunications technologies to democracy is not as simple as is it might look. Technology can impact democracy, but the nature of that impact can be complex and unpredictable. The ideal of the Internet as a force promoting democratic values is not as simple as the reality.
2. Important questions surround the issues of who controls technology, how it is applied, and how it affects the relationship of individuals and groups to the larger community. Technology is more often a mirror of the existing society than it is a determinant of society's direction and values.
3. In the relationship of technology to democracy, we need to clarify what we mean by "democracy." We also need to take active steps to influence the political directions in which new technologies are applied.

36

Benjamin R. Barber

THE NEW TELECOMMUNICATIONS TECHNOLOGY: ENDLESS FRONTIER OR THE END OF DEMOCRACY?

The new telecommunications technologies are everywhere celebrated: celebrated as the key to the new global economy—this was Bill Gates's theme it the 1997 World Economic Forum in Davos, for example; celebrated as the secret of America's new global economic recovery—President Bill Clinton and Speaker Newt Gingrich agree on this much; and celebrated as the beginning of a "new era in American Politics" and of a new stage in the evolution of global democracy. While the first and second claims may be true, the third, linking the new technologies directly to democracy, is far more controversial, palpably dangerous if not entirely false.

To be sure, innovations in communications and information technology do offer new technical opportunities for strong democrats and civic republicans to strengthen civic education and enhance direct deliberative communication among citizens. Only Luddites would dismiss the possibilities of the digital revolution as wholly nefarious. I was myself an early advocate of exploiting the democratic potential of the new technologies, and there are many responsible democrats who today are exploring in theory and practice this potential. Caution has, however, been outrun by techno-Panglossians and cyberenthusiasts who seem to think that with new technologies of communication we can overcome every defect of communication our political system has experienced.

Historically, technology has always had a special if deeply ambivalent relationship to democracy. Jean-Jacques Rousseau believed that the progress of the arts and sciences had had a corrupting effect on morals. . . . The truth seems to be not so much that technology is averse to civic ideals than that it has run away from politics and morals, evolving so rapidly that its impact on democracy and vulnerability to undemocratic forces have gone largely unremarked.

TECHNOLOGY: MIRROR OF DEMOCRACY OR MIRROR OF THE MARKET?

The problem goes deep—to the very core of what democracy means. Democracy depends on deliberation, prudence, slow-footed interaction, and time-consuming (thus "inefficient") forms of multilateral conversation and social interaction that by postmodern standards may seem cumbersome, time consuming, demanding, sometimes interminable, and always certifiably unentertaining. Computer terminals, however, make process terminable, for electronic and digital technology's imperative is speed. Computers are fast as light, literally. Democracy is slow as prudent judgment, which is very slow indeed, demanding silences as well as communicative exchange and requiring upon occasion that days or months pass by before further thought or action can be demanded. Unlike our computers, we humans crash a lot. We often need to cool off, ponder, rethink, and absorb the consequence of previous decisions before we can make prudent new judgments. With human intelligence, "parallel computing" entails sociability and deliberative interaction and slows rather than hastens ratiocination and decision.

Digital reasoning is binary, privileging a simple choice between on and off, a and b, yes and no. It "likes" oppositions and dualism. Political reasoning is complex and nuanced, dialectical rather than digitally oppositional. It aims at escaping the rational choice games that computer modeled decisional processes prefer. To the question "A or B?" the citizen may reply "both!" or "neither!" or "those are not the right choices," or even "I don't care!" Imagine a computer that replies to a question "je m'en fou!" Our tools are in a certain sense out of sync with democracy, out of control. In an epoch of antipathy to government and antiregulatory passion, as the new technologies pass into the hands of corporations organized to secure maximum profits and little else, they are likely to become ever more so. Henry David Thoreau (perhaps in his anarchist incarnation) worried about how easily we can become the tools of our tools.

Perhaps it is even worse: we may be becoming the tools of the tools of our tools—guided not by the technology itself but by how it is being utilized as a consequence of market forces. It has been decades since Fred Friendly suggested Americans might need an "electronic Bill of Rights" to keep pace with changes in information technology that the American Founders could not possible have foreseen. Their Bill of Rights was designed for a world of print in which fast communication meant the pony express or a six-week sea voyage. The Progress and Freedom Foundation has promulgated a Magna Carta for the Information Age (1994), but there has been no serious mainline attempt to update the Federal Communications Act of 1934, devised for the then "modern" world of radio and quite properly concerned to "encourage the larger and more effective use of radio in the public interest." Indeed, the recently passed Telecommunications Bill of 1996 seeks only to move government out of the way, leaving it to the whims of money and markets of how the new technologies will affect our civic lives and our democratic society. The only other advance has been the Communications Decency Act, aimed not at civic enhancement but civic censorship of Internet pornography.

While Europe has traditionally retained greater public control over its information and broadcasting utilities, it is currently under extraordinary pressure (in the name of global competition) to privatize. At the 1997 World Economic Forum in Davos, Bill Gates hectored the French for their cyberbackwardness and reportedly met privately with representatives of the Indian government to push them toward privatization (and perhaps a contract with Microsoft). The Munich Declaration of 1997 promulgated at the Academy for the Third Millennium's Conference on the Internet and Politics calls boldly for greater governmental and popular control and use of the new technologies for civic purposes, but it leans into the hard wind of privatization. Indeed, the information superhighway is being built so fast that whatever residual regulatory powers survive the current regulatory mania, guaranteeing privacy and controlling monopoly are likely to be left far behind. President Bill Clinton has been reduced to high-minded jawboning in trying to persuade the private sector to control entertainment mayhem and link up public schools and libraries to the Internet.

How long will the vaunted "wild west frontier" of the Internet hold out against the colonizing forces of commerce and corporatism? Point-to-point communication systems like the telephone and the Internet are, it has been repeatedly argued, lateral systems and hence more inherently democratic than vertical systems like broadcast radio and television. This is perfectly true, and it offers democrats the very real promise of technologically enhanced forms of civic interaction. But those who own conduits and software platforms, those who write programs and are systems' gatekeepers, still wield extraordinary power. We may wish there were no gatekeepers, although I would argue that there are forms of control and intervention like editing, facilitation, and education that are necessary to democratic utilization of the net and that amount to positive or legitimate forms of gatekeeping. In any case, the alternative to the regulatory state is not the free market but the regulatory market, whose choices and boundaries are powerfully delimiting, but as part of the "invisible hand" of the market, are largely invisible to us. Can any regulatory body hope in the name of the public good to bring a civic dimension to a 500-channel cable system, where the spectrum scarcity that once justified federal regulation has (in theory at least) vanished? Or curtail the inexpensive duplication (pirating) of cassettes, compact disks, and computer programs? Or influence telephone companies that now have the right to compete in cable television markets? Or track and regulate global satellite companies whose stations recognize no borders and can be picked up anywhere by a dinner-plate-sized dish? Such systems are, ironically, more susceptible to corporate than to government control and are likely to serve private rather than public interests.

What these somber reflections suggest is that technology is often less a determinant than a mirror of the larger society. Who owns it, how it is used and by whom, and to which ends: these are the critical questions whose answers will shape technology's role in the coming century. To be sure, technology bends a little this way, a little that, and it has intimations and entailments that obviously can modify human institutions and behavior. But ultimately it reflects the world in which it finds itself. Gunpowder helped democratize a Protestant, urbanizing Europe ripe for democratizing, but in feudal China it secured the hold of grasping elites; moveable type facilitated the democratization of literacy but also made possible mass propaganda and the extended thought control that marked the innovative tyranny known as totalitarianism. Interactive two-way television and keypad voting invite participation even as they expedite surveillance and marginalize thoughtfulness and complexity. But why should we finally expect our technologies to look much different than the society that produces and puts them to use?

Whatever entailments technology may have in the abstract, it still will reflect concretely the premises and objectives of the society deploying it. This is precisely the meaning of the key political idea of sovereignty: politics governs technique, society and culture always trump technology. Ends condition means, and technology is just a fancy word for means. The new telecommunications are less likely to alter and improve than to reflect and augment our current socioeconomic institutions and political attitudes. A commercial culture will entail a commercialized technology. A society dominated by the ideology of privatization will engender a privatized Internet.

Wishful thinkers at outfits like the Electronic Frontier Foundation fantasize an Internet as free and democratic and horizontally organized as their own ingenuity and imagination. For Internet technology is point to point and certainly can be said to have a democratic potential. But it will take political will to allow such tendencies to emerge and modify traditional attitudes and institutions, which in the meantime are likely to be determinative.

The internal combustion engine and electricity did not absolutely mandate a privatized, highway-strip, suburbanized, overmalled America. Those late nineteenth-century technologies suited mass transportation systems (railways and buses, for example) equally well and thus could have also helped anchor an urban and town culture (as they did after World War II in Europe). It was not automotive determinism but specific political decisions taken in the first half of the twentieth century that translated the technologies of internal combustion and electric motors into a suburban society—perhaps most significantly, a critical decision by the U.S. Congress after World War II. Under pressure from the postwar steel, rubber, cement, and automobile industries, and possessed of a spirit of individualism that predated the new technologies, Congress voted to fund an immense interstate highway system that privileged the automobile and the social environment it mandated.

Who knows how different America might look today had that same Congress opted for an equally extensive interstate rail system? During the cold war, Deputy Secretary of State George Ball once justified investment in the Soviet Union's automobile industry by observing that an automobile is an ideology on four wheels. But it was not the automobile that created the ideology but the ideology that created the automobile. A car is radical individualism writ large, the internal combustion engine turned to the purposes of private liberty rather than (to name some alternative ideologies) to such ends as environmental protection, or the preservation of cities, or social cooperation, or war.

Is there then really any reason to think that a society dominated by profit-mongering and private interests will exempt the new telecommunications technologies from the pursuit of profit or constitute them in a more public-spirited manner than the society at large? Bill Gates's vision in *The Road Ahead* omits any reference to the civic good, prophesying instead a "shopper's heaven" in which "all the goods in the world will be available for you to examine, compare, and, often customize" and where "your wallet PC will link into a store's computer to transfer digital money." And even where it can be shown that the technology inherently holds out the promise of civic and democratic potential, is it not likely to reflect the thin, representative, alienating version of democracy that currently dominates political thinking? For without a will toward a more participatory and robust civic system, why should technologically enhanced politics not produce the same incivility and cynicism that characterize politics on the older technologies, radio and television, for example? (Recall that radio too once promised a more egalitarian and democratic form of communication.) Political chatroom banter on the Internet is as polarized and rude as anything you can hear on talk radio.

It remains true that technology can assist political change and may sometimes even point in new political directions. Interactive computer-based television hookups "point" in a certain sense to the feasibility of direct democracy, but unless there is a political will directed at greater participation, the potential remains just that. Nor will interactive technology do anything, on its own, to cure the primary defect of unmediated participatory politics—the danger of undeliberative majority tyranny and thus a kind of plebiscitary dictatorship. One-way information retrieval via the Net may expand for some the orbit of available resources; the Library of Congress has achieved an instant success by making millions of items including Matthew Brady's Civil War photographs, Gershwin's musical scores, San Francisco earthquake pictorials, and theatrical memorabilia from the Yiddish Theater available on its new Net site (www.loc.gov). Yet retrieval is at best an improvement on access to information, not a move towards genuine interactive communication.

. . . If then technology is to make a political difference, it is the politics that will first have to be changed.

THE NEW MEDIA: DIVERSITY OR MONOPOLY?

Much has been made over the apparent diversification of media and the multiplication of communication spectra that have accompanied the evolution of advanced telecommunication technologies. In place of three networks in America, or two or three state networks in many other countries, we now have cable and satellite-based systems that can offer up to five hundred or more channels. . . . Moreover, the multiplication of available channels of communication is clearly abetted by an Internet that offers literally endless millions of interconnected sites that promote point-to-point communication of a kind that seems in turn to promise endless diversity.

In short, the technology is clearly capable of exerting a pluralizing influence on communications. Yet though the technology may be inherently disaggregating and devolutionary, ownership over the technology's hardware and software is aggregating and centralizing. As delivery systems diversify and multiply, program content becomes more homogeneous. . . .

The idea is to gather together the production companies turning out product, the phone and cable and satellite companies transmitting them, and the television sets and computers and multiplexes presenting them to the public all into the same hands. Synergy, however, turns out to be a polite way of saying monopoly. And in the domain of information, monopoly is a polite word for uniformity, which is a polite word for virtual censorship—censorship not as a consequence of political choices but as a consequence of inelastic markets, imperfect competition, and economies of scale—the quest for a single product that can be owned by a single proprietor and sold to every living soul on the planet. (In the United States, the popular C-Span channel that allows Americans to watch Congress around the clock has been forced off some cable systems by the new Rupert Murdoch-owned Fox News Channel); or the search for a "safe image" that avoids all controversy in the name of broad con-sumer acceptance.

. . . Conglomeration had reduced the number of mainstage telecommunications players from forty-six in 1981 to twenty-three in 1991. And of these, a handful like Time Warner/Turner, Disney/ABC, Bertelsmann, and Murdoch's News Corporation dominate—genuinely intermedia corporations with a finger in every part of the busi-ness. So that, for example, when Rupert Murdoch wanted to accommodate the Chi-nese on the way to persuading them to permit his Asian Television Network to broad-cast, he was able to instruct HarperCollins (a News Corporation subsidiary) to withdraw its offer to Harry Wu—a dissident thorn in the side of the Chinese—for his political memoirs.

THE SOFT NEW TOTALITARIANISM OF CONSUMERISM

The new trend toward monopoly signals then not synergy but vulnerability to a kind of commercial totalitarianism—a single value (profit) and a single owner (the monop-oly holder) submerging all distinctions, rendering all choice tenuous and all diversity sham. . . .

WHICH DEMOCRACY? PROGRESS FOR WHOM?

In combination then, the new technologies and the software they support can poten-tially enhance lateral communication among citizens, can open access to information by all, and can furnish citizens with communication links across distances that once precluded direct democracy. Yet there is a formidable obstacle in the way of imple-mentation of these technologies: unless we are clear about what democracy means to us, and what kind of democracy we envision, technology is as likely to stunt as to en-hance the civic polity: is it representative democracy, plebiscitary democracy, or delib-erative democracy for which we seek technological implementation? The differences among the three are not only theoretically crucial but have radically different entail-ments with respect to technology.

Do we aspire to further the representative system, a democracy rooted in the election of accountable deputies who do all the real work of governing? Most advocates of this form of indirect democracy are properly suspicious of the new technologies and their penchant for immediacy, directness, lateral communication, and undeliberativeness. Or is it plebiscitary majoritarianism we seek, a democracy that embodies majority opinions aggregated from the unconsidered prejudices of private persons voting private interests? New technology can be a dangerously facile instrument of such unchecked majoritarianism: the Internet affords politicians an instrument for perpetual polling that can aggravate the focus group mentality that many rue as Dick Morris's political legacy. Will any politician ever again gather the courage to lead in the face of a technology that makes following so easy?

Yet if we are in search of what I have called "strong democracy," a democracy that reflects the careful and prudent judgment of citizens who participate in deliberative, self-governing communities, we will need to tease other capabilities out of the technology. If democracy is to be understood as deliberative and participatory activity on the part of responsible citizens, it will have to resist the innovative forms of demagoguery that accompany innovative technology and that are too often overlooked by enthusiasts, and listen carefully to those like Theodore Becker and James Fishkin who have tried to incorporate deliberative constraints into their direct democratic uses of the technologies. In other words, there is no simple or general answer to the question "is the technology democratizing?" until we have made clear what sort of democracy we have in mind. Home voting via interactive television might further privatize politics and replace deliberative debate in public with the unconsidered instant expression of private prejudices, turning what ought to be public decisions into private consumer-like choices; but deliberative television polling of the kind envisioned by James Fishkin can offset such dangers, while the use of the Internet for deliberation across communities can actually render decisionmaking less parochial.

Strong democracy calls not only for votes but for good reasons; not only for an opinion but for a rational argument on its behalf. Those who once preferred open to secret ballots, who preferred open debate about justified viewpoints to closed votes aggregating personal interests, will today prefer technologies that permit frank interactive debate with real identities revealed, to technologies that allow game playing and privately registered, unsupported opinions.

Traditional proponents of Madisonian representative democracy are likely to find much of the new interactive technology intimidating, since it threatens to overwhelm what they regard as a pristine system assuring government by expert politicians with a free-for-all among "ignorant" masses who swamp the polity with their endless demands and overheated prejudices. Such critics already complain about traditional broadcast television as destructive of party identity and party discipline, and they will properly worry about technologies that further erode the boundaries between the governors and the governed. Plebiscitary democrats will be mindlessly enthralled by interactive instant polling and imagine a time when private consumers make precedent-shattering public choices with no more serious thought than they give to which button to hit when they are surfing a hundred-channel cable system. "Let's see," mutters the glib new Net-surfer, "do I want to play checkers or outlaw abortion? Do I prefer Sylvester Stallone to Bill Clinton? Shall we download the 'Playmate of the Month' or vote to expand NATO to the Russian border? Is it time for a mock battle with Darth Vader on my Star Wars simulation, or should I just declare war for real on Libya?" Deliberative democrats can only shudder at such prospects, insisting that they do more to destroy than to enhance democracy. Deliberation, on the other hand, does require intervention, education, facilitation, and mediation—all anathema to devotees of an anarchic and wholly user-controlled Net.

Technology can then help democracy, but only if programmed to do so and only in terms of the paradigms and political theories that inform the program. Left to the market it is likely only to reproduce the vices of politics as usual. How different is the anonymous flaming that typifies certain kinds of Internet chatter from the anonymous vilification that characterizes talk radio and scream television? Will the newer technologies be any less likely to debase the political currency, any less likely to foster sound-bite decisionmaking in place of sound political judgment?

By the same token, if those who deploy the technologies consciously seek a more participatory, deliberative form of strong democracy and a newly robust civil society, they can also find in telecommunications innovation an extraordinarily effective ally. The trouble with the zealots of technology as an instrument of democratic liberation is not their understanding of technology but their grasp of democracy. They insist that market-generated technology can, quite by itself and in the complete absence of common human willing and political cooperation, produce liberty, social responsibility, and citizenship. The viruses that eat up our computer programs, like sarin in the Tokyo subway, are but obvious symbols of technology's ever-present dark side, the monster who lurks in Dr. Frankenstein's miraculous creation.

With participatory interaction comes the promise of political and economic surveillance. With interactive personal preference modules comes the risk of majoritarian tyranny. With digital reasoning comes the peril of adversarial modes of thought inundating consensus. Computer literacy cannot finally exist independently of lifelong educational literacy. The age of information can reenforce extant inequalities, making the resource and income poor the information-poor as well. The irony is that those who might most benefit from the Net's democratic and informational potential are least likely to have access to it, the tools to use it, or the educational background to take advantage of the tools. Those with access, however, tend to be those already empowered in the system by education, income, and literacy.

And how easily liberating technologies become tools of repression. As consumers tell shopping networks what they want to buy and tell banks how to dispense their cash and tell pollsters what they think about abortion, those receiving the information gain access to an extensive computer bank of knowledge about the private habits, attitudes, and behaviors of consumers and citizens. This information may in turn be used to reshape those habits and attitudes in ways that favor producers and sellers working the marketplace or the political arena. Moreover, the current antiregulatory fever has assured that the new data banks being compiled from interaction and surveillance are subject neither to government scrutiny nor to limitation or control—a sunset provision, for example, which would periodically destroy all stored information. The model of Channel One, an invidious classroom network founded by Chris Whittle's Whittle Communications (and now owned by the K III Corporation) that extorts classroom advertising time from needy schools in return for desperately wanted hardware, suggests that the public is likely to be served by the new technologies only in as far as someone can make serious money from it.

It may be a cause of satisfaction, as Walter Winston insists, that nowadays it is the citizen who is watching Big Brother and not the other way around. But if Big Brother is no longer watching you, nor is he watching those who *are* watching you, and even adversaries of regulation may find reason to be disturbed by that omission. If the classical liberal question used to be who will police the police, the pertinent liberal question in today's McWorld ought to be who will watch those who are watching the watchers? Who will prevent the media from controlling their clients and consumers? Who will act in lieu of a government that has demurred from representing the public's interests? These are issues for democracy deliberation and decision, not for technological resolution. For technology remains a tool: allied to particular conceptions of democracy, if we know what kind of democracy we want, it can enhance civic communication and expand citizen literacy. Left to markets (and that is where it is now being left), it is likely to augment McWorld's least worthy imperatives, including surveillance over and manipulation of opinion, and the cultivation of artificial needs rooted in life-style "choices" unconnected to real economic, civic or spiritual needs.

If democracy is to benefit from technology, then we must start not with technology but with politics. Demanding a voice in the making of science and technology policy is the first step citizens can take in ensuring a democratic technology. The new technology is still only an instrument of communication, and it cannot determine *what* we will say or to whom we will say it. There is a story about the wireless pioneer Marconi who, when told by his associates that his new wireless technology meant he could now "talk to Florida," asked, presciently, "and do we have anything to say to Florida?" Enthusiasts exalt over the fact that on the Net we can talk to strangers throughout the world. But many of today's problems arise from the fact that we no longer know how to talk to our husbands and wives, our neighbors and fellow citizens, let alone strangers. Will our blockages and incivilities locally be overcome by the miracles of long distance computer communication? Will virtual community heal the ruptures of real communities? Will we do on our keyboards what we have notably failed to do face to face?

If in the coming millennium—a millennium in which technology is likely to dominate our lives as never before—we want democracy to be served, then the bittersweet fruits of science will have to be subordinated to our democratic ends and made to serve as a facilitator rather than a corrupter of our precious democracy. And whether this happens will depend not on the quality and character of our technology but on the quality of our political institutions and the character of our citizens.

☆☆☆

There is no doubt that information technologies link people and government in ways never before thought possible. Our political system is one of balanced power and representative government. The Founding Fathers wanted a deliberative government that would act in the national interest. Only the House of Representatives directly represented the people. James Madison wrote in *Federalist 10* that factions, which included political majorities, were evil and by definition would act against the public interest. A large republic and representative government would filter factions and render them politically powerless. Information technologies that have created a new electronic republic make it possible to supersede the Constitution without changing it, as the following reading suggests.

Lawrence K. Grossman is a former president of NBC News and the Public Broadcasting Service. His major points are:

1. Elements of the "electronic republic" are combining with our traditional political forms. Ironically, although cynicism seems to be increasing, individuals are growing closer to their government.
2. The electronic republic has the potential to affect some of the most basic constitutional protections against majority passion. It has already begun to alter the traditional roles of citizenship and political leadership.
3. Unlike the traditional fear of Big Brother controlling the lives of ordinary people, the new technologies make it likely that ordinary people may have too much control over Big Brother. Since the constitutional system was wary of true majority control, this prospect raises a number of concerns.
4. The big losers in the electronic republic have been traditional institutions: political parties, labor unions, civic associations, and the mainstream press.
5. The increasing role of the public in public policy decisionmaking demands organization, education, and preparation of the general populace, if they are to participate in a responsible and intelligent manner.

37

Lawrence K. Grossman

THE ELECTRONIC REPUBLIC

★★★

A new political system is taking shape in the United States. As we approach the twenty-first century, America is turning into an electronic republic, a democratic system that is vastly increasing the people's day-to-day influence on the decisions of state. New elements of direct democracy are being grafted on to our traditional representative form of government, transforming the nature of the political process and calling into question some of the fundamental assumptions about political life that have existed since the nation was formed more than two hundred years ago.

The irony is that while Americans feel increasingly powerless, cynical, and frustrated about government, the distance between the governed and those who govern is actually shrinking dramatically. Many more citizens are gaining a greater voice in the making of public policy than at any time since the direct democracy of the ancient Greek city-states some twenty-five hundred years ago. Populist measures such as term limits, balanced budget amendments, direct state primaries and caucuses, and expanding use of ballot initiatives and referenda reduce the discretion of elected officials, enable voters to pick their own presidential nominees, bypass legislatures, and even empower the people to make their own laws. Incessant public-opinion polling and increasingly sophisticated interactive telecommunications devices make government instantly aware of, and responsive to, popular will—some say, too responsive for the good of the nation. As the elect seek to respond to every twist and turn of the electorate's mood, the people at large are taking on a more direct role in government than the Founders ever intended.

This democratic political transformation is being propelled largely by two developments—the two-hundred-year-long march toward political equality for all citizens and the explosive growth of new telecommunications media, the remarkable convergence of television, telephone, satellites, cable, and personal computers. This is the first generation of citizens who can see, hear, and judge their own political leaders simultaneously and instantaneously. It is also the first generation of political leaders who can address the entire population and receive instant feedback about what the people think and want. Interactive telecommunications increasingly give ordinary citizens immediate access to the major political decisions that affect their lives and property.

The emerging electronic republic will be a political hybrid. Citizens not only will be able to select those who govern them, as they always have, but increasingly they also will be able to participate directly in making the laws and policies by which they are governed. Through the use of increasingly sophisticated two-way digital broadband telecommunications networks, members of the public are gaining a seat of their own at the table of political power. Even as the public's impatience with government rises, the inexorable progress of democratization, together with remarkable advances in interactive telecommunications, are turning the people themselves into the new fourth branch of government. In the electronic republic, it will no longer be the press but the public that functions as the nation's powerful "fourth estate," alongside the executive, the legislative, and the judiciary.

The rise of the electronic republic, with its perhaps inevitable tendency to respond quickly to every ripple of public opinion, will undercut—if not fundamentally alter—some of our most cherished Constitutional protections against the potential excesses of majority impulses. These protections were put in place by the Founders, who were as wary of pure democracy as they were fearful of governmental authority. The Constitution sought not only to protect the people against the overreaching power of government but also to protect the new nation against the overreaching demands of ordinary people, especially the poor.

Telecommunications technology has reduced the traditional barriers of time and distance. In the same way it can also reduce the traditional Constitutional barriers of checks and balances and separation of powers, which James Madison thought the very size and complexity of the new nation would help to preserve. "Extend the sphere, and you take in a greater variety of parties and interests; you make it less probable that a majority of the whole will have a common motive to invade the rights of other citizens." However, as distances disappear and telecommunications shrink the sphere, and as the executive and legislative branches of government become more entwined with public opinion and popular demand, only the courts may be left to stand as an effective bastion against the tyranny of the majority. The judiciary, the branch of government that was designed to be the least responsive to popular passion, will bear an increasingly difficult and heavy burden to protect individual rights against popular assault.

Direct democracy, toward which we seem to be inexorably heading, was the earliest form of democracy, originating during the fifth century B.C. in the small, self-contained city-states of classical Greece. During the two hundred years of Athenian direct democracy, the ancient city-state whose governance we know most about, a privileged few citizens served at one and the same time as both the rulers and the ruled, making and administering all their own laws. "Although limited to adult males of native parentage, Athenian citizenship granted full and active participation in every decision of the state without regard to wealth or class." Democracy in Athens was carried as far as it would go until modern times.

By contrast, representative government—democracy's second transformation—is a relatively recent phenomenon, originating in the United States a little more than two centuries ago. Under representative democracy, Americans—at first a privileged few and now every citizen over age eighteen—can vote for those who make the laws that govern them. Unlike the ancient Greeks, our Constitution specifies a government that separates the rulers from the ruled. It connects the people to the government by elections, but distances the government from the people by making the elected the ones who actually enact the laws and conduct the business of government. As one political scientist put it, that "Constitutional space is the genius of American republicanism. It keeps the process of democratization under control and prevents our democracy from ruining itself by carrying itself to extreme."

Today, that constitutional space is shrinking. New populist processes and tele-communications technologies amplify the voice of the people at large and bring the public right into the middle of the decision making processes of government. As the power of public opinion rises, the roles of the traditional political intermediaries—the parties, the mass media experts, and the governing elite—decline. Institutions that obstruct the popular will or stand between it and the actions of government get bypassed.

Telecommunications technologies—computers, satellites, interactive television, telephone, and radio—are breaking down the age-old barriers of time and distance that originally precluded the nation's people from voting directly for the laws and policies that govern them. The general belief holds that representative government is the only form of democracy that is feasible in today's sprawling, heterogeneous nation-states. However, interactive telecommunications now make it possible for tens of millions of widely dispersed citizens to receive the information they need to carry out the business of government themselves, gain admission to the political realm, and retrieve at least some of the power over their own lives and goods that many believe their elected leaders are squandering.

The electronic republic, therefore, has already started to redefine the traditional roles of citizenship and political leadership. Today, it is at least as important to reach out to the electorate—the public at large—and lobby public opinion, as it is to lobby the elect—the public officials who make the laws and administer the policies. In the words of literary critic Sven Birkerts in *The Gutenberg Elegies*, "The advent of the computer and the astonishing sophistication achieved by our electronic communications media have together turned a range of isolated changes into something systematic. The way that people experience the world has altered more in the last fifty years than in the many centuries preceding ours." The emergence of the electronic republic gives rise to the need for new thinking, new procedures, new policies, and even new political institutions to ensure that in the century ahead majoritarian impulses will not come at the expense of the rights of individuals and unpopular minorities.

We need to recognize the remarkable change that the interactive telecommunications age is producing in our political system. We need to understand the consequences of the march toward democratization. We need to deal with the promise and perils of the electronic republic. It can make government intensely responsive to the people. It also can carry responsiveness to an extreme, opening the way for manipulation, demagoguery or tyranny of the majority that "kindle[s] a flame . . . [and] spread[s] a general conflagration through the . . . States."

Most studies of government, politics, and the media start at the top by examining the qualities of leadership that define political life. . . . [H]owever, in the coming era, the qualities of citizenship will be at least as important as those of political leadership. In an electronic republic, it will be essential to look at politics from the bottom up as well as from the top down. . . .

What will it take to turn the United States into a nation of qualified citizens who are engaged not as isolated individuals pursuing their own ends but as public-spirited members who are dedicated to the common good? In an electronic republic, finding the answer to that question is essential. In the words of Thomas Jefferson, "I know of no safe depository of the ultimate powers of the society but the people themselves, and if we think them not enlightened enough to exercise their control with a wholesome discretion, the remedy is not to take it from them, but to inform their discretion.". . .

THE RISE OF THE ELECTRONIC REPUBLIC

Until very recently, George Orwell's nightmare tale of Big Brother who utilized electronic surveillance technologies to monitor every citizen, hear every word being said, and see everything being done ("Big Brother Is Watching You!") was the prevailing metaphor for the century to come. The frightening vision of Orwell's *1984* evaporated with the disintegration of the monolithic Nazi and Communist regimes.

By contrast, the twenty-first century's defining image is more likely to have ordinary citizens using their personal telecommunications devices to keep Big Brother under continuing surveillance. The tables have turned. For the nation's leaders, as First Lady Hillary Clinton complained, "There is hardly any zone of privacy left anymore." With the push of a teleprocessor button or the stroke of a telecomputer key, citizens can tell their leaders exactly what they think and what they want them to do. In the "smart" media world, information no longer flows only one-way from one to many. Instead, it flows simultaneously and instantaneously in many directions, from the bottom up as well as from the top down.

For many of my well-educated colleagues in the media and public affairs, and, it seems, for most political scientists, this second scenario is not much more reassuring than the first. Though they profess to be enthusiastic supporters of democratic governance, they actually fear the prospect of too much democracy as much as they fear too little. Like most of our nation's Founders, they do not trust the unmediated judgment of the people at large. They prefer "to refine and enlarge the public views, by passing them through the medium of a chosen body of citizens, whose wisdom may best discern the true interest of their country, and whose patriotism and love of justice will be least likely to sacrifice it to temporary and partial considerations." The world is an increasingly complicated and dangerous place, they say. Problems that require solutions are fast-moving and complex, and growing more so every day. To make intelligent decisions about the multidimensional issues that face us, we need experts with specific knowledge, sophistication, experience, and appropriate educational background. Ordinary people do not have the time or inclination to delve into the details of health care reform and crime legislation or become informed about our trade imbalance or Middle East diplomacy. As much as one would like to believe that the people themselves are best qualified to judge what is in their self-interest, the reality is that informed specialists are more likely to make sound judgments. Democracy needs a governing elite. Of course, the people at large tend to have a very different view these days about the "wisdom" and "love of justice" of their "chosen body of citizens."

Twenty-five hundred years ago Plato, drawing on his own experiences in Athens, expressed similar distrust of the common people in *The Republic*. The people, he said, are bad judges in political matters. The common man has no experience with foreign policy, economics, or national issues; to expect sensible judgment and expert knowledge on such matters from ordinary citizens "is to expect the impossible. He will judge on impulse, sentiment, or prejudice, and though his heart may be sound his head will be muddled." Moreover, direct democracy, Plato said, encourages bad leadership. People cannot be trusted to make the best choice of leaders, and since the popular leader depends entirely on popular favor, he "will constantly be tempted to retain that favor by the easiest possible means." How? "He will play on the likes and dislikes, the weaknesses and foibles of the public, will never tell them an unpleasant truth or advocate a policy that might make them uncomfortable. . . . The people care little who their leaders are provided they profess themselves 'the people's friends.'" Thus, "popular leaders are as devoid of true knowledge as are the people they lead." What is worse, according to Plato, in a pure democracy, where "every individual is free to do as he likes . . . , the minds of the citizens become so sensitive that the least vestige of restraint is resented as intolerable." Plato may as well have been describing today's efforts by democratic leaders to placate a restless and dissatisfied public in which "fathers pander to their sons, teachers to their pupils." Therefore, "the public voice pronounced by the representatives of the people, will be more consonant to the public good, than if pronounced by the people themselves." So goes the classical argument against pure democracy.

If the new telecommunications age brings unmediated democracy, what will happen to our carefully contrived constitutional system of checks and balances? Who will protect minorities against the passions and tyranny of the popular majority? Who will protect the majority from manipulation by public opinion experts, political spin doctors, and unscrupulous pollsters? Who will protect the poor from the permanent majority of the "haves?" Who can offset the persuasive power of big money, the often lying and misleading political commercials, the corruption of politics by what *New York Times* columnist Russell Baker and others have called the "legal bribery" of lobbyists and political action committees seeking favors from government, and the pervasive influence of those who control big media? In a pure democracy, how can those who own the means of communications or dominate the media by lopsided expenditures be prevented from overwhelming the debate, slanting the discussion, and unfairly influencing the public at large?

What chance do ordinary citizens have to come to sound public judgments on health care reform, for example, when, given the unlimited sums of money available for lobbying and political campaigns by those with large-scale financial professional interests, even "the Oval Office . . . [was] reduced to just another trade association?"

Opponents of direct democracy cite survey after survey revealing the depth of people's ignorance about public affairs: They cannot name their own state's U.S. senators, nor can they identify the chief justice of the U.S. Supreme Court, or the nation's principal cabinet officers. One survey found that if the Bill of Rights were on the ballot today, most people would vote against it. Political scientists, not without reason, disdain the quality and depth of news and information that people receive from television, their chief source of information about government and world affairs. Critics point to the consistently low ratings for the few remaining serious television documentary programs about important public issues, which invariably rank at the very bottom of television's popularity charts. And in the current commercial television climate such documentaries have all but disappeared from the screen. The quality of information is said to be getting worse, not better. These are not encouraging recommendations for expanding the role of public opinion in major decision making about affairs of state.

As another sign of the dangerous lack of public interest and involvement in politics, direct democracy's opponents recite the abysmally low turnout at elections. A bare majority of those eligible bothers to vote in presidential elections. A paltry minority turns out during bi-election years. In 1994, a record 39 percent of the voters went to the polls but that means more than 60 percent of the electorate did not even bother. Even if many of these dropouts were to be brought back into the political fold, the skeptics ask, are these the people we should entrust with the ultimate power to make public policy and decide our nation's fate—a mass of citizens of unequal and most often inadequate knowledge, training, wisdom, and interest? For most issues, it is unlikely they will take the time to learn all they need to know or deepen their understanding, no matter how inexpensive, accessible, or convenient additional information might be.

By contrast, those who advocate moving closer to "pure democracy," in which all the people govern themselves in public matters all the time, argue that the very process of representation serves to discourage participatory citizenship. By adapting pure democracy to the realities of governing large-scale nation states, representation gains efficiency without sacrificing accountability. But leaving the major decisions on public matters to a few elected representatives leaves the people out of direct decision making and diminishes public participation and involvement.

Nevertheless, stimulated by new and old interactive communications technologies and rising disgust over the way professional politicians, government employees, and elected incumbents function, many members of the public are seeking to gain greater control over the workings of government. They want to reduce the scope of politicians' responsibility through such measures as term limits, balanced-budget amendments, and state ballot initiatives. On the federal level, one-term administrations and split party government have become the rule, not the exception. On the state level, major policy decisions increasingly are being made in the voting booth, bypassing legislatures and governors in California, Oregon, Colorado, Massachusetts, and a growing number of states. Elements of direct democracy are being thrust into the political system. The major political institutions—the presidency, the Congress, state and local governments, the parties, the press, the process for nominating and electing political leaders—have to accommodate to this far-reaching new populist political reality. Even the judiciary is not immune from increasing public oversight and popular attention as courtrooms have been opened to the prying lenses of television cameras.

THE PUSH OF TECHNOLOGY

Each year millions more citizens acquire personal computers, go on-line with computer networks, subscribe to cable and satellite services, and use telephones and faxes to communicate their views on hot political issues to local, state, and federal officials. The spread of computers is changing the political process as radically as it is changing so many other aspects of our lives. Subscribers to CompuServe have a network that puts them on-line with the White House, which is also available to everyone with access to Internet. Members of Congress and state legislators opened computer mailboxes and send messages to constituents through computer bulletin boards and E-mail exchanges. In 1994, Minnesota candidates for governor and the U.S. Senate squared off in the first election campaign debates held by computer, giving voters more direct access than on the old-fashioned campaign trail. "The Internet and other spurs of the information superhighway have emerged as powerful new links between politicians and voters." Politics has invaded cyberspace. A new breed of professional grassroots lobbying firms, using computerized lists and telephone banks in "boiler rooms," has geared up to mobilize the pressure of public opinion at the behest of paying clients. Government officials were always fair game to be bought by special interests. Now that public sentiment plays a central role in the making of major political decisions, it too is being bought and delivered—for a price—to members of Congress and the White House.

But computers are only one part of the story of the revolution in communications. Talk radio and talk television hosts, mostly but by no means all conservative, are proliferating and gaining influence and popularity. Today, most have added old-fashioned telephone lines to their broadcasts, opening the airwaves to members of the audience at home and provoking listeners and viewers to bombard Congress with grassroots opinions on controversial issues—congressional pay raises, abortion, welfare policy, Social Security, immigration, tax policy, and health care, for example. Developing public feedback has turned into a major political and media industry.

The big losers in the present-day reshuffling and resurgence of public influence are the traditional institutions that have served as the main intermediaries between the government and its citizens—the political parties, labor unions, civic associations, even the commentators and correspondents in the mainstream press. Not only are they declining in influence and relevance, but surveys demonstrate that they are losing the public's trust. Sitting before their glass screens at home, people see for themselves what is happening in the world. They judge for themselves the quality and character of the political leaders who parade before them on television seeking their support. Who needs party bosses, union leaders, political columnists, or TV commentators anymore to tell people what to think and which way to vote? Today, the people stay home and make up their own minds while watching television. And the journalists spend a good deal of their time analyzing and reporting what the people think and how they feel.

To its critics, teledemocracy conjures the image of alienated, silent voters, sitting alone inside an electronic cocoon. Like television directors in a sealed TV control room, these modern-day robotic voters absorb virtually all their information about the outside world electronically—through CNN-style live coverage, tabloid-news shows, and sensational newsmagazines; and, increasingly, at programmed computer terminals. The wired public then feeds back its ill-formed, unsophisticated, unmediated opinion instantaneously, without deliberation, following simple on-screen instructions to press Y for yes, or N for no. These isolated electronic citizens never participate in the political community. They rarely discuss issues with fellow citizens face-to-face. Historian Daniel Boorstin contrasts the private, "segregated" experience of watching television, in which each person's experience is separate and silent, with the necessary healthy and vigorous deliberative "public life of a democracy." But is that actually the way electronic democracy will operate, or needs to operate in the future?

THE PLEBISCITE PRESIDENCY: THE CRITICS' VIEW

We shall look back on the 1992 presidential campaign and the live television coverage of the 1991 Gulf War as watershed moments—turning points in the decade-long rise of the American electronic republic. In the 1992 campaign, Perot's mainstream Democratic and Republican rivals for the White House followed his lead, tapping into many of the same direct-to-the-people campaign strategies. During the New Hampshire primary, the press had become so totally consumed with Bill Clinton's alleged affair with nightclub performer Gennifer Flowers that Clinton decided the only way to escape their "feeding frenzy" was to bypass the mainstream reporters and talk directly to the state's potential voters himself. He addressed the issues they were concerned with in a series of well-publicized town meetings on radio and television. Even President Bush eventually awakened to that strategy, when it became apparent that he was in trouble with the voters. Bush invited Larry King to originate his CNN call-in show directly from the White House late in the campaign.

In 1992, political commentators of every stripe, from liberal Anthony Lewis in *The New York Times* to conservative George Will in *Newsweek*, deplored this new populist electronic political trend. They were appalled at the idea that the United States should have a "plebiscite presidency" and "rule by applause meter." Direct electronic democracy, wrote columnist Charles Krauthammer, is the "highway to tyranny," signifying the end of reasoned, experienced, deliberative constitutional political decision making and sure to lead the country down the slippery slope to demagoguery.

These critics echoed the two-centuries-old arguments of Alexander Hamilton in the Federalist Papers. Difficult political decisions should not be left to the snap judgments and popular distemper of public opinion, Hamilton wrote. They should be made only by those who are the "most likely to possess the information and discernment requisite . . . to complicated investigations." In other words, major policy decisions should be left to an informed political elite, what historian James MacGregor Burns has called "the seasoned wisdom" of educated, informed, responsible leaders like the Founders themselves.

Notwithstanding these concerns, however, many of the constitutional roadblocks that originally were put in place to thwart instant responsiveness to majority rule have been pushed aside. The elitist republic has evolved into an inclusive democracy. During the past two centuries, American democracy has progressed inexorably toward greater political equality and universal suffrage. The right to vote, originally limited to a narrow group of adult white male property owners who comprised about 10 percent of the population, has been extended over two centuries to all citizens over age eighteen. The insulating role of the electoral college, originally designed to select presidents by a political elite rather than by popular vote, survives as a kind of quaint—although still potentially disruptive—vestigial political institution. U.S. senators, once chosen by state legislatures, have been elected by direct popular vote since 1913. Since the rise of television in the 1950s, and largely *because of* the rise of television, presidential nominees are no longer picked by party bosses in smoke-filled rooms or even by party delegates in national conventions. Instead, they are elected by rank-and-file voters in direct state primaries and caucuses. As Tocqueville discovered, American democracy "is constantly in the process of democratizing itself further."

THE RISE OF PUBLIC DISCONTENT

Politically, one problem has been that the more television viewers see of their government in action—or in gridlock—the less they like what they find. Whether most viewers are actually being shown more of their government at work, or whether they are being served only with more snippets of government failures and outrages is a question we shall discuss later on. But the fact remains that most Americans have grown increasingly disenchanted with politics, politicians, and political parties. Television has fed their cynicism. According to a Louis Harris poll, taken shortly before the 1992 presidential election, 72 percent of all voters believe their leaders are out of touch with the people, 66 percent feel a sense of powerlessness, and 61 percent say those who run the country don't care what happens to them.

That disillusionment, the deepening sense of alienation and frustration that citizens feel toward government, has served only to accelerate the demand for basic structural changes in the nation's political system. Some people tend to embrace whatever holds out the prospect of empowering them, while others simply withdraw from participation as citizens on the not unreasonable assumption that their involvement will make no difference in their lives. Those who voted in recent elections have consistently supported measures to weaken entrenched officials, narrow the scope of their responsibility (even of those they voted for), and make government more responsive to their views and demands. Hence the dramatic rise in ticket-splitting, term limit and balanced-budget amendments, public opinion surveys, and traffic in faxes, phone calls, and computer messages to the White House and Congress. To get elected, even incumbents feet obliged to run against the government and in favor of cutting their own authority.

To pressure elected officials into doing the job the voters want, people have taken to making their voices heard in record numbers even in the intervals between elections. So many members of the public picked up their phones and called and faxed the White House to protest Clinton's first nomination for attorney general and his proposal to admit gays into the military during his inaugural week that the venerable White House switchboard collapsed from overload. To be sure, many of those calls were orchestrated by political interest groups and stimulated by irate talk show hosts. But millions more were spontaneous. It was not enough that people had just voted in the election, they wanted their newly elected president to know exactly what they thought of his actions and what they expected him to do in the day-to-day job of running the government.

The public's increasing demand for fundamental change in the political system is far from a temporary phenomenon prompted by an emotional reaction to a few highly charged issues like gays in the military or health care reform. It represents a permanent change, made possible, at least in part, by newly empowering interactive telecommunications technologies and by the speed of information that these technologies have spawned.

In a *New York Times* column, Russell Baker—only somewhat facetiously—attributed the record-breaking Republican triumph in the 1994 election, giving the party control of both the House and Senate, to the voters' new sense of personal empowerment. That empowerment, Baker wrote, had been stimulated by the invention of the TV remote control, "the ultimate weapon" of the public's liberation. From zapping television channels at home, people moved on to the voting booths and zapped incumbent Democrats. "Channel-surfing gave millions a taste of power over an old tyrant [television]." It made them "feel comfortable with the idea [that they] . . . could zap a politician" as well. Baker's explanation was not by any means far off the mark.

THE IMPERATIVE FOR SOUND PUBLIC JUDGMENT

The nation's citizens today are being overwhelmed by extraordinarily difficult, seemingly intractable political, social, and economic problems—the high cost of health care, epidemics of crime and drug abuse, faltering public education, lack of job security, pervasive pollution, increasing inner-city poverty, racism, and the breakdown of family life. Well-informed, experienced political elites have made little or no progress solving any of these problems. Out of increasing frustration, some members of the public at large are withdrawing from any participation in politics. But some are beginning to take advantage of their new ability to make their voices heard. Through their rising use of the new mechanisms of direct and interactive communications, many citizens who have not withdrawn in frustration and disillusionment are beginning to have an active and important influence on the making of day-to-day political decisions.

In the electronic republic, as citizens at large gain the power of self-governance, the need to inform and educate the American people about these complex issues and about the workings of our political system has become, if anything, more important than ever. In the words of one political theorist, we need to stem "the decline of a genuine politics in the modern age and to suggest what a form of political association built upon plurality, sheer human togetherness, might look like."

It is obvious that an informed and interested public is the key to successful self-governance. With the public at large playing a critical part in the government's decision-making process, it is essential that the public know what political alternatives are available and what their costs and consequences will be. New methods and new systems must be devised to enable ordinary citizens to reach responsible and informed judgments. Since information has become "society's main transforming resource," the public's ability to receive, absorb, and understand information no longer can be left to happenstance.

No military general would willingly send his army into battle untrained and ill-prepared, no matter how well-equipped. Yet today, the American public is going into political battle armed with increasingly sophisticated tools of electronic decision making but without the information, political organization, education, or preparation to use these tools wisely. Information about public issues can be made immediately accessible to every citizen in a form and at a level to suit each individual's needs. Without a conscious and deliberate effort to inform public judgment, to put the new interactive telecommunications technologies to work on behalf of democracy, they are more likely to undermine the democratic process than enhance it. With citizens an active branch of the government in the electronic republic, they need to know enough to participate in a responsible and intelligent manner. That will not happen without a great deal of work, systematic planning, and significant policy reform.

CHAPTER 9

PLURALISM, DIVERSITY, AND IMMIGRATION

How Do We All Get Along?

America has been variously referred to as a nation of immigrants, a melting pot, and a beautiful mosaic. These and other characterizations indicate the difficulty of defining exactly who we are as a nation, and how groups from different backgrounds are to get along. Questions of diversity, conflict, and compromise are at the core of the Madisonian system of government, which aimed to multiply group allegiances and thereby minimize the potential power of any cohesive majority group.

Today, group conflict remains at the heart of many current issues. Debate concerning racial and ethnic groups is heated and contentious because race and ethnicity strike so closely to how we define ourselves. Too often, however, race and ethnicity are discussed in terms that oversimplify and polarize. When used as rhetorical shorthand, "assimilation" comes to represent a "melting" into a uniform type of American, while "multiculturalism" becomes identified with the maintenance of special racial and ethnic characteristics which preclude full allegiance to the nation. Assimilation and pluralism are abstract ideals about how different groups interact, however, and they do not function well as realistic solutions to group conflict.

Both of these views fail to capture the nuances involved in American group relations. And as difficult as they can sometimes be, group relations and conflicts are a fact of public life in America. The debate over diversity and multiculturalism, concern over immigration, and even misunderstandings about the history of relations between the United States and American Indians—all of these are part of our national commitment to solving complex problems involving a kaleidoscope of interests.

John Higham is a scholar of American history, with special emphasis on immigration, race, and ethnicity issues. His 1955 book, *Strangers in the Land,* is a classic look at immigration to the United States. In this selection, Higham's major points are:

1. "Pluralism" is a concept which is too often left unexamined and taken for granted. "Pluralism" too often refers to a condition, rather than a theory.
2. "Assimilation" is also a misunderstood and under-examined concept. Assimilation and pluralism are not simply opposites.
3. Pluralism at the beginning of the republic referred primarily to multiplicity; now, it often refers to variety, based on the idea that differences are intrinsically valuable.
4. In some senses, pluralism addresses groups above individuals, while assimilation addresses individuals and their right to define themselves. But as abstract ideals, presented this way, neither is wholly desirable.
5. The issue remains one of "rediscovering what values can bind together a more and more kaleidoscopic culture."

38

John Higham

Ethnic Pluralism in American Thought and Practice

For many years writers on American ethnic problems have invoked a vision of pluralism as an ideal all men of goodwill should cherish. Pluralism, we are told, will save us from a foolish belief in assimilation. But what pluralism means in a positive sense—even the extent to which it runs against an assimilationist philosophy—seldom appears. This [selection] is a preliminary effort to examine the chronic indistinctness of the pluralist idea in ethnic relations. That idea has undergone major changes, and I believe it is today in acute need of rethinking. Whatever coherence the idea once had has been dissipated in the course of its popularization during the 1950's and 1960's. Traditional liberals continue to celebrate "our pluralistic society." Those radicals who pay heed to the theory of pluralism denounce it but have nothing to put in its place; and ethnic spokesmen, without much regard to either, pursue their own group interest in whatever ways seem expedient. I propose not to offer a solution to the present confusion, but to explain how it came about.

If my inquiry is not itself to become mired in the confusion it examines, it will have to focus steadily on the problem of intellectual coherence. Several years ago Professor Philip Gleason complained of the mind-boggling ambiguities in the current discussion of a "new pluralism," and since then the situation has become a good deal worse. Seeking unity, former New York Mayor Robert F. Wagner in the election of 1972 contrasted pluralism with factionalism. "The Democratic party," Wagner declared hopefully, "is a pluralistic party, as New York is a pluralistic state, and this will be a pluralistic campaign." Ada Louise Huxtable rejoices that pluralism is superseding the "destructively sterile" architecture of recent years, while a different kind of critic complains that "the fluff of pluralism" has muted "the chord of revolutionary discontent."

For the most part current usage seems to refer to a condition rather than a theory: a condition of diversity, which prevents any one group or point of view from attaining preeminence. In the interest of clarification I will deal with pluralism in a stricter sense. As treated here it is not simply an attitude or a description of reality. It is a normative social theory. As such, pluralism attempts to explain and justify a feasible and desirable social order. It makes a serious claim on our understanding as well as our emotions. It deserves to be judged in terms of internal consistency and compatibility with other beliefs as well as empirical substance and social need.

The history of pluralist theories will, therefore, have to be examined in a wider context of ideas and values. We will have to take note especially of the interplay between pluralism and opposing theories of assimilation. It is customary today to denounce the melting-pot ideal as a false and even bigoted antithesis to the pluralist vision; and it is true that ethnic pluralism arose as a protest against the losses some minorities were suffering under the stresses of assimilation. Pluralism could become a persuasive alternative only when general doubts developed that assimilation was the democratic way. Nevertheless, as we shall see, the relation between assimilation and pluralism was not a simple dialectic of opposition. From the outset the belief that a democratic society should preserve the integrity of its constituent groups has unconsciously relied on the assimilative process which it seemed to repudiate; and now that assimilation has lost momentum, pluralism has lost its sense of direction.

Finally, we will discover that much of the disorientation in the present discussion of pluralism stems from increasing uncertainty about a cardinal assumption of pluralist theory, namely that the persistence and solidarity of ethnic minorities is essential to democracy. The general appeal of pluralism has inhered in its promise of extending democracy. In recent years, however, the most searching inquiries into pluralistic conditions have shown how extensively they serve to perpetuate inequalities. How much pluralism, and what kinds, a good society should have is a question no one has clearly addressed.

Pluralism in all its forms is a philosophy of minority rights. It arises when minorities become conscious of having a stake in the maintenance of their position within a larger society. A pluralist generally identifies himself with a social minority and writes in its behalf. But he also accepts minority status as a legitimate and perhaps even desirable way of participating in the larger society. Thus pluralism posits a situation in which minorities retain their solidarity and effectiveness; but it does not welcome all such situations. A pluralist wants to develop a mutually tolerable relationship between discrete groups and the social system in which they reside. Specifically, he seeks a relationship that will allow the individual groups both autonomy and unimpeded influence. He opposes assimilation on the one hand, because that threatens group survival; but he also opposes separatism, because that will exclude him from the larger society. Accordingly, pluralism addresses itself to the character and viability of an aggregate that has several components, and its special challenge arises from the attempt to define the aggregate in terms that none of its principal components need find unacceptable.

The belief that a well-ordered society should sustain the diversity of its component groups has, of course, deep roots in early American experience, but it became subordinated during the nineteenth century to the quest for unity. The building of a national republic gave central importance to the process of convergence, to the making of a homogeneous future from a heterogeneous past. The dominant American legend—what was later symbolized in the image of a melting pot—said that a continuous fusion of originally disparate elements was forming a single American people. In the attainment of oneness, rather than the persistence of separate identities, lay the promise of American life. After the Civil War, especially, a drive for national integration took priority over other group loyalties. American business and professional leaders built unifying networks of communications and social control. Intellectuals elaborated monistic schemes of thought, which enclosed the processes of nature and the achievements of man within an all-embracing, rational synthesis. If, as Henry Adams charged, his generation was mortgaged to the railways, it also gave its mind to a larger quest for unity, which Adams himself pursued through the eighties and nineties.

Thus the pluralist ideology which emerged in the early twentieth century, though grounded experientially in the earliest facts of American life, represented a significant departure from conventional wisdom. Pluralism was, in fact, part of a profound intellectual upheaval, which Morton White has described as "the revolt against formalism." Conceptually, it was a revolt against the monistic systems that prevailed in the late nineteenth century. It rejected their rationalistic spirit and their inclination toward a stratified view of society. The antiformalists denied a privileged status to any fixed point of view or any social category. They accepted the multiformity of experience and the relativity of values. Their refusal of any single, all-embracing scheme of things acquired a pluralistic bent when it became a positive celebration of irreducible diversity.

Here the modern pluralist has echoed romanticism. The formalistic pluralism of the early republic, as expressed by James Madison, commended the instrumental value of *multiplicity*. Modern pluralism also champions *variety*. It rests on the romantic premise that differences are intrinsically valuable and should take precedence over conformity to a universal standard. In casting off the constraints of late-Victorian America, antiformalists sounded again the rallying cry of their romantic forebears: "*Vive la différence!*" It is significant that pluralism received its philosophical credentials from William James, the American philosopher who, more than any other, incarnated a romantic love of diversity, particularity, and uniqueness. James's late book, *A Pluralistic Universe* (1909), made the most careful statement of the case, though he had already, in *The Will to Believe* (1897), given wide currency to the term.

For modern pluralism diversity has performed a special function, which was often missing in the romantic tradition. It has consistently worked against authoritarian claims to exclusive or preeminent wisdom. Since the democratic aspirations of the Progressive Era colored and shaped the entire revolt against formalism, modern pluralism was initially harnessed to an egalitarian ethic. Pluralists appealed for an appreciation of differences in order to rectify inequalities. . . .

ANOTHER AMERICAN DILEMMA

A season of struggle and hope, of turmoil and guilt, in American racial and ethnic relations has passed. In its place has come a time of apathy, cynicism, exhaustion, and near despair. The civil rights movement has collapsed, a victim at least in part of its successes. The demands for ethnic power and recognition, which exploded in the wake of the civil rights movement, have used up the hectic energies of posture and intimidation. This is a moment, then, for reflection and reconsideration. It is most especially a moment to reckon with an impasse in our thinking about ethnicity. Until the clash between two ways of looking at ethnic problems is resolved, it is hard to see how further advances can take place. The conflict between those contending points of view is paralyzing because it divides the creative minority of Americans who actively seek a more just social order.

. . . The Constitution laid down no explicit guidelines for adjudicating issues of social integration—we have no court of ethnic rights—and an appreciation of the complexities in this troubled area is rarely met. Here the dilemma is both sociological and moral. It has to do with what we are and what we wish to be; with the possibilities of our social heritage and circumstances, and with the kind of identity we would like to have.

I propose, first, to state the crux of the dilemma as we confront it today; second, to review two characteristic strategies American intellectuals have used to escape from the dilemma, and finally to suggest a third strategy which may not suffer from the shortcomings of the other two. Doubtless there are other fruitful approaches to the perplexities of a multiethnic society. I intend not to be exhaustive but to concentrate on the leading tendencies in American liberal thought in the twentieth century. In proposing a third formulation I do not suppose I am settling anything. Fundamentally the issues of ethnic life are never settled. But a clear grasp of unacceptable alternatives and some sense of direction can help us to move beyond the constraints of received opinion.

The essential dilemma, of course, is the opposition between a strategy of integration and one of pluralism. Although the contrast has many dimensions, it can be summed up as a question of boundaries. The integrationist looks toward the elimination of ethnic boundaries. The pluralist believes in maintaining them. Their primary difference, therefore, concerns the scale and character of the community each takes as a model. Integration is pledged to the great community which is yet to be realized: the brotherhood of mankind. Pluralism holds fast to the little community: the concrete local brotherhood which is rooted in the past. Integration in its modern form expresses the universalism of the Enlightenment. Pluralism rests on the diversitarian premises of romantic thought.

From this fundamental distinction others flow. In the United States both integrationists and pluralists claim to be the true champions of democracy; but democracy means different things to them. Consistent with its universal criteria, integration lends itself to a majoritarian emphasis. The integrationist expects a simple majority to approximate the general will. Pluralism, on the other hand, is always a philosophy of minority rights. It represents an effort to generalize the particular claim of a small part of society. It resists the conformity that majorities encourage; it is likely to dispute the legitimacy of any simple majority. Pluralism conceives of democratic politics as a process of building coalitions between minorities.

The democracy of integration is an equality of individuals; pluralist democracy an equality of groups. For the assimilationist the primary social unit and the locus of value is the individual. What counts is his right to define himself. He must therefore be free to secede from his ancestors. This is exactly what happens in the process of assimilation: individuals or families detach themselves one by one from their traditional communities. For pluralists, however, the persistence and vitality of the group comes first. Individuals can realize themselves, and become whole, only through the group that nourishes their being.

The priority one side assigns to the individual and the other to the group affects their respective views of what binds a people together. For integrationists the linchpin of a rightly ordered society is a set of ideals, a body of principles, in our own case what Gunnar Myrdal called an "American Creed." A people who aspire to universality and consist largely of detached and mobile individuals will rely heavily on the beliefs they hold in common. Indeed, they may share little else, for all who subscribe to the official creed should be received into membership. The pluralist cares much less what people believe; he wants to know who they are. The most important social bond is inherited, not adopted; the work of ancestors, not of abstractions. In a multiethnic society, therefore, the assimilationist stresses a unifying ideology, whereas the pluralist guards a distinctive memory.

When the two positions are stated so baldly, the undesirability of either—at least without heavy qualification—becomes manifest. For one thing, both positions are unrealistic. Assimilationism falsely assumes that ethnic ties dissolve fairly easily in an open society. . . . No ethnic group, once established in the United States, has ever entirely disappeared; none seems about to do so. People are not as pliant as assimilationists have supposed.

Pluralism makes the opposite mistake. It assumes a rigidity of ethnic boundaries and a fixity of group commitment which American life does not permit. . . . All American ethnic groups perpetuate themselves, but none survives intact. Their boundaries are more or less porous and elastic. All of them lose people who marry out and whose offspring cease to identify with the rejected strain. This is so patently true that loud assertions of pluralism almost invariably betray fears of assimilation.

Pluralism encourages the further illusion that ethnic groups typically have a high degree of internal solidarity. Actually many of them are unstable federations of local or tribal collectivities, which attain only a temporary and precarious unity in the face of a common enemy. On top of sharp localistic differences, an ethnic group is likely to be split along religious, class, and political lines. For example, the American Dutch, a relatively small immigrant group, belonged in the nineteenth century to three rival churches (Reformed, Christian Reformed, and Roman Catholic), many distinct speech communities (Zeelanders, Groningers, Friesians, Gelderlanders, Limburgers,

Noord-Brabanters, East Friesians, Flemings, Utrechters, people of Graefschap, and those who spoke the Drenthe and Overijsel dialects), and totally dissimilar generations (colonial descendants versus nineteenth-century immigrants). No American ethnic group, Arthur Mann has pointed out, has created an organized community capable of speaking for all its members.

In addition to being unrealistic, both integration and pluralism are morally objectionable. From the point of view of the individual, integration is an ethic of self-transformation—an Emersonian summons to "shun father and mother and wife and brother when my genius calls me." It teaches a rejection of one's origins and a contempt for those parts of the self that resist transformation. It sacrifices love and loyalty to autonomy and mastery, only to find those elusive goals dissolving in a pervasive conformity. In sum, for individuals outside the mainstream the process of assimilation is identical with the pursuit of individual success. It gives an edge to private ambition and a spur to personal aggrandizement. . . .

Moreover, assimilation lays a stigma of failure on those who remain loyal to ancestral ways. The integrationist's assurance that individuals need only an opportunity to prove their worth has led innumerable underachieving ethnics into a blind alley. They must conclude either that they are indeed unworthy or that the proffered opportunity was fraudulent. The result is either self-hatred or alienation from society. It can frequently be both.

The liabilities of a pluralist ethic are equally severe. Whereas assimilation penalizes the less ambitious and successful groups and individuals, pluralism limits the more autonomous and adventurous. To young people fired by curiosity and equipped with a cosmopolitan education, the ethnic community can be intensely stultifying. It is likely to be suspicious, narrow-minded, riddled with prejudices. Pluralism adjures the young to realize themselves through the group to which they belong; but many have little sense of ethnic identity and in any case will not forego individual opportunity in the interest of ethnic separateness and cohesion. While assimilation sacrifices the group for the sake of the individual, pluralism would put the individual at the mercy of the group.

The dangers of the latter course became manifest in the light of proposals from some pluralists for giving legal protection to ethnic differences. Harold Cruse would amend the Constitution to secure the rights of racial and ethnic groups. The Indian activist Vine Deloria has offered somewhat more concrete proposals for "tribalizing" American society by giving corporate bodies full control over local communities. The threat such arrangements would pose to the equal rights of individuals is only part of their difficulty. Raising the walls around unequal ethnic groups must surely sharpen conflicts between them while vitiating the common principles on which all rely to regulate their intercourse. A multiethnic society can avoid tyranny only through a shared culture and a set of universal rules which all of its groups accept. If integration is unacceptable because it does not allow for differences, pluralism fails to answer our need for universals.

The record of American intellectuals in clarifying the issues of race and ethnicity is less than notable. Polemics we have in abundance, but on this subject no contributions to democratic theory compare in depth or complexity with the writings of Hamilton, Madison, Dewey, and Niebuhr. Faced with the antinomies I have outlined, all but a very few theorists have simply elaborated one side of the argument. The other side is either repressed or relegated to some inactive region of consciousness. . . .

In the last decade we have encountered diversity with a vengeance. It is too soon, of course, to say whether the return to ethnicity is a temporary reaction, a mere interlude in the onrush of modernization. Still, it presents an opportunity to reassess the course of history. If the sharpened ethnic assertiveness that erupted in the late 1960's is more than a passing phenomenon, it may indicate that modern history supports the theory of pluralistic integration after all. . . .

In the 1950's, when assimilation was advancing so rapidly, there was much concern over the oppressive featurelessness of a standardized mass culture. Today the weakening of social boundaries does not suggest a further descent into uniformity, but rather a multiplication of small audiences, specialized media, local attachments, and partial identities which play into one another in ways we cannot yet understand. Many who are concerned about ethnic justice feel pessimistic about the ability of our society to develop the necessary appreciation of diversity. But it is possible, in view of the trend I have sketched, that our greater problem in moving toward pluralistic integration may come in rediscovering what values can bind together a more and more kaleidoscopic culture.

The racial divide between black and white continues in American politics. Racial division is the American dilemma that has not yet been solved. The question is where the solution lies among assimilation and policies of ethnic diversity that encourage racial separateness.

Race-based electoral districting is one area that reflects the racial divide. African-Americans argue that they can achieve fair representation only through disengagement from what they believe to be a prejudiced white electorate. However, as the following reading points out, voting evidence does not support their position. White majority districts have elected many African-American politicians at all levels of government. Black candidates must take moderate positions to garner the necessary white votes for election. Once in office these moderate politicians have a far better of chance of making the requisite compromises with their white counterparts to achieve their goals.

Stephan Thernstrom teaches History at Harvard University and is the editor of the *Harvard Encyclopedia of American Ethnic Groups.* Abigail Thernstrom is a senior fellow at the Manhattan Institute in New York City and a member of the Massachusetts State Board of Education. In this selection, the authors write:

1. Writers on both the left and right often distort the realities of race issues for political ends. We have been left without a common language for discussion.

2. Race-based districting is one of today's most contentious issues. Constitutional decisions and the ease with which people can understand maps and bizarre districts have brought the question into the headlines.

3. Writers disagree over whether race-based districts, virtually guaranteeing electoral victories by minorities, are good or bad for blacks. Voting rights and civil rights advocates criticized Supreme Court decisions which questioned the validity of majority black districts. Yet redrawn districts, holding a majority white population, tend to reelect black representatives.

4. Racial classifications imply that skin color is a stronger determinant of voting behavior than character, social class, religion, or other factors. Separate procedures like these overlook the changes in America since the 1960s, and risk grave consequences by separating American citizens by race.

39

Stephan Thernstrom and Abigail Thernstrom

AMERICA IN BLACK AND WHITE

"An American Dilemma," Gunnar Myrdal called the problem of race in his classic 1944 book. He saw a painful choice between American ideals and American racial practices. But in 1944, ten years before *Brown v. Board of Education*, most white Americans were not actually in much pain. Indeed, when asked in a survey that same year whether "Negroes should have as good a *chance* as white people to get any kind of job," the majority of whites said that "white people should have the first chance at any kind of job." Blacks belonged at the back of the employment bus, most whites firmly believed.

"Are they relatives of yours?" a white asks the protagonist in Ralph Ellison's 1952 novel, *Invisible Man.*

> "Sure, we're both black," I said, beginning to laugh.
> He smiled, his eyes intense upon my face.
> "Seriously, are they your relatives?"
> "Sure, we were burned in the same oven," I said.

Burned in the same Jim Crow oven, in the heat generated by overwhelming racial hostility. That brutal world is gone, but some of the scars remain. Both points are easy to forget but essential to remember. On both left and right, writers too often distort the picture for political ends, clouding our understanding of the nation's most important domestic issue. On the right, they frequently dismiss the persistence of racial animus, suggesting, indeed, that "those who look carefully for evidence of racism . . . are likely to come up short." On the left, critics such as Derrick Bell allude to the "bogus freedom checks" that "the Man" will never honor. An enslaved people remains enslaved.

There is no racism; there is nothing but racism. The issue of race sends people scurrying in extremist directions. And thus there is almost no overlap between opposing views, and little sympathy and understanding across the lines of political battle. In October 1994 the Court of Appeals for the Fourth Circuit struck down the University of Maryland's blacks-only Banneker Scholarship program. "I can't get over the irony of the rising African American jail population and then taking away a program like this that tries to bring African Americans into the university," the president of the university remarked. The Fourth Circuit had seen the issue quite differently: "Of all the criteria by which men and women can be judged," the court had said, "the most pernicious is that of race."

Americans committed to racial justice were not always so divided. In 1963, when the Reverend Martin Luther King, Jr., stood at the Lincoln Memorial and spoke of his dreams, blacks and whites marching together pictured the "beautiful symphony of brotherhood" that treating blacks and whites alike would surely create. But that shared vision quickly faded, as many came to believe that race consciousness was the road to racial equality. "In order to get beyond racism, we must first take account of race," justice Harry Blackmun said in the *Bakke* case in 1978. In the civil rights community, by the late 1970s, that much-quoted aphorism had come to seem indisputably right.

Today we argue without a common language. University of Pennsylvania law professor Lani Guinier, a much sought after presence in the media, has repeatedly called for "a national conversation on race." We have not exactly fallen silent on the subject. We talk endlessly, obsessively about the issue, but across linguistic barricades. "Equal opportunity" is a much-used phrase with a much-disputed meaning. In the battleground of ideas, language is part of the territory each side seeks to capture. And thus, while advocates of race-neutral policies equate such equality with basic access—an absence of closed doors—their critics look for outcomes. "As a general matter, increases in the numbers of employees, or students or entrepreneurs from historically underrepresented groups are a measure of increased opportunity," Christopher Edley and George Stephanopolous, advisors to President Clinton, argued in 1995. No opportunity without results.

Definitional quarrels are only the start of the problem. Opposing sides in the debate over race start from different premises, and see American society through very different lenses. The topic of race raises fundamental questions about who we are, where we're going, how we get there. To talk about race is to talk about America—and vice versa. The question pops up everywhere; one can't escape it. Try to name a significant domestic issue that has nothing to do with the status of African Americans: it's a challenge. Crime, family, education, housing, the environment, even foreign military entanglements and border control. Immigration is a good example. Newcomers, immigration advocates say, are good for the country; they contribute to its economic vitality. But are they good for *black* America? And if not, how much does that matter? What do we owe those who arrived on our shores in 1619 and remained members of an oppressed caste for more than three centuries? A relatively narrow question—immigration policy—is hopelessly entangled with the central issue in American life. . . .

Much has changed, but the racial divide has not disappeared. The trial of black celebrity O. J. Simpson, accused of murdering his white ex-wife and Ronald Goldman, was a particularly vivid reminder of that sobering fact. Blacks and whites were equally absorbed by the trial, but from the outset their views were radically different. Most whites concluded Simpson was guilty; most blacks believed his professed innocence. And in the days that followed the October 3, 1995, not-guilty verdict, unforgettable images flitted across the nation's television screens: of cheers, hugs, and high fives among black crowds; of downcast whites and racist graffiti in Brentwood, the traditionally white, liberal, upscale neighborhood in which O. J. and Nicole Brown Simpson both lived. "Whites v. Blacks" was the title *Newsweek* gave its post-verdict story. "Will the Verdict Split America?" *Time* magazine asked. Are we two nations or one? The question assumed still greater urgency when Louis Farrakhan led a Million Man March in Washington, D.C., just thirteen days after the O. J. verdict.

Questions that had moved to the periphery of the civil rights debate have now returned to center stage. How culturally important is skin color? Are blacks a group like no other and likely to remain quite separate? If so, does the drive for integration remain important? "When I got my law degree, I didn't check my blackness at the door," Leonardo Knight, a lawyer living on Capitol Hill, remarked in 1994. "There is very little difference between black Americans and white Americans when you go to the bottom of it. But what little there is, is very important," the literary critic Gerald Early had written a year earlier. Black and white, much more equal, but still separate. It wasn't the vision we once had.

"We cannot walk alone," Dr. King said in his 1963 "I Have a Dream" speech. The destiny of whites and blacks is inextricably entwined. But how to walk together? That question has lost none of its urgency in the fifty years since Gunnar Myrdal wrote *The American Dilemma*. Myrdal's work was full of hope; he believed fervently in the potential for racial decency in most Americans. Our [work], too, rests on that optimistic premise.

CLASSIFYING VOTERS BY RACE

Race-based districting raised constitutional questions, the Court held in *Shaw* [v. *Reno* (1993)]. But when was a state sorting voters along lines of race in such a way as to violate the equal protection clause? Justice O'Connor's answer in 1993 was neither altogether reassuring nor entirely clear. "This Court never has held that race-conscious redistricting is impermissible in *all* circumstances," she wrote. Sometimes it was okay, in other words—just your everyday, garden-variety "reasonable" racial classification. But problems clearly arose when a district was "so extremely irregular on its face that it rationally [could] be viewed only as an effort to segregate the races for purposes of voting, without regard for traditional districting principles and without sufficiently compelling justification." "Bizarre" districts, "unexplainable on grounds other than race," were thus the source of concern. Districts that looked bad *were* bad. Highly irregular contours obviously drawn with race in mind suggested racial stereotyping, reinforcing "the perception that members of the same racial group . . . think alike." . . .

Until the Court's 1993 decision in *Shaw v. Reno*, minority voting rights was perhaps the most debatable, yet least debated, of all affirmative action issues. The enforcement of the 1965 act was controversial policy that stirred no controversy. It was scarcely an exaggeration to say that race-conscious action in the electoral sphere had only adherents. The opposition to busing was loud and clear; behind closed doors, affirmative action in employment was certainly discussed. But protest against racial gerrymandering to increase minority officeholding was confined to the odd academic. Who else was likely to object? Black and white parents cared where their children went to school, but few voters paid attention to the rules by which their county governing board was elected.

The constitutional decisions turned an obscure issue into headline news. Race-conscious strategies are often hard to discuss because the basic facts are so successfully kept under wraps. Districting is different. That is, affirmative action programs at colleges, for instance, also amount to protective racial sorting; by setting racially separate admissions standards, they pit African-American applicants primarily (sometimes only) against other members of the racial group. But almost no school will publicly describe how its affirmative action policy works. With race-conscious districting, on the other hand, a quick glance at the map makes the racial sorting perfectly obvious.

Take the North Carolina map at issue in *Shaw*. When the Justice Department forced the state to create a second safe black congressional seat, the result was a long, exceedingly thin district that stretched approximately 160 miles along an interstate highway. As Justice O'Connor wrote in *Shaw*, the district wound "in snake-like fashion through tobacco country, financial centers, and manufacturing areas 'until it gobble[d] in enough enclaves of black neighborhoods.'" "If you drove down the interstate with both car doors open," one state legislator quipped, "you'd kill most of the people in the district." This seemingly ridiculous situation actually raised serious issues, deeply troubling to a number of commentators generally sympathetic to affirmative action. Stuart Taylor, Jr., a widely respected writer on legal affairs, was among them. The redistricting process has been transformed into a "race-driven spoils system more likely to aggravate than to heal [racial] divisions," Taylor wrote not long after the decision in *Shaw*.

That was not how the civil rights community saw the decisions. The Supreme Court had suddenly threatened black gains. Race-conscious districting had substantially increased the size of the Congressional Black Caucus (and added black members to state legislatures and other governing bodies as well). The number of African Americans in Congress increased from twenty-six in 1990 to thirty-nine in 1993, with almost half (seventeen) elected from the South. What would happen now?

In the Back of a Taxicab

The answer was perfectly clear, in the view of Theodore Shaw of the NAACP Legal Defense and Education Fund. If plaintiffs won in these constitutional cases, he had predicted, the minority members of Congress "could meet in the back seat of a taxicab." It became an oft-repeated image. Laughlin McDonald, an Atlanta-based voting rights specialist for the ACLU, described a Supreme Court "determined to dismantle the structure of civil rights in this country," the result of which would be "a return to the days of all-white government." "Ethnic cleansing," Jesse Jackson called the decisions. The Supreme Court's constitutional rulings "really torch the fundamental right of African-Americans, Hispanics and others to be included as participatory citizens in this democracy," Elaine Jones, director of the NAACP Legal Defense and Education Fund, said. Voting rights scholar Pamela Karlan worried that with decisions like *Shaw*, "the Voting Rights Act may be finished."

Civil rights pessimism—the belief that racism remained pervasive and undiminished—had blinded voting rights advocates to a changed America. In the wake of the 1996 congressional elections, it will take a mighty big back seat of a taxicab to hold the Congressional Black Caucus; in fact, its members would fill a bus. The 104th Congress, elected in 1994, had thirty-eight black members in the House; the 105th has thirty-seven. Louisiana representative Cleo Fields decided not to run after his district was redrawn (following the Court's decision in *Hays*), and Connecticut representative Gary Franks, a Republican, was defeated. But in Indiana, Julia Carson ran in the 69 percent white tenth district and won with 53 percent of the vote.

In short, every member of the Congressional Black Caucus whose constituency had become majority-white in the postlitigation round of districting and who nevertheless chose to run was reelected. In Georgia, Cynthia McKinney whose very liberal politics might have been expected to disqualify her in the South, won with 58 percent of the vote in a district only 35 percent black, although two years earlier she had said that black officeholders faced "the same level of extinction" as they did during Reconstruction. Her Georgia colleague Sanford Bishop also had a constituency only 35 percent black and was elected with 54 percent of the vote. In Florida, Representative Corinne Brown won with 61 percent of the vote in a newly drawn district only 42 percent African-American. The story in Texas was much the same, although the districts were Hispanic as well as white and (minority) black. These victorious candidates—African-American members of Congress who won where they couldn't possibly win—attributed their success to the power of incumbency. But prior to the election, none had mentioned incumbency as an advantage, and indeed they were not incumbents in the redrawn districts in which they were forced to run. The constituencies that sent them back to the House were those that had been (allegedly) "ethnically cleansed."

With the Republican ascendancy in 1994, no group in Congress was more politically marginalized than the Congressional Black Caucus, whose members tend to hover at the left end of the political spectrum. [Earlier,] we suggested that congressional districts that were deliberately drawn to be overwhelmingly black invited the sort of ideological militance that became the model for the black legislative candidate. In contrast to the more heavily white cities in which blacks have been elected mayors, these districts beckoned candidates with racially strident voices. If true, then settings in which candidates are forced to forge biracial coalitions will send representatives to Congress who are more centrist—and thus less politically marginalized.

There is a related point. With fewer majority-black districts and a greater number in which African Americans are the swing vote, the likelihood is *more* black representation—defined, that is, as Democrats (black and white) closely allied with the civil rights community. Race-driven districting, especially in the South, benefited the Republican Party. The concentration of black voters in black districts further "whitened" those that were already majority-white, and overwhelmingly white districts were just what Republican candidates liked. The point has frequently been made with respect to the roughly fifteen seats the GOP picked up in Congress as a consequence of the racial redistricting after 1990; the process was apparent at the local and state level well before that. Thus, in Jefferson County, Alabama, an out-of-court settlement in 1985 replaced an at-large system (under which only whites had been elected) with five single-member districts. Two safe black seats were created, leaving three that were equally safely white—and Republican. Unless unopposed, Democrats could not win in districts drained of black voters, and in 1986 two Democratic incumbents lost.

The civil rights community wanted an absolute guarantee of black officeholding, and politicians, whatever their color, like safe districts in which to run. But the price black voters paid for the race-driven districting (to which the NAACP and the GOP were equally committed) has arguably been high. And thus the Supreme Court's constitutional decisions, reducing the number of majority-black districts, may well have been a political gift to black voters—as some black legislators have acknowledged. "As an African-American," Georgia state representative Calvin Smyre said in 1995, "I want as much black representation in the U.S. Congress as possible. But at the same time, what have we gained? We gained a large Congressional Black Caucus, but we lost all the chairmanships and the subcommittee chairmanships, where the power really lies."

RELUCTANT SWIMMERS IN THE BIRACIAL WATERS

The 1996 congressional elections did not return those chairmanships to black Democrats (Republicans still controlled both houses), but they did send back to the House every black Democratic incumbent who ran. How could civil rights spokesmen have been so mistaken in their dire preelection predictions? In part, they had their eyes glued to the wrong history. Reviewing the debate over white willingness to vote for black candidates, Steven A. Holmes of the *New York Times* noted the skepticism of "traditional civil rights advocates and others on the left." In the early 1970s, they said, 2 percent of majority-white legislative districts in the eleven states of the old Confederacy were represented by black lawmakers; in the 1980s, the figure dropped to 1 percent. But to judge the potential in 1996 by the record in the 1970s and 1980s is to miss the story of enormous change in white racial attitudes, one result of which has been the rise of a black political class many of whose members owe their positions to white support. Between 1967 and 1993 blacks won the mayor's seat in eighty-seven cities with a population of 50,000 or more. In two-thirds of those cities blacks were a minority of the population.

The mayor's office may be more accessible than a congressional seat. Congressional campaigns are hard to launch. The districts are not only large; unlike cities, which usually have only one major newspaper, they contain within them several media markets and many of their residents are often widely dispersed. Get-out-the-vote efforts are thus usually more difficult than in cities even such as New York, whose black poor (prone to low voter turnout) are residentially concentrated. In addition, the distance between city council seat and mayor's office is shorter than from, say, state legislature to Congress. City councils are usually small, and name recognition—an essential ingredient in a successful campaign—is easily achieved. On the other hand, the state representative who has been elected from a constituency of, say, 25,000, is hardly known in a congressional district more than twenty times as large. Are congressional contests, then, exactly like a mayor's race? No. But is the record of black mayoral success relevant? Yes—as the 1996 House returns confirmed.

Successful black candidates for Congress who run in majority-white constituencies must run the centrist campaigns that characterize most municipal elections, however. . . . [M]ost black contenders cannot hope to win if their platform is significantly to the left of the white voters whose support they need. It's a race-blind rule: white candidates also lose if their views are out of sync with those of the voters. David Bositis, a senior fellow at the Joint Center for Political and Economic Studies, and others have nevertheless complained that the burden on blacks is especially heavy. "Why is it there are white leaders who can represent extreme positions within the white community and that's O.K.?" he has asked. "Why is it that black officials have to move to the center?"

The answer should be obvious: they wouldn't have to move to the center if that is where they started out. The center is where the majority of voters are—most of whom are white. And the center is also where the majority of white candidates feel at home, which means they need do no political traveling. To say that the doors of political opportunity are generally open is not to argue that they are open to black candidates with any and all political convictions. Colin Powell can win the presidency, the polling data suggest; Jesse Jackson cannot.

The number of black legislators in Congress and elsewhere will remain limited if African-American candidates are not willing to wade into the biracial waters—to run in majority-white constituencies and put together biracial coalitions. In 1996 a number of black incumbents ran in majority-white districts newly drawn as a consequence of Supreme Court decisions, but prior to that election, few black candidates were ready to do so. Representatives Julia Carson (D-Ind.), Gary Franks (R-Conn.), J. C. Watts (R-Okla.), Ron Dellums (D-Calif.): they have been part of a very small group of African Americans elected to Congress in majority-white settings.

Black candidates cannot win elections in which they do not run. And social scientists who calculate the odds of winning in a majority-white constituency cannot assess contests in which there has been no black candidate in the race. The scholarly literature on voting rights is littered with such statements as "The state's history demonstrates no evidence for the election of African Americans to the state legislature or the U.S. House of Representatives other than in majority-minority districts." But the authors of such statements (often quoted by the civil rights community) are reviewing a history in which potential black candidates, even in recent years, have stayed on the political sidelines.

In fact, had Cynthia McKinney read the scholarly literature and listened to the voices of civil rights activists, she would have known she could not possibly win in a 65 percent majority-white district in Georgia. It's an oddly discouraging line for civil rights advocates to peddle. They have been telling potential candidates, in effect, don't bother to run; it's hopeless. And to black voters they say: don't bother to vote unless you can cast your ballots in a majority-black setting; where whites are a majority, you waste your time.

Even after the successes of the 1996 elections, the drumbeat of self-defeating pessimism persisted. On December 9, 1996 black voters from Georgia, represented by the ACLU and Department of Justice, returned to the Supreme Court where they urged a restoration of one of the two discarded majority-black districts. In winning handily in majority-white constituencies in that Deep South state, Cynthia McKinney and Sanford Bishop had made history; in insisting that they were still in need of electoral arrangements that protected black candidates from white competition, McKinney and Bishop were (in effect) asking the Court to ignore those significant victories. They had remained reluctant swimmers in the biracial waters that just a month earlier had proven so hospitable to them.

THE REAL ISSUES

In voting rights cases the argument between plaintiffs and defendants occurs on two levels, the second often largely hidden from sight. In plain view are disputes over such legal matters as the meaning of "retrogression," the relationship between preclearance and Section 2, and the demands of "strict scrutiny," as well as a medley of technical and normative questions. For instance: the proper benchmark by which to judge the level of black representation; whether white officeholders elected with black support qualify as black "representatives"; how to discern when minority voters have cohesive group interests different than those of whites; whether white support for black mayoral candidates is telling when the case involves city council elections.

Beneath the surface of the fancy legal and social science footwork, however, are the real questions that courts are implicitly asked to address in these minority voting rights cases—questions that go to the heart of how we see ourselves as a multiracial, multiethnic nation. At issue between the opposing sides in these cases are quite different views of American society, the place of blacks in it, its openness to change, and the costs of race-conscious policies. These are, of course, the central questions that run through all debates on affirmative action; in voting rights cases, they are but variations on a common theme.

The assumptions that inform opposing positions are thus familiar and predictable. In [Barnett v. City of Chicago], for instance, the plaintiffs' experts looked only at the racially contested elections for the city council, a decision challenged by attorneys for the city who argued that blacks were electing a candidate of their choice when they cast their ballots for the winner in a white-on-white contest. Plaintiffs assumed that whites were never the true "choice" of blacks; race was the characteristic that counted. White politicians were just as culturally at odds with black voters as white teachers were with black students. It was the two-nations view that permeates much civil rights writing—a view with which the city disagreed.

The belief that blacks and whites are different, that whites are not to be trusted on racial matters, and that historic discrimination continues to affect the status of blacks are the assumptions that run through almost all briefs for affirmative action. Those of voting rights advocates are no exception. What might appear to be strong evidence of white racial tolerance under particular circumstances (white support for Virginia gubernatorial candidate Douglas Wilder, for instance) is thus described as aberrational—nothing blacks can ever count on. Moreover, in those exceptional races in which blacks do win in majority-white settings (the argument runs), those elected officeholders are not truly "black." As one scholar has put it, "black leadership of white majorities is not properly speaking to be regarded as black politics."

In the Chicago case black voters lacked a "realistic opportunity" to elect the candidates of their choice in those wards in which there was not a "sufficient" black population—i.e., where blacks were not a substantial majority and thus protected from (racist) whites. That was particularly the case because "the depressed socioeconomic status of African Americans in Chicago" hindered their ability "to participate equally in the political process." Hence the plaintiffs' demand that the city be carved into wards giving blacks a maximum number of safe city council seats; anything less, it was assumed, would diminish the representation of a group for whom members of no other groups could speak. Again, these were convictions fundamentally at odds with the view of the city's lawyers. Plaintiffs had referred obliquely to the "depressed socio-economic status" of blacks as "related to the effects of past discrimination," while the city saw poverty, crime, and single-parent households as problems with multiple and complex causes. In addition, the defendants believed not only that many whites had shown themselves ready to vote for Mayor Harold Washington and other black candidates, but that (most importantly) individuals, not racial groups, had distinctive voices. Blacks could thus represent whites—and whites blacks.

This last point raised another basic issue. Plaintiffs in *Barnett* argued that blacks on Chicago's south and west sides shared "communities of interest." And, by implication, "communities" did not contain both whites and blacks. But the city's blacks seemed to have a more complicated view. Thus, in the fall of 1995, black middle-class residents on the south side were openly hostile to planned low-rise public housing in the area—to an influx of residents with the same skin color but different incomes. A few years earlier, middle-class blacks and whites had been allied in an effort to keep poor blacks out of their school attendance zone, and thus out of the neighborhood school. In fact, one of the plaintiffs' experts, arguing that race could be used as a proxy for socioeconomic interests, ignored his own scholarship indicating that class, not race, defined a "community."

Whether blacks across socioeconomic lines have distinctive interests and views, whether individuals are defined by the racial groups to which they belong, and whether white racism remains as virulent as ever: these are issues that usually hover between the lines in briefs and judicial decisions. But they did make an explicit appearance in *Shaw* and the subsequent constitutional cases in which the legitimacy of classifying citizens by race was the central question. "Racial classifications of any sort pose the risk of lasting harm to our society," Justice O'Connor said (writing for the Court) in *Shaw v. Reno*. "They reinforce the belief, held by too many for too much of our history, that individuals should be judged by the color of their skin." Race-conscious districts, she argued, carry a special risk. They "may balkanize us into competing racial factions . . . [and thus] carry us further from the goal of a political system in which race no long matters."

That was the central message that ran from *Shaw* through *Bush* [*v. Vera*] and *Miller* [*v. Johnson*]. "All citizens are stigmatized by the notion that their 'interests' can be defined by race or will be represented adequately only if a member of their racial 'group' holds a particular office," the district court in the Louisiana districting case concluded. It was, of course, true as well of the segregated institutions of the Jim Crow South. Blacks and whites were both harmed when drinking fountains carried WHITE and COLORED signs.

Racial classifications deliver the message that skin color matters—profoundly. They suggest that whites and blacks are not the same, that race and ethnicity are the qualities that really matter. They imply that individuals are defined by blood—not by character, social class, religious sentiments, age, or education. But categories appropriate to a caste system are a poor basis on which to build that community of equal citizens upon which democratic government depends. Equal citizens are free to define themselves, and do so differently in different contexts. A voter whose choice of a candidate in a presidential primary is shaped by racial considerations might react to the issues in a school board contest as parents of other races do. It is precisely that fluidity of individual political identity that prevents the formation of castes, which are rigid and hierarchical by nature.

By no demographic or other measures are African Americans truly a people apart. . . . And yet if both they and whites believe they are, it may well become true. This is especially the case if that perception informs the law. Separate admissions procedures for whites and minorities, separate hiring processes, separate legislative districts: when given a stamp of approval by Congress and the courts, they paint an official, influential, and ultimately dangerous portrait of American society.

We have been, from colonial days to the present, a nation of immigrants. The nature of immigration has always shaped politics, and immigration itself inevitably has at various times in our history been a major political issue as the haves attempt to exclude the have-nots. The ethnically diverse immigrant groups assimilated in the melting pot became Americans who viewed "foreigners" with suspicion. The following selection points out, however, that the rhetoric of restrictive immigration is less than the reality.

Peter H. Schuck has taught law at Yale University and New York Law School, and he has served as Assistant Secretary for Policy and Planning at the Department of Health, Education, and Welfare. Shuck argues:

1. American immigration policy is more open and less biased than at any time in the past, despite loud cries calling for more stringent restrictions.

2. Americans are neither blindly pro-immigration nor knee-jerk xenophobes. American attitudes toward immigration, and toward America's immigrant legacy, are more nuanced.
3. Recent legislation has reflected realistic attitudes and approaches toward immigration.

40

Peter H. Schuck

THE OPEN SOCIETY

★★★

To hear many immigration advocates tell it, Americans in the 1990s have slammed the golden door shut in a fit of xenophobic hysteria, bolting it against newcomers and expelling lots of law-abiding, long-resident aliens. Pro-immigrant academics have just published a book ominously titled *Immigrants Out!: The New Nativism and the Anti-Immigrant Impulse in the United States*. Ethnic advocacy groups like the Mexican American Legal Defense and Education Fund depict U.S. immigration policy as nativist and brutal. Amnesty International lumps an attack on American policies together with its critique of dictatorships. Hardly a week goes by without a genuinely heart-rending column by Anthony Lewis of *The New York Times* about the pending deportation of an immigrant who committed some minor crime in his youth.

Is this an accurate picture? Restrictionists have certainly beaten the drums lately. California voters passed Proposition 187 in 1994, and Pat Buchanan campaigned on a nativist platform in 1996. Some recent changes in immigration law do pose real threats to the procedural rights of foreign-born persons in the United States. What's more, federal immigration policies often seem self-contradictory. Congress has amnestied millions of illegal aliens, but it has also enlarged the Border Patrol to the point where it is now the government's largest domestic uniformed service. Congress regularly bashes the Immigration and Naturalization Service's incompetence, but it has doubled the agency's budget over the last four years.

The larger truth is that, even after the recent changes by Congress, American immigration policy is more generous, less racist, and (if we are careful) more politically sustainable than ever before. In 1996, the same year Congress made it easier to deport illegal aliens quickly and without court review and ended public benefits for many legal immigrants, it also admitted a cohort of 916,000 legal immigrants that was the largest and most ethnically diverse since 1914. This at a time when Europe accepts few immigrants and even fewer nonwhites (except refugees). Congress also refused to lower future quotas and facilitated the legalization of over 400,000 currently undocumented aliens. (By contrast, the United States admitted 300,000 immigrants in 1965, the great bulk of them European or Canadian whites.)

How can this be when recent immigration trends have presented restrictionists with explosive political ammunition? The vast majority of today's legal immigrants are nonwhite and non-English-speaking; many come here with few job skills. Their presence makes bilingual education a major curricular and fiscal battleground and sharpens the affirmative action debate as newcomers who never suffered discrimination in the U.S. compete for preferences with the descendants of African Americans who were slaves. Immigration probably accounts for a significant share of the wider wage gap between high- and low-skill workers, especially blacks. The illegal alien population is already at record levels and grows by a quarter of a million each year. Federal indictments allege the falsification of over 13,000 naturalization exams. The General Accounting Office reports that taxpayers bear significant costs because U.S.-born children of illegal aliens are automatic citizens entitled to welfare benefits.

Yet, while Americans are frequently depicted as anti-immigrant, they actually hold nuanced views. Most people want to admit fewer immigrants, oppose illegal immigration, and don't want immigrants to receive bilingual education, affirmative action, or welfare. (As it happens, most immigrants hold similar views.) But, at the same time, Americans also treasure this country's ethnic diversity and immigrant tradition (which means honoring our own ancestors). Generally, Americans admire the immigrants they know personally.

In policy terms, this means that Americans will tolerate relatively high levels of immigration, and even increases in certain categories, as long as they are satisfied that newcomers pay their own way, don't get special breaks, and obey the law. And the policies enacted by the Congress in 1996 and 1997 are largely consistent with this. Congress has tempered the high annual quota of legal immigrants set in the liberal 1990 immigration law with strong measures to exclude illegal aliens, deport criminals, reduce aliens' access to welfare, and limit their procedural rights. This is a hard balance to strike, and there have been some harsh, unjust, and downright foolish excesses. But it's absurd to speak of "a new nativism."

The most extreme of the new laws is the Anti-Terrorism and Effective Death Penalty Act of 1996 (AEDPA), which was passed in reaction to the Oklahoma City bombing. It mandated swift detention and removal of criminal and illegal aliens and secret deportation tribunals for those who could be linked, perhaps tenuously, to foreign terrorist groups. It also cut back traditional hardship waivers and appeal rights for certain categories of aliens and made many of these changes retroactive.

Yet even these often arbitrary provisions do not violate the basic American consensus on immigration. They were anti-criminal in both intent and implementation, not anti-immigrant. They did not aim at legal aliens other than convicted felons and suspected terrorists.

The same is true of welfare reform. Although it made legal aliens ineligible for public assistance, it also cut off millions of *citizens*. Many voters objected to benefits for aliens not out of anti-immigrant animus but because immigrants arrived under the explicit proviso that they have jobs or citizen sponsors. It is not nativist or anti-immigrant to believe that poor citizens have a stronger claim to shrinking resources than immigrants who have been admitted on the condition that they not become "public charges." Though some immigration advocates will never be satisfied with it, the fact is that the savings generated by this compromise helped preserve benefits for destitute U.S. citizens.

Even so, Congress and the Clinton administration recently restored many of the lost benefits to those who had been eligible in 1996 and to the newly disabled, and Clinton vows to restore Food Stamps to immigrant families with children. Meanwhile, high-immigration states have filled some of the remaining gap with their own funds. These changes refute those who claimed that immigrants are so politically friendless that the states, in a headlong "race to the bottom," would cut immigrants' benefits even more in an effort to force them out the door.

This brings us to the 1996 Illegal Immigration Reform and Immigrant Responsibility Act (IIRIRA). Here, the critics of the new laws are on firmer ground. Passed by Congress and signed by President Clinton just before the November 1996 election, IIRIRA is the most radical reform of immigration law in decades—or perhaps ever. It thoroughly revamps the enforcement process and extends AEDPA in ways that even many INS officials find arbitrary, unfair, and unadministrable. For example, it requires the INS to exclude aliens at the border summarily and without judicial review if they seem to lack proper documentation. This gives the lowliest inspector broad discretion, and practically final say, over such life-and-death issues as whether an asylum claimant faces persecution back home. (Since the INS had recently instituted reforms in the asylum process, this hasty change may have been unnecessary as well as unwise.)

IIRIRA bars the INS from granting discretionary relief from deportation to many aliens, even for compelling humanitarian reasons, as the previous law permitted. It mandates detention of many removable aliens—perhaps forever if they come from a country, like Vietnam, that won't take them back. It equates the rights of aliens who entered illegally and live in the U.S. with those of aliens with no ties here. It limits the rights of illegal aliens to reenter legally. It further expands the category of "aggravated felon" aliens who can be deported summarily even if they have been long-term residents of the country. And it bars judicial review of INS administrative decisions to deport them. (The definition of "aggravated felony" was expanded to include even fare-beating on the New York subway system).

To be sure, Congress was properly concerned about the endless procedural delays illegal aliens (or their lawyers) have employed to prolong their stays while they work and search for a way to remain permanently. But fair, accurate adjudication, backstopped by access to the federal courts for those at risk of deportation, is essential not only to aliens but also to the many Americans with strong family, employment, religious, and social ties to them. These high stakes, along with a long history of INS lawlessness and incompetence, make judicially protected due process all the more necessary.

Indeed, the Constitution demands it, providing that the "Great Writ" of habeas corpus may not be suspended except in national emergencies. Congress has also protected this right statutorily since 1789, and aliens have long used it to challenge the legality of detentions and deportations: Federal courts have so far interpreted IIRIRA narrowly to maintain judicial review for aliens in INS custody; otherwise, the law would be unconstitutional. (No relevant IIRIRA or AEDPA case has yet reached the Supreme Court.) Ironically, IIRIRA may increase courts' intrusion as they seek to control more of the frequent INS abuses that the new law encourages.

Still, IIRIRA's excesses should not obscure a fundamental fact about immigration politics: challenges to the high legal-immigration levels set in the 1990 law, such as a proposal by a national commission to reduce them by more than a third, have all failed. Tough on illegals and criminals, and arbitrary toward asylum-seekers and deportation hardship cases, IIRIRA's only serious effect on law-abiding immigrants was to raise sponsors' income requirements.

Perhaps the best evidence of the strength of today's pro-immigration consensus lies in Congress's treatment of *illegals*. Last fall, Congress granted a new amnesty, modeled on the 1986 provision that legalized some 2.7 million undocumented aliens (mostly Mexicans). The new law will protect almost half a million Central Americans who are now in legal limbo. (If President Clinton has his way, thousands of Haitians will soon join them.) It also grandfathered in still other deportable aliens under a now-lapsed rule allowing them to gain permanent residence simply by paying a $1,000 fee and filing for their green cards in the United States.

Even convicted *criminal* aliens enjoy a perverse kind of protection. They manage to remain in the U.S. in large numbers—even when they are already under lock and key and thus should be easy to deport. Though aliens in general are apparently less crime-prone than citizens, the criminal alien population has nevertheless soared. In 1980, fewer than 1,000 federal inmates were foreign-born, 3.6 percent of the total. By 1996, that number had grown to almost 31,000 (29 percent of the total). The foreign-born population in state prisons has risen from 8,000 in 1980 (2.6 percent) to 77,000 (7.6 percent) in 1996. Nationwide, 300,000 or more deportable criminal aliens are in custody or under other legal supervision, at an estimated cost of $6 billion a year. Despite a high-priority INS effort, only 50,000 of these criminals—fewer than 15 percent of the total—were shipped home last year. The real scandal is that this is actually a major *improvement* in the INS's performance.

The pro-legal-immigration consensus that has produced these policies seems likely to endure even if the economy falters. In addition to the continuing strength of the lobbying coalition—made up of ethnic organizations, business, human rights groups, and big agriculture—that helped pass the 1990 law, perhaps the most important reason for this is the split within the Republican Party. In 1994, the Republicans displayed little interest in a balanced approach to immigration. That year, Pete Wilson, the Republican governor of California, had made Prop 187, which proposed to bar illegal aliens from public schools and other state-funded social services, a central motif of his successful reelection bid—and of what was then a prospective presidential run. Although Prop 187 was aimed at illegal aliens, not legal ones, its proponents' coded language (illegals "flooding" the state) helped blur the distinction. Prop 187 was supported not only by a majority of white, black, and Asian voters but, also by many Latinos who resented having to compete with illegals for jobs, housing, and public services. Politicians in other states, emboldened by Prop 187's success, jumped on the bandwagon. On the Hill, Republican Representative Lamar Smith of Texas, the chairman of the House immigration subcommittee, held hearings on proposals to cut back on admissions and even end birthright citizenship for the U.S.-born children of illegal aliens.

In hindsight, however, the passage of Prop 187 was the high-water mark of restrictionism. Similar proposals got nowhere in other states. (Even in California, a federal court promptly blocked Prop 187's implementation, and it remains a dead letter.) Leading Republican politicians realized that, while it is good politics to attack undocumented and criminal aliens, it is politically costly to cut back on legal immigrants who enrich the economy or to deny them public benefits that their taxes support. Cheered on by *The Wall Street Journal* editorial page, Newt Gingrich, Dick Armey, Jack Kemp, William Bennett, William Kristol, and other party strategists argue that restrictionism violated party principles of free markets, economic growth, entrepreneurialism, and social optimism. In contrast to Wilson, Governor George W. Bush praises Texas's many immigrants as economic assets. The Republican chairman of the Senate immigration subcommittee, Spencer Abraham, is now seeking to increase the quota for high-skill immigrants, as is House subcommittee chairman Smith.

These Republicans understand that many legal immigrants will soon become voters and that their friends and relatives already are. They know that in Los Angeles, New York, and other big cities successful Republican politicians are appealing to first- and second-generation Asians and Hispanics. The social conservatism, upward mobility, and entrepreneurial spirit of many immigrants may make them natural Republican voters in the future. Many of the party's corporate allies, especially high-tech companies that depend on skilled foreign-born workers, are pressing Congress to admit more of them.

This feisty Republican debate augurs well for the high-immigration status quo. As the majority party in Congress, the Republican Party is the arena in which American ambivalences over immigration policy are being debated and politically resolved. The results have been good, bad, and sometimes ugly. But even liberal groups exhibit this ambivalence, as evidenced by the fight within the Sierra Club and labor unions over whether or not to support restriction. For advocates of moderate legal immigration expansion (I am one), the best way to sustain the pro-immigration consensus is not to idealize all immigrants as ethnic Horatio Algers but to attend to legitimate concerns about criminal and undocumented aliens, naturalization fraud, welfare abuse, bilingual education, affirmative action, and unfair competition for low-income domestic workers. We should decry the new laws' excesses while celebrating Americans' openness to self-supporting, law-abiding newcomers. And we should stop crying wolf about nativism.

As the millennium approaches, immigration politics differs from politics of the past. Ethnic political bosses in urban areas used to take care of the welfare needs of new immigrants. Public education in most areas was only beginning in the nineteenth century—now it is pervasive. The New Deal created a national welfare state, followed by state governmental welfare systems. Immigration costs the public in dollars and cents far more than in the past.

Ironically, as the following reading points out, economic benefits also flow from immigration as both service workers and highly skilled immigrants come to our shores. Through the hue and cry of immigration politics, a tolerant society continues to accept and assimilate immigrants.

Nathan Glazer is a sociologist whose works include *The Lonely Crowd,* with David Reisman (1950), and *Beyond the Melting Pot,* with Daniel Patrick Moynihan (1963). Glazer is co-editor of *The Public Interest,* and he is one of the nation's foremost writers on issues of race and culture.

Glazer's main points in the following article are:

1. The United States has a long history of anti-immigrant sentiment.
2. America is now more reliant on the welfare state, more tolerant, and less optimistic about its future than at previous periods in its history.
3. Current immigration seems to hurt the job prospects of low-income blacks. Other aspects of the current wave of immigration benefit the country in many ways.

41

Nathan Glazer

THE DEBATE ON ALIENS FLARES BEYOND THE MELTING POT

★★★

The immigration debate is becoming more and more agitated.

We have now seen the passage of Proposition 187 in California, depriving illegal immigrants of public benefits and the passage in the House of Representatives of welfare reform measures that would deprive legal immigrants of some benefits.

Peter Brimelow's *Alien Nation: Common Sense About America's Immigration Disaster* raises sharply for public debate the issue of the racial and ethnic character of current immigration, until now discussed only privately, if at all. [The] deadly bombing in Oklahoma City, too, focused attention on Middle Eastern immigrants and their political activities, though the guilt turned out to lie elsewhere.

Undoubtedly, our immigration laws will be undergoing serious revisions again. The atmosphere of the debate will be less benign and less constrained than in the 1980s.

But why? Haven't we been through all this before? Haven't we had anti-immigration movements every few decades or so, since the founding of the Republic, and didn't we decide, with the immigration reform of 1965, that this is, and should be, a country of immigration, open to the world without restrictions of origin, race or ethnicity? Yes, but it is also true that every time anti-immigration sentiment rises, there is something new as well as much in the way of prejudice, ethnocentrism and racism that is old.

WHAT'S TO FEAR?

It is true that Irish Catholics were looked upon as unassimilable 150 years ago, Jews and Italians and Slavic peoples were considered so in the 1910s and all are now indistinguishable in their integration into a common American society and culture from the oldest settlers. What then do we have to fear from an immigration that is indeed 90 percent or more non-European, but of peoples no more different or foreign in culture, language, religion or hopes than earlier streams of immigrants?

MAKING OF AN AMERICAN

A number of things are different today from what they were in the 1920s and even the 1960s. We have already seen one in the debate—on Proposition 187 and in the House welfare reforms: We are now more of a welfare state, to the degree that people ask whether we should be supporting new immigrants, to what extent and at what cost to public budgets. Public education is more expensive than it once was, and now includes subsidized community colleges. Health care is much more expensive, and much of it is supported through public funds.

We discover to our dismay that many elderly immigrants are now on Supplemental Security Income, a program adopted at a time of low immigration and intended for those native elderly poor who had not accumulated sufficient credit for Social Security. It now serves as an income supplement for many parents of immigrants, enabled to enter through family reunification provisions of our immigration laws and who could well be supported by their children—and indeed would have been in their home countries. But this seems to be the only area in which welfare use by immigrants is exceptional. Most are working and contributing to taxes and to the Social Security fund.

A second thing that is different: We are a much more tolerant country. Ironically, that leads us to worry more about whether immigrants will assimilate. We now protect in law more than we once did differences in language and culture, and provide in most states for education of children for a period of time in their home language, and for services in the language of those who apply for them. What does this do for assimilation, for the making of Americans, which has always been part of our American view of immigration? We don't know.

Very likely the attractions of American culture, the usefulness of English, the benefits of citizenship (in particular now its protection from some of the legislation reducing benefits to immigrants!), will mean that assimilation, overall, proceeds at a rate not very different from in the past. But it will not be assisted by strong measures of "Americanization," as we once called them (remember "I am an American Day"); those are now much out of fashion. Did they help assimilate immigrants? Probably yes. Whatever their effect, we won't have them.

A third difference, and this is harder to put one's finger on: We are a society less optimistic about our future, although there were comparable periods of angst before. We don't think we have any more wide open spaces to settle, however underpopulated we are compared to Asia. We have a powerful environmental movement now. If the Zero Population Growth movement is not as prominent as it was a decade or two ago, how many Americans think 250 million are too few, and that adding 10 million more a decade through immigration, as far as the eye can see, is a good idea?

HUE AND CRY

Yet a fourth factor: There is our own home-grown racial problem, shamefully neglected in the ages of mass European immigration. It has been a priority of national policy now for 30 years, and we are far from overcoming it. Even if the economists can't agree that immigration hurts the job prospects of low-income blacks, common observation suggests strongly that it does. One thing that might be done immediately, however the affirmative action debate comes out, is to remove immigrants from affirmative action protection. They have, like all people in the United States, protection against discrimination through civil rights laws. Affirmative action was intended for our own native racial problem, not for immigrants, who now make up a large share of those entitled to its benefits.

Having said that, there are also aspects of current immigration that are beneficial in ways the older European immigration was not—in the large number of highly skilled doctors, engineers, computer specialists and others who find employment easily in the United States; in the availability of immigrant service workers, which permits highly educated women to work outside the home; in the rejuvenation of half-abandoned inner-city urban areas.

The balance sheet is difficult to draw up. Some restriction, particularly in the family reunification categories that now have preference, seems like a good idea. But a weighing of the costs and benefits does not come down sharply and self-evidently on one side or the other. And however it comes out, it will be driven by sentiments hardly affected by balance sheets. In the hysteria over anarchism and Bolshevism in the wake of World War I—there were mysterious bombings then, too—thousands of East European immigrants were summarily deported. In the current debate, we will all have to keep our heads and remember we all came from someplace else.

The following reading points out that Indians have always occupied a unique place in American culture and politics. Important political issues, such as civil rights, concern Indians as individuals. But Indians are also members of tribal governments, the leaders of which strive to maintain and expand their power. The national government continues to face the difficult task of balancing Indian civil and tribal rights.

W. Richard West is a museum director, a member of the Cheyenne and Arapaho Tribes, and an active participant in Native American issues. Kevin Gover is a member of the Pawnee Tribe and has served as Assistant Secretary for Indian Affairs since 1997.

These are the authors' major points:

1. American Indians have been the subjects of discrimination. Unlike other groups, however, Indian peoples believe that their status as citizens of tribal governments entitles them to a variety of preferences and immunities.
2. Indian civil rights can be divided into two broad categories: civil rights as we usually understand them, and rights that relate to Indians as members of tribal polities, in many senses separate and distinct from the United States as an entity.
3. The Indian Civil Rights Act of 1968 illustrates how these differences can be impacted by federal law.
4. Indian treaty rights are not charity; they are, instead, compensation for cessions of vast tracts of Indian land.

42

W. Richard West, Jr. and Kevin Gover

THE STRUGGLE FOR INDIAN CIVIL RIGHTS

★★★

Like other ethnic minorities, American Indians have been subjected to discrimination by both governmental and private entities throughout the history of the United States. Unlike other minorities, however, Indian peoples' views of their rights under law extend beyond those expected by their fellow citizens, to include a wide range of preferences, immunities, and prerogatives that arise not from their status as a racial minority but, rather, from their status as citizens of tribal governments.

The civil rights of Indian people are best understood, therefore, by separating them into two broad categories. The first category deals with those matters that we ordinarily think of as civil rights: the right to be free from discrimination on the basis of race; the right to vote; the right to due process of law, freedom of speech and religion, etc. And in the case of Indian people, these rights concern not only constitutional limitations on the power of state and federal governments but also limitations on the power of tribal governments. The second broad category includes the rights and disabilities of Indians as members of tribal bodies politic. The United States has established legal preferences, immunities, and disabilities that run directly to individual Indians as well as rights and immunities that flow through the tribal government. In both cases, though, it is tribal citizenship that creates the right or immunity. . . .

As the civil rights movement gained strength, Indian-interest organizations became active participants. Indian demands were the same as those of other minorities in terms of the rights of citizenship. In another respect, however, they were fundamentally different. Indians asserted not only their constitutional rights as members of the American body politic but also their right to maintain distinct political and cultural communities. In short, Indians were asserting a right to be different.

They met with success on both fronts. This success is reflected in both the legislation and the judicial decisions of the sixties and early seventies. Indians routinely were made beneficiaries of civil rights legislation such as the Voting Rights Act, the Fair Housing Act, and the Equal Employment Opportunity Act. The Voting Rights Act, for example, not only prohibits discrimination against Indians but also creates special protections for them as persons whose primary language is not English.

Reflecting the fact that Indian rights go beyond those afforded to other citizens, however, special provisions were included in civil rights legislation. The Equal Employment Opportunity Act, for instance, excludes from its prohibition on discrimination programs granting employment preferences to Indians by employers on or near Indian reservations. On its face, this seems ripe for an attack on the grounds of reverse discrimination. In *Morton v. Mancari* (1974), however, the Supreme Court upheld a statute granting preference to Indians for employment in the Bureau of Indian Affairs and the Indian Health Service. The Court reasoned that the preference was not one based on race but, rather, one based on the unique political relationship between Indian nations and the United States. As a preference based on political status rather than race, it only needed to be "tied rationally" to the fulfillment of federal obligations to the Indians to be upheld as constitutional. It was not subject to the "strict scrutiny" applied to racial classifications under the Fifth Amendment.

The status of tribes as distinct political communities was recognized as well in much of the social legislation spawned by the civil rights movement. New Frontier and Great Society programs such as the Office of Economic Opportunity's Headstart and Community Action programs, the Elementary and Secondary Education Act, and the Comprehensive Older Americans Act all expressly included Indian tribes as governments eligible for participation.

The influence of these heady days of the civil rights movement on Indian tribes and people can hardly be overstated. Aside from placing the weight of the law on the tribes' side and providing economic resources to Indian communities, perhaps the most important aspect was a renewal of Indian confidence and pride. Termination had bred a certain timidity. If a tribe had even modest economic success, it became a candidate for termination. Termination could be avoided, however, if the tribe were poor and docile. The civil rights movement changed all of this. Indians came to learn that they could assert their rights successfully without fear of termination.

An interesting aspect of the combined civil rights movement and the rejuvenation of tribal self-government was the passage of the Indian Civil Rights Act of 1968. Because of their unique political status and the absence of any express limitations on their powers in the Constitution, Indian tribes were not subject to the same restrictions on governmental action as were federal and state governments. As tribal governments began to exercise their long-dormant powers, concern was raised that Indians were unprotected from arbitrary and harmful actions of tribal officials. Congress decided to look into the state of Indian civil rights.

Tribal leaders were not thrilled at the prospect of having their actions reviewed by federal tribunals. Many opposed the legislation on the grounds that it represented an attempt to impose non-Indian values on tribal societies. Others believed that the act would result in costly lawsuits against the tribes by antagonistic non-Indians and dissident tribal members with no genuine complaint. Such fears were well-founded, but Congress deemed unacceptable the existence of governmental bodies without legal restraints on their exercise of official power.

The result was the Indian Civil Rights Act. The act, in essence, requires tribal governments to afford to persons under its jurisdiction the civil rights guaranteed by the Constitution. Tribal concerns, however, were accommodated in several respects. The freedom of religion provision included the right of free exercise of religion but not the prohibition on the establishment of a state religion. A number of tribal governments are theocratic, and Congress protected these governments in the act. Another difference between the act and the Bill of Rights involves the right to counsel in criminal proceedings. By 1968 the Supreme Court required states and the federal government to pay for attorneys for indigent criminal defendants. Tribal budgets could not bear such an expense. Congress, therefore, provided that criminal defendants in tribal courts were entitled to counsel, but only at their own expense.

. . . Even as the general civil rights struggle was winding down, Indians were gearing up for an initiative that would take them beyond even the dramatic gains of the 1960s. Their rights as American citizens were firmly established, in law if not always in fact. The time now had come to assert their rights as tribal citizens, rights born of the tribes' status as domestic nations and confirmed by hundreds of treaties. Treaty rights and the right of tribal self-government would become the new focus of Indian efforts.

Perhaps the primary battleground in the field of treaty rights was a remote site on the Nisqually River in the state of Washington known as Frank's Landing. In the 1850s, the Treaty of Point Mott was signed by Indian nations in Washington Territory and approved by Congress. Among the treaty's provisions was a guarantee that Indians would retain the right of "taking fish at usual and accustomed grounds . . . in common with all citizens of the territory." The Indians exercised this right for one hundred years before non-Indians began to challenge their fishing activities. Despite a 1963 federal court decision sustaining the Indians' rights, state courts enjoined Indian net fishing. A series of protests followed in which Indian fishermen were arrested and jailed by state officials. Allegations of police brutality fell on deaf ears. Despite continuing success in federal court, the treaty fishermen were harassed, threatened and, in one case at least, shot by local non-Indian residents.

The Indians persisted until a dramatic court decision held that they were entitled to nearly 50 percent of the annual salmon harvest. The non-Indian citizenry was enraged, but the decision survived review after review until, in 1979, the Supreme Court itself affirmed the decision in all key respects. Against all odds, the Indians prevailed in protecting rights recognized over a century earlier, and established that treaty rights do not fade with time. The allocation of resources made in the treaties was ruled binding on the descendants of the treating parties, notwithstanding the different circumstances that now exist in Indian country and surrounding communities.

Rights more than a century old were being redeemed in the eastern United States as well. Attorneys for several eastern tribes, including tribes that long had been neglected by federal authorities, discovered a startling fact. Many treaties and other documents taking land from the eastern tribes never were ratified by Congress as was required by the Trade and Intercourse Acts of the eighteenth and nineteenth centuries. Under the plain language of the acts, such transactions were void and of no effect. These cases presented a critical test of America's commitment to the rule of law. Although some claims were nearly two hundred years old, ancient rules of law established for the benefit of Indian tribes, if followed, would result in court victories for the tribes. Despite intense political pressure from the affected states and their residents, the lower federal courts ruled favorably on the Indian claims in case after case. Although many of the claims were settled out of court by the parties (and the settlements approved by Congress), others remained in court until, in 1984, the Supreme Court agreed to hear a case involving title to 100,000 acres in New York state. Finally, in *County of Oneida v. Oneida Indian Nation* (1985), the Supreme Court upheld the Indian claims. Thus, wrongs committed almost two centuries ago still could be addressed by the courts and lost rights restored.

Tribal rights of self-government also were redeemed in the Indians' legal offensive. State power over reservation Indians was curtailed in the areas of taxation, civil court jurisdiction, and Indian child welfare proceedings. Tribal authority over non-Indians in Indian country, though denied in criminal proceedings, was affirmed in other areas. Despite significant defeats in court, the legal offensive generally was quite effective, and the governmental authority of Indian tribes, dormant for so long, was asserted broadly and effectively

Tribal rights of self-government were redeemed in the legislative arena as well. The termination policy was renounced formally through the restoration of the Menominee Tribe of Wisconsin in 1973 and several other tribes thereafter. The Indian Self-Determination Act of 1975 gave tribes the ability to administer federal assistance programs and wrest control of such programs from the government officials who had dominated reservation affairs for a century. The Indian Child Welfare Act of 1978 placed the welfare of Indian children squarely within tribal forums and limited state power in this critical area, state power that too often had resulted in Indian children being removed and isolated from their tribal communities. The American Indian Religious Freedom Act of 1979 recognized the validity of traditional Indian religious practices and pledged to honor and accommodate such practices.

All of these developments during the seventies and eighties resulted from the civil rights movement of the 1960s. Indians built on the progress made in the sixties to register these important legal victories in the seventies. In a very real sense, therefore, it was the civil rights movement that made these victories possible.

Still, the rights claimed by the Indians were different from those claimed by other minorities. The civil rights movement was responsible for the vindication of the rights of Indians as individuals. The vindication of tribal rights, however, could be accomplished only by the Indians themselves. Thus, while the tribal rights movement of the

1970s grew out of the general struggle for civil rights of the previous decade, the struggle for tribal rights was distinctively Indian because the rights claimed were distinctively Indian rights—rights held by no other people in the country. . . .

Indian treaty rights were not created by any act of generosity. They represent, instead, the quid pro quo for cessions of vast amounts of tribal land. The settlers who entered these lands did so on the basis of those treaties. The Indians have made no demand that those lands be returned or that the rights of non-Indians under the treaties be abrogated. Why Indians should be expected to give up their rights under the treaties is most difficult to understand. In the end, the backlash movement was troublesome and worrisome but did not score any major successes, at least in Congress.

One can say quite accurately that legally the American Indians of today are better off than at any time in the past century. Even so, much remains to be done. In its 1979 report on America's compliance with the human rights accords, the United States said that:

> Native Americans, on the average, have the lowest per capita income, the highest unemployment rate, the lowest level of educational attainment, the shortest lives, the worst health and housing conditions and the highest suicide rate in the United States. The poverty among Indian families is nearly three times greater than the rate for non-Indian families and Native people collectively rank at the bottom of every social and economic statistical indicator.

This is the legacy of past failures to honor the rights of Indian people, both as human beings and as members of distinct tribal political communities. America's treatment of Indians, even more than its treatment of other minorities, reflects the rise and fall of its democratic faith. The central issue remains the same. Whether future generations will honor the special rights of Indians acknowledged by past generations remains an open question and a challenge for all Americans.

This selection examines the conflicts that arise between groups as they compete for power and position in the American system. Peter Skerry, following the ideas of sociologist Robet Park, argues that competition and conflict between groups is an inevitable element of American democracy. Such competition has characterized group interactions in the United States for many years, and often reaches its most tense moments just as groups are making their greatest strides. Skerry points out that a commitment to diversity carries with it the demand that we have some tolerance for contention and even for controversy. The selection is an opinion piece written for the *Los Angeles Times* during a contentious state senate race in California, but the author's point is relevant to group relations throughout the country.

Peter Skerry teaches Political Science at Claremont McKenna College, and is a Non-resident Senior Fellow at The Brookings Institution.

Skerry's major points are:

1. Americans today tend to retreat from conflicts between groups. When forced to confront such conflicts, they are usually attributed to irrational prejudice and bigotry.
2. Not all conflict is unjust or avoidable, and not all group conflict is driven by racism. Often, group conflict is driven by "rational conflicts of interest and clashes of world views." While these conflicts can be unpleasant, they are inevitable parts of a competitive political system.
3. Further, tensions are usually at their most heated when groups are making their greatest strides forward. The struggle for advancement and diversity in America demands that we tolerate contention and conflict.

43

Peter Skerry

TOLERATING INTOLERANCE IN AMERICAN POLITICS

★★★

In June 1943, Detroit was the scene of a two-day race riot that left nine whites and 25 African Americans dead. Commenting on those events, University of Chicago sociologist Robert Park wrote to a colleague: "I am not quite clear in my mind that I am opposed to race riots. The thing that I am opposed to is that the Negro should always lose."

The continuing controversy in the San Fernando Valley between former Assemblyman Richard Katz and City Councilman Richard Alarcon over a contested state Senate seat is hardly of such tragic dimensions. Still, Park's blunt realism is a useful antidote to the hand-wringing angst expressed in recent weeks over strained relations between Jews and Latinos. Park, the leading student of race and ethnic relations of his day, believed that competition and even conflict were inevitable stages in the process by which diverse groups learn to accommodate one another in modern societies.

Unlike Park, Americans today tend at first to deny or turn away from intergroup tensions. When we do finally face up to them, we interpret such tensions as the result of irrational prejudice and bigotry. We see them as aberrations, as the despicable excesses of those narrow-minded few who resist change and progress.

Park, on the other hand, viewed intergroup tensions, even animosities, as natural and inevitable. He saw competition and conflict as the quite rational clash of interests that emerge as groups jockey for position and advantage.

There are solid reasons for our contemporary perspective: Our national history has seen a good deal of irrational bigotry directed (Park reminds us) at a few groups that always tended to lose the competition—too often with their lives.

But we Americans have overreacted to this shameful history and high-mindedly decreed all group competition and conflict to be intolerable. Not all conflict is unjust, and certainly not all conflict is avoidable.

When my Irish Catholic forebears arrived in Boston a century ago, there is no doubt that they encountered unthinking, bigoted nativism. Yet as practicing Catholics pledged to obey the pope in Rome, they and their co-religionists did raise legitimate concerns as to their loyalty to their adopted home. When church leaders urged parents to opt out of the public schools and send their children to separate Catholic schools, such fears among Protestant Americans were understandably aggravated. Similarly during this period, when Mormons practiced polygamy and asserted, not unlike Catholics, that they practiced the one true religion, there were legitimate reasons for non-Mormons to be alarmed.

Did such concerns justify the burning of Catholic convents and the lynching of Mormons? Of course not. But an attentive reading of our ethnic and racial past should remind us that quite rational conflicts of interest and clashes of world views have been intertwined with even the most emotional and irrational intergroup battles. Attributing all such dissension to the unenlightened views of retrogrades may gratify those who consider themselves enlightened, but it does not help us to understand the complexities of intergroup relations. These relations are often messy and sometimes quite nasty. But such are the jostling and elbowing that arise among groups in a dynamic, competitive society.

An irony lost upon those who reduce all intergroup tensions to the struggle between the forces of light and darkness is that such tensions typically peak just when out groups are making their greatest strides. For example, Jews encountered the most thoroughgoing anti-Semitism in nineteenth century America after they had made the economic advances that allowed them to seek entry into social enclaves that until then had simply been beyond their means. Similarly, it is understandable, if regrettable, that Latinos encounter resistance today, when they are on the move politically. It would not surprise Park that tensions are emerging now between Latinos and their former Jewish allies. Nor would it surprise him that Latinos are finally getting mobilized politically because they have, since Proposition 187—a 1994 initiative that sought to deny public services to illegal immigrants—felt themselves to be under attack.

The philosopher William James, one of Park's teachers, once remarked that "progress is a terrible thing." Without for a moment excusing any of the political chicanery or vituperation indulged in by all parties in the San Fernando Valley, Angelenos need to face up to the fact that such excesses are to be expected in the struggle for advancement and power in this diverse and competitive society.

If we truly value diversity, then we will need to enlarge our concept of tolerance to include tolerance of contention and outright conflict. Alternatively, if we decide that we value consensus and social harmony more, then we should reexamine our preference for diversity. Our history tells us we can't have it both ways.

CREDITS

Bennett: reprinted with the permission of Simon & Schuster from *The De-Valuing of America*. Copyright © 1992 by William J. Bennett.

Bradley: *Time Present, Time Past*. Copyright © by Bill Bradley. Reprinted by permission of Alfred A. Knopf, a division of Random House, Inc.

Broder: *Behind the Front Page*. Reprinted with permission of Simon & Schuster, Inc. Copyright © 1987 by David Broder.

Brookings Institution: Excerpts from *Courts and Congress* and *A Communications Cornucopia*, reprinted by permission of The Brookings Institution Press.

Carter: *The Culture of Disbelief*. Copyright © 1993 by Stephen L. Carter. Reprinted by permission of Basic Books, a member of Perseus Books, L.L.C.

Cook: *Governing With the News*. Reprinted by permission of the University of Chicago Press.

Cuomo, Mario: Religious Belief and Public Morality, reprinted by permission of the author.

de Tocqueville: from *Democracy in America* by Alexis de Tocqueville. Copyright 1945 and renewed 1973 by Alfred A. Knopf, Inc. Reprinted by permission of Alfred A. Knopf, a division of Random House, Inc.

Fallows: *Breaking The News*. Copyright © 1996 by James Fallows. Reprinted by permission of Pantheon Books, a division of Random House, Inc.

Gergen: "Adapting US Foreign Policy Making to Changing Domestic Circumstances", from *Beyond The Beltway: Engaging the Public in US Foreign Policy* by Daniel Yankelovich and I.M. Destler. Copyright © 1994 by the American Assembly. Reprinted by permission of W.W. Norton & Company.

Glazer: "The Nation; Debate on Aliens Flares Beyond the Melting Pot," *New York Times*, April 23, 1995. Copyright © 1995 by the New York Times Company. Reprinted by permission.

Grossman: "Introduction", "Transforming Democracy – An Overview", from *The Electronic Republic*. Copyright © 1995 by Lawrence K. Grossman. Used by permission of Viking Penguin, a division of Penguin Putnam, Inc.

Holbrooke: *To End A War*, Copyright © 1998 by Richard Holbrooke.

Hoxie and Iverson: from *Indians in American History*. Edited by Frederick E. Hoxie and Peter Iverson, Chapter Twelve: "The Struggle for Indian Civil Rights" by W. Richard Wert, Jr., and Kevin Gover, Copyright © 1988 by Harlan Davidson, Inc., Reprinted by permission.